HOUSE, BUT NO GARDEN

HOUSE, BUT NO GARDEN

*Apartment Living
in Bombay's Suburbs,
1898–1964*

Nikhil Rao

University of Minnesota Press

MINNEAPOLIS ⚘ LONDON

Portions of chapter 5 were published in Nikhil Rao, "South Indians Are Like That Only: Communal Identity in Late Colonial Bombay," in *From the Colonial to the Postcolonial: India and Pakistan in Transition,* ed. Dipesh Chakrabarty, Rochona Majumdar, and Andrew Sartori (New York: Oxford University Press, 2007).

Published by the University of Minnesota Press
111 Third Avenue South, Suite 290
Minneapolis, MN 55401-2520
http://www.upress.umn.edu

LIBRARY OF CONGRESS CATALOGING-IN-PUBLICATION DATA
Rao, Nikhil.
 House, but no garden : apartment living in Bombay's suburbs, 1898-1964 / Nikhil Rao.
  Includes bibliographical references and index.
 ISBN 978-0-8166-7812-9 (hardback)—ISBN 978-0-8166-7813-6 (pb)
1. Architecture and society—India—Bombay suburban area—History—20th century.
2. Suburban homes—India—Bombay suburban area. 3. Apartment houses—India—
Bombay suburban area. 4. Apartment dwellers—India—Bombay suburban area. I. Title.
 NA2543.S6R345 2013
 307.760954'792—dc23

                                                                        2012043822

Printed in the United States of America on acid-free paper

The University of Minnesota is an equal-opportunity educator and employer.

20 19 18 17 16 15 14 13   10 9 8 7 6 5 4 3 2 1

FOR MY PARENTS

Kamala and Raghunatha Rao

Contents

Abbreviations

ACC	Associated Cement Companies
AICC	All-India Congress Committee
BBCI	Bombay, Baroda, and Central India Railway
BDD	Bombay Development Directorate
BEST	Bombay Electric Supply and Tramways Company or (after 1995) Brihanmumbai Electric Supply and Transport Company
BIT	Bombay City Improvement Trust
BMC	Bombay Municipal Corporation
BPCC	Bombay Provincial Congress Committee
BSD	Bombay Suburban District
FDCC	F Ward District Congress Committee
GIP	Great Indian Peninsular Railway
IAS	Indian Administrative Service
ICS	Indian Civil Service
IIA	Indian Institute of Architects
MCGM	Municipal Corporation of Greater Mumbai
MTCC	Matunga Taluka Congress Committee
PCACHS	Parsi Central Association Cooperative Housing Society
RCC	reinforced cement concrete
SIES	South Indian Educational Society
TPS	town planning scheme

Introduction

꒯꒯꒯꒯ TRAVELING NORTH ALONG ONE OF BOMBAY'S ARTERIAL ROADS from the heart of the colonial city in the south of the island is like traversing the history of Bombay's growth and expansion under colonial and postcolonial rule. The showcase districts of the Fort in the south of the city were the heart of British Bombay, with origins in the eighteenth century. Heading north from here entails negotiating the Fort's antithesis in the crowded old "native" city districts of Kalbadevi, Bhuleshwar, Pydhonie, Mandvi, and so on, which grew up as overspill from the Fort as the city expanded in the late eighteenth and early nineteenth centuries. Pressing northward, one enters the industrial districts of Bombay. In temporal terms, the early-nineteenth-century period of Bombay's growth as trading port gives way to the city's late-nineteenth-century flowering as the center of India's industrialization. Upon crossing the factories, workshops, and tenements of Byculla, Parel, and Lalbaug, one encounters a cityscape that remains almost unchanged until one crosses into the very new areas in the extreme north of Salsette Island, about thirty-five miles to the north.

This is a cityscape of apartment buildings, each set within a compound (often barely larger than the footprint of the building itself). The buildings are strung along lanes, which in turn intersect with busier streets, which articulate the neighborhood to the roaring thoroughfares transporting Mumbaikars north and south. Such lower-middle- and middle-class neighborhoods are always interspersed with the slum—often kept to the fringes and edges, along railway lines, in low-lying areas and so on, but sometimes working its way into the middle-class neighborhood. Also interspersed are zoned industrial districts, especially along the northeast industrial corridor flanking Lal Bahadur Shastri Marg, the old Bombay–Agra Road heading northeast out of the city. This is the cityscape as it began to develop from the 1920s onward.

These neighborhoods of apartment buildings have always been known as "suburbs." Beginning with the first "suburbs" of Dadar–Matunga in the 1920s and continuing into the suburbs of Bandra, Kurla, Chembur, and points north on Salsette Island, these areas now constitute the vast majority of the behemoth known as Greater Mumbai. In physical size as well as in the number of people who live there, the "suburbs" of Bombay actually now overwhelmingly constitute the present-day city. Yet, despite the empirical existence of the suburbs and despite the fact that "suburb" has been a meaningful category used by people living in these parts of the city for at least a century, the import of this term in the Indian context has not been sufficiently elaborated.

To appreciate the significance of Bombay's suburbs, consider the difference between the thing called Bombay that historians of the colonial city write about and the other, different, thing called Greater Mumbai that scholars of the present-day city study. Historians speaking of colonial Bombay before 1918 refer to an island city of about 22 square miles, the top third of which was not yet developed. Scholars of the present-day city—anthropologists, sociologists, and geographers among them—speaking of Greater Mumbai are referring to a behemoth of almost 186 square miles. There is thus a significant difference in the referent of the place-names "colonial Bombay" and "Greater Mumbai." The difference between "colonial Bombay" and "Greater Mumbai" raises important questions that this book seeks to address. What were the political and economic implications of changing configurations of power at the municipal level in the middle decades of the twentieth century? In a changing political and economic context, what physical shape did the expanding city assume in the decades after 1918? Finally, how did ideas of urban community themselves transform in changing physical settings?

This book argues that the rise and proliferation of apartment living is *the* distinctive feature of the growth of Bombay from about 1918 to 1960. Understanding apartment living offers a way to begin answering the questions raised above. From the tenures of the lands underneath suburban apartment buildings, to the materials and design of their construction, to the ways in which these dwellings were assimilated into an emerging upper-caste and lower-middle-class framework, apartment living expressed critical features of the expanding city. At the heart of this claim lies the idea that apartment living did not simply present itself, ready-made, as a dwelling option for Bombay's middle classes. The understanding of the apartment or flat as a distinct dwelling type was *constituted* within the matrix created by the political economies of lands and buildings, on the one hand, and by the emergence by the 1920s of a new upper-caste lower middle class, on the other. First appearing as a distinctive mainstream form in the suburbs, apartment buildings subsequently made their way back into the "city" to become the dominant form of living for Bombay's lower middle, middle, and upper classes. In this sense, the suburban apartment building was constitutive of the city.

Suburbs, suburbanization, and suburbanites meant different things in Bombay than they did in the United States, the United Kingdom, Canada, and Australia, which are the principal contexts in which suburbanization has hitherto been studied. For one thing, suburbanization did not result in the evisceration of older parts of the city, as happened in the United States in the second half of the twentieth century. For another, suburbanization in Bombay took place within the city municipal limits, with important implications for patterns of growth.[1]

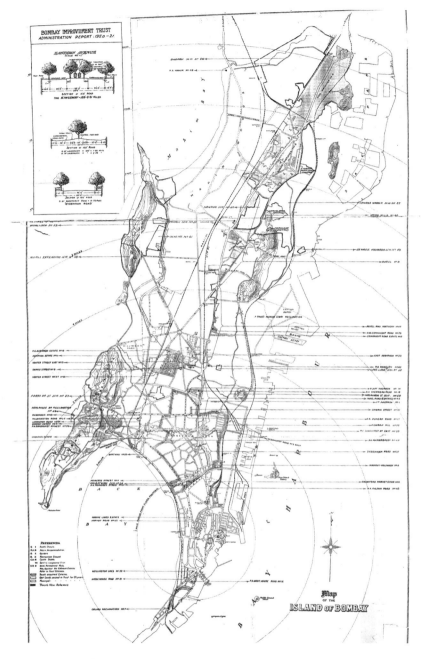

↙ FIGURE I.1. *Bombay in 1909. Development is restricted to the lower third of the island. Courtesy of the Regenstein Library, University of Chicago.*

Finally, for various reasons elaborated in this book, suburbs in Bombay did not consist of single-family houses, the ultimate aspiration of suburban dwellers in Anglo-America.[2] Rather, suburbanites lived in apartment buildings: initially three-story structures with six apartments emplotted within a walled compound, these dwellings have grown over the years as demands on the housing market have driven changes in the regulations on building height.

Yet, as this book will argue, the suburb—and *apartment* living in the suburbs—was a meaningful category and experience for all the various entities concerned with Bombay's growth: the colonial state that originally conceived of suburbs for Bombay in the early twentieth century, the postcolonial Bombay Municipal Corporation (BMC) that annexed large suburban areas in the neighboring island of Salsette to form Greater Bombay by 1957, and, most importantly, the millions of people who lived and continue to live between Dadar and Shivaji Park in the south all the way up to Dahisar, Mulund, and Mankhurd in the north and northeast, who have considered themselves suburbanites. Unlike previous instances of urban spillover, suburbanization in early-twentieth-century Bombay was undertaken with full awareness that suburbanization was a well-established response to the problems of industrialization and urban growth in Europe and North America.

Many middle-class residents of Bombay knew this as well. By the 1920s, living in apartments in the suburbs as opposed to tenements in older parts of the city became critical markers of a new upper-caste, lower-middle-class identity. Beginning in this period, weekly columns, with titles like "Notes of a Suburban Man" and "Suburban Goings-On," in newspapers such as the *Bombay Chronicle* elaborated on the suburban predicament. For the residents of these areas, the physical imperatives of living in such a built environment combined with their class position of working in the white-collar sector and with their upper-caste backgrounds to produce a new kind of lower-middle-class upper-caste identity. The South Indians were one such community who constituted themselves in Matunga, incorporating ideas of caste but combining such ideas with class position derived from white-collar work and, importantly, residence in the apartment buildings of suburban Bombay. Meanwhile, the ongoing daily drama of the suburban commuter trains—where communities of daily travelers are formed and sustained over decades around daily morning and evening card games—continues to reinforce the suburban experience. This book is thus about the lower-middle and middle-class suburbs of Bombay and the people who lived there. It is not about the informal settlements that constitute significant portions of the suburbs. These communities await their historians, but this book suggests that the expansions of the formal city and the informal city are connected and identifies such connections where possible.

⊰ THE SUBURBAN CITY

Suburbanization in a systematic sense in Bombay began at the very end of the nineteenth century. Largely as a response to the disastrous plague epidemic that began in 1896, large numbers of people fled the city and began to settle, in haphazard fashion, along the railway stations of the Bombay, Baroda, and Central India Railway (BBCI) in Salsette. In response to the exigencies of the plague epidemic, which authorities deemed to have been exacerbated by the insanitary conditions of the old city, the colonial government formed the Bombay City Improvement Trust (BIT) to address the problems of the city's infrastructure. The single largest, most expensive, and least studied project of the BIT was its suburban development program. Called the Dadar–Matunga–Sion suburban development schemes (Schemes V and VI of the Improvement Trust), these suburban schemes were undertaken as purely residential developments at the edge of the settled city. They were different from the pattern of suburbanization in other parts of the world because these suburbs fell entirely within the existing city limits of Bombay.[3]

At about the same time in the early twentieth century, the Bombay provincial government also began thinking about the slow but steady and ongoing settlement of Salsette, the larger island lying just to the north of Bombay Island, and outside the municipal limits of the city of Bombay. The suburbanization of Salsette posed certain challenges that were highly specific to the history of the colonization of this part of the continent. Bombay Island had initially been a Portuguese territory and was handed over to the British in 1661. Salsette, meanwhile, had been part of the Maratha Empire and was only fully annexed to the British Empire in the late eighteenth century, more than one hundred years after the British began the settlement of Bombay. Salsette and Bombay thus had very different revenue histories and landholding patterns, which posed very specific kinds of problems for suburban development. While most of this book deals with suburbanization in Bombay Island in Dadar–Matunga, chapter 6 literally covers new ground, discussing the suburbanization of Salsette and showing the continuities and breaks from the patterns established in the island city.

The new suburbs such as Dadar and Matunga introduced novel ideas of "locality." Two important factors—one at the scale of the city and the other at the scale of the dwelling—distinguished the suburb from the older parts of the city. At the scale of the city, the suburbs were designed to strictly separate the residence from the workplace. This was not the first time that residences were separated from workplaces. By its very definition, industrialization meant that from the 1850s onward, new kinds of factory workplaces were assuming increasing significance in Bombay's economy. Factory workspaces could not be accommodated within dwellings the way artisanal workspaces had been until then,[4] and the development of the industrial districts first in Tardeo and Byculla and subsequently in Lalbaug and Parel meant that workers lived in residences and traveled to work in factories. Yet, as Raj Chandavarkar has demonstrated, a physical separation of workplace and neighborhood hardly meant that workplace issues were absent in the neighborhood, or that the neighborhood was not a critical site for work-related labor practices.[5] Perhaps because working-class districts were in close proximity to the factories, there was a fluid relationship between politics on the shop floor and on the streets and in the chawls (multistory structures consisting of several one- or two-room units with distinctive verandahs running along the facades of the buildings at each story; the verandahs provide access to the various units but also serve as an important social space) of Parel and Lalbaug. Dadar–Matunga was different. Constructed on the edge of the city as it was defined in the 1920s, the buildings of Dadar and Matunga were intended solely as residences and were also separated from the white-collar areas of the Fort to the south (where most male residents of Dadar–Matunga worked) by the sprawling industrial districts of Parel, Lalbaug, and Byculla.[6] The Improvement Trust was able to control land use in these areas, and they remained remarkably free of encroachments and were not used for commercial purposes except in the designated areas. Work was thus not "visible" on the streets of Dadar–Matunga in the ways it was in the older parts of the city to the south.

This was very different from the *wadis* and *mohullas* in the older parts of the city to the south.[7] In such older areas, working spaces were closely intermingled with living spaces. Clerks might walk or ride the tram from Bhuleshwar to the nearby commercial districts of the Fort, but artisans and traders lived and worked in the *wadis* and *mohullas,* in close proximity to one another. While recent research suggests that these neighborhoods were not entirely as homogenous in caste terms as has long been presumed, the *wadis* and *mohullas* nonetheless had distinctive communal identities determined by the predominant caste groups living there. Such identities were a function of the religious, linguistic, regional, sectarian, caste, and, perhaps most importantly, occupational arithmetic that characterized the inhabitants of the *wadi* or *mohulla*. In an important way, the caste identity of a *wadi* was closely linked to the fact that work was visible. Since traders or artisans conducted their operations in shops or workshops proximate to where they lived—or even on the street, since buildings had a fluid relationship to the street—a particular area acquired an association with the dominant occupational group (and thus caste group) living and working there. Suburbanization, by enforcing a separation between work and residence, changed the pattern through which spaces acquired community identities.

At the scale of dwellings, the apartment building introduced new relationships between dwellings and the street. People living in apartments in Dadar–Matunga were removed from street life in a way that was very different from life in the *wadis* and *mohullas* of the older parts of the city. Such differences began at the most intimate, bodily levels: because apartment dwellings were "self-contained" and thus had toilets within the dwelling, residents did not have to leave their homes to satisfy bodily functions. More generally, because the state had much greater control over suburban lands than over lands in the old city, municipal power was able to extend its ideas of urban order to a far greater degree in these areas. Life was lived, to a greater extent, "inside" the dwellings of Dadar–Matunga, while the streets were now public thoroughfares principally to be used as channels of communication. This is not to suggest that the built environment of these suburbs created strict distinctions between "private" and "public" space in any simple and mechanical fashion in Dadar–Matunga. But such ideas had to be fashioned, in the novel context of the suburban built environment, regulated as it was by municipal power.

That there was a distinction between the inside and the outside of apartment buildings made these neighborhoods different from older parts of the city. Many *wadis* and *mohullas* were distinctive in that they differentiated themselves from the properly "public" spaces of the city. Although the *wadis* and *mohullas* may not have been strictly homogeneous in caste, the dominant community was nonetheless often able to set the rules governing living and working in the *wadi* through the various trusts and committees that endowed and managed them. Not just the buildings but also the social spaces and the streets within the *wadi* or *mohulla* were regulated by the community trust or *mohulla* community, while municipal power might also seek to extend its sovereignty into these spaces with the goal of establishing sanitary and safety guidelines.[8] There was thus a very gradual transition from the interiors of a small dwelling in the *wadi* to a large thoroughfare outside the *wadi*. For one thing, the dwelling itself was not a strict "inside" since much of life was conducted outside the dwelling in the common spaces of the *wadi*. For another, the lanes and courts within a *wadi* were certainly not "public" in the sense of being universally accessible or governed strictly by municipal regulation. On the contrary, the common spaces of the *wadi* or *mohulla* were often accessible only to or regulated by a much more restricted collectivity than "the public," such as a caste or sectarian association. It was this particular equilibrium of the inside and the outside, expressing a particular caste and communal logic, that was sharply affected by the new built environments of the suburbs. With self-contained apartments serving as more cellular dwellings, on the one hand, and with streets that were more public, on the other, Dadar–Matunga implied different orderings of the inside and the outside. Such distinctions between the inside and the outside were salient not just at the level of dwellings but also at the level of community identities.

A study of apartment living thus opens up the possibility of addressing far-reaching transformations in urban space and ways of being in urban space. In particular, *House, but No Garden*'s study of the apartment building and apartment living in Bombay's suburbs intersects with three broader sets of concerns. Because the historiography of the colonial city—and especially colonial Bombay—has overwhelmingly focused on the nineteenth century, we have little understanding of patterns of urbanization that arose with the changing role of the colonial state in the city from the late 1910s onward. This book introduces some of these patterns of middle-class living—most importantly apartment living in suburban neighborhoods—and argues that such patterns became the norm for middle-class urban expansion in the postcolonial period. Second, *House, but No Garden* suggests that scholarly understanding of the historical urban expansion process has been principally based upon the study of Anglo and European cities through the lens of suburban studies. From the scholarly point of view, peripheral urban expansion in the cities of the south or in the postcolonial world takes place through a series of chaotic, haphazard, and illegal accretions to the existing city. *House, but No Garden* seeks to center the study of the expanding city on the political economy of land and suggests that the scholarship on suburbanization offers useful frameworks for understanding urban expansion. At the same time, this book tries to decenter suburbanization studies from the historical experience of Anglo and European cities. Third, *House, but No Garden* suggests that the novel built environment of Bombay's suburbs became the site for the formation of new kinds of identity. By considering the emergence of the South Indian community in Matunga, *House, but No Garden* shows how older ideas of caste were recalibrated and combined with class to yield new kinds of identity in the context of the suburban apartment-building environment. Such fluid metacaste and class identities became the register on which "community" subsequently played out on the political stage.

COLONIAL POWER AND THE SOUTH ASIAN CITY

Colonial cities in South Asia, Africa, and Southeast Asia have long been viewed in terms of the colonial/indigenous dichotomy. Scholars have sought to identify the respective roles of colonizers and indigenous people in shaping cities or have sought to identify the ways in which colonial cities have been segregated into colonial and native sections. Recent work has complicated the long-standing colonial/indigenous opposition and has shown that it is now increasingly difficult to distinguish unequivocally between "colonial" and "indigenous" cities, or even between colonial and indigenous agency.[9] My book builds on these arguments, but it also departs from them in suggesting that the colonial/indigenous opposition becomes a secondary consideration in understanding late-colonial cities after 1918. The on-going devolution of municipal power onto Indians by the late 1910s and early 1920s decisively changed urban administration. The "colonial," on the one hand, was itself not a unitary agent. There were different wings of government representing different understandings of colonial power that were often in conflict with one other. On the other hand, the meaning of "indigenous" was constantly changing as the city grew. Traditional indigenous elites such as landowners, industrialists, and big merchants vigorously engaged in competition for power with new groups such as the emerging upper-caste lower middle classes, and all these groups colluded with one another against the city's underclasses. While the opposition between the colonial and the indigenous remained significant, it was now one factor among many others—including the emerging real estate market, the jostling for municipal power among Indians, the increasing bureaucratization of urban administration, and the responses of Indians to an increasingly heterogeneous urban environment—that shaped the growth of Bombay from the 1920s onward.

Following the end of World War I, a new political and economic scenario began to unfold in Indian cities like Bombay. On the political front, the Government of India Act of 1919 meant that the colonial state retreated from many aspects of urban development and governance. Local self-government and public works were now "transferred" subjects to be administered by a minister chosen by an elected provincial legislative council.[10] Meanwhile, on the municipal level, the franchise was widened to include not just "ratepayers" (those whose properties were substantial enough that they were paying a municipal property tax) but also persons paying rents of at least ten rupees a month. This bar to municipal franchise was further lowered in 1935 to include persons paying at least five rupees a month. Between 1922 and 1935, thus, a significant new lower-middle-class population was able to formally stake its claims within the emerging electoral public sphere of municipal politics. On the economic front, exigencies during World War I forced the colonial government to step back from its Lancashire-oriented tariffs policy, designed to favor British manufacturing interests, and offer some support to Indian industries. An expansion and diversification of the Bombay economy after 1914 led not only to the emergence of a white-collar lower-middle-class sector but also to increased demands for housing, which in turn led to speculation in lands and buildings.[11]

The changing political and economic relationship between colonial Britain and Bombay after World War I thus was of great significance for land prices, housing prices, and patterns of urban expansion. Yet the problem of urban lands under changing relationships of colonial power in South Asian cities has not hitherto been an important object of analysis.[12] On the one hand, land has been an enduring concern of modern Indian historiography. Because the East India Company transformed itself into a colonial power by winning the right to collect land revenue in eighteenth-century Bengal, both the colonial state itself and subsequent scholarship on colonial India paid great attention to the problems of agrarian land tenures, revenue settlements, and so on. Arjun Appadurai combined the insights gained from the study of agrarian lands with other scholarship on state apparatuses such as the colonial census to arrive at a powerful synthesis. Whereas previously, ideas of agrarian community had been firmly grounded in specific local landscapes, Appadurai argued that the colonial state's obsession with numbers and classification meant that by the late nineteenth century, categories like caste functioned as abstract organizing principles through which the Indian population was understood. As a result, "Indian social groups had become both functionally and discursively unyoked from local agrarian landscapes and set adrift in a vast pan-Indian social encyclopaedia."[13] Space was delinked from ideas of community, and despatialized notions of community and group difference became the organizing principles of Indian politics.

Yet the obverse of despatialized communities must be decommunalized spaces. How are such decommunalized spaces reinvested with ideas of urban community? *House, but No Garden* argues that understanding how ethnic communities constitute themselves in apartment buildings entails close study of urban lands, especially the ways in which agrarian lands are converted to urban lands during suburban expansion. At the urban edge, as industrializing cities such as Bombay sought to exceed their physical limits, the expanding city confronted lands—and landholders—that had formerly been engaged in agriculture. This confrontation between the city and the country at the urban edge yielded far-reaching transformations in the idea of land, in the relationship between people and land, and in the role that states must play in relation to land. While the existing scholarship on South Asian cities has given us excellent accounts of how buildings, streets, infrastructure, and political communities have been shaped by the experience of colonization, the problem of land has receded from the scholarship. This book recenters the history of Bombay's urban growth around the political economy of land. As the city grew, and as the pattern of urban growth was increasingly characterized by residential and industrial suburbs interspersed with slums, the political economy of urban land increasingly became the site of contest between the colonial state and Bombay's middle classes, on the one hand, and between the latter groups and the city's rapidly growing underclasses, on the other. The study of Bombay's suburbanization—and the scholarly perspectives offered by the existing literature on suburbanization—offers a way to investigate crucial yet unexplored patterns of land use in the expanding city. This book thus draws from Sam Bass Warner's approach in the study of expanding Boston. Urging urban historians to "spend more time with the evidence of land ownership and speculation," he suggests that "the Registry of Deeds rather than the Building Department should be the contemporary historian's destination."[14]

✑ SUBURBS AND THE SOUTH ASIAN URBAN PERIPHERY

One important goal of this book is to reassess the significance of the colonial/ indigenous opposition; another is to decenter the history of suburbs. The scholarship on large industrial cities of the nineteenth and twentieth centuries tends to distinguish between metropolitan cities such as London and Berlin, on the one hand, and colonial cities such as Bombay and Calcutta, on the other.[15] The scholarship on suburbanization, meanwhile, would have us believe that suburbs do not exist outside the United Kingdom, Anglo-America, and Australia.[16] These various phenomena are linked: because colonial cities are presumed to have been rigidly divided into "white" and "native" sections, the problem of understanding general urban processes such as suburbanization has been obscured.

To the extent that peripheral urban development in the "cities of the South" is considered at all in the academic literature, it is restricted to the study of informal settlements. From the point of view of the scholarship of peripheral urban expansion, the cities of the developed world have suburbs while the cities of the developing world have squatter settlements.[17] Kenneth Jackson's classic study of suburbanization in the United States has this to say about the peripheries of South Asian cities:

> In Calcutta and Bombay, the only areas with a passable water supply are at the center, where the wealthy live. The depths of squalor can be found in the thousands of legally defined slum districts, known as *bustees,* which are located throughout the metropolises but mostly around the rim of the cities.[18]

Jackson was making this point in order to emphasize the distinctiveness of U.S. suburbanization, specifically the pattern of elites moving to the peripheries. Yet such a point of view represents an inadequate understanding of peripheral urban expansion in the cities of the developing world. At the heart of Jackson's observation lies the assumptions that city centers (or other enclaves such as cantonments and civil lines) were populated by colonial elites while peripheries (or "native cities") were populated by colonized underclasses and that this structure endured in the postcolonial city. Unfeeling colonial authorities made some planning provisions for the elite enclaves but willfully neglected the peripheries or "native cities" where nonelites dwelled. For reasons stemming presumably from corruption, poverty, and plain incompetence, postcolonial municipalities did not succeed in altering such a dispersion of elites and nonelites across urban space. Much of the scholarship on squatter settlements in African and Asian cities, focused principally on the present day, also seems to depend upon such broad assumptions about the enduring spatial legacies of colonial urbanism.[19] An everyday variant of the preceding assumptions is the idea that urban growth in postcolonial cities—or the cities of the South more generally—is largely unplanned, unregulated, and characterized principally by proliferation of slums.

Bombay seriously challenges such assumptions: it does not easily fit into a traditional colonial city model. As scholars such as Raj Chandavarkar and Gyan Prakash have argued, Bombay was always among the most "Indian" of cities within the British Empire, with diverse groups of industrialists and merchants playing important roles in the economy and in urban governance. Indeed, Chandavarkar has argued for Bombay's "perennial modernity," suggesting that the city displayed features of urbanization similar to those unfolding in the modernizing and industrializing cities of the West.[20]

Suburbanization in Bombay was one such pattern playing out in the first half of the twentieth century. Bombay's political economy of land combined with caste and class considerations of suburban residents to make apartment living the dominant form of middle-class suburban dwelling. Rather than playing a subordinate role to the city, the suburbs *pioneered* many fundamental elements of the modern city of Bombay, elements that then made their way back to the older parts of the city. Physical forms of dwelling such as the apartment building, institutions such as the cooperative housing society, and metacaste forms of identity such as the South Indian—now essential attributes of the city called Greater Mumbai—were all initiated and elaborated in the suburbs of Bombay before making their way back into the city.

The study of the expanding city permits us to transcend the static nature of the colonizer/colonized opposition to generate a more dynamic picture of the emerging postcolonial city. The scholarship on suburbanization offers a methodological framework for apprehending the dynamism of urban growth. Unlike previous instances of urban spillover that resulted in urban growth, suburbanization as initiated in early-twentieth-century Bombay was consciously undertaken by a municipal entity with full awareness that suburbanization was a well-established response to the problems of industrialization and urban growth in Europe and North America. This book introduces the category of suburbanization into South Asian urban historiography as a compelling ensemble of categories through which to understand urban expansion; on the other hand, the book also seeks to widen suburban studies and challenge some widespread assumptions about peripheral urban growth in the cities of the global South. Despite disagreements and the absence of a consensus, the debates within suburban studies have yielded a very productive set of categories through which to approach the problem of peripheral urban expansion. Three important frameworks in particular are useful for the study of Bombay: the political economy of land and land-use conversion is the first step in urban expansion; the development of transportation, building, finance, and regulatory technologies, in conjunction with the political economy of land, places constraints on what kinds of dwellings can be built and where; the nature and meaning of such suburban dwelling is constituted by the cultural pre-occupations—including religion, caste, class, and gender—of suburban residents. I turn now to considering some of these cultural preoccupations.

◢ CLASS AND COMMUNITY IN THE SOUTH ASIAN CITY

In arguing for the *constituted* nature of urban community identity in Bombay, this book intervenes in ongoing debates on the nature of cosmopolitanism in South Asian cities. One long-standing narrative of Bombay's cosmopolitanism portrays the city of the 1950s as, more or less, a model of communal harmony that began to break down by the 1970s under the pressures of economic transformation and rising communal discord.[21] Such studies presume the existence of large urban community identities that transcend particularities of caste and class. From the point of view of the assault on Bombay's cosmopolitanism, some such meta-identities include "Muslim," "South Indian," and "Maharashtrian." My book joins other recent studies in arguing that the nature of communal identity in large heterogeneous urban settings—where people encounter unprecedented diversity and unprecedented imperatives—is different from that obtaining in smaller cities, towns, and villages. Such forms of identity, swiftly and sometimes violently mobilized in the present-day urban political context, are potentially volatile composites of religion, caste, class, region, and language. As Thomas Blom Hansen brilliantly demonstrated in his study of the Shiv Sena in Bombay, politically significant categories such as "the Marathi *manoos*," in whose name the Sena acts, only acquire specific meaning in acts of "plebian assertion" carried out in the social spaces of Bombay.[22]

House, but No Garden argues that the South Indian identity fashioned in the apartment buildings of suburban Matunga was an exemplary instance of such urban identity. South Indian identity was not the outcome of some simple and universal process of "suburbanization" that had already taken place in Europe and the United States. Specifically, enduring concerns of caste, community, and family remained salient but were often recast in new forms in the context of the new built environment and were also combined with class. Such forms of identity were highly flexible depending on the contexts thrown up by the heterogeneous and changing urban environment. In some situations, they might refer to very specific and orthodox subcastes; in other cases, they might refer to very broad regional identities. The book suggests that such fluid and flexible forms of identity became the norm in the expanding suburbs of Bombay after Independence, with the fashioning of "Sindhi," "Punjabi," and even "North Indian" identities.

In arguing for the constituted nature of South Indian identity, this book elaborates one important conclusion arrived at in a new collection of essays on the middle class in colonial India.[23] The middle class, as the collection's editor Sanjay Joshi asserts, is *made* rather than simply objectively *there* as an expression of systems of production. The essays in Joshi's collection explore the ways in which caste, gender, and white-collar work become important foci around which the middle class—now seen as an entrepreneurial group seeking to distinguish itself from the lower classes as well as from the upper classes—fashions itself.[24] One such important urban setting was the new world of white-collar "office work," which Prashant Kidambi has shown to be the context within which traditional service-caste Saraswat Brahmins refashioned themselves as Bombay middle classes.[25]

An important question is raised by studies such as these: what are the roles of the changing urban spaces in middle-class self-fashioning? Anyone living in a large South Asian city today will appreciate how housing and the provision of basic amenities—running water, electricity, sewage connections—have become critical indices of social class. Yet we have only a limited historical understanding of this link between the materiality of urban living and the development of urban identities.

A theoretical framework for thinking about the connections between urban spaces and urban identities is offered in the writings of Partha Chatterjee and Sudipta Kaviraj.[26] While these scholars have different positions, in general they argue that European urbanism, including ideas like "public space" and "private space," did not encounter a conceptual vacuum during colonial rule. Indians in cities like Calcutta had their own understandings of urban spaces, inflected with notions of caste and community rather than predicated upon ideas of the individual and the bourgeois family, as were European ideas of public and private. The colonial encounter thus produced a wide range of Indian responses to urban spaces, usually entailing complex negotiations and compromises between Indian and European ideas of urban space. These essays focus on social spaces and publicity and offer no equivalent working out of a range of understandings of "the private" over the nonsocial spaces of the colonial city.

Chatterjee and Kaviraj also offer accounts of the changing dynamics of class power in postcolonial cities and of the resultant changes in the ways in which social spaces were used. Initially the domain of hegemonic middle-class elites who inherited the mantle of British power, the social spaces of cities like Calcutta became, by the 1970s, the terrain upon which recently mobilized and enfranchised nonelites flaunted their new status by using social spaces in conspicuously non-public—what Kaviraj might call "pablik"—ways: sleeping, cooking, eating, bathing, and conducting their livelihoods on sidewalks, in parks, and in other social spaces. For Chatterjee, such practices are spatial expressions of the emergence of political society as a sphere of action distinct from that of civil society.[27] Kaviraj suggests that such "plebianization" is the form that the spread of democracy in India takes.[28] Both scholars offer sophisticated analyses of the changing meanings of social spaces, suggesting ways in which caste considerations might structure Indians' understanding of space, while also showing how the changing use of social spaces in postcolonial cities reflects the changing structure of class hegemony.

Both essays also beg a question: what are the implications of changing urban spaces—and changing class control of urban spaces—for ideas of caste and community? Neither Kaviraj nor Chatterjee explicitly explores this vector in the urban space–class–caste matrix. These two superb accounts tell us how class is contested and refashioned in urban social spaces while also transforming the meaning of those social spaces. They also tell us how particular "cultural" considerations might structure Indian appropriations of urban spaces. Yet they assume an uncharacteristically ahistoric and nonspatial position when considering how caste and community, also, might be transformed by new kinds of practices in new kinds of urban spaces.

But the link between Chatterjee's and Kaviraj's arguments about the changing class control of public space, on the one hand, and Hansen's fine account of the Shiv Sena's flexing of its nativist Marathi *Manoos* muscles in the public spaces of Bombay through "plebian assertion," on the other, cannot be established without a better understanding of how ideas of community, too, are recalibrated in the context of the urban spaces of South Asian cities.[29] *House, but No Garden* draws upon the insights of Kaviraj and Chatterjee and extends the inquiry into questions of how changing spatial contexts, such as apartment living in the suburbs, might affect and transform ideas of caste and community.

Such transformations in the idea of caste combined with class, as Joshi argued, in the new urban middle-class identity. Beginning in the late 1910s, demands for housing and basic urban services became the context in which a new lower-middle-class upper-caste identity constituted itself. As these groups increasingly gained representation and voice in municipal matters beginning in the 1920s, the provision of transportation, housing, water, and other services to the emerging suburbs became the object of middle-class demands, and the satisfaction of these demands offered new ways in which they began to understand themselves.[30] Here, the object of Bombay's upper-caste lower middle classes was not so much to fight colonial rule as, rather, to demand services from the municipal state. *House, but No Garden* shows how in Bombay, apartment living, pioneered in the suburbs of Bombay, was an expression of the convergence of a variety of factors: the expansion of the city under the aegis of an increasingly Indianized municipal power; the emergence of new upper-caste lower middle classes who worked in white-collar office jobs in the older parts of the city to the south and who increasingly associated their middle-class status with living in apartment buildings; and the recalibration of caste identities under the imperatives of suburban apartment living through the embrace of institutions such as the cooperative society.

✌ PLAN OF THE BOOK

Read through from beginning to end, this book proceeds in roughly chronological fashion. Chapter 1 begins with the formation of the Bombay City Improvement Trust in the aftermath of the plague epidemic in 1896—and the subsequent genesis of the suburban vision—and chapter 6 concludes with the suburbanization of Salsette Island and its annexation to the Bombay municipal limits in the late 1950s. Intervening chapters deal with the formation of Bombay's new lower middle class and the emergence of Dadar–Matunga as a lower-middle-class suburb in the 1920s and 1930s (chapter 2), the rise and spread of the Bombay apartment building as a distinctive dwelling typology in the 1920s and 1930s (chapters 3 and 4), and the emergence in these suburbs of new forms of metacaste identities such as the South Indian by the 1940s (chapter 5). Thematically, the book moves from the ground up to explore the formation of communities in apartment buildings on suburban lands. Bracketing the book, chapters 1 and 6 are principally about land. Chapters 2 and 5 are principally about class and community. Chapters 3 and 4 are about the emergence and proliferation of the apartment building, a way of living produced by the political economy of land and the class and caste concerns of Bombay's new lower middle class.

Chapter 1 examines the production of a suburban landscape by the Bombay City Improvement Trust in the early years of the twentieth century. Dadar–Matunga–Sion constituted a major intervention in the built environment of Bombay. Yet the decision to develop vast new swathes of land on the outskirts of the existing city was not undertaken and executed in some kind of planner's vacuum. The suburb emerged as an option not so much because the Trust embraced Garden City principles (although it was later couched in these terms) as because the Trust's planners were simply unwilling and unable to undertake the necessary massive urban improvement projects in the old city. The precedent established by the city's previously lax regulatory practice and the increasingly empowered and vocal Indian landowners of the city combined to thwart the Trust's ambitions of urban renewal in the old city. The scholarly verdict has thus condemned the Trust's incomplete efforts, especially its failure to construct adequate housing to replace the buildings torn down in the name of urban renewal. This chapter argues that such a focus on buildings obscures the Trust's mightiest achievement: by physically acquiring land held under a variety of tenures and then leasing it out in standard 99- and 999-year leases, and by building a network of roads, the Trust conceptually and physically linked the spaces of the city. This contributed greatly to the emergence of the land market in the twentieth century.

Acquiring lands to build suburbs was difficult, but the problem of determining who was to live in the suburbs was no less significant. Indian critics of the Trust pointed out that caste was as significant as class in Indian society and that it was thus unrealistic to imagine, as the Trust did, that Bombay's middle classes would abandon their ties to the old city and move to the suburbs. Chapter 2 examines the formation of a new lower-white-collar middle class in the early decades of the twentieth century and argues that migrants from southern India, an important sector of this class, made the space of Matunga into their place in the city. Through a variety of ways that included participation in the broadening arena of municipal politics, Matunga's lower middle classes made Matunga into a South Indian suburb. The chapter elaborates the meaning of this last category by discussing three demarcations: the consolidation of Matunga as a suburb through its residents' campaigns for the improvement of communications with the commercial districts to the south; the development of Matunga as a South Indian neighborhood through the establishments of markets, housing, restaurants, temples, cultural institutions, and sports clubs; and finally, the emergence of Matunga as a political entity as evidenced by disputes in Matunga in local elections in 1934.

Chapter 3 argues that the apartment building and flat living was pioneered in the suburbs of Dadar–Matunga. It examines how, contrary to the Trust's original vision of a district of bungalows and villas, Dadar–Matunga–Sion became an apartment-building suburb in response to pressures in the land market. While it was a new dwelling type for the lower middle classes, the apartment building did not merely present itself, ready-made, for adoption by the residents of the suburbs. Rather, the chapter argues, the form of the apartment building and the associated form of the single-family flat or apartment was produced in the Bombay setting. Unlike in Europe and North America, the Bombay flat acquired social meaning through being self-contained, through the fact that, for the first time, the toilets were within the dwelling. The toilet within the flat became a key site where the built form of the apartment was incorporated into an upper-caste lower-middle-class framework. Apartment living presented itself as a compromise between the class considerations of the inhabitants of the suburbs and their caste considerations. It served to mediate between the community as class and the community as caste in the suburban setting.

Even though the Bombay flat had emerged as a concept by the 1920s, the depression in the building industry meant that not much actual construction took place for most of that decade. It took a combination of certain contingent developments in the building trade as well as a domestication of the apartment form to generalize the practice of apartment living by the 1930s. Chapter 4 begins by considering three developments in the building industry that resulted in the proliferation of the Bombay flat in the 1930s and 1940s: the generalized availability of cheap cement and reinforced cement concrete, the emergence of a new generation of Indian architects who were willing and able to build according to Indian needs, and, finally, the development of municipal bylaws that led to the standardization of the Bombay flat. As important as the physical proliferation of apartment buildings was the spread of ways of living in apartments. The chapter moves to considering the implications of the organization of space within the apartment—with its presumption of the bourgeois nuclear family—for the upper-caste and lower-middle-class families who lived in them. The chapter argues that residents, through their living practices, domesticated the apartment and the apartment building to make flat living the quintessential Bombay form of dwelling.

Chapter 5 investigates the constitution of South Indian identity. "South Indian" was a highly fluid and novel category that was generated in the context of Matunga's residents' efforts to consolidate themselves as a community in the context of Bombay and the subsequent redrawing of boundaries of inclusion and exclusion. Specific economic and political imperatives dictated that Matunga's residents widen their older caste understanding—the formation of cooperative housing and credit societies was one such economic imperative. Politically, the need to present a unified front against a perception, even by the late 1930s and early 1940s, that South Indians were dominating the white-collar professions meant that even Christians from Kerala could sometimes count as South Indian. On the other hand, in other contexts, highly specific forms of differentiation obtained among the South Indians of Matunga. Not just the expected axes of caste and subcaste but also considerations of native place and food (a function of native place) could mean that the Palakkad Iyers, for instance, perceived themselves as totally different from Thanjavur Iyers. The upper-caste South Indians of Matunga also distinguished themselves from the low-caste residents of Dharavi, which lay literally across the train tracks from Matunga. Many residents of Dharavi also came from southern India, but they were never considered "South Indians."

Chapter 6 examines the suburbanization of Salsette, the large island to the north of colonial Bombay that was annexed in large part to Bombay city to form Greater Bombay by 1957. A changing political scenario—specifically the increasing vocal opposition by Indians to the Trust and the gradual retreat of the colonial state from extensive urban intervention—meant that the suburbanization of Salsette followed a different pattern from that in Dadar–Matunga. Town planning, a new form of converting land from agrarian to urban use, was pursued in Salsette and remained the principal mode of land use conversion until the 1960s. Town planning (distinct from a more general notion of urban planning) was a form of suburbanization in which landowners retained ownership of their lands but consented to land-use conversion through the imposition of street layouts on agrarian lands. Town planning–based suburbanization, initiated in the late 1910s and early 1920s but pursued with gusto after Partition in 1947, offers a look into the changing pattern of relationships between city authorities and suburban residents, on the one hand, and between municipal power and provincial/regional level power, on the other. Though the pattern of land-use conversion was different in Salsette than in Dadar–Matunga, certain other patterns pioneered in the earlier suburb were reproduced in the suburbs of Salsette. Specifically, the apartment building and the cooperative housing society became the dwelling and social institution of choice as large numbers of refugees from Sindh and Punjab and other migrants flooded into Salsette from the late 1940s onward, leading Bombay city to annex large parts of Salsette to form Greater Bombay in 1957.

1 *An Indian Suburb*

IT IS DIFFICULT INDEED TO VISUALISE FROM DRY FACTS AND FIGURES the extent of the operations in progress, but a visit to Worli or the Sion–Matunga and Dadar areas must impress upon the most casual observer the great change that our operations are making in the geography of the island. Hills are disappearing, low-lying ground is being raised; land from the sea is being reclaimed and unhealthy tracts of land are being converted into well laid out building plots. 2,400 acres of land or about ⅙th of the entire island are comprised in the Trust's larger undertakings in progress, which will provide sites for the accommodation of nearly half a million people.[1]

With this rather breathless passage, the annual report of the Bombay City Improvement Trust—not a document generally known for its purple phrasing—captured the scale of the suburbanization project in the Dadar–Matunga–Sion areas of early-twentieth-century Bombay. While noteworthy for the scale of the operation—no less than one-sixth of the surface area of the city was involved—the suburbanization project of the BIT was more important in introducing new ways of thinking about land and space in the colonial city of Bombay.

The notion of the suburb suggests the idea of planning. While the suburbs of Bombay in the early twentieth century were certainly "planned" in the sense that the Trust started off with a suburban vision, the history of Bombay's suburbs points to a less confident and far more contingent trajectory than the word "planning" suggests. In particular, the history of suburban planning and development was embedded within a larger history of transformation in the sphere of municipal governance, as Indian elites increasingly contested the project of the colonial state. This chapter charts the history of the suburban vision—from its genesis in the plans of the Bombay City Improvement Trust and through its vicissitudes over the turbulent first two decades of the twentieth century, when the Trust became caught up in a swift-moving and complicated tide of self-assertion by Indians.[2] It was the Trust's fate to have an ambitious vision that ultimately bore fruit, but because of the intervening history of political transformation, there has always been a strange disconnect between the Improvement Trust and the cityscape that came to characterize post-Independence Bombay.[3] The Trust seems complacently located in the high noon of colonialism, circa 1900, while the cityscape that came to represent middle-class Bombay seems associated with the city after 1947. Elaborating the suburbanization project establishes links between the Trust's vision of the early 1900s, its struggles through the 1910s, and the slow emergence by the late 1920s of the dominant cityscape in the subsequent expansion of the city. Understanding and elaborating the suburban project, in other words, unearths connections between the political and the built forms of the colonial city of the early twentieth century and the postcolonial city.

While the notion of mass suburbanization as a response to the challenges of rapid industrialization was obviously a widespread current of urban thinking in the late nineteenth century, and while the BIT certainly drew inspiration from instances of suburbanization in Britain and Germany, ultimately it was Bombay's own dynamics that shaped the course of suburbanization. Specifically, three factors were decisive in shaping the suburbs of Dadar and Matunga. First, the peculiar revenue history of early colonial port cities such as Bombay led the East India Company to adopt extremely lenient land policies in order to attract settlement. Such leniency had set a troublesome precedent by the second half of the nineteenth century, when, as the need for "urban planning and development" arose, the state found it exceedingly difficult to enforce regulation. A second factor had to do with the rapidly changing politics of municipal governance. At every stage, the Trust's planners were confronted with a vocal and active citizenry, increasingly conscious of the power it wielded in shaping the city. The "citizenry," however, was far from some democratic ideal; consistently, certain kinds of landowning, industrial, and mercantile elites were able to assert their own specific interests in the name of the people. A final decisive factor shaping the suburbs was, paradoxically, the effect of the Trust's own land-acquisition activities. In a peculiar way, while acquiring lands and buildings streets and roads for its suburban project, the Trust transformed the nature of the land market in the city and thus encouraged a new wave of Indian speculators whose activities ultimately undermined the efforts of the Trust.

The project of suburbanization, with its attendant mandates of land acquisition and construction on a large scale, must be understood in the context of a distinctive moment in Indian cities such as Bombay in the first two decades of the twentieth century. Sandip Hazareesingh has shown very well the peculiar predicament that colonial urban authorities found themselves in in the early twentieth century.[4] In discussing the transformation of politics in Bombay in the first two decades of the twentieth century, Hazareesingh distinguishes between concurrent discourses of political, civil, and social rights. Political rights pertained to the right to self-determination, civil rights pertained to such rights as the right to property, and social rights pertained to rights to public goods, such as housing, public transport, sanitation, and so forth. Until the early twentieth century, "rights" in the context of colonial Bombay had been confined to civil rights. Over the later decades of the nineteenth century, political rights were slowly emerging as, with the growth of the Bombay Municipal Corporation, certain landowning elements of Bombay society began to exercise some control over local matters. Between 1900 and 1925, however, as Hazareesingh has shown, the colonial state was confronted with an onslaught of demands for political and social rights as well. "If the colonial administration often seemed to be out of its depth during this period," Hazareesingh argues, "it was largely because, unlike the historical experience of Western Europe, the clamour for civil, political and social rights did not occur gradually over the course of three centuries, but was arriving on its doorstep virtually simultaneously."[5] The debate and conflict over the BIT's suburbanization project constituted an important platform upon which these various kinds of rights were exercised. Bombay's citizens proved adroit at exploiting newly available political rights to self-determination to maximize their claims to civil and social rights.

Such an increasingly strident "clamour" by Bombay's residents meant that suburbanization stalled and sputtered and ultimately took a very different form from that imagined by the Trust in the early twentieth century. Perhaps for this reason, the Trust's suburbanization project has not received the same attention as the Trust's works in the older parts of the city.[6] The consensus on the Trust's work in the old city has been that the colonial nature of the Trust ultimately hobbled its efforts, resulting in partial and incomplete attempts at redeveloping parts of the old city such as Nagpada. If we focus at the level of buildings constructed by the Trust, then the BIT appears to have failed or to have acted as a weak colonial entity. The most common critique of the BIT has been that in prosecuting its "improvement schemes" in the old city, it ultimately dishoused more of the poor than it rehoused in new and sanitary dwellings—that it destroyed more dwellings than it erected and thus exacerbated rather than ameliorated the housing crisis.

If we shift our perspective to the level of urban land, however, we can begin to appreciate the extraordinary transformations wrought by the BIT. Two changes in particular will be elaborated later in the chapter. First, the Trust managed to effect a change in the way in which people perceived the lands lying at the urban edge to the north of the built-up city of Bombay. Despite the fact that the villages of Matunga, Sion, Dharavi, Mahim, Worli, and so on were jurisdictionally part of the "Town and Island of Bombay," they were perceived by most city residents as agricultural villages lying outside the city. The Trust managed to change that perception and cast these areas as parts of the city that were merely awaiting development. Just as crowded slums in the south such as Nagpada and Agripada needed to be "attacked" by the Trust, so the "insanitary villages" of the north needed intervention. Suburbanization, in this sense, entailed a very important change in people's minds as to what was the territory of the city and thus subject to "urban" intervention.

The Trust's activities also greatly accelerated the process of commodification of land. By physically acquiring a vast quantity of land at great expense and effort (more than 20 percent of the surface area of the city), the BIT succeeded in unyoking lands in Bombay from the variety of tenures under which they had been held. By then subsequently inserting itself and its rules and regulations between the holders of land and the land through the issuance of standardized long-term leases, the BIT stabilized the meaning of "property" in land. Since the BIT succeeded in getting its own standards adopted by the Municipal Corporation as well, this meant that a very large portion of the island consisting of BIT and BMC lands was now subject to a high degree of regulation. Finally, by constructing an extraordinary network of streets and roads linking the older city to the suburbs in the north of the island, the BIT not only extended control over building (by linking the height and form of buildings to the width of streets) but also physically connected discrete parts of the island. These were formidable achievements that resulted in the production of the island city of Bombay as a set of commodified and fungible spaces.

The chapter begins by describing the circumstances leading to the setting up of the BIT in 1898 and the genesis and evolution of its suburban vision. It then considers the implications of Bombay's specific revenue history and demonstrates the manner in which the latter affected the Trust's operations in the old city. Only then is it possible to understand the central thesis of the Trust's suburban vision: taking control of lands and using the street to order a new urban landscape. All along, the Trust had to respond to the claims of Bombay's residents, often modifying and sometimes rejecting aspects of its suburban agenda as a result.

THE BOMBAY CITY IMPROVEMENT TRUST AND THE GENESIS OF THE SUBURBAN VISION

When the city of Bombay experienced a withering plague epidemic starting in 1896, one of the outcomes was the establishment, by the provincial Government of Bombay, of the Bombay City Improvement Trust. The Trust was an interesting and controversial body right from the moment of inception, and before it could even come into existence through the enactment of the City of Bombay Improvement Act of 1898, it was the focus of contestation between the colonial authority represented by the Government of Bombay and the increasingly confident and Indian-dominated Bombay Municipal Corporation. (The BMC was dominated by a cartel of three elites: landlords, industrialists, and rich merchants.)[7] The constitution of its board of trustees already revealed its somewhat eclectic character, straddling the domains of colonial power and surging Indian ambitions.[8] The issue of the composition of the board had already provoked criticisms from the Indian residents of Bombay, with the newspaper *Mumbai Vaibhav,* for instance, criticizing as unnecessary the inclusion of the chief military officer and the municipal commissioner as ex officio members of the board.[9]

Modeled after the Glasgow Improvement Trust, the Bombay City Improvement Trust had a broad mandate of urban development. But its main goal was to attack the problem of overcrowding and attendant disease in parts of the old, "native" city. Areas such as Nagpada and Agripada, home to various Hindu and Muslim communities in the late nineteenth century, were seen as breeding grounds for plague and other diseases. Since disease was believed to proliferate through miasmas that thrived in close, dense habitations, building sanitary housing was perceived as a way in which urban interventions could combat disease.[10] To achieve this central goal, the Trust deployed a three-pronged strategy:

1. So-called improvement schemes, for example, the creation of housing along modern "sanitary" lines in the older parts of the city, such as Nagpada and Agripada.
2. So-called street schemes, which were of two sorts:
   a. The building of broad west–east boulevards that would bring breezes, deemed healthful, from the ocean to the west into the neighborhoods of central and east Bombay, such as Nagpada.
   b. The opening up of new areas, hitherto undeveloped, for settlement and urban habitation. Two kinds of new areas were envisaged: on the one hand, areas that were to be reclaimed from the sea, and on the other, areas in the northern parts of the island that were sparsely populated by rice cultivators, Bhandari toddy-tappers, and Koli fishing communities.

The Trust prosecuted its mandate through the agency of such schemes. Through the City of Bombay Improvement Act of 1898, which brought the Trust into existence, large areas of imperial lands (Schedule C in the act) and municipal lands (Schedule D) were vested in the Trust. Further, using as an instrument the recently promulgated Imperial Land Acquisition Act of 1894, it sought to acquire all the land in an area designated as blighted (or slated for new development) and then go ahead with the execution of the scheme. Such a method would permit radical and comprehensive interventions over relatively large areas. The dire situation seemed to render such interventions necessary.

The Trust was very active in executing its plans between 1898 and 1919. All along, however, criticism of the Trust by Indians, especially the Municipal Corporation, was mounting. By the end of the 1910s, the decisions of the Trust were being challenged at every turn, even by the Indian members on its board. Government responded to such pressure by creating a new body in 1919, the Bombay Development Directorate (BDD), an entirely executive body and an actual department of provincial government. The Trust, for all its faults still in principle a body that included Indian representation, was reduced to a minor role in the planning and development process. The BDD proceeded exclusively on executive authority

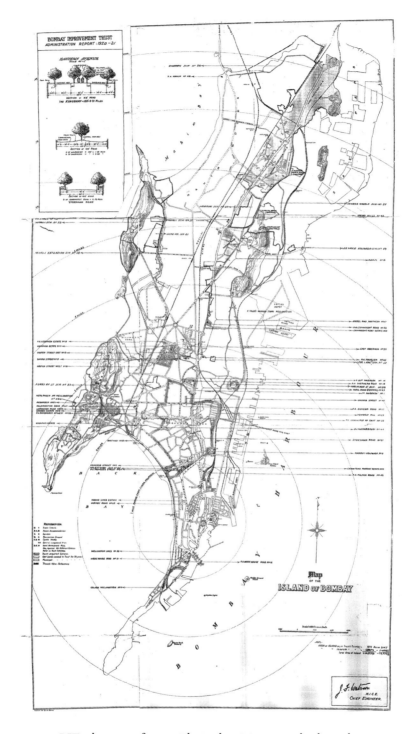

FIGURE 1.1. *BIT schemes as of 1921. The Dadar-Matunga suburban schemes are in the extreme north of the island. BIT,* Annual Administration Report, *1920–1921. Courtesy of Maharashtra State Archives.*

until, floundering over its expensive, corrupt, and failure-ridden reclamation and industrial housing schemes, it ran out of steam in 1925. (It was not actually terminated until 1929.) Over the course of the 1920s, the assets and properties of the Improvement Trust were transferred to the Bombay Municipal Corporation, and on October 1, 1933, the Improvement Trust was formally absorbed into the Corporation as the newly formed Improvements Department. The period from 1919 to 1933, coinciding with the withdrawal of the colonial state from urban intervention that began with the Montagu–Chelmsford reforms of 1919, thus represented the dramatic increase of municipal (and thus Indian) power in the planning process. From 1933 onward, planning operations in the city of Bombay were in municipal hands, in the form of the Improvements Committee (consisting of elected municipal corporators) and the Estates Department (consisting of bureaucrats) of the BMC. These two aspects of the BMC—one elected, one executive—oversaw the legacies of the BIT.

For the first ten years after its founding in 1898, the Trust's energies were mostly caught up with the first two items on its agenda: the building of sanitary housing for the working classes in the older parts of the city and the building of new crosstown boulevards linking the congested southeastern parts of the city with the ocean to the west.[11] As a result, the third item on its agenda—the development of new suburbs in the northern parts of the island—did not receive much attention. Although the initial City of Bombay Improvement Act included two schemes— Schemes 5 and 6—that were designed to acquire and subsequently develop lands in the north of the island, primarily in F Ward, these aspects of the Trust's agenda were not accorded a high priority, the emphasis being on "direct attack" on the slums of the old city. Further, the Trust's northern suburban schemes were almost immediately challenged by the persons living in those areas. (Some of their petitions are considered in detail later in the chapter.) Partly for reasons of the Trust's different priorities and partly because of opposition from Indians residing in the north of the island, the suburban schemes did not receive much attention in the first decade of the Trust's existence.

In 1909, however, with the ascendance of the energetic J. P. Orr to the chairman's position, the Trust announced a major strategic shift in its approach to the housing crisis. Rather than continuing its direct attack on the slums in the south of the city, Orr and the Trust now proposed to emphasize an "indirect attack" on the housing problem by making available new tranches of building plots and thus dramatically increasing the supply of housing.[12] The goal of indirect attack was to attract residents of the slums of Nagpada, Agripada, and Pydhonie to the new building sites, thus alleviating the overcrowding in the south. Within this new strategic vision, the suburbs in the north of the island now assumed heightened significance, since it was in these newly developed areas that building plots could be made available. Suburbanization was now reframed as indirect attack on the city's housing problem.

Indirect attack was viewed with suspicion by the public of Bombay and with outright hostility by the Indian representatives of the Municipal Corporation on the Trust's board. The argument of the Corporation's representatives on the board, prominent landowners such as Dinshaw Vacha and Ibrahim Rahimtulla, was that suburbanization would only add more housing stock for the upper classes and would not really address the problem of housing the poor. Of course, the landowning Indians from the Corporation had a different interest as well: they owned lands in the south of the city, so the Trust's works in those areas would improve the value of their lands. Adding new housing stock in areas where they did not own land, on the other hand, would only diminish the value of their property.

In order to quell such opposition, figures such as Orr and Sir Lawless Hepper (the future chairman of the Bombay Development Directorate) effected a stunning epistemological transformation. In a new list of "slum areas" in the city drawn up by the Trust's executive health officer, villages such as Vadala, lying adjacent to Scheme 5 in Dadar–Matunga, were now represented as "slums."[13] Thus some 4,200 acres of the Sion section of F Ward in the north of the island were now categorized as slums deserving of BIT attention. This represented an extraordinary variation of what William Glover calls the "colonial spatial imagination" that guided colonial urban intervention in the nineteenth century.[14] In that earlier period, the older parts of the native city were represented as epistemologically opaque and unsusceptible to European intervention, while the bucolic villages on the urban periphery were considered more amenable to transformation. In the Trust's new way of thinking in the 1910s, villages such as Vadala and Sion on the urban edge were now outposts of the very same urban malaise that characterized Nagpada or Agripada, but in smaller and more manageable form.

The transformation of villages on the urban edge into slums was part of a larger epistemological transformation implicit in the Trust's recasting of suburbanization as part of the strategy of indirect attack on the slum problem. In effect, the Trust was bridging a long-standing cognitive chasm between the physical territory of Bombay Island, which coincided with the municipal definition, and the reality of the built-up city, comprising only about half the island at the end of the nineteenth century. By recasting suburbanization as part of the indirect attack on the slums of the old city, the Trust was effectively reaching beyond the edge of the built-up city in the mills of Parel and Lalbaug and incorporating the northern third of the island into the proper ambit of intervention for an urban entity such as itself. In order to understand why the Trust was compelled to turn from direct to indirect attack on the slums, however, we must turn to the problems of precedent it encountered in its attempts at direct attack.

◌ *THE BURDEN OF PRECEDENT*

To appreciate the problem of what I am calling the "burden of precedent" when it came to dealing with land in Bombay, consider the following notice, which appeared on the Classified page of the *Bombay Chronicle* newspaper in 1938. The notice announced the sale of a piece of land between two parties and was posted by the buyer's solicitors. It asked that any third party who might have any claims or rights to the piece of land in question make themselves known to the solicitors. After announcing the names of the parties, the notice proceeded to describe the piece of land as follows:

> All that piece or parcel of Pension and Tax tenure land or ground (now redeemed) with the messuage, tenement or dwelling house standing thereon, situated lying and being on the Eastern side of First Kolbhat Lane . . . and according to Cadastral Survey Register 133 sq. yds. or thereabouts and registered in the Books of the Collector of Land Revenue under Old No. 225, New No. 1714, Old Survey No. 226, New Survey No. 1/142 and Cadastral Survey No. 746 of Bhuleshwar Division and in the books of the Collector of Municipal Rates and Taxes under C Ward No. 3171 and Old Street No. 6 and New Street No. 13 and bounded on or towards the East by the property of Pestonji Ardeshir Bomanji Wadia, on or towards the west by First Kolbhat Lane, on or towards the North by the property of Pallonji Rustomji and on or towards the South by the property secondly described.[15]

In the absence of clear titles to land, anyone engaging in a property transaction would have to post such notices to minimize the risk of some other person presenting a claim to the property. Such notices appeared daily and by the dozen on the Classified pages of newspapers like the *Chronicle,* referring to lands in various precincts of the older parts of the city, suggesting the lack of clarity of title to lands. These notices were quite astonishing—they used no fewer than six administrative classificatory grids in seeking to completely and totally apprehend the piece of land in language. The notice begins by specifying the tenure of the land as "Pension and Tax," a precolonial form of land tenure that, as the notice points out, has been "redeemed."[16] It then proceeds to give an "Old" number and a "New" number, which are the house numbers corresponding to the "Old Survey" (the Tate–Dickinson Survey of 1811–1828) and the "New Survey" (the Laughton Survey of 1865–1872). It then gives the survey numbers of the plot corresponding to the Old Survey and the New Survey. Since neither of these surveys were considered satisfactory, it also gave the numbers corresponding to the Cadastral Survey of 1915–1916. Dissatisfied with these surveys, all of which bore the mark of the colonial Collector's Office, it moves next to a different administrative grid altogether—that of the Municipal Corporation, which collected "Rates and Taxes." Here too, there are two street numbers, an "Old Street No. 6" and a "New

Street No. 13." Finally, abandoning all such classificatory grids, it moves to a literal description of the property, trying to define where it lies in terms of adjacent properties.[17]

Such "Schedule[s] of the Property," as they were described in the notices posted in the newspapers, were nothing less than terse encapsulations of the revenue-administrative history of the city of Bombay—from the precolonial "Pension and Tax" regime, through various stages of the colonial Collector's Office, through the transfer of power to the Indian-dominated Municipal Corporation, and finally into some Borgesian retreat from symbolic representation. Such schedules, with their desperate attempt to cover all possible avenues in legally apprehending the relevant piece of land in language, were necessary because of the peculiar pattern of development of Bombay and the burden of precedent that it entailed.

As is well-known, Bombay and the other colonial port cities—Calcutta and Madras—originated as European settlements. There were no significant indigenous urban formations at these sites. After the Portuguese handed Bombay over to the British as part of Catherine of Braganza's dowry on her marriage to Charles II in 1661, the islands were in turn passed on to the East India Company for a nominal rent.[18] In truth, no one was overly excited about the malarial and swampy expanse of seven islands that constituted Bombay: in the late seventeenth century, the "city" consisted of a small British fortification containing the houses and factories of East India Company representatives, a few Portuguese forts with sparse populations, and various small villages all scattered across the seven islands.

In order to facilitate its trading operations, the Company tried to attract settlers to the islands, especially to the vicinity of the fort, by offering land on the most favorable terms it could come up with: property holders were able to build on their property under no restrictions whatsoever; persons who were already occupying lands were permitted to retain their properties under the very terms under which they and their ancestors had held them. (In other words, there was no attempt to disturb the status quo and introduce newer, more modern forms of leases.) The rights of the Company to resume land were left quite murky, the presumption having been that there could not conceivably have been any reason for the Company to want the land back. Property holders thus held land under a variety of tenurial systems, some of them allegedly dating back to the thirteenth century.[19]

By the early nineteenth century, the East India Company was not merely one of many European competitors struggling to fight disease and to do business with the mighty Mughal Empire, but in fact had established itself as ruler of large parts of the subcontinent. As is well-known, part of the process by which the Company consolidated its position was by imposing uniform revenue settlements over the disparate parts of what was beginning to resemble an empire.[20] Yet despite the fact that much of "Bombay City" resembled agricultural land in the 1820s and 1830s when the Bombay [Presidency] Revenue Survey was being conducted, the city and island were excluded from the standardizing thrust of the survey.[21] Because the Company had followed a laissez-faire policy with regard to tenures on the island since the seventeenth century, it was unable, in the nineteenth century, to alter the relations that the Bombay islands' landed classes had enjoyed for almost two hundred years with the Company's sanction.

Yet another sensibility was also unfolding, one in which certain elements of the administration felt deeply uneasy about the lack of clarity with regards to the Company's relationship to its lands. In 1843 the Government of Bombay charged the collector of Bombay with furnishing a map of the island of Bombay,[22] "distinguishing particularly the portions which are the acknowledged property of Government as well as those which are admitted to have been encroached upon."[23] In his response, the collector concludes with the following astonishing admission: "In fact, I believe that there is little or no ground on the Island [of Bombay] which I could report to be the acknowledged property of Government."[24] The government's "property" could not be established precisely because of the staggering range, complexity, and antiquity of tenures that obtained on the island, most of which did not have clearly demarcated notions of "ownership" and "property" attached to them.[25]

Such a state of affairs provoked much anxiety in the administration, especially from the 1860s onward. In this period, the administration's (by this time the British Crown) laissez-faire attitude toward lands began to change. In the 1860s Bombay underwent its first "boom" period. In 1853, the first rail link in India had already been established, connecting Bombay to Thana. The first cotton mill had opened in Bombay in 1851. During the U.S. Civil War, when the supply of cotton from the American South to Britain was interrupted, Bombay experienced a windfall as the demand for Indian cotton soared. Accompanying the spike in demand for cotton was a speculative frenzy, primarily in the stock market but also, importantly, in lands.[26]

Such energetic exchanges in the property market caused the state to worry that it was not getting its due. Most importantly, the state worried, with some justification, that people were buying and selling government lands without the government's knowledge and without the government receiving any portion of the proceeds. Effectively, the state was kept out of the circuit of exchanges in the emerging real estate market. Hence, a second survey of the town and island of Bombay was commissioned: that of Colonel G. A. Laughton, whose team surveyed the island between 1865 and 1872. While the primary purpose of Laughton's survey, as he wrote in his final report, was to gain an accurate picture of the nature of landed property following the speculation of the early 1860s, a second important goal was to accurately survey those parts of the island that were either "new," having been reclaimed from the sea since the last survey, or, "chiefly in the northern districts," for which "no detailed plans were to be found at all."[27] Hence, an important goal of Laughton's survey was to clearly map out those northern parts of the island that could possibly increase greatly in value if the speculation in lands continued.

A further consideration that emerged after the 1860s had to do with the state's abilities to control urban development. Whereas the problem initially had been to attract people to Bombay and to get them to remain there, the industrialization of Bombay beginning in midcentury posed migration as a problem in another way: how to regulate Bombay's growth? How to plan for development if government had no clear idea of its status with regards to the lands of Bombay? Hence, the most important consequence of Bombay's revenue history was the proliferation of different forms of tenure, leading to a situation where almost no one had clear title to any piece of property. This meant that the state had no clear mandate to resume lands in the public interest.

When the Trust actually began its operations in the older parts of the city in the late nineteenth century, the complications arising from speculation and indeterminate ways of pricing the land were astounding. The following discussion illustrates the problems encountered by the Trust in its attempts to acquire land in older parts of the city in order to execute various improvement and street schemes. These acquisitions were not part of the suburbanization project, but as I argued at the beginning of this chapter, the resistance encountered in the executions of these schemes was an important factor that led the Trust to turn to suburban development as a perhaps easier way to address the problem of overcrowding in Bombay. (However, land acquisition in the suburbs posed its own problems, as discussed later in the chapter.)

In the older parts of the city, where lands were needed to prosecute sanitary housing schemes and to build new streets to "ventilate" the congested areas, the Trust encountered extraordinary resistance. Generally speaking, the Trust's initial practice in 1898 and 1899 in assessing land was first to ascertain the net rental yield on the land and then to pay the owner a sum that represented the capitalized net rental over a certain number of years.[28] The number of years over which the net rental was capitalized, as well as the rate of interest, was determined by the nature of the property and the interest that such a property might be thought to yield.

However, as soon as the Trust sought to acquire land on this basis, it faced alternative modes of assessment offered by landholders, invariably resulting in much higher sums being demanded of it. One technique used by landholders was to claim compensation on the basis of "valuation on land and buildings." In this method, landholders computed the cost of the building that stood upon the land, less depreciation, and added to that sum the cost of the land itself, calculated independently. This form of valuation was ultimately rejected by the Tribunal of Appeal, which was constituted under the City of Bombay Improvement Act to arbitrate in disputes over land valuation. The tribunal ruled that such a form of valuation was specious because it falsely assumed a "direct and necessary relation between cost and value"—that is, a direct and necessary relation between the costs of building a structure and the present market price of that structure.[29]

Subsequently, landholders came up with a different method of valuation that raised the issue of the "potentiality" of land. Many plots contained buildings of only one floor, often improvised, built of *cutcha* materials such as sticks and rags instead of bricks and mortar. Landholders claimed that it would be unfair to assess the land on this basis, and that instead lands should be assessed on the basis of the potential yield were the land to be fully developed. Hence the true value of the land would be the capitalized net rental the land would yield were it to be developed to its fullest extent less the cost of building the new structures plus the debris value of the existing structure. The Trust adopted this form of valuation for a while, until it realized that it was taking a severe beating. Landholders would come up with "paper schemes for the erection of magnificent buildings upon sites which were already often fully developed according to the requirements of the neighbourhood" and would then claim "an altogether fictitious value for the land upon this basis."[30]

After a period in which the Trust was forced by the Tribunal of Appeal to pay out sums far larger than the initial assessment proposed by the special collector, the tribunal finally ruled that this form of valuation—known as "valuation by a hypothetical building scheme"—needed an important qualification. If the purchaser of a parcel of land paid out the full value of the land once the hypothetical building scheme was carried out, then the purchaser was basically handing over all the profits to the vendor (in the form of the enhanced capitalized net rental of some future development), while also assuming all the risk (in the event that the scheme did not yield the projected returns). Hence the tribunal now ruled that in any future such transaction, the price of the land must be discounted to reflect not only the cost of building future structures but also the potential risks and profits associated with the buyer's investment. In practice, however, this discounting did not amount to very much and probably did not really reflect all the risks borne by the Trust, nor the possible profits that it might gain.

A final form of land valuation, which appears to have become generalized by about 1907, was on the basis of "plotting schemes." This form of valuation was exceptionally common in areas in the north of the island, where the Trust was busy acquiring large "vacant" plots for its proposed new suburban developments.[31] In a plotting scheme, the owner of a large, vacant plot of land would hypothetically lay out the land in plots, allowing for the construction of roads and passages, and would then calculate the value of each plot. He would then demand a sum equivalent to the aggregated gross of all such plots, less the actual cost of laying out the land in plots. In other words, he would demand retail prices for what amounted to a wholesale transaction.

The Trust objected furiously to this method of valuation, contending that this amounted to exactly the same speculative pricing as that which obtained in the valuation by hypothetical building scheme. Yet, curiously, the courts appeared invariably to have sided with landholders in this matter. In the wake of these setbacks, the Trust sought to have its act of incorporation amended to reflect a clearer understanding of what market value was, one that acknowledged a reasonable potential value to land but yet checked what it viewed as the rapacious predilections of Bombay landholders (and the vagaries of the courts that led them to rule in the landholders' favor). Predictably, this led to an energetic correspondence among various luminaries. Generally, the difficulty lay in getting to a figure that represented the true value of the land, something that lay anterior to the present standard of "market value." The Trust seemed willing to acknowledge that there was some "potential value" to the land, and hence that the price of the land should be higher than what it would fetch if it were sold "as is," but yet it seemed to believe that there was a better way to get to this figure than the one adopted by the courts. Eventually, this elusive quest was shot down. Doubting the efficacy of legislative actions, the Trust's counsel argued, "I doubt whether it will be possible to find any better criterion of the amount that ought to be paid than the present one of 'market value.' That is clear enough, and no refinements of legislation will avail to restrain the vagaries of the Courts."[32] The proposal to amend the City of Bombay Improvement Act was dropped on the grounds that no legislative changes would help further clarify the true meaning of market value.

The problem seems to have been that not only did the Trust face severe opposition from Indian landholders who were seeking to uphold their property rights, but also, more surprisingly, the British courts seemed to side very often with Indian landowners in their assertion of property rights. The "burden of precedence" came to have two meanings. First, the East India Company recognized the precolonial and premodern forms of tenure—forms of landholding that were not, in principle, fungible—existing on the island of Bombay without the gradual process of imposing property-like settlements as had been common elsewhere in the country. But on top of that, the British courts upheld older notions of "private property" and were less open to the kinds of eminent domain–like acquisitions that the Trust was making. In other words, while the Trust represented a novel kind of state power claiming to speak and act (and acquire property) in the name of something called "public interest," the British courts only recognized private interests.

These examples have served to illustrate the problems the Trust faced in acquiring land in the old city. Consistently, the Trust's valuations on pieces of land, often no more than a few square yards in size, were challenged by landholders, leading to an extraordinarily litigious process in which the (colonial) judiciary often ruled against the (colonial) Trust. Much of the problem seemed to arise from the absence of uniformity in the market for land. Different pieces of land had different kinds of tenures, with various groups claiming an interest. As a result the market worked on a principle of proximity and adjacency: the price of a piece of land was determined by the lands in the vicinity. It was not likely that potential buyers might consider buying land in a distant area, especially in the north of the island, since the wide range of tenures and the absence of street linkages made such investments highly uncertain. It was only when speculators gained advance knowledge of the Trust's acquisitions—and thus the existence of a buyer of last resort—that they would invest. This was precisely the sort of investment that the Trust did not want to take place.

The shift from direct attack to indirect attack in 1909 was thus an important move by the Trust to take control of *all* the land in the north of the island. By taking possession of lands and then leasing these very lands out with consistent regulations and conditions, the Trust hoped to create a smoothly functioning land market in the north, where investors could invest with full knowledge of the conditions under which land was held. By linking the north to the city with streets and roads, the Trust sought to stabilize property values.

✎ PLANNING THE SUBURBS

Although Matunga was loosely envisaged as a garden suburb, no comprehensive urban planning vision appeared to underpin the Dadar–Matunga–Sion enterprise. Control of land and control of streets were the two principal features of the suburban program. Since the whole enterprise spun out of the devastating plague epidemic of 1896, which was thought to have been caused by overcrowding and the resulting lack of light and ventilation in the old city, the main idea was to construct housing that would be spacious, well lit, and well ventilated. There was a loose and unsystematic attempt to model the suburbs along the great innovations taking place in Europe at the time: it was common practice, for instance, for senior Trust officers to make little study trips while on their home leave and share their observations with other senior Trust officials.

W. C. Hughes, for instance, an engineer who did the rounds of postings in various establishments before becoming the chairman of the Port Trust in Bombay, wrote a little pamphlet titled *Notes on City Improvement Schemes in England*.[33] Hughes noted that the schemes he had visited in Manchester were not, in fact, as comprehensive as those envisioned for Schemes 5 and 6. Indeed, the administrators at the Blackley scheme in Manchester were especially admiring of the all-encompassing nature of the Trust's schemes in Bombay—the fact that, by purchasing all the land beforehand, the Trust could control every aspect of the scheme in a way that was quite unprecedented. But the English settlements were especially to be noted for the great advances they had made in land evaluations—systems of determining how best to price the land fairly prior to acquisition. The key element here was not some rarified technique of calculation but rather the more prosaic measure of secrecy—Hughes notes how well planners in Britain had succeeded in keeping the details of a scheme secret, most importantly the areas to be affected, in order to avoid speculation and resulting higher prices.

Such attempts to study the global process of suburbanization notwithstanding, the process as it actually unfolded in Bombay was a piecemeal and contingent affair. The Trust never really worked out a comprehensive plan for its suburban estates. The key discriminating feature of the suburb was that it was to be the negation of the city. Whereas neighborhoods like Nagpada and Pydhonie had crowded, multistory tenement buildings, Dadar–Matunga would have bungalows laid out on spacious plots. Whereas the old city was overcrowded and had no "healthful" open spaces, Dadar–Matunga would have plenty of spaces reserved for gardens and parks. Whereas the streets in the old city were narrow and crooked and difficult to traverse, the streets in Matunga would be straight, and their widths would be calibrated to accommodate the specific roles they would play in the neighborhood: Was a given passageway to be a lane along which residences were to be strung? Was it to be a street linking such lanes? Was it to be a road connecting such pockets to bigger thoroughfares leading into and out of the neighborhood? (However, as will be discussed later, Trust officials also campaigned successfully for more-stringent municipal building bylaws, which proved important in determining the final shape of the suburban environment.)

The Trust's suburbanization project proceeded at two levels. Most importantly and prominently, the Trust physically acquired and transformed all the lands needed: an epic task, as suggested by the quotation from the BIT annual report at the beginning of the chapter. As argued below, control of the land was the key instrument through which the built environment was to be shaped. Second, the Trust sought to control the suburb by controlling the use of the street. Indeed, the control of the street was the primary instrument through which the Trust sought to shape the form of its suburban development. As indicated above, the Dadar–Matunga project was envisaged as a street scheme, which might appear contradictory when one considers that the suburb was actually a housing development more than it was a street development. Yet in fact the laying out of streets and the control of the size of plots were the only means the Trust had to shape the development. It did not have a strong mechanism for controlling exactly what kind of residences would be built in the suburb, but it imagined villas and cottages with a smattering of chawls for the lower end of the middle class. Through control of the lands and of the streets, it sought to channel private building in the desired direction. The following discussion is thus structured around these aspects of the Trust's suburbanization strategy: the attempts by the Trust to acquire and thus control the lands, and the attempt to control the street.

Suburban Lands

As early as 1827, the villages of "Matoonga" and "Sion" appeared in the collector's rolls as small villages paying a few rupees in assessment.[34] When the East India Company acquired the islands of Bombay in the seventeenth century, these lands were uncultivated or "waste" lands, but the Company gradually proceeded to alienate the lands to Kunbi cultivators. The land was alienated under a *toka* tenure, a term that refers to the share of the produce that was due the Company as landlord. By 1751, the Company had introduced a revenue-farming system, with the hope of boosting the produce of the land—every seven years, a public auction would be held and revenue farming rights would be sold off, with the condition that the revenue farmers were not to extract from the Kunbi cultivators more than the agreed upon *toka*. This measure introduced another intermediary layer of "ownership" between the Company and the lands, in addition to the mediations created as a result of the Kunbi cultivators alienating the lands among themselves.

These lands and their cultivators do not appear too frequently in the archival record over the course of the nineteenth century, except as and when the colonial state sought, in its sporadic way, to try and flex its muscles by trying to reassess the revenue rate on various kinds of lands. The *toka*, or revenue assessment, varied from year to year, depending on the market price of crop. From 1837–1838 onward, however, the rate of assessment remained fixed, at twenty rupees per *moora* of crop, without any links to the market price.[35] The delinking of the assessment from the market price marked an important shift: this was a moment when the value of the land was beginning to be determined less on the basis of its agricultural productivity and more on the basis of its proximity to an expanding city.

In 1876, shortly after the completion of Laughton's survey of the town and island of Bombay, the collector of Bombay sought to reassess the *toka* lands on the basis of the new survey and hence, as argued above, on the grounds that these lands had a new kind of a potential created by the land speculation taking place. The collector, F. F. Arbuthnot, wrote to the Revenue Department asking permission to

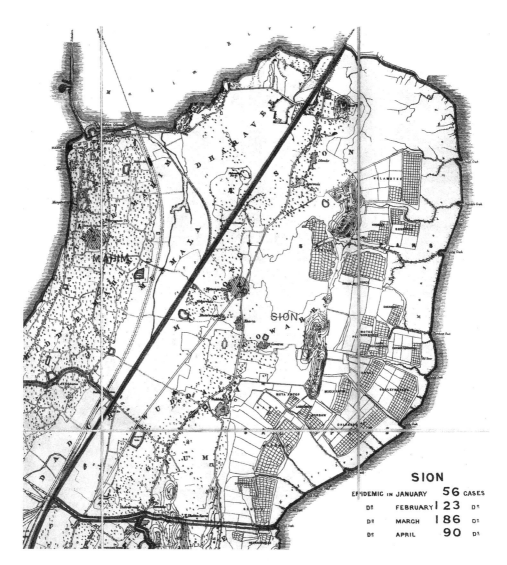

SION

EPIDEMIC IN JANUARY		**56**	CASES
D͟ᵒ	FEBRUARY	I **23**	D͟ᵒ
D͟ᵒ	MARCH	I **86**	D͟ᵒ
D͟ᵒ	APRIL	**90**	D͟ᵒ

⤳ FIGURE 1.2. *This detail of the northern portion of Bombay from 1897 shows the villages of "Matoonga" and "Sion" in the top right portion of the map, just east of the railway line in the northeast part of the island. The area that became the suburbs contained the settlements Colwada, Agurwada, Bhunderwada, Maharwada, Gowaree, and Kharra. Presumably these were inhabited by Kolis, Agris, Bhandaris, Mahars, and Gowaris. "Map of the Island of Bombay," in* Report on the Bubonic Plague in Bombay, 1896– 97, Medical History of British India, *http://www.digital.nls.uk/74580550. Courtesy of the National Library of Scotland.*

assess lands in Sion, Matunga, and Wadala at a rate of half a paisa per square yard in Matunga and Sion. (The rate would be one paisa per square yard in Parel and Naigaum, which were closer to the city and hence had more potential value.)[36] When this proposal was sanctioned, it marked a very important point in the passage of the lands in Matunga and Sion from agricultural land to urban land: they were now being assessed purely on a cash basis, with no connection whatsoever to the agricultural productivity of the soil.

This remained the somewhat placid state of affairs until the late 1890s, when most of the Dadar–Matunga–Sion area was notified under Schemes 5 and 6 of the Improvement Trust. Almost immediately after the plan to acquire lands in Sion and Matunga were announced, however, it became clear that land acquisition in the north of the island was not going to be especially easy. For one thing, the fact that the land was held on *toka* tenure, an ancient and archaic form of landholding, meant that establishing the Trust's rights to acquire such land was not going to be easy. While exchanges of property had obviously taken place previously, they had been confined to exchange of usufructuary rights, with the buyer merely acquiring from the seller, for cash or some other form of compensation, the right to continue using the lands. The Trust was trying to do something different: it was trying to purchase land outright and establish a freehold on it, which it then proposed to lease out on 999-year leases.

One of the challenges faced by the Trust in establishing such freehold property was that the British Crown, through its representative, the collector of Bombay, still held a feudatory interest in the land. The acquisition of *toka* lands by the Trust thus entailed working out formulas of monetary compensation to resolve these older rights and obligations. This particular problem was elaborated by the Trust's land manager, M. S. Bharucha, in a note written in 1908. By that year, Scheme 6 involved 1,300 cases of land acquisition, and at the time of his writing, only 148 awards had been made, and of that number, 90 had been challenged and referred to the Tribunal of Appeal:

> I have the honour to inform you that most of the land included within the limits of the above Scheme is held of Government under Toka Tenure and that the assessment on it is liable to enhancement in 1929/30 when the term (50 years) for which the present assessment was fixed expires. . . . The grounds on which the appeals have been lodged deal mainly with the question of the claim by Government in respect of its interests in the land to be acquired.[37]

In other words, what were the terms under which the land could be resumed by the Trust if the land was held by landholders on *toka* tenure from the British Crown, whose representative was the collector? Since the Trust was not, technically, an organ of government, the latter entity was concerned that when the

Trust went ahead and acquired lands, which it subsequently would lease out for building purpose, then government would lose the "revenue" it was accruing through these lands. As indicated earlier, the revenue was not substantial: Sion and Matunga, the areas alluded to here by the land manager, were fixed at a half paisa per square yard in 1877 (hence the expiration, fifty years later, in 1929, as alluded to in Bharucha's note). The government was ceding control over the land, though, which would now vest in the Trust, and it wanted compensation.

This seemingly minor affair actually pointed to important changes occurring in the way these lands were perceived. In particular, two problematic aspects of the increasing fungibility of land were cast into relief. First, the Trust's acquisitions in the *toka* tenure lands of Sion was clearly a first step in converting lands from agrarian to urban use. If this change took place, then what was the basis for the collector to continue claiming an annual share of the produce as "land revenue"? Second, as described earlier, the Trust's acquisitions and development in the suburbs were part of its indirect attack on the housing problem. Toward this end, its goal was to create an efficiently functioning market in land in the suburbs, a market that would be able to meet the demand for housing by supplying building sites. To enable this market to function efficiently, the Trust sought to impose consistency and uniformity in landholding patterns, most obviously by establishing a single party as the landholder. From this point of view, the Crown's feudatory interest in some lands but not others constituted a disturbance of the uniform stable land market that the Trust sought to fashion. From the Trust's point of view, thus, the Crown's claim to a share of the value of *toka* lands was an atavistic encrustation that it sought to sweep aside.

Eventually Bharucha proposed a settlement in which the Trust's award for each plot was apportioned between the *toka* tenants and the government.[38] Even after such a settlement, however, the diversity of landholders with different arrangements, even on small patches of land, made apportioning shares of the Trust's award extremely arduous. Consider the following case of the Trust's attempts to acquire a patch of land in Matunga known as the "Matunga Maharwada," a Mahar settlement that appears on late-nineteenth-century maps of Bombay but that had disappeared by the time the Trust generated its own maps of its schemes in the 1910s.[39] The entire patch of land was "notified" as required for Scheme 5. This was a patch of land consisting of forty-seven small holdings that had been held by the Mahars to pursue their occupation of small cultivation and, in this instance, basket weaving. But by 1908, only eleven of the holdings were still held by Mahars; on two other holdings were a temple and a Catholic church. Thirty-three of the remaining thirty-four holdings were in possession of persons other than the original Mahar holders, as sublessees. The remaining occupant had already had his land attached by the collector for revenue default.

The problem faced by the collector was how to arrive at a settlement on this one patch of land, consisting of forty-seven small holdings, in which there were three categories of occupants. The case of the sublessees was easiest to negotiate—they were clearly tenants-at-will of the government. The Collector's Office not only served notice on them to vacate the lands but also assessed them arrears of revenue from 1889, when they had subleased the land from the Mahars. The temple and church were being used by the Mahars but were not deemed permanent structures. Hence the Collector's Office offered the Mahars the value of the land on which they stood, and then went ahead and resumed it. The Mahars themselves constituted a special case. There was no record of the Mahars ever having paid assessment, even though there was a record of a correspondence dating from 1849 in which the collector had attempted to extract a nominal payment, and the fact that they had never actually made any payments meant that their lands had now acquired more of the character of a freehold. Since this would mean that it would be very difficult for the collector to claim any share of the land at this late date, and "having regard to the fact that the Mhar holders are basket makers, possessing no means or resources of any kind," the collector proposed making no claims whatsoever on the eleven Mahar holdings. Note that this did not mean that the Mahar holdings were not to be acquired; it just meant that the collector was making no claim on these lands and thus was claiming no part of the compensation offered by the Trust.

An excellent account of the pattern of land alienation and speculation that took place in advance of the Trust's acquisitions is provided by the case of the Matunga village near the railway station whose population were Kutchi Bhatias. Many Bhatias and other Gujarati speculators from older parts of the city to the south had purchased plots of land in Matunga and Sion from 1898 onward in advance of the Trust's proposed acquisitions. While many of these land purchases were scattered around the large plain that became the suburbs of Dadar–Matunga–Sion, the densest settlement of houses was in an area near the railway station and came to be called the "Bhatia settlement" by the Trust's officers. In the Trust's original plans, this settlement was to have been included in Scheme 6 and redeveloped into orderly building sites. As a result of the haggling and counterbidding of the settlement's residents, however, the Trust was forced to exclude it from the scheme altogether. The account of this settlement's exclusion thus provides a window into the speculation that was rife in these lands in advance of the Trust's acquisitions.[40]

The original Scheme 6 clearly indicates that the Bhatia settlement was to be part of the scheme.[41] Among the property owners in this area, however, was an extremely litigious and combative Bhatia landowner by the name of Keshavlal Sanghani. Along with his partners Bai Hemkuvar, Vacharaj Mohanji, and the latter's son Nagardas Vacharaj, Sanghani had acquired a whole group of properties in this area between 1899 and 1906.[42] The map from 1898 in Figure 1.2 shows no sign of the "Matunga village" near the train station, confirming that Sanghani and his associates began their speculative acquisitions in this area shortly after the Trust's formation in 1898 and the initial announcement of the intention to develop Matunga into a suburb. The Trust sought to acquire these properties from 1905 onward, but Sanghani bargained tenaciously.[43] Sanghani sought to bypass the conventional process of land acquisition, in which the special collector came up with a figure that the landowner either accepted or contested in the Tribunal of Appeal. Instead, he attempted to negotiate a private settlement, at much higher rates than the special collector was awarding elsewhere.[44] His tone became increasingly strident when it started to become clear that the Trust was about to call his bluff and exclude the older Bhatia settlement from Scheme 6, which would result in his failing to profit from his speculations. Finally, a bland note from J. P. Orr concluded that there was no real need to include the settlement in the scheme. Later maps of Scheme 6 show the areas around Lakshminarayan Lane and Vacharaj Lanes as "excluded from the scheme."

Sanghani and his fellow Bhatias may not have been successful in their speculations, but they were able to modify the Trust's agenda in more ways than getting their own settlement excluded from Scheme 6. Consider the proposed meat-and-fish market near the Matunga railway station. At a meeting of the trustees on January 31, 1913, the chairman of the Trust proposed the building of a market:

> With a view to attracting people to our Dadar–Matunga Estate it is important that we should make the first comers as comfortable as possible and remove or abate as far as may be the inconveniences they have to put up with as things are. Amongst these the one I have heard most inquirers speak about is the absence of a market. In the sanctioned development plan a site is reserved for a market close to Matunga Station; it was not originally intended that the market should be built at once, as it might not pay to invest much money in a pukka market long before the vicinity is fully populated; but with the population already on the ground and the population attending the new Railway workshops close by, I think a market would certainly pay.[45]

Although the suburban population was not growing as fast as expected, there was still a demand for a market: the already-existing "population on the ground"—by which the chairman referred to the small population of Kutchis scattered along Lakshminarayan Lane and Vacharaj Lanes and the various small villages and households scattered around Matunga and Sion—was not entirely insignificant. There was also a new population of workers who visited the area every day in order to work in the newly opened Great Indian Peninsular Railway (GIP) workshops. Most importantly, the area had to be made attractive for prospective settlers, and a market would significantly boost the area's desirability.

Shortly after the Trust decided to go ahead and sanction the opening of a private market near the Matunga railway station, the Trust's land manager received a letter from the Matunga Residents' Association. The association was objecting to the proposal to have a "flesh market" near the Matunga station since all the residents in the vicinity were "Vegetarian Hindoos."[46] As described by the land manager, there was a pocket of bungalows "to the north of the market site," which were "not included in the Scheme," whose owners had covenants in their deeds requiring them to "sell only to vegetarians." The land manager was referring to the houses that lined Lakshminarayan Lane and Vacharaj Lane, the core of the Bhatia settlement.

The land manager met with members of the Matunga Residents' Association, who persuaded him that the residents of "the northern portion of this Scheme (Scheme V) and the southern part of Scheme VI" would mostly be Hindus and thus vegetarians.[47] In the northern parts of Scheme 6, on the other hand, in areas that fell within the range of the old Portuguese Sion fort and settlement, where there was a Roman Catholic church, there were also Catholic residents. Hence, the land manager "anticipate[d] that in the future a large number [of meat eaters would] live in that locality."[48] The meat-and-fish market was moved to Sion, and Matunga featured a vegetable market. In this case, the Bhatias of Matunga were able to use their peculiar type of claim on the land—leases that included covenants to sell only to vegetarians—to persuade the Trust that it was prejudiced against them in its efforts to introduce a meat-and-fish market. Such covenants thus served to resist and transform the Trust's wish to create an abstract space that could be fashioned into a suburb where calculations about the location of meat markets could be made on purely rational bases.

The vegetarian clause in the covenants of the Bhatias was one way in which older ties to the land were used by residents to modify the Trust's attempts to create abstract space; another example was provided in the efforts of Ranchodlalji Ghanshamlalji Maharaj to enhance the Trust's valuation of his property. This man was an important leader of the Vaishnav community of the city and was the head priest of the temple in Bhuleshwar, where he had his permanent residence.[49] In Matunga he had constructed what he called his suburban residence, where he spent a few months of the year. He had made an effort to decorate his bungalow in keeping with his beliefs and his position as a spiritual leader, with the front of the bungalow having an "ornate porch of the Hindu temple style of architecture." The fruits and flowers in the garden were grown for use in the main temple in Bhuleshwar, and overall, an "attempt was made to invest this property with a quasi-religious character."

In valuing this property for acquisition, the Trust sought to ascertain the value of the lands and the cost of building, as was customary practice. They denied that it was a "suburban residence" since Matunga was not yet a suburb and since this property was not near the railway station. It was thus more like a country house, according to the Trust, and should be valued correspondingly lower. In contesting the Trust's valuation with the Tribunal of Appeal, Maharaj insisted that his property was his "suburban residence." Further, although this claim was not made explicit in the Trust's reporting of the case other than as implied in the detailed description of the religious paraphernalia on the property, I suggest that Maharaj tried to make an issue of the fact that the place was special. Since it was *his* suburban residence, not just that of any other person, it was invested with a special aura, as indicated by the religious appurtenances. It was not just his place, but a place of significance for the entire Vaishnav community. The land and buildings, thus, were not simply land with a physical structure upon it; they were also invested with the beliefs of the Vaishnavs of Bombay.

Undoubtedly Maharaj was out to get the best price he could for his property. If the Trust was not willing to accept his claim that it was his suburban residence, he asked them to consider it as a potential industrial site, which would be valued more than a country residence but less than a suburban residence. Yet it would be a mistake to characterize Maharaj's machinations as purely cynical manipulation of his spiritual status to maximize his compensation. He was not a speculator like the landowners of the Bhatia settlement. His bungalow had been built more than forty years prior to the Trust's acquisition attempts in the 1910s and had never been rented out. Rather, I suggest that Maharaj believed that his land was invested with the emotions of his community and felt that if he was to be uprooted, he would demonstrate the degree to which he embodied his community's spiritual investment by maximizing his compensation. Eventually the Tribunal of Appeal decided on a figure that was higher than the Trust's valuation but much lower than what Maharaj sought. Nonetheless, this example illustrates ways in which land was invested with sentiment, which the Trust had to contend with in its efforts to create the abstract space of suburban building plots.

While the most common challenges to the Trust's efforts came in the form of such contests over valuation, sometimes landholders would try and lodge petitions before the provincial Government of Bombay. Since such petitions were interrogating the Trust's mission and mandate at a fundamental level, they merit a closer look. Before considering the petitions, however, it is important to understand exactly how petitions were received and the consideration they received. In other words, all petitions were not equal. An important element of the original Trust Act had been the manner in which the legislation countenanced challenges to the Trust's activities. There were, in essence, only five sorts of challenges that the Trust had to take seriously:

1. A representation by the municipal commissioner
2. A representation passed by the Municipal Corporation
3. A written complaint by the municipal health officer

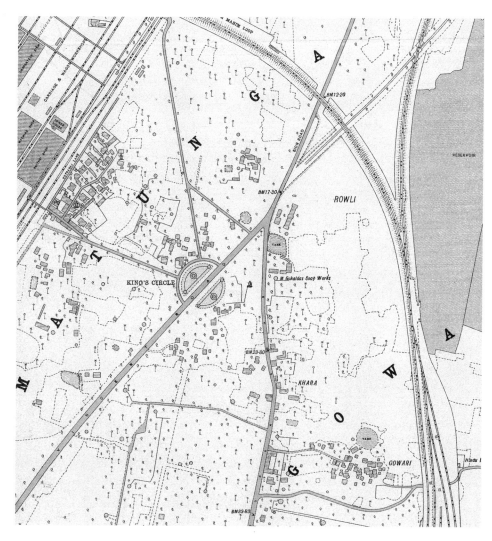

FIGURE 1.3. *The Dadar–Matunga–Sion sector as developed up until the 1910s. The Bhatia settlement by the GIP east of King's Circle is the most developed part of Matunga; King's Circle is the most noteworthy physical manifestation of the suburban project. The marked plots are still irregular in shape, but the beginnings of alignment of regular-edged building plots oriented along streets can be seen. Bombay City Survey 1919, Sheets 11–12. Courtesy of the Regenstein Library, University of Chicago.*

4. A written complaint signed by three or more justices of the peace residing in the area affected

5. A written complaint signed by twelve or more persons liable to pay any property tax leviable under the Municipal Act and residing in the affected area.[50]

Such a structure surely affected the manner in which the Trust's proposals were challenged and modified. Indeed, as an examinations of various petitions reveals, the Trust was able to have its way over smaller landholders or powerful individuals, but it was unable to fight organized groups of larger landholders or ratepayers.

The "landowners" of the Sion village petitioned the government to reconsider Scheme 6.[51] The petition is interesting for what it reveals about the Trust's perception of the villages of Matunga and Sion lying at the edge of the city. The petitioners challenged the notion that the new suburbs would actually provide cheap housing for the working classes, which, it will be recalled, was the primary task with which the Trust had been charged. The petitioners charged that instead of producing cheap accommodations, the Trust's plan to create a garden suburb would actually result in the conversion of the fields and palm groves into "residential villas for the well-to-do," who would "prefer a cheap bungalow in Dadar [on the Dadar–Matunga–Sion Estate] after the place is improved with roads and parks to their expensive residence in Bombay."[52] The real solution, the residents of Sion believed, was to construct cheap housing in the industrial areas where the workers were employed, and the employers should be charged with such construction.

The petitioners claimed that Schemes 5 and 6 would deprive them of their livelihoods, which were not very substantial but were adequate, and of lands that they had cultivated for centuries. The petitioners were composed of Kolis, Agris, and Bhandaris. They claimed to be market farmers, surviving on the basis of their proximity to the city of Bombay, which enabled them to bring their goods to the Bombay markets at a lower price than if they had been based in Salsette Island. Interestingly, they invoked the periodic guarantees that were made to them by the Portuguese and British governments, which was why these Agris, Kolis, and Bhandaris had chosen to settle here in the first place and give up their traditional caste occupations as toddy-tappers and fishermen. Hence, the Trust's actions in seeking now to evict them from Sion were essentially a betrayal of those earlier guarantees. This would be especially unjust since the Kolis, Agris, and Bhandaris had cultivated land that hitherto had been waste land and had successfully transformed it into rice fields. The Sion villagers thus presented at least three arguments for why they should be permitted to remain in their villages: First, by terming themselves the "landowners" of Sion, they were clearly invoking a proprietary right to defend their holdings against the claims of the Trust. (Note, however, that they did not designate themselves as ratepayers, probably because their holdings were too small.) Moreover, they claimed to have "improved" the property from waste to agricultural land, thus enhancing their claim. Finally, they invoked the older *toka* tenure linking them to the land, extended to them by the East India Company in an effort to attract settlement to the area. Such a tenure was characterized by reciprocal obligations and was not subject to termination on the payment of cash compensation.

In rejecting outright the claims of these petitioners, the chairman of the Trust, G. O. W. Dunn, issued a terse and brutal statement that captured, better than any other available material, the inexorable path of urbanization that the Trust envisioned. The petitioners, he began, "appear to be the inhabitants of the small and insanitary villages included in Scheme VI," and he continued to explain why their cause was futile:

> The gradual absorption of their lands for the extension of the City must in the nature of things have been merely a matter of time and . . . the proposed action of the Improvement Trust will merely be to quicken this natural expansion and to ensure that the new Suburbs that will be so created will be constructed with due regard to sanitary principles. It is highly probable that a large number of those who are not engaged in Agricultural operations in the North of the Island will when their holdings have been acquired by the Trust be absorbed into other occupations in the City. Others will possibly migrate elsewhere and with the compensation money received for their properties in the Island of Bombay will be able to obtain larger areas elsewhere.[53]

Critical to Dunn's ability to reject the petition of the Sion villagers was his representation of them as dwelling in "small and insanitary villages," a characterization that was just a short step away from the characterization of these villages as "slums" in the list of slums prepared by the executive health officer of the Trust in 1918 (discussed earlier in this chapter). Dunn and the Trust were thus projecting a new cartography of the city of Bombay as a necessary first step in their land acquisitions. The northern villages of Sion, Matunga, Dharavi, Wadala, and so on, previously perceived as villages on the urban periphery, were now cast as "insanitary villages"—instances of blight—and, by 1918, as "slums" in a new cartography of the city of Bombay that was coterminous with the island.

Despite representing themselves as "landowners," and thus as part of that group of the population that the Trust was obliged to hear out, the villagers of Sion did not get much consideration by the Trust. Dunn went on to offer an explanation for why the Trust sought to acquire all the lands in the notified area before commencing with any infrastructural projects:

> The petitioners would no doubt have preferred that the Trust or the Municipality should confine themselves to merely making roads and drains so that they might benefit by the unearned increment that would accrue to them in the enhancement of the values of their lands, which, under those circumstances, they would probably not have objected to convert into building sites as they have done already wherever the situation

is suitable for the purpose; and that they will not have this advantage is no doubt the main reason for their opposition to the Schemes of the Trust.

The provincial government agreed with the chairman of the Trust and decided not to intervene on behalf of the Sion petitioners.[54]

Yet the Trust could not always ride roughshod over petitioners. Consider, for instance, the petitions of the ratepayers of G Ward, who successfully managed to block the Trust from acquiring their lands to execute Schemes 5 and 6 as originally conceived.[55] The original scheme proposed by the Trust was intended to include large swathes of land in the Mahim Woods, in G Ward to the west of Dadar–Matunga–Sion, which lay in F Ward. The Mahim Woods consisted of coconut plantations, and the landowners controlled substantially more valuable properties, which made them ratepayers and hence entitled them to challenge the Trust's schemes. In the original proposed scheme, large portions of these lands were to be included so that Dadar–Matunga–Sion could be linked to the sea and thus be well "ventilated":

> The Trustees' idea was that with this suburb [Dadar–Matunga] fully opened towards the sea and connected by good roads to the sea front, and with large areas as recreation grounds, the middle classes would at once see the advantage of scoring cheap healthy residences in so favourable a situation, and that as they settled down they would take with them their servants and dependants, that shopkeepers and others of that class would naturally follow in their wake, and that along with those a considerable population of the poorer classes would naturally be also attracted to the suburb. It was for these reasons that the Trustees laid such particular stress upon the importance of not having any of the attractive features of the scheme as proposed by them in any way reduced.[56]

The ratepayers challenged the Trust's plan to acquire lands to the west of the railway lines, in G Ward. The Trust's reasoning was that they needed to acquire, at the very least, strips of land in G Ward along which they could construct boulevards, which would suitably ventilate the bulk of Schemes 5 and 6, which lay to the east of the railway lines. As one Trust official noted in response to the ratepayer's petition, "the area west of the B.B.C. & I Railway . . . is necessary to acquire for providing building sites for the expansion of the City and with a view to the suitable ventilation of Schemes V and VI and to render these Schemes attractive to a mixed population."[57]

The ratepayers mounted a series of astute challenges to the Trust's position. They argued, primarily, that the main source of overcrowding was the high density of persons within houses, and hence high densities per acre, rather than a high density of houses. More land for buildings sites was thus not needed. What was needed instead was cheap housing, for the high densities within houses were caused by the high rents, which forced people to cram into houses. They also argued that the Trust should proceed with the acquisition and reclamation of the rice fields in Matunga rather than the coconut plantations of Mahim. The latter had been granted to the owners "since antiquity," and the seizure of the properties would place their owners in "great hardship." The ratepayers had more clout with the government and were able to block the Trust from acquiring lands to the west of the railways lines in G Ward. This meant that a fundamental bulwark of the Trust's suburban vision—the existence of open boulevards linking the new suburbs of Dadar–Matunga to the ocean and thus enabling through winds—was compromised by the ratepayers' opposition.

Sometimes, even powerful individuals were unable to stand up to the acquisitive energies of the Trust. The great industrialist J. N. Tata, for instance, challenged the Trust's original vision for Schemes 5 and 6 on the grounds that some lands belonging to him, located between the GIP and the BBCI, had been notified for acquisition.[58] Tata insisted that he had intended to build a flour mill on this land, which, he claimed, was eminently suitable for that purpose because its location between the two Matunga stations on the two lines would make distribution much simpler. He petitioned the Trust to omit his lands from the notified areas. The Trust was not swayed by his pleas. Arguing that while it was not inclined to obstruct industry, it could not permit him to continue with his plans since this would "prejudice the neighbourhood as a residential quarter." "The object of the Scheme," it wrote, "is to provide building sites for the expansion of the City, and the area has been laid out with a view to its being occupied for residential purposes."[59] This was the most explicit statement of the Trust's radical aims: to create residences that were separate from workplaces.

In the face of such challenges, the attempts by the Trust to acquire and develop the land in Dadar–Matunga for Schemes 5 and 6 proceeded slowly and feebly. For most of the 1910s, the efforts of the Trust were directed toward painstakingly acquiring the land, parcel by parcel, and then draining and improving the land before laying out an infrastructure of streets, drains, and lighting. A look through the annual reports of the Improvement Trust through these years reveals that, typically, the work in this period consisted of activities such as dredging and draining. In 1921, for instance, the Trust reported that the progress on Schemes 5 and 6 for the previous year consisted of leveling and filling in, some work on the construction of a light railway, some work on drains between Kingsway and Matunga Road, some construction of semipermanent sheds for laborers and dishoused tenants, and the construction of a new office for the Engineering Department.[60] The Trust complained about the difficulties: promised machinery did not arrive, delaying important construction activities. Most irksomely, getting possession of lands for the execution of the various schemes remained difficult and long drawn out. In some cases, in addition to the "obstruction of the occupying tenants," there was the additional "handicap of the law's delay."[61]

To adequately grasp the magnitude and complexity of the land-acquisition process, it is worth considering in some detail an example of what the Trust had to deal with. The proceedings of the Trust's meetings contain a schedule that indicates the awards made by the special collector in connection with each of the Trust's various schemes. For a typical such meeting, that of January 11, 1910, there were no fewer than fifty individuals whose lands were required by the Trust for Schemes 5 and 6 and who had received an estimate from the land manager of the Trust. Not satisfied with this estimate, they had appealed to the special Tribunal of Appeal, constituted for this purpose, and this schedule detailed the awards made by the special collector of the Tribunal of Appeal. Hence this schedule listed only those cases that moved to the special collector's Tribunal of Appeal; doubtless there would have been some who elected not to contest the original estimate made by the land manager, just as this schedule included several who were going to contest even the award made by the tribunal, which meant that those cases would move up to the High Court. Many individuals had multiple pieces of land that had been requisitioned, and the size of the land manager's estimates ranged from 63 rupees for a small plot belonging to Damail Dharma Bhoir to 40,877 rupees for a set of plots belonging to Vinayak Shamrao Laud. Interestingly, the names on the schedule indicate a wide diversity of landholders in the Dadar–Matunga–Sion area. While many of the names are traditional caste names of communities that might be expected to occupy such lands, such as Bhoir and Koli, there were also Parsis, Catholics, and a variety of Maharashtrian and Gujarati caste names, possibly reflecting the entry of speculators in advance of the Trust's acquisition. Most of the lands seem to have been used for the cultivation of rice or vegetables.[62]

The Boulevard and the Street

Physically acquiring the land, freeing it from older forms of tenure, and then leasing it out on standardized leases was one important aspect of the Trust's suburbanization strategy. By doing so, the Trust sought two things. First, it wished to create a more uniform and smoothly functioning land market that would respond to the demand for housing. Second, by imposing conditions and covenants in the plots subsequently leased out, it tried to control and regulate the nature of the buildings that would emerge in the suburban landscape. These two goals—creating a uniform land market and regulating building—also underpinned the Trust's street strategy.

At the macro level of the city as a whole, the Trust's strategic turn to suburbanization can be represented by a shift in its emphasis, from east–west streets to south–north streets. In its early years, when the Trust sought to transform the old city, one major means for doing so was through the use of major "ventilating" east–west boulevards such as Princess Street and Sandhurst Road. These roads were to deliver fresh air from the ocean to the west of the city into the crowded districts of the native city in the east. With the "suburban turn" after 1909, the Trust's emphasis turned to south–north streets such as Lamington Road and Sydenham Road/Parel Road/Eastern Avenue, which connected the older parts of the city to the south with the new suburbs to the north. By establishing physical linkages between the city to the south and the new suburbs to the north, the Trust hoped to reassure potential investors that the suburbs would indeed be physically integrated into the city and that investments in the suburbs were thus stable.

At the more micro level of the neighborhood, on the other hand, the Trust used the street as a sort of battering ram for its vision of orderly and regulated building. If the *wadis* and *mohullas* of the older parts of the city were marred by insanitary and ill-ventilated housing, it was because such areas were not penetrated by municipal street patterns that bore modern sewers, drains, and ventilation. The street also served as an index and regulator of building activity by determining building heights and setbacks. In this way, the creation of neighborhoods that were entirely penetrated with street patterns had the effect of stabilizing property values.

The debate over the construction of Eastern Avenue was the principal instance of the first street strategy discussed above. Eastern Avenue was to be a broad boulevard originating in Crawford Market in the south, cutting through the crowded areas of the old native town in Pydhonie, Dongri, and Byculla, reaching through the newer industrial districts of Parel and Lalbaug to culminate in the new suburbs of Matunga and Sion. The road existed, more or less, in rough form. It was known by different names as it meandered its way northward, but the "Eastern Avenue Scheme," as it was called, conceived of a single boulevard, constructed according to standard specifications for each zone that it went through, firmly linking the south of the island with the north. Such a scheme represented perhaps the most comprehensive attempt to anchor the Dadar–Matunga–Sion development firmly to the older parts of the city to the south. It would serve to firmly imprint the former as suburbs of the latter, not merely as satellite settlements loosely linked to the city. The debates over the "improvement" of this road, which was crucial to the success of Schemes 5 and 6 since it was the main access to Dadar–Matunga from the southern parts of the city, indicate the different priorities of the British and the Indian members of the Trust's board.[63]

This road existed in rough form, but the main boosters of the suburban vision, such as Chairman Orr and Chief Engineer R. J. Kent, were in favor of constructing a grand boulevard, "an amenity intended to make the north of the Island attractive."[64] For the planners in the Trust, the boulevard had many advantages. Importantly, it served as an automatic and indirect strategy for "improvement." It also shifted much of the costs of improvement onto the landowners. The position was articulated by H. V. R. Kemball, then chief engineer of the Trust, in a "Note" of 1907.[65] Kemball's "Note" is an extraordinary document, in that more than most other documents, it explicitly articulates the Trust's thinking. Kemball begins by emphasizing the importance of such long arterial roads, especially for long and narrow cities such as Bombay, where most of the traffic will always flow along the length. (In Bombay's case, this would mean a north–south direction.) The important thing to note, Kemball argued, was that the capacity of such roads always needed to increase at a higher ratio than the growth of the population.[66]

In addition to these more obvious advantages in facilitating communications, however, the boulevard and street schemes in general had another, possibly even greater advantage. In effect, they provided a way for the Trust to indirectly effect "improvement" in the quality of the housing stock. As Kemball argued, "The effect of driving a good street through a slum is the general improvement of the district through which it passes."[67] In other words, when a good street is "driven" through a neighborhood, it has the effect, in both literal and figurative senses, of blasting through the slums in the vicinity. Simply put, the land becomes too expensive for landowners to persist in erecting slums, and they are driven by market forces to upgrade their housing stock. Such reasoning explained why the Trust came to favor street schemes over improvement schemes: the former contrived to shift the burden of "improvement" onto landowners. Thus, the Eastern Avenue plan and street schemes in general became the primary target of the landlord-dominated Corporation. While these arguments between the Trust and the Corporation were ostensibly about priorities and better ways to proceed with development, actually they were about battles between the BIT and the landlords about who should bear the cost of raising the value of lands. Both were in the same game: making money from land.

Before turning to these critiques, however, it is worth considering in further detail the minutes of Orr, chairman of the Trust, and R. J. Kent, the chief engineer after Kemball. Taken together, the minutes of Orr and Kent constituted a classic restatement of the modernist view of the street. The street was now to be an efficiently organized machine in itself, to be devoted to pure movement. It was to be as broad as possible so that any future infrastructural enhancements to the mode of communications—in this case the tramway that was to run along the center of the boulevard—could be accommodated. Challenging Dinshaw Vacha's argument that the road did not need to be so broad, Orr argued:

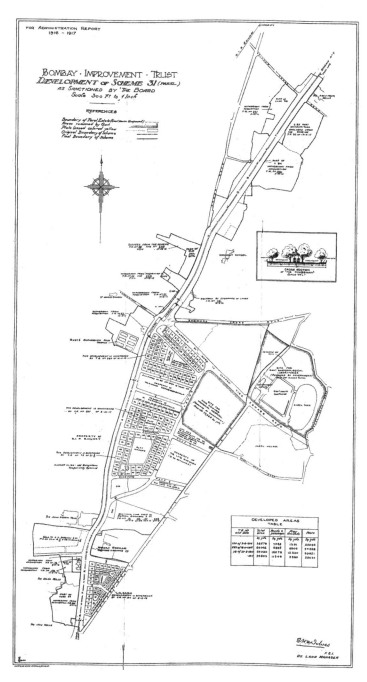

FIGURE 1.4. *Parel Road, also known as Eastern Avenue, making its way northward to Dadar–Matunga. One goal was to physically link the northern suburbs with the old city to the south, but another was surely to establish a continuity of property values between the suburbs and the city by controlling the pattern of development along the road. BIT,* Annual Administration Report, *1916–1917. Courtesy of Maharashtra State Archives.*

Eleven years have now passed since the Board first decided to lay out the North of Island in order "to provide fresh space for building to relieve overcrowding in congested parts" [Orr quotes the text of the Bombay Improvement Trust Act of 1898] and now that they are at last in a position to commence the work of filling in and laying out the land they have acquired at a cost of 20 lakhs for this purpose, their object seems likely to be defeated by the lack of means of cheap and rapid transit between the congested areas and the new suburbs.[68]

Any attempts to lessen the width of the street, and hence slow down the velocity of communications, would lessen the attraction of the expensively acquired and developed Dadar–Matunga Estate. Further, the boulevard was not to be marred by the usual agglomeration of pedestrians, animals, carts, and automobiles that characterized the typical Indian street: Orr and his engineers sought to use trees and other "edges" to distinctly demarcate those areas that were meant for trams, those meant for automobiles, and those meant for pedestrians.[69] A small cross-section of the proposed Kingsway featured in the Trust's annual report, for instance, shows four rows of trees. Two rows near the center of the boulevard would sandwich and separate the tramway from the carriageway lying just outside. Another pair of rows of trees would separate the carriageway from the footpath.[70]

Orr was careful to present the boulevard as part of a "strong indirect attack on the prevailing insanitary conditions which are largely due to overcrowding."[71] The suburbs were presented not as an escape from the crowded city for the privileged classes, but rather as part of a comprehensive citywide strategy to attack the problem of overcrowding in the older parts of the city by attracting some residents northward.

Kent, meanwhile, attacked the suggestions made by Vacha that the amenities of the boulevard—benches, trees, strips of green to separate different functions, and so on—should be relegated to the parks that were also envisioned in the schemes.[72] Kent argued that such suggestions were "based on the false premise that boulevards and parks fulfill the same purpose, and it may be as well to compare the two and examine the points of similarity and difference." While the park and the boulevard might have some features in common, parks were essentially static places. They provided the "lungs" of the city, and they were also pretty to look at and an "attractive amenity to those living within easy reach." Boulevards, on the other hand, were of greater importance than parks since they constituted the channels through which "the life of the place must pass." In thus privileging the boulevard over the park, Kent and Orr displayed an extraordinary and novel way of understanding the neighborhood: not on its own terms, but rather in terms of the ways it articulated with other parts of the city.

Yet while they clearly enunciated a dichotomy between the boulevard and the park, there was to be one place where the two functions were to be subsumed

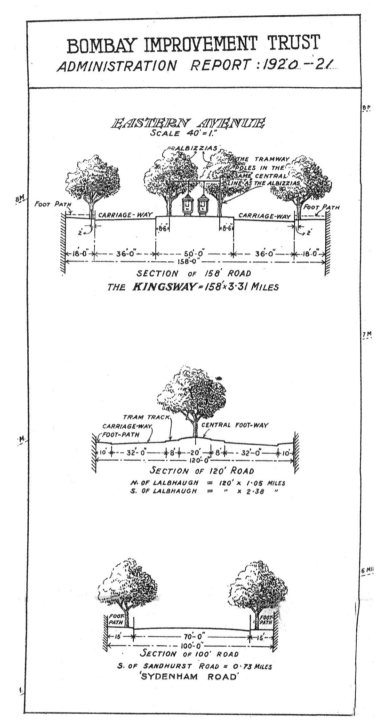

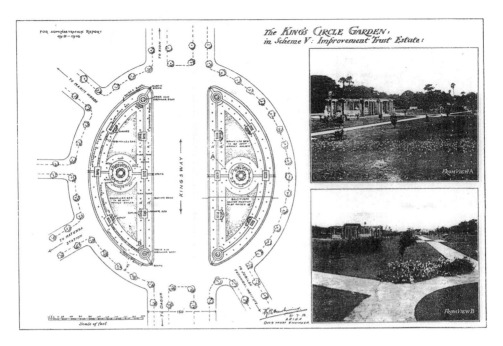

~ FIGURE 1.6. *King's Circle plan. With its parklike arrangement around tram lines, King's Circle marked the focal point of suburban development.* BIT, Annual Administration Report, *1915–1916. Courtesy of Maharashtra State Archives.*

into one grand edifice: the grand King's Circle, the center of gravity of the entire Dadar–Matunga–Sion development.[73] In this development, the attributes of the garden and the boulevard were to be held in delicate balance. While the boulevard would clearly still have the right of way, as it were, and would cut clean through the circle, there would also be elaborate arrangements of flowers, shrubs, and gravel beds on either side of the boulevard. Such a layout would bring together a balance of boulevard and garden and would serve as a suitable centerpiece to the development.

Meanwhile, the Indian members of the board of trustees were extremely suspicious of such suburban development. In response to Orr and Kent's proposal to construct a grand 150-foot-wide road, lined with villas, through Sion and Matunga, Dinshaw Vacha, one of four Indian members of the Trust at this point, proposed a counter amendment condemning the Eastern Avenue plan.[74] Essentially Vacha argued that the southern parts of the city remained congested and insanitary and that the construction of a grand boulevard in the north would be a needless diversion of energy and resources from the paramount goal of improving the older parts of the city. Further, such "ambitious and expensive roads," which "are of no paramount or urgent necessity for many years to come," constituted a further heavy burden on the municipal ratepayers, whose contributions partly underwrote the activities of the Trust.[75] Yet this amendment, as well as another amendment proposed by Sir Ibrahim Rahimtulla (another board member), were rejected.

The thrust of the critique by the Indians on the Trust's board and in the Corporation was that the Trust was merely engaged in beautification. A newspaper report of Pherozeshah Mehta's attack in a meeting of the Corporation illustrates the position well: "The official members on the Trust had ambitious greeds [sic] to make the City look enormously fine and in that greed they neglected the sanitary regeneration of the City."[76] This more or less captured the positions on the issue of Eastern Avenue: supporters, such as Orr, urged that Eastern Avenue provided essential access to the new suburbs in the north of the island and hence constituted a far more cost-effective "indirect attack" on the problem of overcrowding and insanitary housing in the old city. Because of the high cost of land in the old city, he argued, money would be much better deployed in constructing the avenue and hence opening up huge new tracts of housing; the same sum of money would have only very limited impact on some direct improvement scheme in the old city.[77] The following excerpt from his speech is illuminating:

> I look upon these main Avenue Schemes much in the same light in which every one now looks upon the "Munitions problem" in connection with the war. I look upon direct slum improvement methods much in the same light in which our Military leaders look upon trench warfare. A small advance here and a small advance there, however gratifying locally, can have little effect in the widespread war against insanitary conditions until we have solved what corresponds to the "munitions problems," namely, the problem of facilitating the sanitary development of outlying estates in the Island by constructing this main avenue. It undoubtedly requires courage to leave things at a deadlock in those trenches—the slums—and to devote the bulk of the Trust's present resources to this one spine road, but I feel convinced that this bold course is the right one and that there is no alternative promising anything like the same measure of ultimate success in our campaign against slums.[78]

Orr and his associates, viewing themselves as generals fighting a war against the slums with scarce resources, saw Eastern Avenue and the subsequent development of the suburbs as a strategic weapon that would inflict maximum damage on the enemy.

The Corporation's critique, meanwhile, consolidated itself around a few positions. Most scathingly, the Corporation argued that the Trust's obsession with grand boulevards catered to the pleasures of a tiny and exclusive minority who would get to ride their big cars at great speed. More temperately, they also argued that the Trust's focus on broad roads and suburbs was misplaced, when the slums in the old city were still more or less unchanged. It is difficult to separate the Corporation's critique from the class interests that dominated it. As A. D. D. Gordon showed in his *Businessmen and Politics,* the Corporation was controlled by landowning, industrial, and mercantile elites, all of whom had different visions of the city.[79] The point of this discussion has been to demonstrate that the fate of the suburbs depended crucially upon the politics of the city.

The Eastern Avenue project represented in most explicit terms the attempt to physically integrate the new suburbs to the north with the old city to the south and thus create a stable range of property prices in the suburbs. Control of the street also functioned in more subtle ways to transform the cityscape. Consider the Trust's street strategy in older parts of the city (Figure 1.7): in this neighborhood near the present-day area of Dhobi Talao, the Trust sought to use the street as a battering ram through the older urban fabric of the *wadi*. The Trust's principal concern with the *wadi* was that it was not regulated. Even though it was a social space, it was not public space subject to state rules. Thus building could continue indiscriminately to fill up all available space. Not only did this have the effect of exacerbating public health issues, but it also had the less obvious effect of distorting the property market. Without the street serving to regulate the extent and density of building, potential buyers of property were subject to a version of the tragedy of the commons. Individual property owners would have a short-term incentive to build more intensively on their plots in order to maximize income from rentals. In doing so, however, property owners on adjacent plots would slowly eat into the open spaces between the buildings, which had been one of the factors that had imparted value to the plot to begin with. Furthermore, any individual property owner could not control the extent to which adjacent property owners might develop their own sites, thus slowly decreasing the open space between buildings and detracting even from the property value of the owner who did not build intensively.[80]

The street could be used as an index to control the intensity of building, which would have the beneficial effects of promoting sanitary standards and of stabilizing property prices. In the Trust's first city-extension scheme, in Gamdevi (see Figure 1.8), this is precisely what was achieved. Note how every single plot in this scheme is subject to the surveillance of the street, so to speak. All building activity was now to be indexed to the street. Gamdevi was a relatively small city-extension scheme. Dadar–Matunga–Sion was of a different order altogether: in the suburbs, where the Trust had acquired all the land at great expense, it was able to impose a street grid. By the 1930 and 1940s, much of the agrarian landscape of Dadar–Matunga–Sion, still overwhelmingly in evidence in the 1919 survey image (Figure 1.3), was replaced by a grid of streets and building plots (Figure 1.9).

The Trust did not have a very strong vision for what kinds of buildings it would erect in the new suburbs. It was more concerned with controlling the lands and the

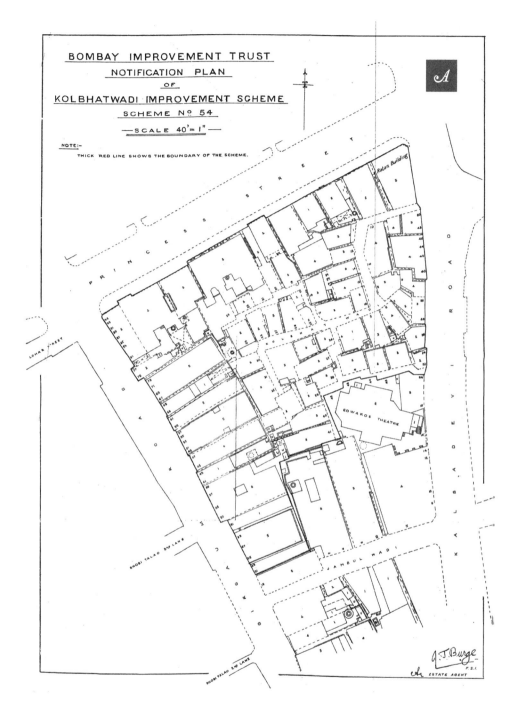

FIGURE 1.7A & B. *Kolbhatwadi Street scheme before* (A) *and after* (B) *orderly development was imposed on an existing older pattern. BIT,* Annual Administration Report, *1918–1919. Courtesy of Maharashtra State Archives.*

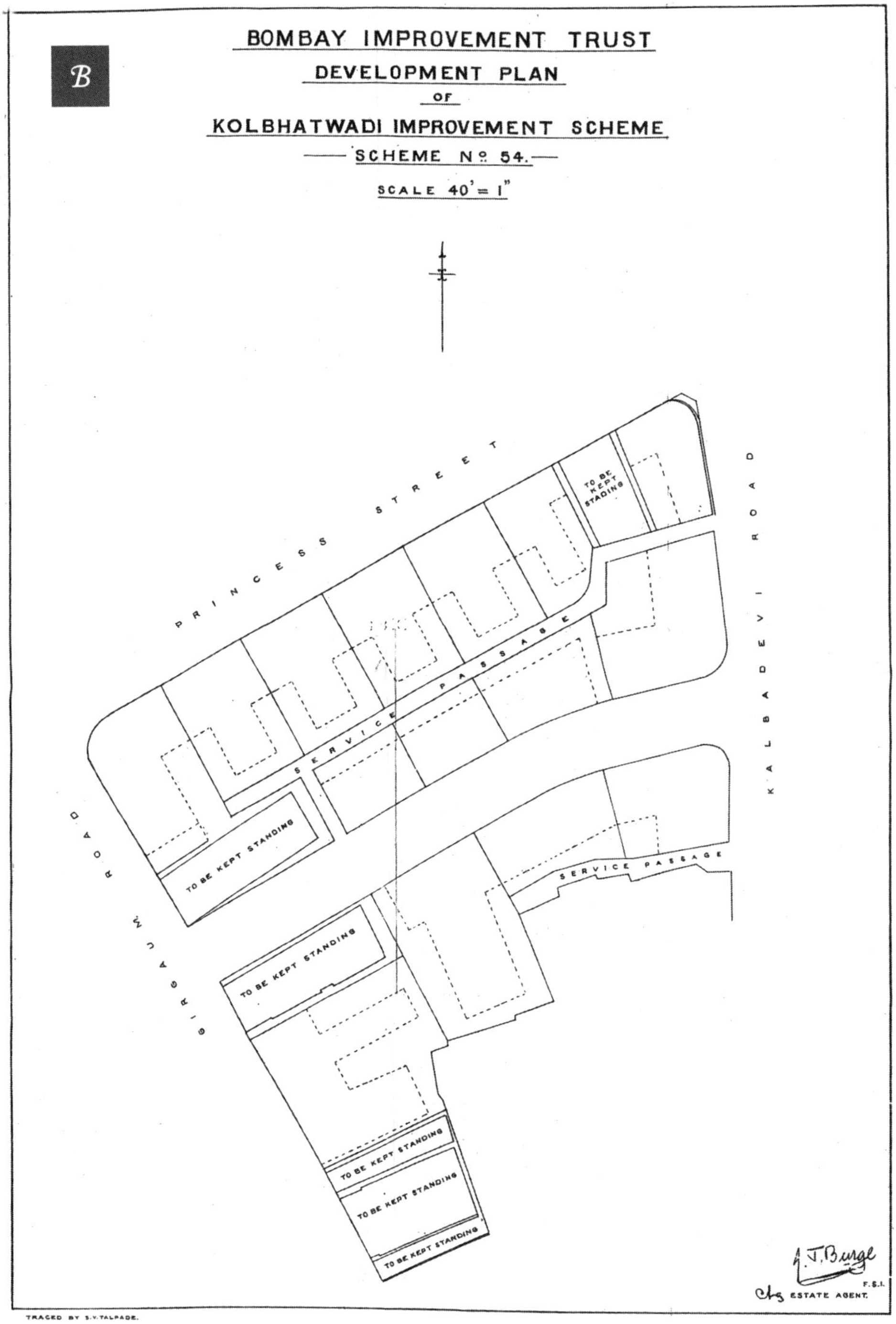

BOMBAY IMPROVEMENT TRUST

DEVELOPMENT PLAN

OF

KOLBHATWADI IMPROVEMENT SCHEME

—— SCHEME No. 54. ——

SCALE 40' = 1"

PRINCESS STREET

KALBADEVI ROAD

GIRGAUM ROAD

SERVICE PASSAGE

SERVICE PASSAGE

TO BE KEPT STANDING

TO BE KEPT STANDING

TO BE KEPT STANDING

TO BE KEPT STANDING

TO BE KEPT STANDING

TO BE KEPT STANDING

A. J. Burge
F.S.I.
Estate Agent.

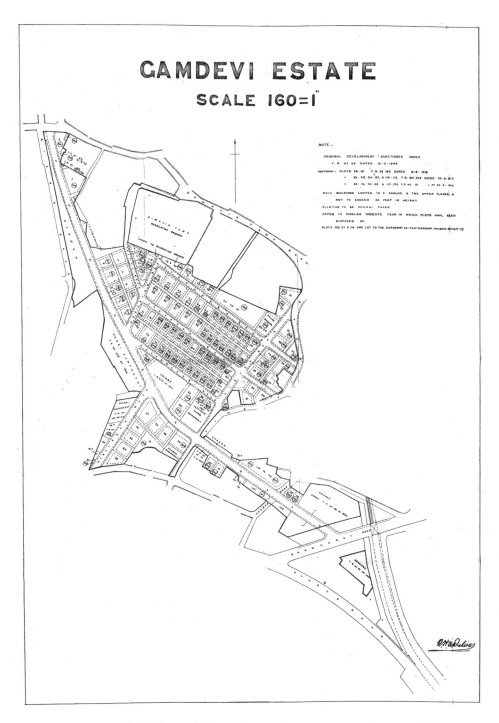

❁ FIGURE 1.8. *Gamdevi Scheme, the first substantial city-extension scheme, in which an entire neighborhood street pattern was laid out in advance of settlement. BIT,* Annual Administration Report, *1915–1916. Courtesy of Maharashtra State Archives.*

streets. Originally, in keeping with conventional European notions of the Garden City, the Dadar–Matunga–Sion estate was supposed to contain a mixed residential pattern dominated by bungalows and villas. Consider, for instance, the plan submitted with the proposed Scheme 6 in Matunga–Sion.[81] It includes proposed areas for a playground, which later became the Indian Gymkhana (discussed in greater detail in chapter 2). It contains a reference, in the southwest corner of the plan, to the Kutchi Bhatia community discussed earlier, which still exists today in the southwest portion of Scheme 6, along Lakshminarayan Lane.

Next to the Bhatia settlement is a space designated for cheap cottages. A little further from the settlement is an area designated for chawls. On the opposite side of the site, on the high ground surrounding Rowli Hill, are areas designated for bungalows. Large areas are designated as "playgrounds" or "open spaces." There is even a "village green." In addition to spaces designated for meat and vegetable markets, the plan shows a zone slated for "trades and industries."

The Trust made only sporadic efforts to more directly impose its vision of the built environment: it built, for instance, a series of "cottages" very near the Bhatia settlement. It also built some slightly larger cottages near King's Circle. By 1916, these cottages were already being featured in the Trust's annual report and were being referred to as "workingmen's cottages."[82] In addition, they built at least two blocks of tenements—one in the vicinity of the old Bhatia community,[83] and the other near the open area that is now the ground of the Indian Gymkhana. Through such scattered interventions, the Trust sought to ensure that the neighborhood would have a mixed-income quality to it. The assumption was that the wealthier groups would not need the Trust to build for them, but would rather build from their own initiative.

CONCLUSION

The manner in which the Trust tried to bring about its vision of bungalows and villas provoked much bitterness. As late as 1934, an observer reminisced about the way the Trust had imposed its scheme in the Dadar–Matunga–Sion area:

> Under the name of "public purpose" vast areas of land have been acquired in the North of the city by the abuse of the Land Acquisition Act. I have deliberately used the word abuse because instead of saving newly built bungalows in airy surroundings over there the Trust destroyed them and after acquiring the land at their prices they now turn to the very same owners to lease the land and build bungalows over again.[84]

This observer was clearly resentful, and it would appear that he had been one of the owners who had been forced to vacate and then were offered the very same

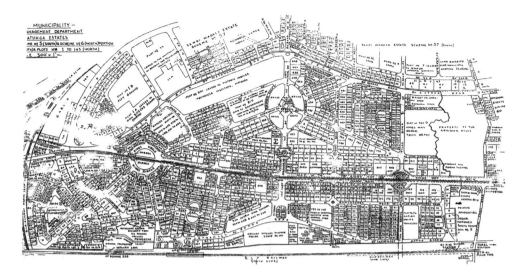

⤙ FIGURE 1.9. *Dadar–Matunga, Schemes 5 and 6: the BIT's most elaborate effort to impose a street pattern on a large area of land. Design Cell, Kamla Raheja Vidyanidhi Institute for Architecture and Environmental Studies, "Documentation and Preparation of Heritage Conservation Guidelines for Dadar–Matunga Scheme V—Parsi Colony & Hindu Colony Precincts."*

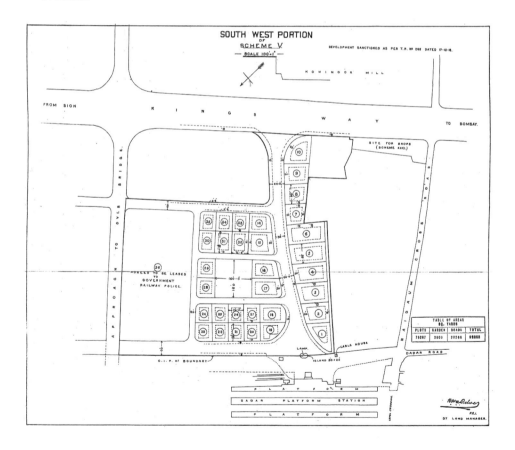

⤙ FIGURE 1.10. *Detail of southwest portion of Scheme 5. BIT,* Annual Administration Report, *1916–1917. Courtesy of Maharashtra State Archives.*

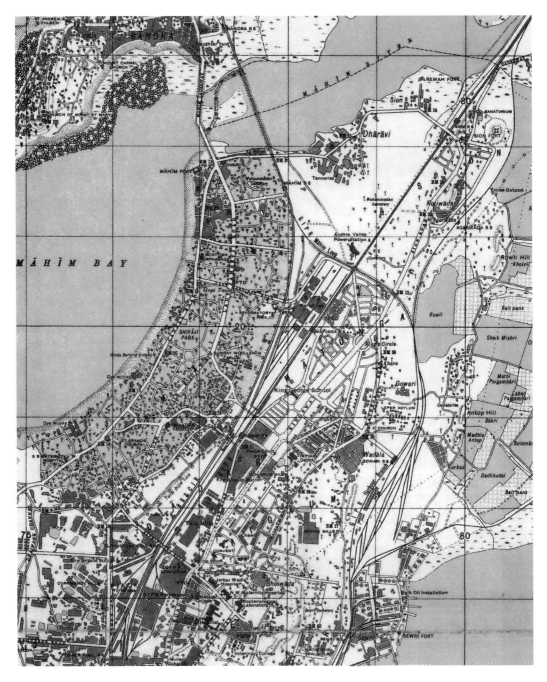

FIGURE 1.11. The northern part of Bombay in 1933. Compared to the representations in Figures 1.2 and 1.3, there is now a more extensive street pattern in Dadar–Matunga. From Bombay Guide Map. _Courtesy of Regenstein Library, University of Chicago._

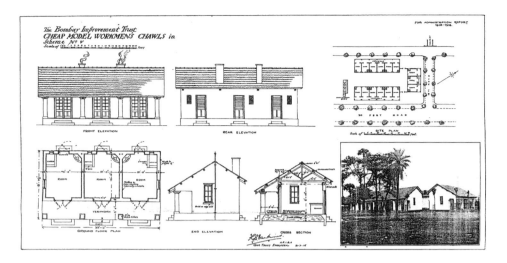

FIGURE 1.12. *BIT's "Workingmen's Cottages" in Scheme 5. BIT,* Annual Administration Report, *1915–1916. Courtesy of Maharashtra State Archives.*

plot at the "improved" rates. Yet the complaint is instructive in that it indicates that the real goal of the Trust was to *take control of the land*—to wrest it from the various uncertain tenures and to alienate it once again, but this time as leasehold property. Property alienated under such leaseholds was more susceptible to a regulatory regime than were lands held under the *toka* and other tenures. Further, buildings on such properties were now subject to the regulating influence of the extensive street pattern. The specifics as to building typologies remained fluid and, as we shall see, changed quite significantly between 1900 and 1930, when Dadar–Matunga finally started getting occupied on a large scale.

Bombay's increasingly vocal indigenous elites were able to stall the Trust's direct attack on the slums in the older parts of the city to such an extent that suburbanization gained importance after 1909 as part of the Trust's new strategy of indirect attack. Through suburbanization, the Trust achieved two major transformations in the perception of land in the city. Places such as Matunga, Sion, Dharavi, Mahim, and Worli were now seen not as outlying villages but rather as suburbs of the city that were, moreover, slum-like and in need of intervention by the Trust. Such a transformation in the perception of these places went together with—or served as a precondition for—the material transformation of the lands on which these villages stood. The Trust's acquisitions unyoked the land from older forms of tenure and introduced standardized leaseholds. The uniformity of such leaseholds combined with the imposition of a street pattern and the construction of roads linking the suburbs to the city to render the new suburbs an attractive option for investors from the city.

For investment in housing to yield returns, however, tenants were needed for the new buildings emerging in Dadar–Matunga from the 1920s onward. Attracting people proved harder than expected. Older communities of the city were reluctant to move to the new suburbs. The common refrain over the course of the 1910s and into the 1920s was that while the Trust sought to develop new suburbs in the north of the island for the middle classes, the middle classes themselves appeared to be actually living in the chawls and tenements that were supposed to be for the lower classes, leaving the lower classes to fend for themselves in the lowest grade of tenements and slums. It took the arrival of a new wave of migrants for the suburbs to finally start gaining in popularity.

2 Peopling the Suburbs

✒︎⁓✒︎⁓✒︎ BY THE LATE 1910S, THE BIT'S SUBURBAN VISION HAD EVOLVED and transformed in response to various kinds of pressures. Yet who would live in the new suburbs? This, it turned out, was not an easy question to answer. In 1907, on behalf of the Government of Bombay, Indian Civil Service (ICS) officer R. E. Enthoven issued a questionnaire soliciting the opinions of various prominent persons on the question of the "development of Bombay and the improvement of communications within the island."[1] The survey questionnaire consisted of questions regarding housing, land reclamations, roadways, and rail communications. It was sent to the usual stakeholders—the Port Trust, Improvement Trust, Municipal Corporation, Millowners Association, Chamber of Commerce, and so forth. The unusual thing about this survey, however, is that it seems to have found its way into the hands of various citizens of the city who did not necessarily belong to these bodies but who took the trouble to offer their opinions on these matters.[2]

One important element of the questionnaire solicited opinions on what class of people might best be suited to living in the new suburbs emerging in the north of the island. The responses to the survey exhaustively considered this question and provided an interesting perspective on views of the suburbs in Bombay at the time. The volume of correspondence by various groups of middle-class Bombay residents suggests that "the suburb" and "suburbanization" were understood by Indians to be planned, organized responses, developed through a global conversation, to the challenges of industrialization and urbanization.

The first possibility was that the rich could live in the new suburbs, where they could build big bungalows, and they could afford the motor vehicles or carriages that would be necessary to move to and from the commercial districts in the south. This option was rejected, however, because it was believed that the rich would never want to leave the leafy and well-ventilated precincts in the west and southwest of the island, that they would want to be very close to the commercial centers in the Fort area, and that they would also want to live close to the sea. The working classes, on the other hand, were simply working too many hours of the day to be able to spare the time to commute; moreover, they were also too poor to afford even the modest sums that tram and rail demanded. The middle classes, hence, were settled upon as those who would be "forced" to the north of the island, since they would be able to afford the rents and the costs of commuting.[3] Perhaps the strongest statement in this regard was the minute by R. J. Kent, the Improvement Trust's chief engineer, in which he was most concerned with what he called "the clerk class." Even though famous British developments such as the Hampstead Garden City had flourished by such groups empowering themselves, in India the clerk class could not be counted on because "the people have little enterprise compared with Western nations," he argued.[4] As a result, government would have to take more of an initiative. The clerk class should be encouraged to move to the new suburbs. Indeed, since some of them had already fled to the suburbs following the plague epidemic, that temporary exodus should be made permanent. The Trust, Kent argued, should construct "suitable cottages" and rent them out to the clerk class, who would have the opportunity to purchase them on an installment plan.[5]

Such discourse, while simplistic, nevertheless suggests that the nature of the suburbs was not some preordained repetition of a European pattern. Rather, the discussion centered on Bombay, with its specific topography and its specific population. Nowhere was the local context of the discussion on suburbanization better underscored than in the contribution of Vishvanath P. Vaidya, a civil engineer in private practice.[6] Vaidya's letter might well be the most intelligent and farsighted comment on the past, present, and future of the Bombay of 1908. He considers many topics, including the pattern of railway and road traffic, the location of the cotton exchange, and so on, but of interest in this context is Vaidya's comment on the project of suburbanization. For Vaidya, Enthoven's formulation in the original questionnaire would have appeared absurd: Enthoven wrote that "it appears in the first place necessary that an attempt should be made to divide the Island into natural areas for the accommodation of the upper, the middle and the lower classes with special reference to occupation."[7] The idea of simply chopping up the island of Bombay into zones on the basis of class would be an utter misapprehension of the sociology of Bombay, according to Vaidya. "It is difficult to divide Bombay into the West Ends and East Ends of London or even . . . to create Hampstead in the midst of our city," he wrote, referring undoubtedly to the newly created Hampstead Garden City.[8] In addition to the bonds and divisions of class, Indian society also had other axes of difference, such as caste and community. Even though the wealthy Hindus and Muslims of Bombay might live in fashionable areas such as Malabar Hill, they were still intimately linked to their communities in less fashionable areas. Here is Vaidya indulging a flight of eloquence: "The tie of caste and relations is so very strong that however much one may like to live on the breezy hill-top, he cannot help coming down to mix with his poor relations who are very often useful to him and to whom he is also a great help."[9]

In other words, Vaidya noted that Indians in cities were going to form communities on the basis of a complex network of associations, including class, religion, caste, language, and family. It was unlikely that the existing middle classes of the old city would simply abandon their caste fellows and live in the new suburbs as members of the "middle class." His solution was to call for a mixed-income, mixed-class neighborhood, where "rich people will build suitable houses for themselves and also chawls and flats, round about in such a way that they can remain in the midst of their people."[10] Through a completely different reasoning process, Vaidya had come to a conclusion superficially resembling the Trust's, described at the end of the last chapter, as to the ideal demographic constitution of the suburb. For the Trust, the idea of the mixed-income suburb emerged from a utopian urban-planning vision that sought to mitigate the reactionary bonds of class by progressive urban design. By mandating that a particular suburb have dwellings of different grades for the different classes of people, the Trust sought to create the harmonious community. For Vaidya, on the other hand, class would be secondary to caste and community: if caste, community, and family were merely permitted to do their work of social organizing, then the multiclass suburb would more or less result automatically. The multiclass suburb, for Vaidya, derives from the more or less conservative recognition of the primacy of caste and community in Indian social relations. From Vaidya's point of view, however, since the existing communities of Bombay already had their bases in the older parts of the city, it was unlikely that any particular class segment of any particular community would uproot itself and relocate to the suburbs.

As such debates regarding the ideal demographics of the new suburbs were taking place, there was also a parallel discussion regarding the proper dwellings for the middle classes. The prevailing wisdom held that tenements were not, in fact, suitable for the middle classes (although they were considered okay for the working classes). An interesting study from 1923, conducted by H. L. Kaji, a professor at Sydenham College, with the assistance of his students, indicates that for these observers, "middle-class tenement" was, in a sense, a contradiction in terms.[11] Middle-class people, and especially middle-class morality, required more space and privacy than tenements afforded.[12] On the other hand, housing shortages in the older parts of the city were quite dire, leading the government to pass the first of many rent-regulating legislations in 1917. Such a confluence of circumstances might lead one to think that the suburbs presented an attractive opportunity—more space to accommodate concerns of class and caste, at lower rents. Yet even with all these attractions, Kaji noted in his study that, as late as 1925, the suburbs were not really an attractive option for the middle classes.[13]

The problem appeared to be the way in which new migrants—who, especially in the boom years of 1918–1922, constituted the main pressure driving up rents—perceived their own relationship to the city. Many of them viewed their time in the city as temporary, as a brief interlude in which they would earn enough money to be able to retire to the villages. Hence, they were not willing to pay even the slightest premiums for more comfortable accommodations in the suburbs, opting to tough it out in the chawls and tenements in the older parts of the city and remitting every single rupee they could spare back to the villages. (South Indian immigrants, for instance, appear to have taken at least a generation before they fully gave up the idea that they were going to return to the south and hence began to consider actually purchasing flats in the city rather than renting them.)[14]

There is scattered evidence to suggest that the Trust imagined that middle- and upper-middle-class people would primarily live in bungalows and villas. As was discussed in chapter 1, the petitioners of Sion were skeptical about the whole notion that the development of the suburbs would lessen congestion in the southern parts of the city—they believed that, instead, it would merely offer cheaper bungalows for the middle and upper classes. The Trust seemed to have had a scheme to make houses available for the middle classes, for which they would make payments over the course of twelve years and which they would end up owning.[15] But some newspapers echoed the opinion of the Sion petitioners that it was crazy of the Trust to think that the lower middle classes—the people who really needed housing—would ever want to live in the new suburbs. Even high-grade clerks were finding it difficult to make ends meet in the city, argued the newspaper *Jam-e-Jamshed*. They were more than willing to live in chawls as tenants at moderate rents rather than to "cherish unrealizable hopes of owning their own bungalows" in the suburbs. Furthermore, these new suburbs were not suitable—they lacked police protection, markets, schools, and accessibility.[16] Similarly, other publications scorned the Trust's attempts to build broad boulevards linking the older parts of the city to the new suburbs in the north: why did the Trust not build affordable chawls and tenements for the middle classes in the older parts of the city, rather than expending energies on "extraordinarily wide and fashionable roads" to the north of the island, which was never going to be inhabited by the middle class?[17]

As V. P. Vaidya pointed out in 1908, it was going to be difficult to pull members away from any particular community living in the older parts of the city and attract them to the suburbs. A new population was needed, and one was created by transformations in Bombay's economy and demography over the 1920s. This chapter examines the constitution of the new suburban middle class in Matunga. It consisted primarily of migrants from southern India. Yet those class and ethnic identities were not simply available prior to the experience of living in Matunga. This chapter seeks to demonstrate the way a new kind of neighborhood identity emerged through the experience of living in the novel urban space of Matunga. I consider four aspects in particular: the nature of the middle class in the 1920s and 1930s, the emergence of Matunga as a distinct suburban entity, the ways in which migrants to Matunga made themselves at home by forming various kinds of institutions, and the emergence of Matunga as a political community.

✣ A NEW (LOWER) MIDDLE CLASS

By the 1920s, the idea of what constituted the middle class was changing. Earlier understandings of "the middle class" in nineteenth-century India tended to emphasize its English education and subsequent employment in the "learned professions," such as law and medicine.[18] These middle classes were derivations of Thomas Macaulay's mediating classes, those he proclaimed, in 1835, "Indian in blood and colour, but English in taste, in opinions, in morals, and in intellect." By the post–World War I period, I suggest, a diversified and heterogeneous economy meant that a much broader variety of occupations were available to educated groups. With the professionalization of existing enterprises and the growth of sectors such as banking and insurance, there arose a demand for large numbers of educated men who would be willing to work in office settings for relatively modest salaries. Increasingly, as in the case of many Brahmins from southern India, the path to upward mobility in cities like Bombay meant becoming a clerk.

Clerks, ordinarily an innocuous segment of the population, seem to have occupied an extraordinary profile in various kinds of public discourse in the Bombay of the 1920s and 1930s. The state's Labour Office conducted two studies to analyze the conditions of the clerk population,[19] clerks featured extensively in newspapers such as the *Bombay Chronicle,* and clerks were even the subject of an extraordinary M.A. thesis from the University of Bombay's Sociology Department.[20] Part of the reason for anxiety on the part of the colonial state no doubt arose from the specter of the educated unemployed and the threat they posed to colonial rule.[21] Yet, as I demonstrate below, clerks also featured prominently in the news because they *were* the news—representatives of a new kind of middle class that was asserting itself as the ascendant class in the city of Bombay by the 1930s.

The *Report on an Enquiry into Middle Class Unemployment in the Bombay Presidency* recognized both the problems entailed in defining the middle class and the fact that the meaning of the middle class had changed by the mid-1920s when the enquiry was conducted. "The term 'middle class,'" it argued, "is one of those expressions in common use, the general significance of which is understood by all, but which is somewhat difficult precisely to define."[22] It went on to exclude the groups who, in the nineteenth century, would have been the front-runners in any understanding of the middle class in India—"those following one of the learned professions, i.e., doctors, lawyers, etc."[23] It concludes with an admittedly weak definition of "middle class" as referring to educated people engaged in nonmanual occupations, and eliminates small traders and businessmen, as well as nonmanual workers in "traditional" trading concerns. Indeed, roughly 65 percent of the report's sample of "the middle class" consisted of clerks and typists.[24]

The 1931 census of India also acknowledged the difficulty of properly apprehending the clerk population. It identified no less than 50,017 men and 2,411 women engaged in what might be understood as clerk-like capacities that, in the census, fell under the general subclass titled "General terms which do not indicate definite occupation."[25] This represented an increase of about 17 percent in the number of people identified as engaging in clerk-like occupations since the previous decennial census of 1921. The discussion of these figures identified the very existence of this category—of clerks, cashiers, bookkeepers, and so on—as "a measure of Census inefficiency of classification." "Were it possible to classify this kind of employment more satisfactorily," it continued, "much of this employment would be relegated to many different orders."[26] The census recognized that the work that clerks do cannot be simply slotted into the various other major headings of occupations: "Exploitation of animals and vegetables," "Exploitation of minerals," "Industry," "Trade," and so on. But what it did not quite fully recognize was that the difficulty in classifying the work of clerks actually spoke to the emergence of a new kind of service class, a class where competence in English, typing, shorthand, and perhaps some accounting translated into a wide range of possibilities for employment in fields ranging from industry through trades to the classic "service" industries such as banking and insurance. By the end of the 1930s, the city's clerks, fighting retrenchment throughout the decade of the 1930s, met at the Blavatsky Lodge Hall (home of the Theosophical Society) to form the Bombay Clerks' Union. At this meeting, they estimated that there were more than fifty thousand clerks living in the city.[27] It was this class that was ascendant in the first three decades of the twentieth century.[28]

R. N. Bhonsle's "Clerks in the City of Bombay" came to a slightly different conclusion in trying to determine the meaning of the middle class, although in a way that suggests that an understanding of the clerk population is crucial to understanding the trajectory of the middle class. The middle class, for Bhonsle, consisted of "those persons who have received some form of secondary or higher education and are not sufficiently well off to dispense with earning their own living."[29] For Bhonsle, clerks, while not quite yet a part of the middle class, were on the verge of stepping into this category. I quote him here at some length, as he has a vivid feeling for his subjects and makes several important points:

> Theirs is one of the white collar professions which requires more of obedience to orders and less of initiative. They have to maintain a certain standard of dress and personal appearance. They have a definite social status. Money is the primary instrument of their life. They hold no power and very rarely property in the city. . . . Educationally, they present a much more uniform front than any other class in the city. They are always above the secondary education stage, majority of them undergraduates, and many graduates with a double degree holder here and there. Their greatest endeavor is to maintain a respectability which would approach that of the middle class but for

the economic inferiority in which they stand. An attitude of "humble submission" in life because of the very nature of its work demanding faithful execution of what the superior requires and giving no opportunity for independent initiative, sensibility to injustice without power to redress, inability to take an active part in economic production and distribution resulting in a pitiful crushing of the spirit, a stifling of its pride and helpless dependence upon the administration, the capitalist or his agent are some of the common characteristics of the members of the class. They lead a moderate life, avoiding the vices of the poor, the evil consequences of which they cannot ignore, and luxuries of the rich, which they cannot afford. They take a mild interest in politics and social controversies and, while siding with progressive thought in words, in action will stick to the old. Their conditions of work, emoluments and prospects of promotion vary very little and socially they form a solid block in the general middle class having more points in common among themselves than with other members of that class.[30]

The peculiar intensity of Bhonsle's feelings regarding this class—especially their alleged docility and keen instinct for self-preservation—needs to be flagged. Note the edge position that the clerk population occupies in Bhonsle's representation. Suspended between the somewhat financially secure middle class and the very proximate (and financially insecure) working class, the clerk class must strive to pass comfortably into the former group and avoid sliding into the latter. To consolidate its position, it clings tenaciously to its main asset: higher education, usually in English, as well as accoutrements such as proficiency in typing and shorthand. Furthermore, it strives to cultivate respectability. It avoids those commitments—such as "politics and social controversies"—that might distract from its efforts at establishing itself.

What accounts for Bhonsle's tone of contempt for clerks? He seems, on the one hand, to despise clerks and their allegedly servile nature, yet, on the other, he grudgingly acknowledges their instincts and capacities for survival. Indeed, he appears to regard them as a new and especially virile species of cockroach that has proliferated, unknown to others, throughout the city. Part of Bhonsle's attitude might arise from the condescension of an upper-caste and upper-middle-class person toward an arriviste group. Part of it almost certainly arises from the specific regional composition of this class. Bhonsle's account is unique and invaluable in that he provides a look at the caste and regional composition of the clerk class in a way that none of the census reports or other Labour Office surveys provide. The *Report on an Enquiry into Middle Class Family Budgets in Bombay City* had already suggested that the "middle class" of the mid-1920s, even if not financially secure, still remained largely upper-caste in composition.[31] But Bhonsle actually gives us a sense of the rough correlation between caste/region and sector of employment. For instance, he notes that Brahmins and Kayasthas dominate government employment; Saraswats dominate the Municipal Corporation; Gujaratis deal in export/import, piece goods, and stationery; Pathare Prabhus control the banks and insurance; Parsis are cashiers and storekeepers; and Madrasis are stenographers and accountants and are the clerks of choice in commercial offices and in those with foreign management, but in general "Madras superimposes all without distinction."[32]

A remarkable attribute of Bhonsle's thesis is his perception of the powerful South Indian/Madrasi presence in the overall clerk population, even though only 24 respondents to his survey of 886 clerks had their origins in Madras Presidency.[33] He attributes the South Indian/Madrasi presence in Bombay to the Justice Party's sweep of the Madras Presidency legislatures in 1920, as a result of which the Brahmins no longer had access to the government employment in Madras that had been their primary source of livelihood. Meanwhile, Bombay was going through its post–World War I boom period and hence was able to absorb "hundreds and thousands of Madras youths" into the booming and diversifying Bombay economy.[34] Indeed, the Bombay industries needed this supply of white-collar labor, and hence the controversy when, owing to a dispute between them, the University of Bombay and the University of Madras temporarily ceased to recognize each other's degrees, leading to a situation where "a great mass of students from Madras," drawn to Bombay by its promise of opportunity, now "[found] themselves stranded" in the city.[35] The dispute appeared to be resolved when, through the efforts of the South Indian Association and of the many students from southern India, the Bombay University agreed to recognize Madras University degrees.[36] But it refused to go away, and in 1935, the *Bombay Chronicle* reported, "Bombay and Madras Universities Quarrel Again."[37] In any case, the youths from Madras seemed to have been willing to work harder and for less money than the young men of the Bombay Presidency, and hence "with their acumen for accounts, better command of English, proficiency in shorthand and typewriting and willingness to begin at the lowest rung the Madras clerk at one time bade fair to *keep out the sons of the Presidency from all jobs in government and private offices.*"[38] Bhonsle's locution—his use of the phrase "sons of the Presidency"—is remarkably prescient in prefiguring the rhetoric of the early Shiv Sena thirty years later. It points to what has obviously been a long-standing grievance on the part of "natives" of the Bombay Presidency against the invading clerks from Madras.

Two important points emerge: by the early 1930s, the educated Brahmin and other upper castes from southern India had already established themselves in the city; second, they had captured a significant position in the large army of clerks that worked in Bombay's various trades, industries, and services. Over the course of the 1930s and the 1940s, this group had begun to populate the Matunga and Sion areas of the city, located in F Ward.

An exact tally of the number of people who might be considered South Indian in 1931 is difficult to generate from existing data.[39] Some 21,415 reported having been born in Madras Presidency, amounting to 1.8 percent of the total population and representing an increase of 6,259 over the previous census of 1921. Another 15,914 reported having been born in the state of Hyderabad, a fraction of whom would have been of the high-caste background and with the education required to enter the clerkly ranks.[40] Telugu was claimed as their mother tongue by 17,142, with another 8,300 reporting Kannada.[41]

Of those born in the Madras Presidency, 3,025 males and 1,664 females lived in F Ward, the single largest concentration in the city of persons born in Madras. Another 1,232 males and 807 females from the state of Hyderabad and 425 males and 220 females from the state of Mysore also lived in F Ward, yielding a total of 7,373 persons born in the regions of southern India living in F Ward. In addition, there would have been more from these areas who had been born in Bombay as the children of immigrants.[42]

The picture becomes a little clearer when we consider the 1951 census.[43] The total population of the city of Bombay was now 1,489,883.[44] Almost 60,000 people reported Tamil as their mother tongue, with the single largest concentration of Tamil speakers—approximately 19,000—residing in F Ward. In addition, there were almost 9,000 Kannada speakers, about 22,000 Telugu speakers, and about 6,500 Malayalam speakers also residing in F Ward, making for a total of some 55,000–56,000 persons from southern India in the ward.[45] F Ward also contained more than 40,000 Gujarati speakers and almost 200,000 Marathi speakers. This heavy presence arose in part because the Dadar–Matunga Estate was divided into three distinct regions—Matunga proper, which was primarily a South Indian area; Dadar Hindu Colony, which was primarily a Maharashtrian area; and Dadar Parsi Colony, which was primarily a Gujarati-speaking Parsi area. In addition, F Ward included the areas of Lower Parel and Worli, which were the heart of the industrial districts and hence contained very large numbers of Marathi speakers. These figures should not obscure the extraordinary concentration of South Indians in Matunga proper.

By 1951, F Ward also contained significant numbers of non–South Indians; for instance, it was the single largest concentration of Sindhis and Punjabis in the island city, many of whom settled there after arriving as refugees in 1947 and 1948. It also had the second-largest concentration of Kutchi speakers in the city, many of whom were the original inhabitants of the area and predated the Improvement Trust development of the area.[46] All told, F Ward contained the most extraordinary linguistic and regional diversity; however, the diversity manifested itself in quite homogenous terms. Each region in F Ward was marked by a specific kind of linguistic/regional/caste/religious identity.

In 1951 the overwhelming majority of the residents of the Matunga and Sion tracts of F Ward reported their occupation as "Other services and miscellaneous sources," which, as discussed earlier, was the category under which clerical services most probably fell.[47]

✌ CONNECTING THE SUBURB TO THE CITY

The Matunga section of the Dadar–Matunga Estate was probably the last area of the Scheme 5 plan to develop into a populated suburb. As has been discussed earlier, northward suburban expansion was strictly a function of the extension of communications networks. By 1914, around the time of the *Report of the Bombay Development Committee* (the published version of the questionnaire on the development of Bombay and the resulting correspondence), the Bombay Electric Supply and Tramways Company (BEST) had already applied to the municipal commissioner for government approval to extend the tram service northward from Parel to Dadar along the Kingsway. This proposal was approved by the Municipal Corporation, and on June 5, 1917, the extended section was opened for service.[48] Although this extension of the network was a mere 1.2 miles long, conceptually it represented a far-reaching extension of the idea of the city: now, stretching northward from the already-developed industrial working-class neighborhoods of Parel and Lalbaug, with their amalgamated form of factories and chawl dwellings, the new residential suburbs of Dadar and beyond were incorporated into the city's transportation grid.

Yet the proposed penetration of the transportation network still further northward into Matunga remained stalled for a long time. On March 26, 1920, the managing director of BEST applied to the municipal commissioner for permission to continue the northward expansion of the tram lines as far as King's Circle. While the Municipal Corporation gave its blessings to this extension in 1921, with construction scheduled to begin in 1924, the whole project stalled over the question of a dispute between BEST and the Corporation over the fare structure. The company argued that it could not operate at the rates the Corporation sought to compel it to charge.

The deadlock continued until 1927, when the Municipal Corporation forwarded a letter from the Matunga Residents' Association to the general manager of BEST, pleading for the company to consider extending the line to King's Circle, since the residents of that area were greatly inconvenienced by the lack of tram service. BEST's general manager wrote back with regrets that it still did not make economic sense for the company to extend the line since it believed "that this tramway extension would induce very little additional traffic" to recover the capital costs. The general manager further pointed out that the company had had to discontinue its omnibus service, begun only the previous August, due to inadequate demand. Hence the company felt that the population of the Dadar suburban area did not as yet merit an extension of transportation services.[49]

By 1933, the situation appeared to have changed, for the general manager of BEST now wrote to the municipal commissioner seeking permission to extend the line, with a reduced increase in the fare being charged to any passenger traveling any portion of the extension. The Municipal Corporation swiftly acceded to this, and on June 16, 1935, the extended tram service to King's Circle was opened for traffic.[50]

Indeed, this period from 1933 to 1935 appears to have been a momentous time in the development of the communications infrastructure of Matunga. From 1933 onward, the "office-going public" of Matunga had been agitating for an omnibus service linking Matunga with Parel or to the Byculla Bridge to the south. One resident wrote to the Corporation, "The residents in Matunga and Dadar are feeling the necessity of the extension of bus or tram services to Matunga and beyond. I would, therefore, suggest to the Bombay Corporation to make a beginning, and it should have its own bus service."[51] From Parel or Byculla, commuters could avail themselves of a variety of options to travel to points within the industrial area around Byculla and Parel or to points further south in the commercial areas of Kalbadevi and the Fort. Apparently the Matunga area had developed sufficiently that there were now buildings that were far enough removed from the two main communication hubs of the neighborhood—the GIP station at Matunga and the tram line along the Kingsway—to make the walk to either of these hubs a great inconvenience. In July 1934, commuters succeeded with their petitions, and an omnibus service linking Matunga to Byculla Bridge was initiated.[52]

A few years after these landmark events, the residents of Matunga adopted increasingly militant measures in order to further enmesh the neighborhood into the city's transportation grid. The following episode is instructive in illustrating the peculiar way in which Matunga's residents were "politicized" by what would have been, in late 1938, a very dynamic moment in the anticolonial struggle.

In November 1938, the management of the Great Indian Peninsular Railway decided to cut down on the suburban train service that had been linking Matunga and points further north to the city's commercial center in the south. The GIP's decision was based on a claim that it had been running at a loss of two million rupees a year and that this suburban service was especially contributing to the losses. Such a scaling back of services provoked some resentment among the "office-going public" of Matunga, but initially in early December of that year, the anger surfaced merely in the form of written complaints. On December 24, 1938, however, an accident up the line in Mulund forced a delay in the 8:43 AM train that took commuters from Matunga down to the Victoria Terminus and the commercial district, and the train only arrived in Matunga at 9:13 AM. Here the train confronted a mass of irate passengers, many of whom were unable to board the train because it was already very crowded.

At this point the commuters' simmering resentment seems to have escalated dramatically. Those passengers who had been able to board the train began to repeatedly pull the chain in order to prevent the train from moving on, bringing the entire traffic on the GIP line to a halt at rush hour. Two railway officers had to make their way to Matunga and negotiate with the irate commuters. Only after thirteen hours was the train allowed to move on. The GIP agreed to scale back its retrenchment, as it were, and to reintroduce two additional trains and increase the capacity on some of the other trains.[53]

However, the crowds of people heading south on a daily basis were not satisfied with these measures. A few short days after this event, on the night of January 11, a massive disturbance took place on the same line, but at the Byculla station. This time, the commuters' rage appears to have been triggered by the fact that the outward-bound 9:50 PM Kalyan local from Victoria Terminus arrived in Byculla with only four carriages, utterly inadequate for the large numbers of people waiting on the platform. Soon the crowd at the station approached three thousand persons, and once again passengers resorted to pulling the chain in order to prevent the train from continuing onward. The passengers had been agitating against the crowded conditions from the onset of the journey at Victoria Terminus, but they had been appeased by the promise of more carriages at Byculla station. When none materialized at Byculla, the passengers resorted to what began to be reported as *satyagraha* (the Gandhian form of nonviolent campaign through the force of truth). It was only after politicians and "social workers" such as B. A. Khimjee (a member of the Legislative Assembly) and B. N. Maheshwari rushed to the scene and negotiated between the irate commuters, on the one hand, and the Byculla station master and police, on the other, that the situation was defused.[54] Following this episode, the GIP pleaded with commuters to refrain from such actions and to resort to the standard procedure of making written representations through suitable spokespersons. It claimed that no such written representations had been made, and that had they been made, the GIP would surely have addressed the commuters' grievances.[55]

Still the commuters were dissatisfied. On January 15, "thousands of people offered mass 'Satyagraha'" at the Matunga station on the GIP line, bringing traffic to a halt for five and a half hours.[56] This was the largest such action yet. Once again, the occasion was sparked by inadequate capacity, this time on the 10:22 AM Kurla local, which pulled into Matunga at 11:07 AM already full. A few passengers were able to squeeze into the train, while the rest clung precariously to the outside by standing on the footboards. At this point, someone started pulling the chain and those passengers who were left standing on the platform jumped onto the tracks, making the progress of the train impossible. Passengers stopped all traffic on all the tracks, thus stopping even long-distance trains such as the Northeast Jhansi Passenger, which was due to pass en route to Victoria Terminus. When police and senior railway officials arrived on the scene, "the platform presented a solid mass of demonstrators and 'satyagrahis' clamouring for their grievances to be heard and redressed."[57]

At this point, the authorities tried to switch tactics. Police boarded each car of the train to ensure that the chain was not pulled. The train started to move, and the "people who had gathered on the platform looked on in consternation," but the "satyagrahis" on the tracks started shouting slogans and did not move, bringing the train to a halt. Matters seem to have gotten quite tense at this point, as more and more people swarmed to the station and scuffled with policemen trying to block their entry and seal the station. Soon police reinforcements arrived in the form of trucks full of armed police. At this point, the affair began to assume the aspect of a carnival, with "the attention of all holiday makers riveted to the Matunga Railway station that day." The onlookers began jeering and ridiculing the ranks of policemen, and buckets of water were supplied to the sweating satyagrahis. Ever enterprising, several hawkers and peddlers "pushed their way into the station yard and made a brisk sale of edibles."[58]

The standoff continued for several hours until no less a figure than Bhulabhai Desai, president of the Bombay Provincial Congress Committee (BPCC), "rushed to the scene" and began negotiations between the satyagrahis and the authorities, represented there by Dr. N. B. Mehta, the divisional traffic superintendent. He asked the satyagrahis to suspend their action, and "immediately, the people got up, followed him outside the station and formed themselves into a meeting," at which Desai exhorted the people to "maintain discipline." Eventually services were restored by 4:30 PM, almost five and a half hours after the train first pulled into the station. The protesters made clear that their main complaint was the overcrowding resulting from the scaling back of services beginning on December 1, 1939; the authorities claimed that no formal written complaints had been made and that, in any case, two additional trains had been added since the day direct action had first been taken (December 24, 1939).[59] Needless to say, the GIP subsequently issued an appeal pleading with passengers to follow standard procedure and express their grievances in writing, whereas an entity calling itself the Passengers' and Traffic Relief Association expressed surprise at the statements of the GIP, since they were under the impression that they had lodged numerous written complaints with the GIP on this matter.[60]

The episode was resolved with a triumphant victory for the satyagrahis. Pending final resolution of the matter, railway authorities determined, after negotiations with Bhulabhai Desai, to restore services to the pre–December 1, 1938, level.[61] In his statement to the people, Bhulabhai Desai appealed to the people to accept this settlement and said that he hoped cordial relations between the commuting public and the railway company would resume.[62]

This episode is remarkable for how quickly the clerks' and office-goers' protest against inconvenience caused by a scaling back in commuting services appears to have escalated into the dimensions of a *satyagraha,* with all the evocations of critique of colonial rule that that term suggests. What were the residents of Matunga protesting? The fact that decreased suburban rail service was interfering with their ability to get to work on time and in reasonable comfort. Yet such a bureaucratic matter was quickly transformed—through the use of specific practices and the deployment of specific terms—into a critique of colonial rule.

The transitional character of Matunga—its suspension between the urban and the rural or even, sometimes, the wilderness—was integral to the feeling of the neighborhood in this period. It would have been strange to live in chawls and apartment buildings—forms of dwelling that typified urban life—in a setting that did not exactly resemble the city but more closely resembled a sparsely developed outpost. This sentiment comes across strongly from several informants: K. V. L. Narayan, for instance, who moved into the BIT tenements in 1932, told me that most of the plots in the area were vacant in his first few years there.[63] A young boy in those days, he used to play cricket with the "only other group big enough to form a team"—the Kutchi boys who lived in Lakshminarayan Lane near the Matunga railway station. The boys from the BIT tenements—exclusively South Indian—would play against the Kutchi boys from the only lane in the neighborhood that predated the Improvement Trust development of Matunga and that actually looked like a "typical" bazaar-like street: narrow, winding, with buildings almost providing an arch.

M. T. Rayan, who moved to Matunga in 1934, used a very powerful metaphor to describe the feeling of living in Matunga. When I spoke to him in his house, he gestured in the direction of his lane—Brahmanwada Road, one of the oldest developed lanes in Matunga—and said "here all was *nadu,* everywhere else was *kadu.*" Drawing upon a powerful binary opposition from Tamil Sangam literature—between *nadu,* or suitably cultivated dwelling space, and *kadu,* the negation of cultivated land—Rayan was trying to make the point that, other than the few settled plots along his lane and in a few other spots in the development, much of the rest of the land in the middle 1930s was "open" or, in a northerly direction, was actually jungle. In fact, he insisted that the lands immediately to the north of Brahmanwada Road, just past the rail spur that linked the Harbour Line of the GIP to the main line, was populated with leopards and other predators that posed a threat to the residents of the suburb.[64]

The following three complaints about the Dadar–Matunga area, two appearing in the same year, illustrate the transitional character of the space. The first is a letter to the editor, which appeared in the *Bombay Chronicle* on July 11, 1934, in which the writer, calling himself "A Resident of Dadar Matunga," complained of a "Cattle Menace on Dadar–Matunga Estate." The writer points out that until very recently, the Dadar–Matunga Estate had mostly consisted of empty plots and observes,

> But now a large number of buildings have sprung up and still more are under construction. People from the southern parts of the City are slowly shifting to this area because of the apparently healthy surroundings. But unfortunately for them hundreds of cattle are allowed to graze all over the area day in and day out. This has become a grave danger to the lives of pedestrians, particularly children, apart from the menace to the health of the residents of the locality.[65]

The writer goes on to point out, not without wit, that not only are there cattle mingling with pedestrians, but "many of the buffaloes are fresh from up-country and they move about the roads in dangerous moods." Here the writer's complaint is of inadequate urbanization. Having taken the trouble to develop Dadar–Matunga as a suburb, and having lured residents with the promise of an Arcadian idyll, the Municipal Corporation must now deliver on its promises and prohibit stable owners from allowing their cattle to graze on these lands. Otherwise, the tenants on the estate, "who have laid out gardens at considerable expense," risk finding them "ruined the next morning whenever the gates of their compounds happen to be kept open." Even though much of the land on Dadar–Matunga might still be vacant in the form of unbuilt plots, still, something about its character had changed, and it had now transformed into a suburb. Animals may be permitted now only in strictly controlled circumstances.[66]

A different complaint appeared on August 8, 1934, in the section of the newspaper focusing on the lurid and the spectacular. Titled "Mawalis Active in Dadar: Several Cases of Theft and Smash-and-Grab Robberies Reported," this letter takes the familiar tone of middle-class outrage at the growth in crime: "It seems as if house-breaking, theft, and smash and grab offences are rapidly taking an aspect of almost daily occurrence in and about the Dadar–Matunga quarters."[67] The article details a series of petty crimes, including a "chain-snatching" episode in which a miscreant snatched the gold chain of the four-year-old daughter of one N. P. Krishna Iyer, a South Indian resident of Matunga. What is noteworthy is the presence of urban petty crime in the same area where, as the previous example demonstrated, herds of cattle also took their bucolic pleasures.

By the end of the decade, crime had increased to the point that the Public Grievances Committee of Matunga made an effort to keep track of the numbers.[68] Cases of burglary were becoming common, including one in the Laxmi Nivas building that was clearly planned, committed when the householder was away at the market in the afternoon. In another instance, burglars entered a flat on Brahmanwada Road by bending the bars on a window; they "removed many boxes" from the flat, "though three or four persons were sleeping inside the room." (The phenomenon of entering apartments by bending the protective bars on windows became known, with the quick familiarity of Indian newspapers, as "barbending." Practitioners of the craft came to be known as "barbenders.") Most intriguingly, a group of people from southern India, desperate to return to their homes, "made their attacks in family residences and demanded money for their passages to go home. On refusal, they bolted with whatever was within their reach."[69] The manner in which the Public Grievances Committee of Matunga articulated their concerns is noteworthy:

> In view of the increased population and *the absence of majority of male members who will be generally out in their offices* it is hoped in the interest of public safety [that] the public vigil will be strengthened and a close watch kept on those of suspicious movements.[70]

The request for greater vigilance noted the increase in population in Matunga, and hence the increased likelihood of crime. But the complaint also made the connection between the physical form of Matunga, the commuting patterns of its male residents, and the incidence of crime: because Matunga was a residential suburb, most male residents would leave the neighborhood during the day to go south into the city to work. This left the community "unprotected" during the day, when criminals could strike. Such an analysis would have been inconceivable in the older parts of the city, where neither the density of a neighborhood nor its gender composition changed much during the course of the day. People either worked near where they lived (or they worked in the place where they lived, or they lived in the place where they worked), or the movement of people out of the neighborhood to work was matched by an equal movement of people into the neighborhood to work.

This is the period of transition for Matunga, the time when it goes from being a very sparsely populated outpost of the city to becoming a fast-growing suburb into which young South Indian men, especially, move.

✕ AT HOME IN MATUNGA

Life for a young migrant from the south could be difficult. The experience of Irunjalakuda G. Gopalakrishnan illustrates the epic of upheaval, migration, uncertainty, and resettlement that comprised the urbanization experience in Bombay, and indeed, in the world generally.[71] He grew up in grinding poverty in the village of Irinjalakuda, in what is now Kerala. He somehow educated himself and obtained his B.A. from St. Thomas College in Trichur (the only one of five siblings to do so). But employment conditions for Brahmins in the south were extremely bad, and faced with the exigency of supporting himself and his family, he undertook, in 1931, the grueling forty-hour train ride to Bombay. He was lucky enough to have a brother already somewhat established in the city, but unfortunately for him his arrival in Bombay coincided with the onset of the Depression. He spent many days drifting in search of work, including spending many hours in a public library near the Victoria Terminus, where he and others like him would read several newspapers every day. Graveyard humor mitigated their circumstances somewhat: phrases like "Apply, apply, no reply" and "Morning appointment, evening disappointment" were circulated to make light of their travails.

Until the Depression hit, there had been a very high demand for clerks, stenographers, and typists from southern India. Apocryphal stories abound—for instance, of recruiters from English firms crowding into Victoria Terminus around the time when trains from Madras Presidency were expected. As soon as passengers started disembarking, the recruiters would start hustling them—"Do you speak English? Can you type? Good, I have a job for you"—and, thrusting a typewriter (available at hand) into the bemused arrival's hand, would hurry them off to a waiting desk in some office in the Fort or in Flora Fountain. Alternatively, the prospective job seeker needed simply to go to the entrance of an office: if there were vacancies, then there would be a typewriter—the iconic signifier of the clerical class—placed near the entrance, and all the applicant needed to do was to pick it up and make his way in. Sometimes the applicant needed to be more enterprising, as was the young man who advertised as follows in the Situations Wanted section of the *Bombay Chronicle* Classified pages: "Smart young Madrasee clerk ten years European firm service. Spare time work. Accounts Correspondence—Office routine."[72] Krishnamachari Padmanabha Chari, one of my main informants, who came to Bombay in 1927, told me that South Indians had no problems finding clerical jobs because of their proficiency in English. "When someone asked me my name I'd always reply 'My name is Chari' in a complete sentence," he told me, to emphasize the pride he took in his English proficiency and in his diligence with the language.

Gopalakrishnan eventually succeeded in getting a job as a stenographer at New India Assurance at a salary of fifty rupees per month. Four rupees were deducted monthly for his provident fund, and he repatriated fifteen rupees monthly to his family in the south. This left him with a meager thirty-one rupees per month on which to survive.

Gopalakrishnan survived the way most others survived: by depending upon family (in his case, his older brother) and by not eating very much. He lived for a while in a chawl or tenement in Dadar before finding his way to Matunga and an apartment there. The move from chawl to apartment was fairly typical: many new migrants would have lived for a while in a chawl in Dadar or in the famous Paanch Buildings of Matunga—a series of five chawl-type buildings that appear to be among the oldest buildings in the area.

In such dwellings, several men might share tenements of one or two rooms. Those who could not afford even these humble lodgings might consider options such as the boarding house of Viswanatha Iyer. Within one of the Paanch Buildings, Viswanatha Iyer, according to reports, provided cheap boarding and lodging facilities for half a century. Here up to twenty or twenty-five men might occupy a single large room, each with a patch on the floor for a bed and a segment of wall on which to hang up his few possessions.[73] Alternatively, one might consider the Trichur Mess, a society formed of people from Trichur, where one could get a bed in a large room and a coupon for two meals a day for two and a half rupees per month. The coupon was called a "meal ticket." Two meals and two cups of tea a day were all that this fare purchased, and it was not a lot of food. It was a mark of upward mobility when a young man could afford a "full ticket," which entitled one to consume unlimited quantities of food with each meal, as opposed to the restricted portions of the meal ticket. "Meal ticket or full ticket?" became a discriminating question that men would use to assess each other's status.[74] Many young men who set forth from districts in Palakkad or Thanjavur or Tirunelveli might spend several weeks or months in such establishments before moving to less dense living situations.

Food was of special significance for the large number of Brahmins in the South Indian community, and very soon a variety of specific eating establishments arose to provide a range of dining services. Some Brahmins were so nervous about the havoc that Bombay cuisine might wreak upon their rigorous dietary regimes that they went to extraordinary lengths to ensure that their needs would be met. The great journalist Salevateeshwaran, who represented the *Hindu* and the *National Herald* in Bombay, was so skeptical about Bombay food that he brought his cook from his college days at National College in Trichy to Bombay. This individual set up Appadorai's Mess, which provided "meal sets" for single young men for several decades in Matunga.[75]

Establishments such as the Trichur Mess and Appadorai's Mess catered primarily to single young men. As the young men got married and set up domestic establishments in the apartments of Matunga, a range of establishments arose to cater to these new families. The first such operation was the South Indian Consumer Cooperative Society, which was among the earliest cooperative societies in the city of Bombay, probably founded in the late 1920s.[76] This institution did provide meals for single men, but it was also established in order to supply the South Indians of Matunga with specifically southern Indian provisions, utensils, and so on. Yet another such society, established in about 1935, was the pithily named Model Co-operative Society, which was more commonly known by the literalist name of the Sappadu Society.[77] However, apparently both these societies were dominated by Iyers from the district of Palakkad, which led to friction with other South Indians. Probably this split occurred initially because of the different ways of treating food. Since the original founders of the South Indian Consumer Cooperative Society and the Sappadu Society were from Palakkad, Trichur, or other parts of Kerala, they tended to use coconut oil to prepare food, whereas the Iyers of Thanjavur and Tirunelveli tended to use groundnut oil. Further, the Palakkad Iyers tended to use coconut in preparing sambhar, but the other Iyers tended to use a ground powder. In any case, differences over preparation techniques came to a head at the daily meal sets, and this led eventually to the establishment of the South Indian Concerns, for instance, which was founded by Tamil Iyers from Thanjavur, where food was prepared according to the techniques of that region. Established in 1935 in the heart of Matunga on Telang Road, right next to the Consumer Society, the South Indian Concerns offered everything from general provisions to board and lodging. It also offered mill cloth and was the sole distributor in Bombay of the Tamil magazines *Ananda Vikatan* and *Naradar*. In addition, it was selling stainless steel utensils especially designed for southern Indian cuisine and specific brands of cookware from southern India such as the Rukmani cooker.[78] Hence, differences that emerged when young men from different Iyer communities ate together in canteen-like settings carried over into later life, when they were eating food cooked at home but were still purchasing their provisions from the establishments that used to serve the kind of food that they liked to eat.[79]

Education was a crucial aspect of the South Indians' understanding of themselves. The first educational institution in Matunga was the appropriately named South Indian Education Society (SIES), started in a garage near King's Circle. This school, which now is a comprehensive institution offering education from the first grade all the way to postgraduate degrees, had humble beginnings. By 1934, it was already looking to expand, and its administrators placed the following advertisement in the *Bombay Chronicle* Classifieds:

> Applications in writing are invited for 5 new teachers for the S.I.E.S. school, King's Circle, Matunga: 2 lady teachers—graduate or undergraduate trained in Montessori or Kindergarten methods. Knowledge of Tamil at least speaking knowledge essential. Salary, Rs. 60 p.m. 3 male teachers—Matric trained. Second language—Tamil, Kanarese and Telugu, one for each. Salary Rs. 50 p.m.[80]

In addition to the obvious fact that this advertisement indicates a planned expansion, which points to a growing demand, it also suggests the linguistic composition and priorities of the South Indian community in Matunga. Quite clearly the education would be administered in a Western style, possibly also in English.[81] Tamil would have been the most important language for the students; hence, it would have been mandatory for the teachers to have at least a speaking knowledge of Tamil. Kannada and Telugu would have been the languages next in significance. Thus the constituency for the SIES school would have been dominated by Tamil speakers, with Kannada and Telugu also playing an important role. Yet what this advertisement does not reveal is the great importance of Malayalam. As discussed in greater detail in chapter 5, Malayalam was an important language in Matunga since many of the migrants were Iyers from the district of Palakkad in what is now Kerala, where they developed a syncretic linguistic culture incorporating elements from Malayalam and Tamil.[82]

Almost as a corollary to the arrival of these young men from southern India to take up clerical positions, the 1920s and the 1930s also witnessed a mushrooming of institutes where prospective clerks could learn typing and shorthand and earn more-advanced qualifications. Davar's College, the long-standing bulwark in this field, by 1929 had already been offering courses in various clerical and managerial skills for thirty-five years. "India's future depends on banking, insurance, commerce, and joint stock company expansion," an advertisement announced. In addition to typing and Pitman shorthand, Davar's College also offered courses for bank managers, accountants, insurance managers, and company secretaries—the upper echelons of a ladder whose lowest rung was the clerk.[83] The South Indians of Matunga, many of whom arrived in Bombay already having a background in shorthand and typing, became inextricably involved with these practices. Under the aegis of the Laxmi Tutorial and Commercial Institute in Matunga, several new recruits were drawn into the ranks of the typists and the stenographers. For these young men, shorthand became nothing less than a metaphor for life in a large and unfamiliar city. How else to interpret the following remarks of M. A. Subba Ram of the Bombay Presidency Shorthand Writers' Association in a lecture titled "Shorthand Typist," delivered in 1934? He maintained that "one should possess adaptability, preciseness, a keen sense of duty and common sense in a good degree to satisfactorily discharge the duties of a shorthand typist." In a demonstration following the lecture, R. Skandasastri Venkatarama Iyer, the principal of the Laxmi Tutorial and Commercial Institute, read out a passage, and Subba Ram typed a record 250 words per minute.[84] This same R. S. V. Iyer was known in Matunga for reading out dictation selections to his students from the pages of the *Hindu*, a prominent newspaper from Madras, rather than from local newspapers such as the *Times of India*, the *Free Press Journal*, or the *Bombay Chronicle*.[85] By 1938 the Bombay Presidency Shorthand Writers' Association was so completely dominated by South Indians that, to simplify things, they started holding the annual general meetings of the association in the Asthika Samaj Hall in Matunga, demonstrating yet again the immense flexibility of this meeting space and the importance of the role it played in Matunga life.[86]

Still, there were amusements and distractions in the life of the young men who worked as clerks. On a given day in the 1930s, for instance, one had the opportunity to view a variety of cinematic offerings. If one wanted a Hollywood film, *Tarzan and His Mate,* starring Johnny Weissmuller, played at the magnificent new art deco cinema house in Colaba called the Regal. More local fare, *Suvarna Mandir,* starring Hirabai Barodekar, was available in more modest settings at Krishna Talkies on Charni Road.[87] The South Indians had very specific regional offerings available to them as well: initially, cinemas in the working-class areas, such as the Surya cinema in Parel, might screen the occasional Tamil-language film.[88] Gradually cinema houses such as the Aurora near King's Circle, in the heart of Matunga, though screening something like the Marx Brothers comedy *The Big Store* during the week, on Sunday mornings at 10:30 AM would offer, "for South Indian patrons," a showing of something like the Tamil-language film *Aryamala,* starring P. V. Chinnappa and R. M. Santhananlaxmi.[89] In addition, cinema houses such as the Broadway and the Rivoli occasionally featured Tamil films, while the Aurora cinema would also rotate in the occasional Malayalam film on Sunday mornings to complement the Tamil offerings.[90] By the early 1940s, there was a steady supply of Tamil- and Malayalam-language films available on a regular basis in Matunga and in the adjoining areas of Dadar and Parel.

Films were popular, of course, but the Brahminical residents of Matunga also aspired to more lofty aesthetic pleasures. By the 1930s, there were at least three cultural *sabhas,* or societies, engaged in promoting South Indian music and dance— the Shanmukhananda Sabha, the Sangeetha Sabha, and the Fine Arts Sabha, which, in 1952, consolidated to form the diplomatically titled Shanmukhananda Sangeetha and Fine Arts Sabha. This remains a preeminent venue for cultural performances in Matunga.[91] Indeed, the progression from watching films to watching and listening to live performances of music and dance appears to be a quintessential way in which the community understands its progressive consolidation and assimilation. When I asked my informants what made Matunga a South Indian neighborhood, the first two things they would point to would be the temples and, closely associated with religious practice, the prolixity of musical and dance performances available in the neighborhood. It is difficult to determine to what extent the clerks of the 1930s could have indulged a passion for live music, but many clearly seem to have tried, as indicated in notices such as the following, which appeared in the *Bombay Chronicle*:

Attempts are being made by the south Indian residents of Bombay to get Bombayites interested in Karnataki [sic] music. The south Indian Association have been inviting well known artists from south India and concerts are being held practically every week in Matunga. . . . Master C. S. Krishnan, graduate of Annamalai University at Chidambaram (College of Music) to perform.[92]

This is a remarkable frequency of cultural performances, given the extremely constrained resources of the community. Indeed, exactly one week after this notice, another notice appeared announcing a discourse on a particular section of the *Kamba Ramayana,* to be led by a learned scholar from southern India named Sriram Thothadri Ramanujachariyar and to be conducted at the Asthika Samaj Hall.[93] The Asthika Samaj had been recently designed and built by the firm of Master, Sathe, and Bhutia and had received a special notice in the *Journal of the Indian Institute of Architects (JIIA)* for the design of a "community space" for its patrons. The members of the South Indian community of Matunga had raised the funds for the building through a chit fund—a sort of revolving-door lending scheme.[94] The Asthika Samaj Hall remained the most important venue for cultural events until the construction of the hall for the Shanmukhananda Sabha, although venues such as the Byramjee Jeejeebhoy Hall were also commonly used, as on the occasion when the South Indian Sangeetha Sabha hosted a vocal performance by D. K. Pattamal.[95]

By the end of the 1930s, the neighborhood could boast of an annual devotional festival in honor of the great composer Thyagaraja, called the Thyagaraja Utsavam, which lasted for a full fifteen days. The event was organized by the Sri Ranjani Sabha of Matunga and was staged on various *pandals,* or platforms, erected for the purpose in the various open spaces of Matunga.[96] In addition to daily renditions of *bhajans* and other religious ceremonies, local amateur singers and dancers would have the opportunity to entertain the crowds with renditions of devotional songs, especially those composed by Thyagaraja.[97] These performances were acknowledged to be among the top cultural offerings in the entire city, as can be seen in a notice in the *Bombay Chronicle* titled "High Class Music Performance in Matunga." The performance by Vidwan Sri Vishwanatha Sastri was acclaimed as "easily the best attraction [in town] last weekend." The site of the venue, Nappoo Hall, "was packed to capacity," and local luminaries, such as V. K. R. V. Rao, at that time the secretary of the Bombay Economic and Industrial Committee, were in attendance.[98]

By the 1940s, performances were being given larger advertisements in the newspapers rather than small announcements in the papers' Happenings sections. A performance by the great M. S. Subbalakhsmi, for instance, was advertised almost a week in advance, and specific information was given regarding the cost of tickets and where they could be purchased. This was clearly done so that nonlocals could also plan to attend.[99] In this way, the South Indian community was able to put an imprint on the public spaces of Matunga.

Culture was not the only domain in which the Matunga population exercised itself. From the very beginning, the South Indians laid great emphasis on sports and physical activity as an essential attribute of urban life. The center of sporting activities in Matunga was the Indian Gymkhana, founded in 1935 and situated on a plot of land leased from the Bombay Municipal Corporation. It was originally named South Indian Gymkhana, but the founders decided soon after to change the name to the more ecumenical Indian Gymkhana.[100] Volleyball, ball badminton, basketball, and tennis were played there, with the basketball and volleyball teams, especially, serving as nuclei around which the youth of the neighborhood consolidated their feelings of belonging. For instance, in early 1939, the Matunga Athletic Club, consisting of South Indians from Matunga, inaugurated the Indian Gymkhana basketball court with a match against a team from Khalsa College.[101] At almost the same time, a ball badminton tournament was being held on the grounds of the Hindu Gymkhana in Matunga, made possible through the good offices of T. V. Ramanujam, a prominent resident of Matunga. The final was contested between a team from the South Indian Association and a team from the Hindu Gymkhana, captained respectively by M. S. Kandaswami and Chelappa, both South Indians.[102] There seems to have been almost a ball badminton circuit in Matunga, for the very next week, more than a thousand people witnessed a match in the Southern Star Cup Singles Ball Badminton Tournament, conducted by the South Indian Association of Matunga.[103] At the same time, the Indian Gymkhana hosted the Indian Gymkhana Tennis Tournament, at which almost all participants were South Indian.[104] Further evidence of the importance that the residents of Matunga placed on sporting activities may be derived from the structure of the community associations that were formed in the 1930s. Invariably, each institution would have two "wings," or branches, usually defined as "literary" or "cultural," on the one hand, and "sports" on the other. The South Indian Association, for instance, had precisely this structure.[105] The Mysore Association, whose members were Kannada-speakers from Mysore (many of them Iyengar Brahmins), established a Sports Section and a gymnasium as early as 1931. Initially the Mysore Association was constrained owing to a lack of space and was only able to support indoor sports such as table tennis. From 1938, however, the association was able to rent some land in Matunga from the Municipal Corporation, and it immediately started fielding sports teams, first in volleyball and then, in 1948, in basketball.[106] A very similar trajectory can be seen in the history of other local institutions, such as the Keraleeya Samaj.[107]

It was not only in sports that the youth of Matunga busied themselves. The emphasis on physical culture also manifested itself in organizations such as the South Indian Volunteer Corps, which was active in Matunga by the close of the decade. The full range of this group's undertakings remains unclear, but its members certainly performed social service activities, through which they were able to garner support and presumably mobilize voters and other resources in times of need. On January 18, 1939, for example, the corps performed what the *Bombay Chronicle* reported was "its most humanitarian service" yet, which "justified the formation of such an organization for the Matunga area." The incident was relatively minor—a Maharashtrian man, who ran one of the Matunga messes on the Telang Cross Road, passed away in the mess in the presence of his family. Some students who were eating their meals there heard about this and informed the South Indian Volunteer Corps, who "rushed to the scene" and made the necessary arrangements.[108] Thus the corps was able to convey that their help and services were available to all; yet, ultimately, the agency delivering the service was South Indian.

A comparison between the upbringing of Kamu Iyer and S. Ramachandran illustrates the spectrum of positions taken with regard to Matunga by the South Indians who lived in or around it. Both men's fathers had lived in tenements in Matunga when they first migrated to Bombay as young unmarried men—Iyer's father in the BIT tenements, and Ramachandran's father in a boarding house in one of the famous Paanch Buildings. Both men had also briefly moved out of Matunga upon first acquiring some prosperity—Iyer's father moved to Bandra, and Ramachandran's father moved to Vile Parle. Such a move, from the island city into the far suburbs on Salsette Island, appears to have been very common; usually it was only in the distant suburbs of Salsette that men could first afford accommodations that were more spacious than the tenements of Matunga. But usually, if increasing incomes permitted it, they would move back to the Matunga area, as these two men did upon marriage: Iyer's father moved into a building in Dadar Hindu Colony, at the very edge of Matunga, and Ramachandran's father moved into a building close to where he now lives, in the heart of Matunga. One more move followed: in 1941 Iyer's father moved into the more "cosmopolitan" part of Matunga across from King's Circle, to a building next to the building where the famous Kapoor family (of the film industry) lived, whereas Ramachandran's father moved at around the same time into a slightly larger flat but still in the heart of Matunga.

Iyer's father thus appears to have always skirted around Matunga, never straying too far away from it (except for the brief stint in Bandra) but without fully committing himself to the heart of the community. Indeed, this is reflected in the manner in which he chose to educate his son, Kamu Iyer. Although Iyer attended the SIES school as a young boy, his father soon shifted him to the St. Xavier's School in south Bombay. According to Iyer, his father wanted him to have the benefit of a "cosmopolitan education," which he would receive in south Bombay. The education would be cosmopolitan because he would not have been surrounded just by other South Indians. From St. Xavier's School, Iyer proceeded to the J. J. School of Architecture, where he received the best architecture education available in Bombay.

Hence, while Iyer has lived in the Matunga area his whole life, his experience of it has been different from that of Ramachandran, who also lived there his whole life. Ramachandran grew up in the heart of Matunga and then studied at the SIES school, from which he graduated. He then studied at Podar College, also in the heart of Matunga.

Yet it is not possible to deduce from these decisions regarding education that Iyer's father was more "progressive" or "modern," and that Ramachandran's father was more "traditional." Indeed, in many ways, Ramachandran's father was very radical. Educated until the inter matriculation level (equivalent to about two years of college), he had worked for a firm called Havro Trading as secretary to the managing director. Havro Trading was an agency that represented several German manufacturers of dyes, chemicals, and intermediaries. When World War II broke out, the agency folded up, and Ramachandran's father—Shivaraman Subramaniam Iyer—faced unemployment. In Ramachandran's words, Subramaniam Iyer at this point "boldly took the initiative" and did what few South Indian Brahmins would have done: abandoning the security of salaried employment, he went into the textile trading business. Further, he took the radical step of discarding his caste name and began calling himself S. Mani. ("Mani" is a common abbreviation of the name "Subramaniam.") He then set up a *pedhi*—a small trading shop—in the Masjid area in the older part of the city, "sitting with the Gujaratis." This would have been an extraordinary move in 1940—just when, as I have been arguing, South Indians were consolidating a certain kind of identity in Matunga, in which caste and occupation played an important role, S. Mani chose to divest himself of his caste name and also of the kind of white-collar occupation that would have been proper to the South Indian community. Thus demonstrating his willingness to take risks and diverge from the trajectory of his fellow southern Indian migrants, S. Mani became a successful cloth trader.

Kamu Iyer's father, on the other hand, appears to have moved in the opposite direction. After arriving in Bombay, he secured a good job with the Thomas Cook travel agency. Yet despite the fact that he had a high-paying job, he found the prospect of working for a private firm "too risky," since such firms were always susceptible to collapse. Hence he quit this job and took up another job in the government's Accountant General's office.

These two accounts illustrate a wide range of attitudes toward residence, education, and employment that southern Indian migrants to Matunga would have held. While there is clearly a commitment to the Matunga area among the migrants, there could also be a wide variation in how exactly an individual or family might relate to the neighborhood, or how the relationship to the neighborhood might articulate with a relationship to the larger world in general.

Through such institutions and practices, the South Indian community was able to stamp its imprint on the spaces of the neighborhood. As I have tried to describe, the sense of the neighborhood as South Indian was derived from the totalizing thrust of the community's institutions: institutions such as the South Indian Association sponsored a wide range of activities, involving food, music, theater, education, sports, and religion. I turn now to consider the way Matunga began to demarcate itself as a distinct political space.

⊰ A POLITICAL COMMUNITY

Both the physical articulation of Matunga to the city and the emergence of South Indian everyday life there have suggested ways in which the suburban communities were becoming politicized. A more explicit sense of how Matunga was starting to establish itself as a distinct political entity can be discerned in the dispute that arose within F Ward in the heated campaigning leading up to the Bombay Provincial Congress Committee elections of August 1934. As indicated earlier, Matunga was a neighborhood within the city's F Ward, an extraordinarily diverse area in terms of both class and community. Some regions in F Ward, such as Lower Parel and Worli, constituted the very core of the industrial district called Girangaon (literally, "village of mills"). Other districts, such as Dadar and Matunga, were staunchly in the lower-middle- and middle-class categories. As the earlier discussion of census figures indicates, F Ward was also extremely diverse in terms of the linguistic and caste communities that inhabited it.

The dispute began at a meeting held on June 30, 1934. The main contenders were the F Ward District Congress Committee (FDCC) and another entity that called itself the Matunga Taluka Congress Committee (MTCC). The Congress Party organization, as is well known, consisted at the city level of various ward committees that were under the umbrella authority of the presidency-level BPCC. The various provincial committees, in turn, were under the authority of the All-India Congress Committee (AICC). Yet in the lead-up to the Congress elections of August 1934, the Matunga Taluka Congress Committee sought to register voters on forms bearing the title of the MTCC rather than on forms bearing the title of the FDCC, as was being used elsewhere in the ward (and presumably in various parts of the seven wards of the city).[109] In effect, this was an attempt by Matunga to "secede" from the jurisdiction of F Ward. There are many interesting things about this episode, not least the fact that the MTCC chose a nonurban administrative designation—*taluka*—to underscore its difference from the urban, ward-type designation FDCC.

The issue came to a head at a stormy meeting on June 30, 1934, at Napoo Hall in the heart of Matunga under the aegis of the FDCC. A sense of the weightiness of this event is conveyed by the fact that all correspondence relating to this topic bore the heading "The Matunga Meeting." According to the report of B. N. Maheshwari, president of the Matunga Vyayam Shala[110] and one of the leaders of the separatist MTCC, the FDCC attempted, at this meeting, to deny the legitimacy of the MTCC. But, according to Maheshwari, there were sufficient supporters of the MTCC present at the meeting to successfully challenge this attempt at dismissal, and allegedly the meeting ended in the FDCC's utter failure to achieve its goal and hence its subsequent humiliation. Maheshwari saw this as an indication of the legitimacy of the MTCC.[111] This version of events was challenged by others, such as K. Rajagopalan, who argued that in fact the supporters of the MTCC, instead of voicing their opposition in an orderly fashion, had resorted to "yelling and whistling whenever a speaker got up on the platform." Rather than representing an organized opposition, they were merely "a handful of rowdies [who] could break up a big meeting."[112]

Another correspondent wrote expressing his dismay that the FDCC might even consider seeking to abolish the MTCC. Yet this writer, who called himself "Subra" (presumably short for "Subramaniam," a very common Tamil name), took issue with the way the MTCC and its supporters had conducted themselves. If there were disputes between various regional subcommittees, Subra argued, then those committees should have negotiated with each other and called in the higher authority—in this case the BPCC—to negotiate if necessary. Such unregulated squabbling, argued Subra, should be checked: "It is dangerous to the Congress to encourage the policy of revolt by subordinate committees against one another, which is against the principle of Congress discipline."

What was noteworthy about this whole dispute so far, at least in terms of the way it was represented to the public of Bombay, was that there was no real indication as to the actual origin of the dispute. What exactly was the dispute between the MTCC and the FDCC? B. N. Maheshwari merely alleges vaguely that the FDCC wanted to do away with the MTCC, and he resents the fact that the FDCC called the Matunga Meeting without ascertaining whether B. G. Horniman and Maheshwari (the two leaders of the MTCC) were going to be available (although they were invited). The two letters from Rajagopalan and Subra primarily take issue with the procedural aspect of the conflict, without necessarily rejecting the MTCC position. Indeed, Subra is openly sympathetic to the MTCC but regrets that the way its members and supporters carried out their protest violated Congress Party discipline at a time when discipline needed to be observed more than ever.

The issues only start to become a little clearer with a letter to the editor by N. Iyer of July 11, 1934. Iyer points out that "Congress activities are flourishing in Bombay, while Matunga is silent." He notes that the conflict arose because the FDCC's secretary had declared the MTCC an "unauthorized institution" and had stated that only those members enrolled on the FDCC books would be entitled to vote. He urged K. F. Nariman, the president of the BPCC, to bring about some kind of resolution of the matter between the leaders of the FDCC (one Mr. Kondaye and Abidali Jafferbhai) and the leaders of the MTCC (B. N. Maheshwari and B. G. Horniman).[113]

But it was only on July 16, 1934, that the matter was articulated more clearly. At a meeting in Matunga in which the national flag was unfurled and raised and in which he offered thanks for the providential escape of Mahatma Gandhi from a bomb attack in Poona, Horniman made the most explicit statement of the MTCC's position:

> I defy Mr. Nariman and Mr. Abid Ali to disprove our right to exist on the basis hitherto existing, and of having the right to have members on our own forms. We have documentary proofs to say that our committee has been in existence at least for the past 5 years, even though in fact it goes as far back as 1923.[114]

Horniman then went on to state that the only recourse open to them was to resort to *satyagraha* if the BPCC did not recognize members enrolled on the forms of the MTCC. He claimed that members of the latter institution would carry out *satyagraha* before the polling booths to challenge such "unjust, unconstitutional, and arbitrary decisions."[115]

Here is the clearest and most explicit articulation of the feeling that Matunga had now become a bounded community, with a need to determine its own political future. Horniman's proclamation, once again deploying the seemingly limitlessly flexible political weapon of *satyagraha,* asserted that enrolling members on its own forms was an expression of the MTCC's right to exist. By extension, it was an assertion of Matunga's existence as a community.[116]

K. F. Nariman, the president of the Bombay Provincial Congress Committee, acting with the senior Congress Party leader Sarojini Naidu, was eventually able to broker a deal between the two groups. Nariman commended the two sets of leaders—Maheshwari and Horniman acting for the MTCC and Jinabhai Joshi and Kondaye acting for the FDCC—for displaying the "accommodating spirit of give and take befitting true Congressmen" in coming to a resolution. In brief, the compromise was that those members who had already been enrolled by the MTCC would remain enrolled, but the MTCC would cease to use its own name on its enrollment forms and would function under the FDCC. In return, the FDCC would "afford facilities to the M.T.C.C. for enrolment of members" by handing over to them twenty enrollment books at a time, books that would have the name of the FDCC at the head.[117]

This compromise, however, appears to have been short-lived. When the leaders of the FDCC sought to pass Nariman's compromise by their own members, some members, led by S. B. Mahadeshwar, vigorously objected to and ultimately rejected the compromise, which, in turn, led to the resignations of Jinabhai Joshi and Kondaye and to further chaos in F Ward.[118]

Even here the squabbling between the two entities did not cease. A few days before the election, representatives from the MTCC wrote a letter to the BPCC in which they complained that the FDCC was not allotting them a physical polling station in the Matunga neighborhood. Noting that in the previous election F Ward had had two polling sites—one in Parel at the southern edge of the ward and one in Matunga near the northern edge—they stated that on this occasion the F Ward authorities (that is, the FDCC) had not provided the polling booth in Matunga, despite the MTCC having sent a representation to the FDCC for this very purpose. Not having their own polling booth in their own neighborhood would "cause great inconvenience and difficulty to Matunga voters."[119] This request was met with a refusal from the FDCC, who argued that two polling booths within the same ward posed the danger of "double voting" and hence could not be permitted. The MTCC, not to be put off, responded with biting sarcasm:

> It appears to me that the reason put forward by your committee for refusing to have a polling station at Matunga is a mere subterfuge. . . . Are we to suppose that in the "G" Ward, where there are three polling stations, there will be danger of triple voting?[120]

Once again the president of the BPCC, K. F. Nariman, had to intervene in this dispute between the MTCC and the FDCC. The compromise called for only one polling booth, not in Parel, at the southern edge of F Ward, but at a Montessori school called Balak Mandir near the Dadar station on the GIP line, exactly in the middle of F Ward.[121]

The earlier dispute, over the MTCC's right to enroll members in Matunga under its own letterhead, was an assertion of Matunga's existence as a political community; the latter dispute, over the location of the ballot box, was an attempt by the people of Matunga to physically locate themselves in a space. Taken together, the demand for the right to enroll members along with the demand for their own ballot box constituted an attempt to set up an equivalence between political community and physical space. These political squabbles suggest that by 1934 Matunga was beginning to emerge as a distinct political space.

∼ CONCLUSION

While the suburbs had emerged as a physical entity consisting of uniform plots, street patterns, and some buildings by the 1920s, populating the suburbs posed very specific problems. The suburbs were intended to attract middle-class residents, but it turned out that those members of the city's older communities who might be termed "middle-class" actually preferred to live in the older parts of the city among their lower- and upper-class fellows. In other words, while the planned suburbs of Dadar–Matunga had created a kind of abstract space by vanquishing older forms of tenure and instituting uniform leaseholds, the older communities of Bombay remained tied to particular places in older parts of the city where the bonds of caste and community trumped emerging class distinctions. Transformations in the city's economy after World War I attracted a new wave of migrants from southern India who did not have the same ties to places in older parts of the city. These migrants began moving into the buildings in Matunga from the 1920s onward.

By the 1930s, Matunga had developed a clear identity as a physical, ethnic, and political community. Campaigns to improve communications to the commercial districts to the south, efforts to create a familiar cultural context in Matunga, and political campaigning all contributed to the demarcation of Matunga as a South Indian place. Yet the novelty of the emerging suburbs was not restricted to the uniformity of its leaseholds, plot shapes, and street patterns. In particular, a distinctive form of dwelling emerged in the suburbs of Dadar–Matunga, a product of aspects of the housing markets combined with the caste and community considerations of the new migrants. I turn now to consider the physical environment in further detail. In particular, I focus on the apartment building, the dominant dwelling form in Matunga.

3 The Rise of the Bombay Flat

⟣⟣⟣⟣⟣ IN A RECENT ARTICLE IN *INDIAN EXPRESS,* A MUMBAI NEWSPAPER, the journalist Manju Mehta explored the proposed redevelopment of Dharavi, the gigantic informal settlement in the heart of the island city, which, for generations of middle-class Mumbaikars, has held the distinction of being the "largest slum in Asia."[1] Much has since been written about this controversial and often maligned redevelopment project, but I focus here on the form of housing that "rehabilitated" slum dwellers will receive. As S. A. Sunder, a twenty-five-year Dharavi resident interviewed for the article by Manju Mehta, said, "Flats with all the trappings of an upwardly mobile lifestyle [will be] available here itself."[2] Following redevelopment, each former shanty owner will get a "225 square foot flat for free, with middle class lifestyle attached."[3] What links the middle-class lifestyle to such a flat? It turns out that middle-classness is literally attached to the flat in the form of the attached toilet, as further elaborated in Mehta's account of Syed Yakkubhai, another longtime Dharavi resident:

> Every morning, as he treks half a kilometer to complete his morning ablutions, Syed Yakkubhai (52) remembers a dream. It's a dream that he and 60 other families of Islampura colony in Dharavi have been chasing for eight years now. From their 250 square foot shanties which open into 4-feet-wide lanes, Yakkubhai and others have dreamt of life in a "self-contained" flat.[4]

Manju Mehta's uncritical celebration of the proposed Dharavi redevelopment is problematic, but her account of Syed Yakkubhai's dream is extraordinarily evocative of a defining feature of middle-class life in urban South Asia that, nonetheless, has gone largely unremarked: the attached toilet. To have one in the dwelling—or, in other words, to live in a self-contained flat and to not have to walk half a kilometer to "complete [one's] morning ablutions"—is what, in many ways, sets even a modest slum dweller on the path to the middle class. Indeed, the self-contained feature is so critical that in accepting the standard 225-square-foot flat as part of the slum rehabilitation scheme, residents of Dharavi will often be getting *less* space than they previously had in their shanties: Syed Yakkubhai, for instance, in accepting a 225-square-foot flat will actually lose 25 square feet, or 10 percent, of his previous 250-square-foot hut.

Syed Yakkubhai's dream of owning a "self-contained flat"—and thus embarking on the "middle class lifestyle"—began in 1920s Bombay. Yet the connection between middle-classness and flat living was a contingent one, and Bombay's middle classes did not take to flat living in a self-conscious embrace of modernity. Rather, a conjuncture of factors combined to send Bombay's new lower middle classes into multistory, multiroom, multifamily dwellings in the 1920s. This move co-incided with the advent of indoor plumbing to create the self-contained Bombay flat by the 1930s. Once the Bombay flat had acquired its social meaning as the "self-contained flat," it became an important marker of middle-class identity, a way in which the empirical middle class became self-consciously middle class. Two important features thus distinguished the Bombay flat from flats in other parts of the world: first, it was pioneered in the early suburbs of Bombay before mak-ing its way back into the older parts of the city; second, the social meaning of the Bombay flat—the way the category was popularly understood from the late 1920s onward—was constituted through its "self-contained" nature. The preoccupation with the self-containedness, further, signaled the way the flat was appropriated into a Bombay lower-middle-class framework.

In the *Gazetteer of Bombay,* which he compiled between 1906 and 1909, S. M. Edwardes wrote of the pressures on land prices generated by the boom of 1861 to 1865 and indicated that "the old style Hindu house with its *otla* and *masaghar* (middle hall) [is beginning to] disappear under the pressure of space and high rents."[5] Only the wealthiest Indians still lived in houses: Parsis lived in European-style houses, and "Bhatias, Banias, and Jains" lived in "traditional" houses that allowed for separate women's apartments in the rear of the house. While the very poorest lived in huts scattered around the city, the majority of the working classes and the lower middle classes were making do in chawls. But for the more affluent middle classes, a new form of dwelling is announced:

> The richer middle classes, both Muhammadan and Hindu, are found residing in what for want of a better term may be called flats, the most prominent feature of which is the *divankhana* or reception-room. Around this are grouped the kitchen, washing room, sleeping rooms and women's apartments, which vary in size and number in proportion to the wealth of the owner.[6]

Such dwellings represent a verticalization, so to speak, of the traditional Indian house in response to the economic pressures that Edwardes alludes to. Thus the *divankhana* of these dwellings is an attempt to re-create, within a multistory, mul-tiunit dwelling, the *masaghar*—also called the *baithak*—of the traditional Hindu house of Bombay. It is clear that this type of dwelling is somewhat new at the time Edwardes was writing, and "for want of a better term," he calls them flats. They do not contain toilets and would probably have had such facilities on the floor landings or on the roofs of the buildings. Edwardes distinguishes such flats from dwellings that he calls "flats on the English model," which he says "have sprung up in large numbers in the Fort" in recent years and in which much of the European population actually resided. Such flats too do not appear to have necessarily contained toilets, but they featured a different organization of interior space that had already been developed in Europe, with functionally specific spaces such as living rooms, dining rooms, and bedrooms.

Compare Edwardes's description with the following extraordinary account by Hansa Mehta, an educated woman belonging to the "richer middle classes" alluded to by Edwardes. Mehta lived in Kalbadevi, in the old native city, had run for municipal office in the mid-1930s, and would later go on to become chancellor of M.S. University in Baroda. Addressing an audience at the Indian Institute of Architects (IIA) on the topic of domestic architecture in India, she said, "If any country needs attention to domestic architecture today it is India, and I hope the new woman architect will remember it." She had lived in Bombay for eleven years by the time of her address in 1936 and claimed to have changed flats a number of times:

> I am not very happy about these constant changes but I have done so because I could not find a single flat that would come up to my expectations of comfort or convenience. During my flat hunting I have seen flats and flats. Those which are styled Hindu flats have certain peculiarities. The front room generally extends to the whole length or breadth of the flat. It is more like a durbar hall. The rest of the rooms, bedrooms, etc., are too small in proportion. One can hardly move in them. . . . Those, therefore, who have some conception of beauty and proportion and also comfort are unable to live in such flats in spite of their being Hindus.[7]

Hansa Mehta complained here of the large "durbar hall"–type room, which Edwardes called the *divankhana*. In more traditional settings, this would have been the principal space of the house, but Mehta here clearly felt that this space was too large in proportion to the other spaces and felt constrained by the small size of the bedrooms. Such a concern with the size of bedrooms might lead the present-day observer to classify her as Westernized, in the sense of having acquired notions of conjugal privacy, but while this might have been true, Hansa Mehta's case was actually more complicated. After having delivered her critique of the Hindu flat, she went on to describe the experience of seeing European-style flats:

> The house agent takes [prospective renters] round to see flats built in what he would call the European style. These flats have generally low ceilings where one feels like being in a box and a feeling of suffocation comes over. The drawing-room and the dining room are generally combined, which can suit only those who are actually living in the western style. The sanitary arrangements are good, and yet bath tubs are not particularly desirable. From the point of view of health and cleanliness, the Indian system of bathing in running water is much more commendable. The real drawback to such flats, however, is that hardly any provision is made for the servants' quarters. Those of us,

therefore, who are neither Europeans nor are orthodox enough to live anyhow find it extremely difficult to get suitable places to live in or else have to pay very much beyond their means.[8]

Hansa Mehta was that rare person who seemed to have been self-conscious about straddling two worlds and two different ways of dwelling. She did not like the lower ceilings of the modern flats that were coming up, especially in Dadar–Matunga. She did not like the combined dining/living area, which she felt was too Westernized; Indian families would either eat on the floor in the kitchen or, in the case of larger houses and larger families, in a separate room closer to the kitchen, but still on the floor. She did not like the bathtub system of bathing favored by Europeans, and she found fault with the lack of separate servants' quarters in the compact modern flat. Despite this litany of complaints, however, she liked one thing: the "sanitary arrangements" of the "European" flats, by which she meant, of course, the presence of toilets within the dwelling.

Spanning almost thirty years between Edwardes's 1909 description and Mehta's 1936 lecture to the Indian Institute of Architects, these two accounts frame a period in which the Bombay flat coalesced as a distinct entity. Although "flat" as a general term for a multiroom dwelling in a multistory, multifamily dwelling had existed in Bombay from the early twentieth century, by the 1930s the flat had become "domesticated" as a category. Or, in other words, what Edwardes and Hansa Mehta respectively term the "English-type" or the "European" flat becomes by the 1930s, with small modifications, the Bombay flat, which increasingly became the dwelling of choice of Bombay's lower middle classes. The Hindu flat, meanwhile, was not built anymore.[9] Dadar–Matunga, the first suburb of Bombay, became the site where the Bombay flat received its earliest expression on a mass scale.

What marked the domestication of the flat-type dwelling—the way in which it was appropriated into a Bombay lower-middle-class framework—was its "self-containedness," or the presence of the toilet within the dwelling. Subsequently, living in self-contained flats became constitutive of middle-class identity. As the present-day story about Dharavi recounted at the beginning of the chapter underscores, the "self-containedness" of the flat remains the feature that distinguishes it from other forms of multistory living and is a critical indicator of middle-class identity. While Hansa Mehta might have been ambivalent about the European flat because of its low ceilings, bathtubs, lack of servant quarters, and so on, in fact a version of such a flat was already becoming the predominant dwelling of Bombay's lower middle and middle classes by the time of her lecture in 1936.

The conventional argument for the rise of apartment living elsewhere in the world is tied to scarce land, expensive real estate, and a grudging concession by middle classes seeking privacy to live vertically instead of in a house.[10] In Bombay, though, neither land nor dwellings were in scarce supply in the 1920s when apartment living first gained wide currency among Indians: the Improvement Trust was developing vast new estates on the north of the island, on the one hand, and the Bombay Development Directorate had a huge housing project underway in the early 1920s, on the other. Hence neither land nor dwellings were scarce in any absolute sense. Land was scarce and expensive in the older part of the city to the south but available in the new suburbs. The particular way the land market worked in the late 1910s and early 1920s meant not only that Dadar–Matunga developed quickly in this period but also that dwellings were driven upward. And housing stock was not exactly scarce. The BDD built more than sixteen thousand one-room tenements between 1920 and 1924. But the BDD's misapprehension of the demographics of housing demand meant that their vast new projects were never more than half occupied, while the new lower middle class sought alternative accommodations. As a result of these two factors, Bombay's lower middle classes started living in the apartment buildings of Dadar–Matunga. Through a contingent set of circumstances, thus, middle-class apartment living was pioneered in the suburbs of the old city: beginning in a small way in the Improvement Trust estate of Gamdevi and then reaching mass expression in Dadar–Matunga before making its way into older parts of the city.

Just as a contingent set of circumstances yielded the physical buildings in Dadar–Matunga, the social meaning of the flat also was produced in the specific cultural context of the demand for housing in Bombay. In the cities of Europe and North America, the social meaning of the apartment or flat, as opposed to a tenement, was derived more from emerging ideas of public and private in the early and middle nineteenth century and the associated emergence of a middle-class bourgeois sensibility.[11] Hence, what distinguished the apartment from the tenement in mid-nineteenth-century Paris was whether a dwelling was large enough to afford suitable functional segregation, so that one did not sleep in the same room where one cooked, say, or so that parents and children did not sleep in the same room. The toilet had never been the decisive feature distinguishing apartments from their humbler cousins, the tenements. Even though sewerage systems and indoor plumbing had developed to a stage recognizable today by as early as the 1860s, when the first apartments arose in New York, the distinctiveness of the latter was never closely linked to the presence or absence of toilets within the dwelling.[12] Elizabeth Cromley writes of New York that "bathing facilities and water closets (toilets) were usual in middle-class apartment buildings from the first," but while this feature might have physically distinguished the apartment from the tenement, it was not what gave the apartment its social meaning.[13] In a different setting, writing of apartments in Budapest of the 1920s, Gábor Gyáni suggests that bathrooms did play an important role in determining the status of a particular apartment. Higher-class apartments would have bathrooms, while more modest apartments would not necessarily have one.[14] Yet even here, the bathroom did not play the decisive role in differentiating the apartment from the tenement the way it did in Bombay. Rather, as the title of Maureen Ogle's outstanding book on indoor plumbing indicates, the bathroom/toilet became one of "all the modern conveniences" that apartments promised and that apartment dwellers began to expect.

The discussion of the social meaning of the Bombay flat is not merely about semantics or about correctly establishing the emergence of a particular building typology. Identifying the self-contained nature of the Bombay flat as central to its social meaning suggests that flat living was intimately connected to emerging notions of middle-class identity in 1920s and 1930s Bombay, which will be further elaborated in chapters 4 and 5. Flat living—and specifically negotiating the toilet and the urban problem of disposing of bodily wastes—became critical issues in relation to which the new upper-caste white-collar migrants to the city discussed in chapter 2 renegotiated their caste identities and began to understand themselves as an urban lower middle class.

In other words, this chapter seeks to explain the "dream" of Syed Yakkubhai discussed by Manju Mehta, the dream of being rehabilitated in a self-contained flat, to show how dwelling in self-contained flats starts to become a defining feature of middle-class life in Bombay by the 1930s. For it was not simply the case that a preformed upper-caste lower middle class simply existed, ready to hand, with established tastes and preferences for housing. Rather, the new demographic group whose arrival in the city was discussed in chapter 2—the upper-caste, clerk class—constituted a powerful but as yet amorphous force in the housing markets. The demand for multiroom dwellings originated in the rising profile of this lower middle class in the city's housing markets, but eventually, as the cases of Syed Yakkubhai and countless others—Hindu, Muslim, upper caste, lower caste—demonstrate, living in self-contained flats became constitutive of middle-class identity, regardless of whether caste considerations were salient or not.

In the first section of this chapter, "Land Prices, the Lower Middle Class, and the Pressure to Build 'Up,'" I elaborate the process by which the Bombay apartment or flat emerged as a concept and as a built form in the late 1910s to middle 1920s. It begins by examining an important change that took place over the late 1910s and early 1920s. In the last years of World War I and in the few years immediately following, the Bombay economy surged, with an accompanying boom in land prices. This created a great demand for land, boosting sales of the Improvement Trust's newly developed plots in Dadar–Matunga. Yet, as I go on to argue, the boom was short-lived, and from 1922 onward the land market slumped, with significant consequences for the nature of housing that came up in Dadar–Matunga. It was this particular boom-and-bust movement of the land market that drove buildings in Dadar–Matunga upward, as it were, and made it a suburb of multistory dwellings.

The demographic change in Bombay's workforce described in chapter 2 constituted a major shift in the nature of demand for housing. As the next section, "The Bombay Development Directorate and the Multiroom, Multifamily Dwelling," goes on to show, the newly emergent upper-caste lower middle class—or clerk class—did not find a suitable dwelling option in a housing market where the choices were confined to either larger dwellings that were too expensive or one-room working-class tenements that were perceived as unsuitable. Brahmin migrants from southern India arriving to work in white-collar jobs constituted a significant portion of this new upper-caste but lower-middle-class market for housing. This section examines the failure of the massive tenement-building project of the Bombay Development Directorate in the early 1920s and suggests that the project failed not only for the conventional reasons offered—poor design, high rents, and so on—but because it severely misjudged the nature of demand for housing.

At about the same time, roughly between 1920 and the mid-1930s, a variety of changes in the infrastructure of the city, the increasing proliferation of flushing technology, and a gradual acceptance of the concept by lower middle classes meant that the toilet began to move "into" the dwelling from its former exilic location outside. Outlining various aspects of this inward migration is the subject of the next section, "Toilets and the Emergence of the Bombay Flat," which argues that accompanying this inward migration of the toilet is a coalescence in the understanding of the idea of the "flat" to encompass its self-contained nature, which became constitutive of middle-class identity.

LAND PRICES, THE LOWER MIDDLE CLASS, AND THE PRESSURE TO BUILD "UP"

Although the Improvement Trust originally envisioned Dadar–Matunga as a villa suburb, by the end of the 1920s it was populated principally by multistory, multifamily apartment buildings. Specific movements in the Bombay land market in the period 1916–1924—especially in Dadar–Matunga—created a pressure to build upward that resulted in the multistory dwelling replacing the cottage. Meanwhile, the emergent lower middle class created a demand for housing that was not being met either by the single-room tenement or by larger dwellings. The multiroom dwelling in the multistory building became increasingly common in response to these pressures.

Boom and Bust in the Land Market

The Improvement Trust, as was shown in chapter 1, envisioned a garden suburb–type setting populated mostly by villas and bungalows punctuated by the occasional multistory tenement. As late as in 1923, the architect and town planner W. R. Davidge assessed the housing schemes of the Improvement Trust and the ongoing massive chawls being built by the Bombay Development Directorate. He noted that almost every single public housing scheme in Bombay consisted of multistory tenements and attributed this to the high cost of building land in the island city. An absolute scarcity of space in the island city was not, however, the only or even the principal reason for the high cost of land; rather, it was the speculative practices of private landowners, invariably accompanying public authorities' announcement of attempts to purchase land, that drove up the cost of land. The price of land in the newly emerging northern suburbs in the island city could get as high as 10 rupees per square yard, or about 3,250 British pounds per acre, not high by Bombay standards, Davidge argued, but much higher than what would be paid for similar lands near large English towns.[15]

Such speculative practices had already been noticed and attacked both by colonial authorities and by leaders in the Indian community seeking to secure cheap housing for the working classes and, especially, for the rapidly growing lower middle classes. The land manager of the Development Department, E. M. Gilbert-Lodge, pointed out the ways in which the post–World War I economic boom had resulted in rampant speculation in land.[16] Gilbert-Lodge urged public officials seeking to acquire land for public purposes to approach the land-acquisition process with caution. Landowners, he argued, were engaging in speculative malpractices to inflate the perceived market value of lands in the city.[17] Since public authorities bought land for its perceived market value, and since the market value of a given piece of land was based on recent transactions within that part of the city, landowners sought to manipulate the recent record of property transactions. For example, a recorded recent sale at a seemingly high price might not be a sale at all but, rather, merely an agreement to purchase, without any money actually changing hands. Or the buyer in a seemingly large land deal might merely have been acting as a dummy, and no actual exchange of funds might have taken place. As a result Gilbert-Lodge urged public officials to take certain precautionary measures in determining market values. Isolated high or low sales were to be disregarded; any sales taking place shortly after an area was notified for acquisition by a public authority were to be viewed with caution; and finally, if a previous sale price seemed exceptionally high, then the buyer and seller should ideally be summoned and the contract and the transfer deed should be investigated to ensure that the sale did, in fact, take place.[18]

A. G. Viegas, a leader in the city's Catholic community and a member of the Municipal Corporation's Standing Committee, also deplored speculative practices in the land market. Writing in 1919, he noted that land prices had soared from about six to eight annas per square yard to six to eight rupees per square yard (sixteen annas made a rupee), even in outlying parts of the island city and in Salsette. He argued that plans for suburbanization were all well and good, but nothing would happen with land prices so high. He urged the government, in vain, to act swiftly and acquire large swathes of land in Salsette and to check land speculation and profiteering by legislation.[19] O. K. Bhuta, a civil engineer active in property valuation in the city at this time, took his analysis a step further in an address to the Bombay Cooperative Housing Association. He identified the Improvement Trust as the single largest landholder with alienable land and blamed specific policies of the Trust for contributing to the "contagion" of speculation. Two practices, in particular, he found objectionable. First, the Trust's introduction of an auction system to dispose of plots of land—which replaced an earlier system in which the Trust simply alienated land at a "scheduled" price on a first-come, first-served basis—was contributing to the steep rise in prices. Second, the Trust's monopolist practice of controlling the supply of land by only releasing plots at a slow dribble based on the perceived demand was also driving up prices. Bhuta felt that it was absurd that there should be such a steep rise in land prices when the Trust's vast estates in Dadar, Matunga, and Sion were basically lying uninhabited. He urged the Trust to release more land onto the market and thus deflate the bubble.[20]

A variety of Indian critics were thus seeking to curb the speculation in land that was driving the price of housing upward. But the market plummeted of its own accord after 1922. As M. Visweswaraya, engaged by the Bombay Municipal Corporation in 1924 to serve as retrenchment adviser, portentously announced:

> In the boom period immediately following the war, the commercial prospects of the city, for a time, appeared particularly rosy, property values rose high and the Municipal revenues showed a sudden expansion. It was at such a time that the Corporation started large schemes of development and expansion, and sanctioned funds and establishment on a liberal scale for the execution of schemes. But when the tide turned and the trade depression set in about 1922 and 1923, when it was seen that municipal income was falling, while the expenditure continued to increase, the thoughts of the corporation turned to retrenchment and reform.[21]

As a result of this "trade depression" and the ensuing collapse in municipal revenues, the city's chief developmental agencies—the Improvement Trust and the Development Directorate—faced a difficult predicament. On the one hand, constrained resources meant that they were less able to develop lands for urban use. On the other hand, they felt compelled to relax their strict control over the pace at which new land was released for building, a practice Bhuta had criticized, hoping to encourage investment. Flustered investors, however, who had invested in new lands in the boom period, now reconsidered their investment and started to rethink the kinds of buildings they were going to erect on these lands.

It was in the context of such a steep rise in land prices between 1916 and 1922, followed by a collapse, that Davidge surveyed the housing scene in Bombay in the early 1920s. For him there was no question that the multistory tenement was far from ideal and that something needed to be done by the government to control land prices and ensure that subsequent house construction in the new suburbs of Worli, Dadar, and Matunga took the form of small cottages instead of tenements. For Davidge, the cottage possessed several advantages over the tenement, from the point of view of both the occupants and the state:

> It will be readily agreed that, whenever and wherever possible, the one storey self contained cottage, with its private garden and enclosed yard, so dear to the home loving Indian of the country districts, should be provided and, at any rate in the suburban districts, the height limit of two storeys should be rigidly kept. . . . The difficulties of securing any measure of privacy in a single room tenement, occupied by a family, but forming one of twenty or so on the same floor and using the same sanitary conveniences, are almost insurmountable and the moral and social effects, and probably too, the political effects, on the rising generation brought up entirely under such conditions, are extremely serious to contemplate. The dangers from epidemics from so great a concentration of the population are also considerable, although against this may be set the greater facilities for control which certainly exist.[22]

Davidge might well have formulated here the classic colonial statement on the advantages of the cottage over the multistory dwelling. A vastly varied assortment of reasons are mobilized to make this point, ranging from well-worn clichés such as the "home loving Indian" to the improving qualities of "privacy," and including admittedly contradictory effects of at once fomenting insurgence while facilitating control of potential insurgency, all along paying respects to that old warhorse of legitimation for housing reform, public health.

The multistory tenement, while seemingly cheaper to construct than the cottage, was actually less efficient according to Davidge. In particular, he argued that the space taken by stairs, corridors, and other "general conveniences" of the multistory dwelling tended to offset its seeming cost-effectiveness, and that in fact it would be possible to build cottages that would more efficiently house Bombay's middle and working classes. To ensure this, he proposed a strict system of zoning within the city, using building regulations to restrict the height of new buildings to two stories (ground plus one) and also to limit such cottages to residential use.[23]

Davidge's zoning proposals were resoundingly criticized by various city officials engaged with housing matters. E. G. Turner, the chairman of the Improvement Trust, effectively dismissed both Davidge's assessment of the housing scene and his recommendations. Turner pointed out that much of Bombay was already effectively under some sort of zoning or other, especially in the Improvement Trust's estates in the north of the island and in the Development Department's new housing schemes in Worli and south central Bombay. The Municipal Corporation, meanwhile, had already instituted zoning in the older parts of the city to the south by refusing to permit new mills there and by resolving to relocate stables and tanneries out of the island city into Salsette.[24]

More revealing of the implications of the cyclical movement of land prices upon the building industry was the response of J. W. Mackison, an engineer in the Development Department. He noted that a large swathe of land in F Ward was being developed under the Trust's Schemes 5 and 6, the Dadar–Matunga and Sion–Matunga schemes. The Trust had originally stipulated that buildings should be limited to two stories so as to secure cottage-type construction. Despite the Trust's efforts to lease the land out at reasonable rates, the overall buoyancy in land prices between 1916 and 1922 had meant that investors were saddled with expensively acquired lands when recession set in after 1922. They felt they would be unable to recover their investment if they were to be compelled to build cottages on these lands, in part because house seekers were less likely to pay higher rents for cottages in recessionary times. As a result,

> instead of erecting buildings of the cottage type [the Trust's lessees in Dadar–Matunga] approached the Trust with the request that they should be allowed to erect an additional storey on their buildings. The arguments adduced resulted in the Trust granting the concession asked for, and *in place of the cottage type of house so much desiderated, there are now detached buildings with ground and two upper storeys on this estate. With a view to economy, some of the buildings have been constructed on the flat type.*[25]

These last sentences are exceptionally revealing, for they indicate the way the movement of the economy in a particular period shaped the pattern of housing in the newly emerging suburb of Dadar–Matunga, setting a precedent that would have profound ramifications for the future of housing in the city. It was a particular movement in land prices—rising high from 1916 to 1922 and plummeting thereafter—that rendered the cottage unviable and boosted the multistory dwelling instead. And already, as Mackison notes, some of these multistory dwellings were taking the shape of the flat. In a peculiar way, then, the movement of buildings upward was *not* driven by an absolute scarcity of lands, as is commonly assumed. Rather, it was a *surplus* of lands at a particular moment following the economic slowdown from 1922 onward that created a condition of diminished confidence among landowners. Having invested in expensive land at the height of the boom, investors were disconcerted to observe plentiful cheap land available after 1922. Further, they began to worry that house-seekers would shy away from the more impressive cottages. Together, these factors led investors to eschew the riskier cottage and embrace the multistory dwelling as the preferred building type for Dadar–Matunga.[26]

In permitting them to construct an additional floor the Trust did not, to be sure, act only with the interests of their lessees in mind. As Mackison went on to point out, had the Trust not conceded to the request to put up multistory dwellings, they would not have been able to lease out the remaining vacant plots and would have subsequently faced a debilitating loss in revenue, especially since much of the work of readying the land for construction had been expensively conducted in the boom period of 1916 to 1922.[27] In the long run, even concessions such as these did not save the Trust from financial meltdown. By the end of the 1920s, the Improvement Trust's finances were in disastrous shape, showing an income of 43 lakhs of rupees (4.3 million rupees) and outgoings of 93 lakhs of rupees (9.3 million rupees), creating a deficit for that year of 50 lakhs of rupees (5 million rupees). The Trust's annual report from 1930–1931 noted that this shortfall was "mainly due to the fact that nearly eight crores [80 million] of rupees had been locked up in the Trust schemes in the North of the Island," incurred through ruinously expensive costs of acquisition and development. With the slowdown of the building industry over the 1920s, the report gloomily concluded, "the Trust has been burdened with vast areas of land for which there is very little demand."[28]

The pattern of boom and bust in the land market in Dadar–Matunga between 1918 and 1924 can be illustrated by considering the investments of the Parsi Central Association Cooperative Housing Society (PCACHS) in Dadar–Matunga. The PCACHS had been the most active player in acquiring plots from the BIT in the southeast quadrant of the Dadar–Matunga Estate and putting up apartment buildings for lower-middle-class and middle-class Parsis. In the scramble for land in the boom years of 1916–1922, the PCACHS, like many other buyers, had paid a high price to acquire plots from speculators, who had grabbed them when the BIT first made the plots available. Such was the anxiety to get in on the land market that the PCACHS had simply grabbed whatever was available, even though the plots included some that were not entirely suitable for the PCACHS's purposes. But it acquired them anyway "to guard against the likelihood of other more suitable plots being not available in future."[29] What made some plots unsuitable? It was surely with reference to misadventures such as those of the PCACHS that a group of Parsis petitioned the governor of Bombay in 1924 to extend the rent restriction regulation that had been passed at the end of World War I in 1918. The petitioners of the Zorastrian Association argued:

> It has to be borne in mind that during the trade boom, people were in so great a hurry to invest their surplus income that they madly went in for the purchase of existing houses at exorbitant prices instead of building new ones. It has been the depressing

experience of your Memorialists that many of the Parsi tenants, who leased plots in the Dadar–Matunga schemes of the City Improvement Trust, at the time of the trade boom, with a view to erect their own buildings thereon, now find that their capital has so far depreciated that they have to abandon their plots even forfeiting their deposits.[30]

Providing a pithy summary of the boom and bust of the land market between 1918 and 1922, the association's petition also suggests that some plots were "unsuitable" for Parsi lessees such as the PCACHS because they already had houses on them, houses that were almost certainly of the cottage type. The PCACHS went ahead and acquired them anyway because it was worried that if it did not act then, it would be shut out of the market. But the PCACHS had no intention of permitting cottages on its lands—it clearly wanted to erect apartment buildings, which would consist of A-, B-, C-, or D-type flats, ranging in size from two rooms to five rooms.[31]

The discussion above has demonstrated the specific way the working of the land market in Dadar–Matunga in the period 1916–1924 drove out the cottage and introduced the multistory dwelling as the preferred choice of investors in this large new suburban development. It was not just a simple scarcity of lands that drove buildings upward; rather, it was the boom-and-bust phenomenon of scarcity of land followed by surplus, creating uncertainty in the land market, that drove investors to build multistory dwellings. Some of these investors, such as the PCACHS, had already settled on the apartment or flat as the form that multistory living would take. I turn now to consider housing practices in the city more generally during this same period by examining the single largest public housing project undertaken by the colonial government in Bombay, the Industrial Housing Scheme of the Bombay Development Directorate. Originally intended to fill the "deficit" in housing for the working class, the BDD chawls failed dismally in this respect. But critique of the chawls and the ensuing discussions demonstrated, as the following section will show, the emergence of a consensus that the emergent new lower-middle-class population of the city constituted a new and powerful force in the housing markets.

THE BOMBAY DEVELOPMENT DIRECTORATE AND THE MULTIROOM, MULTIFAMILY DWELLING

The most dramatic illustration of the chasm between perceptions of the housing shortage in Bombay and the changing nature of the demand in the market was provided by the (mis)adventures of the Bombay Development Directorate. The BDD awaits its comprehensive chronicler, and a brief account must suffice here.[32] Formed in 1919 at the height of the boom in the Bombay economy at large and in the real estate market in particular, the BDD was supposed to oversee the orderly development of the city in a time of overall growth. It was entrusted with three tasks: the reclamation and subsequent development of large swathes of land in the foreshores to the west of the island from Malabar Hill to Colaba (the so-called Backbay Reclamation Scheme); the construction of fifty thousand single-room tenements in the industrial districts of Bombay to meet the shortfall in housing (the Industrial Housing Scheme); and finally, the development of suburbs on Salsette Island (the suburban schemes).[33]

Among other things, the BDD was interesting because it appeared to represent a last-gasp attempt by the colonial state to exercise direct control over urban development. Following the Montagu–Chelmsford reforms of 1919, urban development would normally have been a transferred subject, and hence the project of building new tenements would have come under the Public Works ministry of the Government of Bombay. (And indeed, in many other respects urban governance did devolve from the colonial state onto the provincial government with greater Indian representation.) Instead, however, the BDD was constituted as an executive organ of the colonial state. Further, the advisory committee to the BDD was effectively powerless, and its advice was usually disregarded.

The BDD chawls were noteworthy for the innovations in chawl design, about which officials regularly boasted in the early stages.[34] Overall, it would appear that the Industrial Housing Scheme failed miserably, at least in its stated goals of housing the industrial working classes. The original scheme called for constructing fifty thousand one-room tenements to meet a perceived "deficit" of sixty-four thousand one-room tenements.[35] Owing to what the manager of the BDD chawls coyly termed "changed circumstances" by the mid-1920s, building was stopped after only sixteen thousand–plus tenements had been constructed.[36] In fact the cessation in building had to do with the fact that the BDD was mired in controversy over its reclamation schemes; at the same time, the tenements were never more than half occupied (until after World War II). The BDD also came in for heavy criticism from the Bombay public for its relentless—and allegedly reckless—building activity. One whole strand of criticism had to do with the way the "deficit" of single-room tenements was calculated. If the chawls were never more than half occupied, was there really a shortage? Another strand stemmed from the peremptory fashion in which the BDD went about the whole process. Yet a third line of criticism faulted the BDD for not doing more of the work under contract, which would provide local businesses the opportunity to bid on the projects, rather than departmentally.[37]

But the criticisms that are of greatest relevance here had to do with the modifications in the design of the BDD chawls, initially trumpeted by officials as great innovations but later used to explain the chawls' failure to attract and retain tenants. These criticisms came predominantly from the middle-class intelligentsia, who claimed that the BDD had misunderstood the tastes and needs of the working classes. It will be argued, however, that such critiques said more about the middle class than they did about the working class. Two aspects of an emerging consensus regarding the middle class were discernible. First, it gradually came to be realized that a surprising number of the tenants of the BDD chawls were actually not of the working class but were, rather, of the lower middle class. A second developing idea was that such a lower middle class constituted a new kind of market for cheap, multistory, multifamily, multiroom dwellings, and that the real failure of the BDD lay not in misgauging the housing shortage but, rather, in misgauging the demographic of the market that was seeking housing. I turn now to considering some of these discussions over the design of the chawls.

The best-known modifications of the BDD involved the decision to remove the *nahani,* or washing place, from the tenements. The *nahani* consisted of a tap and small tiled area separated from the rest of the room by a low wall or partition. It had played an important role within these tenements and had been used for everything from washing clothes to cleaning dishes to bathing, including occasionally, presumably under duress, as a toilet. As Lawless Hepper, the rakishly named director of the BDD, declared in his speech inaugurating the first complex of BDD chawls at Worli, the *nahani,* formerly a fixture of even the meanest tenement, had been taken out of the tenement and relocated in a central block on each floor, an arrangement that "[had] the advantage of being more sanitary as well as more economical."[38] The emphasis on cost cutting came in for its share of criticism. But more importantly, the notion that external *nahanis* were more "sanitary" was based on what Conlon calls "an old erroneous plague-combatting measure," namely, the notion that the spread of plague could be controlled by eliminating dampness.[39] The removal of the *nahani* was a big step and provoked much opposition.

Another important modification in chawl design was undertaken by the BDD in an attempt to create more "private space" for residents of the chawls. It decided to enclose the space normally occupied by the external verandah into the individual units, thus providing slightly larger rooms at the expense of the verandah. (As described previously, each story of a chawl had a verandah that allowed access to the building's small units.) Access to the units was now to be through a narrower internal corridor. This design decision, undertaken by the BDD with the intent of facilitating bourgeois values, was seen as making the chawls even less appealing to Bombay's working classes. The most vigorous criticism appears in a letter to the editor of the *Bombay Chronicle* from Jamshedji P. Mistri, a civil engineer:

In India a house or a *chawl* is not perfectly designed if there is no verandah. Verandah to a poor man is his breathing space; it is his parlour; it is his cosy corner; it is his diwan; it is there he sits and enjoys, there he imagines himself to be monarch of the world; it is there he can entertain his guests and his friends; it is there he can smoke his cigar and ruminate when his family is busy cooking his food inside the room. To remove the verandah from the dwelling place of a poor man is to remove all amenities from his dwelling. To throw that space into his room is to allure him to keep more boarders.[40]

Mistri's letter has an undeniably patronizing upper-middle-class tone, enthusing as it does over the verandah as a "cosy corner" and "parlour." While there is some truth to his observation that previously the verandah had served as an important multifunctional space where both "private" activities, such as resting and sleeping, and more social interactions could take place, note that all the verandah pastimes he quotes are middle-class pastimes. Such practices—the man of the house entertaining guests, relaxing with a cigar on the verandah while his family cooks his dinner, and so on—would have been inexplicable in the context of working-class housing patterns of the early 1920s, when five or more men might share a single room while their families, if they were married, were probably in the village. Mistri is really saying more about how significant a verandah is for a middle-class family living in a multistory dwelling.

The labor leader S. K. Bole had an interesting critique of the whole concept of multistory living. Writing a dissenting minute in the report of the Special Advisory Committee to the Industrial Housing Scheme, he noted that specific design flaws could be redressed, but "what is fundamentally wrong cannot be corrected by subsequent additions and alterations."[41] Bole was suspicious of multistory housing. In the villages where people came from, he wrote, they lived in cottages and huts, and "each caste live[d] in a particular locality." This arrangement allowed them to live without "offending the sensibilities of their neighbours of another religion." But what would happen when all these different kinds of people lived on top of one another? Living in what he called "these huge piles which are supposed to accommodate people of different castes, religions, languages and of different parts of the country," they would definitely impinge on each other's various religious beliefs. Ultimately Bole learned that there was a de facto practice of restricting tenancy on any given floor to members of a particular community, which led him to grudgingly accept the multistory tenement.[42] Bole's note is interesting because it indicates the sorts of fears that multistory living provoked, fears that went beyond specific design flaws, as well as the sorts of unofficial measures being taken to counteract these fears.

There was still plenty to complain about with the design, though. In a letter to the editor of the *Bombay Chronicle,* a group of self-professedly middle-class Christian residents of the BDD chawls on DeLisle Road voiced a plaintive complaint. The single-room tenements, they claimed, were airless, hot, and dark. They were

FIGURE 3.1. *BIT chawl under construction, Love Lane, Byculla. The verandah is beginning to be enclosed but is still present. Courtesy of Gammon India.*

FIGURE 3.2. *DeLisle Road BDD chawl under construction. Note the lack of a verandah. Courtesy of Gammon India.*

just like pigeon holes, but we think pigeon holes are far better than these rooms, as the former get sufficient breeze. Sorry we human beings are not treated even like birds. . . . At present [we are] in a state of being roasted live in an oven, but nobody hears our cry.[43]

Such letters drew attention to the fact that the educated lower middle classes were living in chawls supposedly built for the working classes, as well as to the often-mentioned design flaws in the BDD chawls. The letter also drew attention to the fact that the chawls did not have regular windows but instead had a reinforced cement concrete (RCC) lattice, which, supposedly, was to let in air but keep out the sun. Obviously, as the complainants' letter indicated, the lattice was not performing its role in a satisfactory fashion. The response of the BDD to this particular letter is instructive. The BDD's land manager argued that regular windows had not been provided because tenants were using windows to dispose of rubbish. He suggested that Muslims, Christians, Jews, and high-caste Hindus could have open windows but that it would be better to keep the present system for lower castes (which would presumably include lower classes) until they had been "educated to use a window as a means of fresh air and not as an ever present outlet for refuse, both solid and liquid."[44] Such a remark indicates a complex and overlapping mapping of caste, religion, class, and practice in the mind of this particular BDD official. But one clear implication is that the BDD chawls contained certain residents who, by virtue of birth, education, or occupation, were able to live in a "civilized" fashion. By implication, such people needed to live separately from those who were not able to live in "civilized" fashion.

Another instructive complaint came from within the BDD: the junior assistant land manager pointed out that the imperfect working of the chimneys in the one-room tenements, combined with the inadequate ventilation of the latticed windows, caused smoke and soot to collect in the rooms and form a black coating over everything:

> We are asking the tenants time after time to keep their rooms neat and clean, but the rooms in the majority of cases have been darkened through no fault of theirs, but through defective chimneys. This is really unfortunate as the tenants who desire to live with clean habits cannot do so on account of the above nuisance.[45]

In the previous instance it was tenants' malpractice that impeded the civilizing influence of BDD design; in this instance, it was imperfect design that was obstructing the civilizing endeavors of BDD tenants.

The BDD chawls may have had flaws in their design, but even after these flaws had been rectified, the occupancy rate did not climb over 50 percent.[46] This suggests that the real problem of the one-room tenements of the BDD chawls was that they were betwixt and between, so to speak. They appeared to be too expensive for the working classes, yet at the same time the single-room tenement was increasingly perceived as unsuitable for the lower middle classes. The problematic nature of housing Bombay's lower middle classes in one-room tenements was most explicitly stated in a study of housing conditions undertaken in 1923 by students of Sydenham College under the supervision of Professor H. L. Kaji. The study found tenement living to be especially difficult for the lower middle classes, who were more likely to live in family groups including wives and children than were the working classes, who, in the city, were more likely to live as single men:

> A middle class man requires, for common decency, at least two rooms one of which can be used a cook room, store room and bathroom, while the other can be used as a living room and bedroom. . . . One room life so thoroughly militates against the ideas of comfort and decency that essentially constitute the middle class man, that it is only through the impossibility of affording more roomy quarters that he puts up with it, though even then he tries to make two rooms out of one by a sort of a partition by almirahs, cupboards or cloth curtains.[47]

The study remarks here upon a common practice in one-room tenements of dividing up the space for different uses through makeshift partitions of curtains or furniture. But what is interesting here, again, is the observation that a new lower middle class was seeking housing in a city that did not yet have a category of dwelling for it: the upper middle classes and the wealthy lived either in houses or other dwellings with three or more rooms, while the working classes were forced to live in single-room tenements.

The matter of housing the lower middle classes came to a head when a deputation from a body calling itself the Non-Official Housing and Tenant Ownership Institute paid a visit to R. D. Bell, deputy director of the Development Department, in April 1925. The delegation included housing luminaries such as Mancherji Edulji Joshi, the founder of the Parsi Colony in Dadar–Matunga, and Captain E. M. Gilbert-Lodge, land manager of the Development Department. Since the BDD tenements were more than half vacant, Mancherji Joshi, the leader of the delegation, urged the Development Department to consider converting some of these single-room units into two- and three-room units to meet "the pressing needs of the poor middle classes." Such multiroom units should then be handed over to leaders of the Hindu, Muslim, Christian, and Parsi communities, who would dispense them among their respective constituencies and would also guarantee that the units would be occupied and that the rents would be paid. One of the members of the delegation, a British resident of Bombay named E. Woodfall, urged that the poor middle class, "viz. the poorly paid clerk" in various kinds of employ, "should be provided cheap house accommodation at once" since, according to Woodfall, "they were the backbone of the services and public life."[48]

On the face of it this seemed like a good arrangement, since, as already noted, the BDD was facing vacancy rates of 50 percent and at the same time, as described above, Bombay's lower middle classes were seeking multiroom dwellings. However, a legal problem arose: the subsidy offered on BDD rents—the difference between economic rents and the rents actually charged—was financed by a tax on cotton imports into the city. There was thus a legal obligation to use these resources only to subsidize housing for workers associated with the cotton industry, which would be the traditional working classes. This constraint engaged the Development Department for a while, but it appears to have resolved the legal challenge for itself, for by April 1926, almost exactly a year following the visit of the delegation led by Mancherji Joshi, the Development Department effectively sanctioned, in principle, the conversion of some single-room units into two- and three-room units. They argued that even though the chawls were theoretically only for people of the working class, "in point of fact [the Development Department] do nothing to exclude clerks, shopkeepers and others who, by a narrow interpretation of the words 'working classes' may be said not to belong to these classes."[49] The Development Department concluded that if rents were dropped to an irreducible minimum and there were still vacant units available, then there was no reason not to convert some of those vacant units into two- and three-room tenements for the lower middle classes. Not only were the conversions sanctioned, but *nahanis* were permitted back into the units, both because of the storm of protest against their exile and because it was felt that the lower middle classes needed water taps within their dwellings even if the working classes did not.

The decision to permit the conversion of multiroom tenements was significant since it represented an acknowledgment of the housing needs of the burgeoning new lower middle class. Not only did this lower middle class merit a multiroom dwelling, but such dwellings also needed to be spatially separate from the single-room dwellings of the working class. Thus, shortly after sanctioning the conversion of some single-room tenements, A. W. Mackie, secretary to the government, Development Department, announced:

> In order to attract the lower middle class of people who we like to inhabit the two and three room tenement it is desirable that complete *chawls* should be tenanted by the same class (and therefore converted) and that the *chawls* should be so selected as to be practically separated as far as possible from those occupied by labourers.[50]

By the end of the decade two chawl buildings—one in Naigaum and one on DeLisle Road—had been converted into two- and three-room tenements "as an experimental measure." The one at Naigaum, especially, had been almost entirely occupied, and one floor in the Naigaum chawl had been rented out to the Parsi Federal Council, no doubt in response to the petitions discussed earlier. These rooms had been fitted with interconnecting doors to facilitate great flexibility in the size and layout of units.[51] By the early 1930s, three chawls in Naigaum and one in DeLisle Road had been modified in this fashion.[52] Indeed, the manager of the BDD chawls, a Brahmin by the name of T. A. J. Ayyar, announced that "the department of late has been doing its best to popularize the Worli *chawls* among the lower middle class people," and that he himself had moved into the Worli chawls to lead by example, as it were.[53]

By the mid-1920s, thus, it was clear that the lower middle classes constituted a discrete market for the multiroom dwelling. It was this market whose needs were not met either by the single-room tenements in the chawls of the working-class districts or by the larger dwellings in the older parts of the city. The latter were too expensive while the former were deemed unsuitable for a class that, while modest in resources, nonetheless prided itself on its proprieties. Meanwhile, as was demonstrated at the beginning of the chapter, the movement of land prices by the 1920s had been such that investors in plots in Dadar–Matunga eschewed the cottage and started building multistory structures. Lower middle classes were beginning to reside in multiroom dwellings in multistory structures. Meanwhile, the toilet was slowly making its way into the dwelling, both at the level of building practice but also, importantly, at the level of popular understanding, to yield the Bombay flat. It would be the inward migration of the toilet that would finally yield a kind of dwelling that catered both to the modest economic resources of the new lower middle class while also accommodating their notions of propriety. I turn now to consider this process.

TOILETS AND THE EMERGENCE OF THE BOMBAY FLAT

Writing in 1939, R. S. Deshpande, a civil engineer and popularizer of house designs, defined the flat as a "self-contained, convenient, small dwelling, within a large building."[54] In describing the flat as "self-contained," Deshpande was referring to the fact that all essential functions were contained within the walls of the dwelling, including the kitchen and, crucially, the bathroom and the toilet. Such an understanding of what constituted a flat had become commonplace by this time and, indeed, the "self-contained" nature of the flat was what distinguished it from its humbler cousin, the tenement or chawl. Deshpande explicitly made this distinction: "Flats are quite different from *chawls*, which are perhaps peculiar to Bombay," he wrote. Whereas the flats were self-contained, chawls were "provided with a few washrooms and w.c.'s, usually inadequate in number, for common use in a separate appurtenance" to the dwelling.[55]

The process by which "self-containedness" became what distinguished the flat from other kinds of multistory, multiunit dwelling was slow and gradual. Both technological and social transformations were involved in producing the flat: sewerage networks had to extend into the dwelling and flushing technology had to become more widespread, while the notion of urinating and defecating under the very roof where one slept, ate, and prayed also had to become acceptable. In this section I explore this extraordinary transformation in living practices, which took place in the two decades between the late 1910s and the late 1930s. I begin by considering the way the concept of the flat began to achieve a stable meaning between about 1916 and the early 1920s; I then examine the changes in the city's infrastructure between 1918 and 1939 that enabled the inward migration of the toilet; and I conclude the section by considering some of the political and cultural implications of the inward movement of the toilet.

By about 1910, the concept of the "flat" or "block" appears to have made its first appearance on the Bombay real estate scene. The first residents of flats in Bombay appear to have been poorer Europeans. Claude Batley, mandarin of the Bombay architecture scene for four decades from his arrival in 1913 until his death in 1956, identified Grant's Buildings and Kamal Mansions as two of the earliest instances of flat dwellings in the city; both were located in the European precinct of Colaba.[56] Early references to flats seem to underscore their suitability for Europeans. Consider the following rental advertisement:

> "To let: Colaba Reclamation. A thoroughly English flat for Europeans. Two bedrooms etc. Ground floor enjoying Westerly breeze. Latest sanitary arrangements."[57]

Colaba Reclamation, in Colaba, was firmly in the European part of the city. The advertisement underscores this point by explicitly proclaiming the suitability of this "English flat" for "Europeans." And finally, the announcement of the "latest sanitary arrangements" promises something different—the attached toilet. Such advertisements became increasingly common from about 1916 onward, although it was not always the case that the modern flat mapped precisely onto an exact social form such as the nuclear family. The "paying guest" arrangement was already practiced, as witnessed by an ad seeking "paying guest by European family in modern flat on Apollo Bunder, room large and airy with bathroom attached."[58]

Yet the concept of self-contained multistory living was not entirely restricted to Europeans in this period. In this as in other areas having to do with becoming at home in Bombay, the Saraswat Brahmins were ahead of their time. As early as 1915, the Saraswat Cooperative Housing Society had been established on the Improvement Trust's Gamdevi Estate, just to the west of older parts of the city such as Girgaum and Khetwadi.[59] There were several pioneering features to this development: it was the first cooperative housing society in Bombay and perhaps in India, and it represented a very early use of RCC elements in the form of pillars to support the arches. Yet what was utterly remarkable, not least because it was presented almost as a matter of course despite the fact that it must have been quite novel, was the fact that the dwellings were all "self-contained" and consisted of two bedrooms, hall, kitchen units, and a bathroom and toilet within the dwelling.

To my knowledge this would have been the first building for middle-class Indians where the toilet was contained entirely within the dwelling. To put it in the terms used by Edwardes and Hansa Mehta at the beginning of this chapter, the Saraswat Society was a case of "European" flats built for Hindus. The toilets are all provided with a "full flushing system." What is also interesting is that the term used in 1916 to describe the Saraswat dwellings is "tenement," suggesting that the term "flat" had not yet come to be associated with being "self-contained" and may simply have referred to larger, multiroom dwellings in multistory structures occupied by Europeans or very wealthy Indians. Indeed, the very fact that the Saraswat buildings in Gamdevi were so unusual, if not actually unique—a case where the built form preceded a category adequate to it—perhaps meant that no other term than "tenement" was available for describing a lower-middle-class Indian dwelling in a multistory, multiunit structure.

The precise meaning of "flat" as a dwelling distinct from a tenement or chawl remained unclear until well into the 1920s. Consider, for instance, the range of allusions contained in the following rental ads in the Classified section of the *Bombay Chronicle* from 1920. All three are from the same day and same page of the newspaper:

> To be let: . . . and also a bungalow on block system three minute walk from Matunga Road station (G.I.P.)

> To be let: FLATS of most suitable accommodation near Club Road, Byculla, at Agripada Chawl Street, Plot number 147. Improvement Trust, rent reasonable. Apply to Salemahomed Peermahomed & Co.

> To be let: two FLATS, consisting of Dining, Drawing, two Bedrooms and bathrooms, cookhouse, W.C. and electric light. Top floor, "Vasant Building." Opposite G.I.P. Parel.[60]

In the first example cited above, there appears to be a categorial blurring: the advertisement is for a bungalow, which, however, has been modified, to be on the "block system," a common term in Bombay for flats. This structure, once a single-family house, had presumably been internally modified and divided into several multiroom units resembling flats, although it is not clear from this advertisement whether the flats were "self-contained" or not. Such a structure would, thus, have been an intermediate stage between the house and the apartment building. The second advertisement appears to be a case of a chawl masquerading as a flat. No flats were built in this area at that time, and the address suggests that the unit in question was quite probably on the BIT's Agripada Estate with chawls. But the attempt to represent a chawl as a flat indicates that the meaning of the latter was not entirely stable and that it might have been possible to extract higher rents by passing off a two- or three-room chawl as a flat.

The third advertisement contains a more specific definition of the flat with the crucial feature that differentiated it from the multiroom tenement: the WC, or water closet, a common term for the toilet. This particular flat also appears to be significantly larger than many other dwellings, with dining and drawing rooms, two bedrooms and bathrooms, and a kitchen in addition to the toilets.

Some advertisements were even more specific about precisely what distinguished the new dwelling type, with attached WC, from previous forms:

> Commodious FLATS for Europeans in new building, "Adorn House," opposite G.I.P. Railway Institute, Suparibaug Road, Parel, facing West with electric fittings and full flushing system, good for officers of a Railway Company, Mills, or large limited companies. Apply Cassam Karmally & Co., #204 Khoja Mohalla, Mandvi.[61]

This particular advertisement is even more explicit about sanitary conveniences on offer, promising "full flushing system" instead of older systems such as the "basket privy," which would have necessitated manual removal of waste from the premises. These various advertisements suggest that while there was some ambiguity in the meaning of the term "flat" at this moment in 1920, there was, nonetheless, a gradual movement toward an understanding of the flat as a form of dwelling that was part of a multistory building and "self-contained," in that the toilet was located within the dwelling.

Such a discursive coalescence of the meaning of the flat should be understood in the context of the extension, between 1920 and 1940, of the citywide waste-removal infrastructure *into* the dwelling. This, in turn, was accompanied by active attempts by the Bombay Municipal Corporation to standardize the form of the toilet and to replace older systems with the newer flushing system.[62] In older parts of the city to the south, the BMC sought to increase the connectivity of existing houses to the sewerage network, which began to be laid in the early twentieth century.[63] From 1918, the Corporation included an entry in their annual reports titled "Street and House Connections" in order to tabulate the rate at which older houses were being plugged into the sewerage system through "sullage" connections, thus marking an important step in the entry of the sewerage network into the dwelling.[64] In 1922, the BMC's chief engineer announced that work had commenced on "removing the old pattern latrine and reconstructing on the new pattern full flushing system" in BMC buildings in Mahim, in the north of the island.[65]

Meanwhile the Trust sought, from the beginning, to plug the new suburbs in Dadar–Matunga into the waste disposal network. But in 1917, as the work of developing the BIT's estates in Dadar–Matunga picked up in the wake of a booming land market, the Trust announced that urgent action needed to be taken. It looked as if plots were to be sold and houses built in this area before the sewerage system was in place. The Trust constructed a temporary infrastructure of septic tanks and biological filters until the proposed sewerage scheme was put into place.[66] In 1919, J. W. Mackison, special engineer, Development Works (the same engineer whose remarks on land speculation in the early 1920s were discussed earlier in this chapter) drew up a comprehensive scheme for a new network of sewers and drains for the northern part of the island, including, significantly, a brand-new outfall to be situated in the northeast of the island.[67] At the same time, the BMC invited John Watson, engineer to the city of Birmingham, England, to conduct a thorough study of the city's existing sewerage and drainage systems. Watson endorsed Mackison's proposals, especially for building new sewerage and drainage works for the northern parts of the island in view of the impending development of that region.[68] Then, as now, the BMC moved slowly: in 1932, more than ten years after Watson submitted his proposals, the Corporation approved a large new sewerage scheme for the north of the island and sanctioned almost 2.4 million rupees for it.[69]

In 1922, the BMC's chief engineer announced that work had commenced on "removing the old pattern latrine and reconstructing on the new pattern full flushing system" in BMC buildings in Mahim, marking the entry of the sewerage network into the dwelling.[70] Meanwhile work had already commenced in replacing basket privies with flushing toilets in other parts of the city.

By 1939, seeking to fully eliminate the old basket privy system altogether, the BMC offered a subvention of sixty rupees per seat of basket privy converted into a full flushing water closet in F and G Wards. This was sanctioned on August 10, 1939, and put into operation.[71] By the late 1930s, sewage and wastewater treatment facilities had also sprung up in the northern parts of the island, and the Dadar Purification Plant reported annually on the smooth functioning of the "Sludge Digestion Process."[72] By 1939 the Matunga Pumping Station had "developed into one of major importance and the amount of sewage to be dealt with [had] exceeded expectations owing to the very rapid development of the surrounding areas."[73] In conjunction with the carrot of the subvention to convert to flushing toilets was a stick: action began to be taken against house owners who did not swiftly connect the drains in their buildings to the new sewerage system coming into existence in the northern parts of the island.[74] In general, the annual reports of the Municipal Corporation

YEAR	Basket privies replaced by WCs
1919–20	215
1920–21	440
1921–22	128
1922–23	110
1923–24	88
1924–25	108

FIGURE 3.3. *Annual numbers of basket privies replaced by WCs. Bombay Municipal Corporation,* Annual Administration Reports, *1920–1921, 17; 1921–1922, 17; 1923–1924, 15; 1924–1925, 15.*

between 1920 and 1940 indicate that the city in this period was gradually acquiring a network of drainage and sewerage pipes that connected buildings into a citywide mechanism for the movement of wastewater, especially from the new toilets. The incentives to convert to flushing toilets combined with the penalties for not converting meant that by the 1930s, the flushing toilet was slowly becoming the norm in old buildings in Dadar–Matunga, and new buildings almost certainly would have been built with the flushing toilet.

An interesting inversion of the pattern observed by William Glover in the old city of Lahore was taking place. Glover notes that colonial Lahore (and other colonial cities, for that matter) displayed a paradoxical feature. On the one hand, buildings were built in extremely close proximity to one another, sometimes even sharing a wall. Functionally, however, these structures were discrete units, in that they did not partake of a network of pipes, drains, or cables for gas, water, or electricity.[75] The cityscape rising in Bombay from the 1920s onward, by contrast, was one of highly discrete structures separated from one another by compounds and walls, which nonetheless were actually highly interlinked through an elaborate network of infrastructural connections.

The actual movement of the toilet inward was a gradual process and took place in stages. Advertisements for modern bathrooms with toilets were appearing in newspapers from as early as 1921. Consider, for example an advertisement that appeared for "Shanks' Modern Bath-Rooms" in the *Bombay Chronicle*.[76] The firm of Armitage Shanks had been an early pioneer of ceramic bathroom fittings in nineteenth-century Britain and in fact continued to supply furnishings to Bombay flats until quite recently. The photograph in this advertisement (Figure 3.4) features a very modern looking complete bathroom: a sink, bathtub, and toilet attached to a flush, all dispersed through an airy room with a large window.

Bathrooms were differently organized in the majority of apartment buildings coming up around Bombay, especially in Dadar–Matunga. A rich archive of flat-building practices is provided in the works of R. S. Deshpande, a pioneer of housing construction in the 1930s who published several books—in Marathi, Hindi, and English—instructing the middle classes in the techniques of modern building construction. Deshpande wrote at least ten books on building, with titles like *A Textbook of Reinforced Concrete, Disposal of Domestic Sewage,* and *Cheap and Healthy Homes for the Middle Classes.* I consider here two of his works that bracket the boom period of apartment building construction in Bombay: *Residential Buildings Suited to India,* which appeared in 1931, and *Modern Ideal Homes for India,* which appeared in 1939.

In the earlier volume, the relevant chapter in the book is titled "Flats or Semi-detached Houses," suggesting that Deshpande viewed these as belonging to the same category in that they were distinct from the free-standing house. One of the ten designs is of a "semi-detached house" of two stories, while the remaining nine

Shanks' Modern Bath-Rooms.

We Keep Large Stock of Baths, Water Closets, Lavatories, Sinks and all Kind of Sanitary Goods.

Of Messrs. SHANKS & Co., Ld., Barrhead.

Sole Agents :—

GARLICK & Co.,

Engineers, and Iron Founders, Jacobs Circle, BOMBAY.

FIGURE 3.4. *Advertisement for Armitage Shanks bathroom fittings, showing an "integrated" bathroom. Bathrooms in the flats of Dadar–Matunga were disaggregated, with the three principal elements (toilet, washbasin, bathing area) occupying different but adjacent sites.* Bombay Chronicle, *February 21, 1921.*

designs are for flats.[77] The location of toilets or WCs in these flats is interesting. Clearly each flat has a toilet associated with it, thus differentiating these dwellings from previous multistory structures in which many dwellings would share a few toilets. However, the toilet, while associated with the flat, is not actually inside the flat. Eight of the nine designs for flats feature the toilets in the rear verandah area, thus "cut off by a small passage" from the living areas.[78] The one flat design of the nine that actually had the toilet within the flat located it in the extreme corner, surrounded by the window to outside, the bathroom, a passage, and the toilet of the neighboring flat, separated by a shared wall (Figure 3.6). Of this one design Deshpande notes that "the back verandah which is a great convenience is omitted," suggesting that it would be preferable to have the toilet in the verandah rather than in the house. In one design, the toilet and bathroom are actually in a separate block connected to the building by a passage.[79] To use the toilet, thus, a person would have to step out of the flat interior and into the verandah. But the user would still be within the property of that flat, and only residents of that flat could use the toilet. Some of the designs, however, advertise their flexibility and display even greater variety in the location of toilets. Buildings of two stories could either house four flats (two flats on each floor) or two flats (one large flat on each floor); or, indeed, the whole structure could be occupied as a house (Figure 3.8).

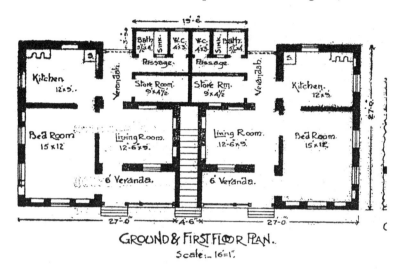

FIGURE 3.5. *Attached toilet, accessed through verandah.* R. S. Deshpande, Residential Buildings Suited to India, *240.*

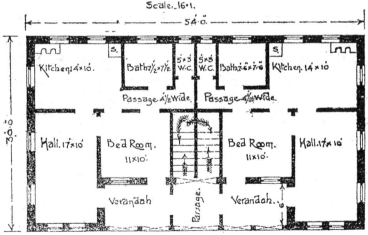

FIGURE 3.6. *The only early design with the toilet actually within the house, rather than accessed through the verandah.* R. S. Deshpande, Residential Buildings Suited to India, *241.*

In these designs, to accommodate this potential flexibility, the toilets are all in the back verandah, which would mean that were the floor divided into two flats, then each flat would have its own toilet but potentially the toilets could be adjacent to one another and accessible through the same passage.[80] Thus, when *Residential Buildings Suited to India* was published in 1931, the idea of a toilet uniquely associated with a given flat was firmly established, but the location of the toilet was more likely to be in the back verandah, separated from the other living spaces by the verandah itself. Furthermore, to accommodate flexibility in design, it was sometimes possible for toilets associated with two different flats to be adjacent to one another and accessed through the same passage, even though each toilet was uniquely associated with one particular flat. The toilet had thus taken steps in its journey into the flat, but it was yet to be completely "internalized."

Compare the designs above to the designs in Deshpande's 1939 *Modern Ideal Homes for India.* In his preface to this latter book Deshpande writes that he "originally intended to bring out a revised edition of *Residential Buildings Suited to India,*" but

> on account of the very common use of concrete in building construction, and the advent of a number of new materials, since the publication of that book in 1931, not only have the domestic architecture and also building materials been revolutionized, but *even our very ideas of living have undergone a considerable change.*[81]

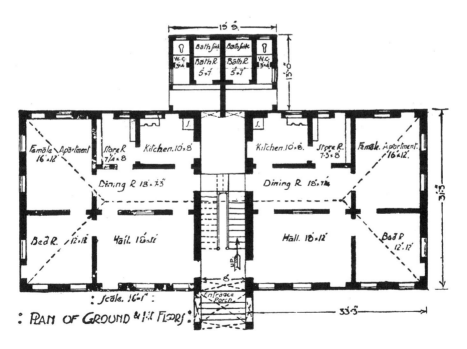

FIGURE 3.7. *Attached toilet located in separate block. R. S. Deshpande,* Residential Buildings Suited to India, *244.*

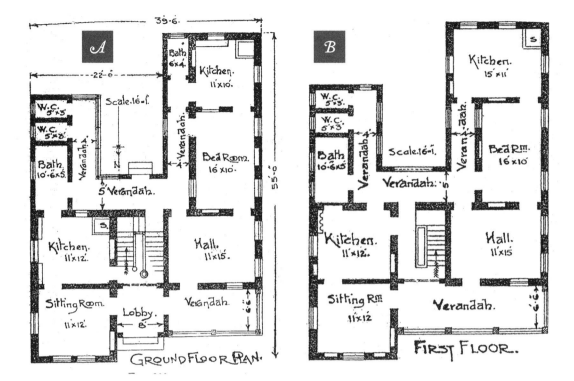

_→_ FIGURE 3.8. _Flexible design showing ground floor (A) and first floor (B) plans. This building could be a house for one large family, or could be two, three, or even four separate flats depending on how the toilets were used. Each floor offers either one large flat with two adjacent toilets, or two smaller flats accessing toilets through shared verandah._ R. S. Deshpande, Residential Buildings Suited to India, _247, 248._

In writing what ended up being an almost entirely new book, Deshpande signaled the revolution in dwelling practices that had taken place over the course of the 1930s. One important shift had to do with the increased use of concrete in building construction, some implications of which will be discussed in chapter 4. But a revolution in the "idea of living" had also taken place: in all the new designs, the toilet had now firmly moved inside the dwelling from the intermediate zone it occupied in 1931, when _Residential Buildings Suited to India_ was published. Desphande explicitly links this to the widening infrastructure of drainage, noting that in larger cities "where underground drainage is constructed" and toilets can be flushed with water, thus eliminating "noxious smells," the toilets "could be built close to, or even inside, the house."[82]

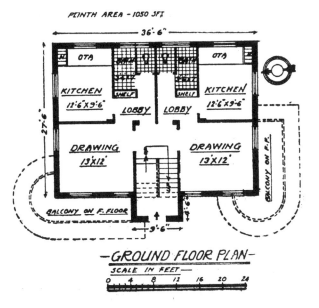

PLINTH AREA - 1050 SFT

GROUND FLOOR PLAN

SCALE IN FEET

⊰ FIGURE 3.9. *The toilet is firmly within the space of the flat. Architect: Marathe and Company.* R. S. Deshpande, Modern Ideal Homes for India, *135.*

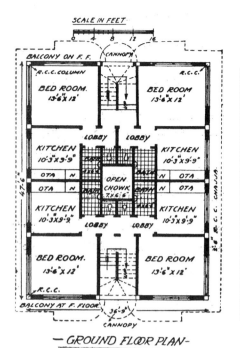

SCALE IN FEET

— GROUND FLOOR PLAN —

FIGURE 3.10. *A typical late Deshpande design, with the toilet accessible immediately on entry into the apartment from the outside landing. A person entering to clean the toilet could access it without traversing the rest of the dwelling. Architect: Adalja and Noorani.* R. S. Deshpande, Modern Ideal Homes for India, *137.*

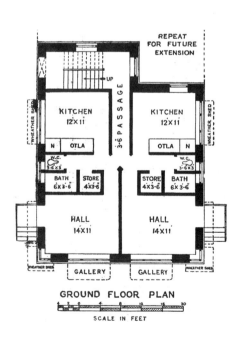

GROUND FLOOR PLAN

SCALE IN FEET

FIGURE 3.11. *Deshpande was critical of the location of the toilet next to the kitchen in this design. Architect: Kamtekar and Bhivandikar.* R. S. Deshpande, Modern Ideal Homes for India, *139.*

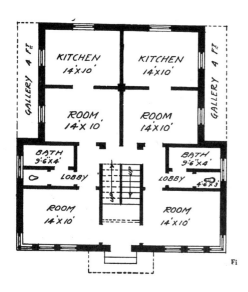

FIGURE 3.12. *There are two doors from the stairwell into the flat: one leads into the lobby and directly to the toilet and could be used by servants and cleaners, while the other leads into the drawing room and could be used by family and guests. Architect: N. S. Gupchup. R. S. Deshpande,* Modern Ideal Homes for India, *141.*

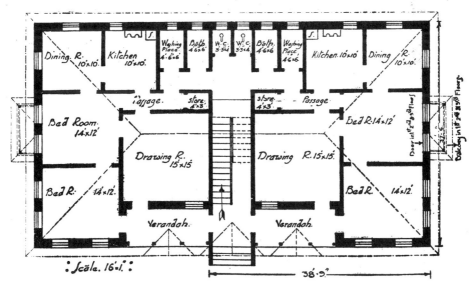

FIGURE 3.13. *A more complex design. R. S. Deshpande,* Modern Ideal Homes for India, *161.*

Yet the technological innovation of drainage and the flushing toilet is only one part of the revolution in the "idea of living." The revolution also had a social aspect to it. Prior to the advent of flushing technology in Indian cities, towns, and villages, all toilet functions would have been performed outside the living, eating, and sleeping spaces, for all classes of people.[83] For higher-caste Hindus, bodily waste would have been ritually impure and best disposed of at a distance from the dwelling by, as is well known, cleaners of night soil, who would also have been considered ritually impure.[84] Thus middle-class reformists such as R. S. Deshpande, in identifying the source of the problem of urban filth, drew upon two distinct discourses: "poverty and ignorance of the most fundamental principles of hygiene, coupled with conservative and religious prejudices" were the two main reasons for the paucity and misuse of toilets and latrines in Indian towns, according to Deshpande.[85] Both the ignorance of the principles of public health as well as the caste-based stigma against dealing with such bodily products—the "conservative and religious prejudices"—would need to be addressed in order to achieve urban order with latrines and toilets that were not only adequate in number but, importantly, properly used. This last point was crucial for Deshpande. He noted that the problem was not confined to a sheer paucity of toilets but also reflected the fact that people did not seem to use them properly. Even where toilets were available, "the people are so slovenly in their habits that most of them do not take the troubles of walking a few steps to take advantage of them."[86]

To combat the "conservative and religious prejudices" against bodily waste and the handling thereof, Deshpande recommended a program of teaching-by-example that closely resembled Mahatma Gandhi's famous efforts at Sabarmati Ashram to overcome the stigma of untouchability by compelling all residents to clean latrines. Gandhi, of course, had long been engaged with the question of latrines and their intimate links to ideas of caste and pollution in India. As early as 1896, following his first return from South Africa in the very year that the plague epidemic broke out in Bombay, Gandhi volunteered his services to the sanitation department in Rajkot and was assigned to a committee to inspect latrines in that town. The committee's attempts to inspect latrines in upper-caste homes always met with resistance, and the latrines, when successfully inspected, were always "dark and stinking and reeking with filth and worms." The untouchables' quarters, on the other hand, where there were no latrines—"we go and perform our functions in the open," one resident told Gandhi—were neat and clean.[87]

Writing of his own efforts to organize a "volunteer corps," Deshpande argued that youthful participants in such a corps would bring the necessary energy:

> If under proper guidance they are taught to clean up with their own hands the stink left by insanitary householders and if they have once absorbed the spirit of social service and do it whole-heartedly not only would those responsible for the filth be put to

shame and taught a lesson, but the gospel of the dignity of labour and social service would be brought home to them in a more telling manner against the age long habits and religious prejudices.[88]

Following Gandhi's example, thus, Deshpande sought to transform the perspective of upper-caste "insanitary householders" through his volunteer program. Where previously they viewed toilets and bodily functions as associated with ritually impure functions and ritually impure bodies (those of the night-soil gatherers), Deshpande sought instead to introduce a discourse of public health and sanitation. If "insanitary householders" viewed bodily functions and bodily wastes from the perspective of sanitation, then perhaps their attitudes toward toilets could be transformed.

The lower middle classes moving into flats in Dadar–Matunga in the 1920s and 1930s were not necessarily explicitly thinking in Gandhian (or Deshpandian) terms about sanitation. But the preceding discussion on sanitation and bodily waste has established the way in which the handling of bodily wastes presented a specific kind of problem in cities such as Bombay and the way in which figures like Gandhi and Deshpande, famous and obscure, were attempting to work among the Indian upper castes to change their views. It was not just the case that residents needed to be educated in the latest thinking on the connection between the correct treatment of bodily wastes and good sanitary practices. Rather, their whole view of bodily wastes needed to be transformed—bodily wastes and toilets would have to be viewed principally from a sanitary point of view rather than from the point of view of caste purity/pollution, what Deshpande called "age long habits and . . . prejudices."

The toilet migrating into the dwelling, thus, was not simply a matter of increased convenience as it was in the cities of Europe and North America; rather, it entailed a conceptual transformation in how the disposal of bodily wastes was perceived by upper-caste middle classes. Efficient plumbing replacing the night-soil gatherer meant that the disposal of bodily waste was increasingly starting to be viewed from the point of view of sanitation as well, rather than just from the point of view of caste. Once the disposal of bodily waste began to be viewed in terms of a discourse of sanitation and public health, then exercising greater control over such disposal—through an efficiently functioning toilet within the dwelling, for instance—became desirable. For the upper-caste, lower-middle-class residents of Dadar–Matunga living in self-contained apartments in the 1920s and 1930s, perceiving bodily waste from the point of view of sanitation was a critical step through which it went from being a middle class "in itself" to a middle class "for itself," to use a famous phrasing in a different context.

Yet it was not the case that the sanitation perspective entirely replaced the caste perspective of bodily wastes. Rather, the residents of Bombay flats recalibrated their caste-based view of bodily waste to accommodate the sanitary perspective.

The gradual movement of the toilet into the dwelling—underscored in the difference between Deshpande's designs in *Residential Buildings Suited to India* and his designs in *Modern Ideal Homes for India*—reflects this process of negotiation and recalibration. The privileged status of the toilet in the understanding of the Bombay flat thus reflects this dual position of the occupants of such flats: as upper castes for whom the toilet and bodily waste was polluting, on the one hand, and as a newly emergent self-conscious middle class for whom clean toilets indicated sound sanitary practice (and thus sound middle-classness).

Such a suspended position between different perceptions—bodily waste as polluting versus bodily waste as object of sanitary practice—became critical to middle-class identity. This suspended position was represented spatially in the location of the flat within the dwelling. Consider, for instance, a particular feature of the location of the toilet in the early flats of Dadar–Matunga. As is indicated in the Deshpande flat floor plans in Figures 3.5–3.13, the toilet was usually separated from the other rooms of the flat, either by a verandah (the plans in *Residential Buildings Suited to India*) or by a lobby (the plans in *Modern Ideal Homes for India*). Indeed, many flats had two entrances. One entrance led into the main living room; another led into a passage or lobby that led directly to the kitchen, toilet, sink, and bathroom. The living room, in turn, was connected by doors with both the passage and the bedroom.

For the early Brahmin migrants to the flats of Dadar–Matunga, this feature was appealing for a specific reason. M. A. Rajagopalan, who came to live in a flat in Dadar–Matunga as a young man in the late 1920s, told me that this design feature meant that any sweeper or servant could come into the house and proceed directly to clean the *nahani* or toilet without actually entering the living room or the bedroom.[89] (He insisted that these sorts of things did not matter to him any more.) Such an arrangement permitted the dual sensibility I have alluded to above: the polluting space of the toilet was still "separated" from the other living spaces by the lobby, and the polluting body of the toilet cleaner would not have to enter the other living spaces. On the other hand, having the toilet within the dwelling meant that the toilet could be kept spotless, through daily visits by the cleaning person, in accordance with the best sanitary (and middle-class) principles.

The significance of this design element—of flats having two doors, one leading into the living room and the other leading into the lobby—was underscored by Deshpande, who remarked of one design that had only one door leading into the living room that the feature was "a blemish to the design" since the living room "in consequence [became] a passage" through which domestics made their way to the kitchens, *nahanis,* bathrooms, and toilets.[90] Ashok Kulkarni, whose father's firm Marathe and Kulkarni designed many of the buildings in Dadar–Matunga, assured me that this particular passage or lobby, off of which the bathroom, *nahani,* and toilet were located, was a very conscious design element in his father's buildings:

You can't have anybody entering directly from outside into the living room. That's why that lobby would be a space where people would come in first. That's why if you compare it with flats in England—that sort of thing is because of the weather. To keep the entire thing warm. When you come from outside the weather is too cold. When you open the front door, the entire house will get the gust of wind.[91]

The door leading from the landing into the lobby—which played an important role both in facilitating the flexibility of use of the various rooms and in regulating the use of domestic space by permitting domestics and servants to proceed to the cleaning areas without needing to traverse the principal living areas—was not entirely an innovation of the Bombay flat builders of the 1930s. What Kulkarni suggests here is that a design element that had served a different function in European flat designs—minimizing the loss of heat once the front door was opened—was assimilated and redeployed to different effect in the Bombay flat. Thus was the flat or apartment—a building typology in long-standing worldwide circulation by the 1920s—appropriated into a specific South Asian context to produce the Bombay flat.

One final detail of toilet location is worth discussing. Ashok Kulkarni vividly explained to me, from the architects' point of view, the perils of toilet design and location in the apartment buildings of Bombay in the 1930s:

Our people had their sensibilities. And not only that, the architects who didn't know about these sensibilities . . . failed in their designs. Like never locate a WC in such a way that there is a common wall between the kitchen and the WC. *First of all having the WC in the house is a wrong idea.* Then having the WC near the kitchen is the worst idea. First you should design the bathroom near the kitchen and then the WC. Never have the WC next to the kitchen. There is a wall, but if it leaks—all sorts of problems.[92]

Kulkarni underscores here the revolutionary nature of the "self-contained flat" and the constraints imposed on architects, like his father, by the Hindu middle-class sensibilities of his clients in the 1930s. Kulkarni's injunction against locating the toilet next to the kitchen echoes Deshpande, who, while remarking upon a particular design by the Bombay firm of Kamtekar and Bhivandikar, noted that "the close proximity of the w.c.'s to the kitchen may not be liked by some people, but if there is a water-flushing system available there is no objection" (Figure 3.11).[93] Note that this injunction goes directly against the advice of the famous modernist English architect F. R. S. Yorke, who, writing at almost the same time as Deshpande, advocated locating the bathroom and toilet "back to back with the kitchen, in order that plumbing and other services may be grouped in a vertical duct, and have branches of minimum length."[94] Hence, whereas in English flats of the 1930s the emphasis was on minimizing costs by having the bathroom and the kitchen share plumbing facilities, in Bombay at the same time, even though economy would have been important, the toilet and the kitchen were to be kept separate if at all possible. Thus, again, the peculiar position of the toilet as express-ing a suspended sensibility in these flats was underscored: on the one hand, it sig-nified a polluting presence that needed to be kept away from food (and the images of gods, which were housed in the kitchen, as discussed in chapter 4); on the other hand, it was a site where bodily waste could be effectively disposed in a controlled fashion in accordance with sanitary principles.

To illustrate the way Bombay's upper-caste lower middle classes began to per-ceive bodily wastes and toilets from the point of view of sanitation, it is worth considering the "politics of toilets," so to speak, in this period of the late 1910s and early 1920s. Throughout the period of escalating land prices and rents in the post–World War I years, landlords' control of the water supply to buildings (and hence of the conditions of toilets) had been a thorny issue. Especially after the first rent-restriction legislation was passed in 1918, landlords used their control of the water supply to harass tenants. Consider the case of Dr. B. S. Shroff, the owner of a chawl on Mount Road in Mazagaon. In April 1918 he sought to raise the rents of the units in the chawl. When his tenants pointed out that he was not permitted to do so according to the rent-restriction legislation, he responded by stopping the water altogether to the three upper floors of the chawl.[95] This particular chawl was already equipped with a flushing water closet, so no water meant no flush-ing, with predictable results. Astoundingly, there appears to have been no water supply from April 15 to May 7, at the very least, and bodily waste accumulated in prodigious quantities, as there were at least twenty persons living on each floor of the building. When one tenant asked Shroff to resume supplying water, Shroff told him that if he was dissatisfied with the water supply, he should simply vacate the premises.[96] Upon being investigated, Shroff claimed that the water supply had stopped because the handle on the pump had broken, not because he had willfully strangled the supply in order to harass his tenants into accepting the rent increase. However, the investigating magistrate did not believe him, and he was fined twen-ty-five rupees.[97] Such instances of harassment were not isolated: shortly after Dr. Shroff was convicted, Narayandas Goculdas, another landlord of a chawl on Clare Road in Byculla, near Mazagaon, was accused, investigated, and convicted of sim-ilar harassment while seeking to increase rents.[98]

Even in the absence of such harassment, water supply to the chawls under "normal" circumstances posed problems. Water supply might have been scarce elsewhere in Bombay or in other cities, towns, and villages for that matter, but what was interesting about some complaints was that they identified the specific structure of the chawls as the problem. Complaining specifically about the reduced water supply to chawls in the Dadar area—water was only available between 4:30 and 7:00 AM and between 7:00 and 10:00 PM—one complainant by the name of N. R. Iyer pointed out that this restricted water supply was "keenly felt by thousands who reside in Chawls, containing on an average about 20 rooms, each room holding about 3–4 souls." The situation was so dire that

> [on] almost all days [the tenants] have been obliged to continuously stand at the tap room, insufficiently supplied by the landlords, in almost every case with no separate connections to the top floors, waiting for an opportunity to get at the tap and when one manages to do so, he goes on utilizing it till his requirements are over, which at times takes about 15 to 30 minutes. . . . *The present difficulty for water especially in chawls, where there are only one or two taps in each floor and water will not rise when the tap on the ground floor is opened, is such that every day can witness a miserable and despairing scene.*[99]

There are a number of suggestive aspects to this letter. The complainant identifies the water problem as especially acute in the chawls, where the taps are located in a common area. Furthermore, the multistory structure of the chawls poses a particular problem, since often the higher floors have no taps at all, or if they do, the pumps are not sufficient to ensure adequate water pressure.

Finally, note that the letter writer is N. R. Iyer, a Tamil Brahmin residing in a Dadar chawl. For Iyers and other high-caste but lower-middle-class residents of chawls, standing around at a common tap to collect water or dealing with accumulating bodily waste in toilets that they shared with others would have generated all kinds of contradictions: bodily waste as polluting in the caste sense, on the one hand, versus bodily waste as dirty and unhealthy, in the public health sense. In such a context, moving to a self-contained flat in Dadar or Matunga provided a way to negotiate such a contradiction by, at the very least, taking control over the disposal of bodily waste.

A rare perspective on the transformation of Dadar–Matunga from a bucolic space peopled with a few bungalows and mostly empty plots into an emerging landscape of buildings with self-contained flats—in other words, the transformation discussed in this chapter so far—is offered in an article from a newspaper announcing the successful efforts of the South Indian Cooperative Housing Society to secure a lease from the BIT for plots in Matunga. The article notes that middle-class housing is a "knotty problem" in Bombay and that rents are much higher than what the middle classes were willing to pay. At the same time, the existing accommodations for the middle classes in older parts of the city were not quite satisfactory either:

> The local South Indians who form a considerable number of the city's middle class population not having been accustomed to the chawl life with its concomitant scanty water and sanitary inconveniences in crowded parts of the city have more or less monopolized the newly developed northern part known as Dadar–Matunga Estate.[100]

The description of chawl life as filled with "sanitary inconveniences" is striking, for it implicitly associates Dadar–Matunga flat living with sanitary conveniences. The buildings in the Dadar–Matunga estate were attractive to the Brahmin lower-middle-class South Indians because they were apartment buildings and hence offered certain crucial conveniences, such as bathrooms and toilets within the flats, that were of great importance to the Brahmins who constituted the South Indian community. The self-contained nature of the flats meant that residents could have greater control over the supply of water, say, and certainly far greater control over who used toilet facilities and how they were kept. Such a move to take control over the disposal of bodily waste thus represented the negotiated position of the new middle classes of Dadar–Matunga, negotiated between a perception of bodily waste as polluting, on the one hand, and of bodily wastes as insanitary and needing proper disposal, on the other hand.

At the same time, the apartment buildings were not bungalows and villas and hence were much more affordable for the middle classes. Living in the apartment buildings of Dadar–Matunga, with their self-contained flats, thus constituted a compromise in two senses: first, the flat was an economic compromise between the cottage and the tenement, and second, the attached toilet represented a negotiation between the community as caste, for whom bodily waste was polluting, and the community as class, for whom bodily wastes should be treated according to proper sanitary principles best achieved under circumstances of maximum control. It is essential to understand how this innovation in the built environment offered a compromise between the lower middle class's economic concerns and their caste considerations as Brahmins or other upper castes. In other words, the self-contained flat in the apartment building was a compromise that mediated between the community as class and the community as caste in the urban setting.

The first section of this chapter showed how the land market in the early years of the 1920s pushed buildings upward. At the same time, as argued in the discussion of the BDD chawls in the second section, the need of a newly emergent lower middle class for affordable multiroom dwellings became pronounced in this period. The last section sought to show the gradual process by which, over the course of the 1920s and 1930s, the toilet moved into the multistory dwelling to create the Bombay flat. Yet as we saw at the beginning of this chapter, after about 1922 the building industry in Bombay entered a deep slump, and new areas like Dadar–Matunga did not, in fact, have many buildings. To understand how the situation changed over the course of the 1930s, I turn now to consider changes in the building industry in the 1930s that resulted in the proliferation of the Bombay flat. Chapter 4 will thus examine how flat living became a generalized feature of middle-class living by the end of the 1930s, looking both at the changes in building practices that led to a building boom in that decade, and at dwelling practices in Dadar–Matunga through which flat living was further domesticated.

4 The Spread of Apartment Living

꿈꿈꿈꿈 "HUNDREDS OF MODERN BUILDINGS ARE UNDER CONSTRUCTION IN BOMBAY."

So screamed the caption underneath an image of a modern apartment building on the March 15, 1939, cover of the *Indian Concrete Journal*. Following the boom in land prices between 1916 and 1922, a dramatic slump in the land market ensued, severely restricting building activity in the city. By the 1930s, however, building activity had picked up dramatically, creating a building boom that lasted through the decade and until the wartime government began to restrict building materials from 1940 onward. It was during this building boom that Dadar–Matunga decisively assumed its character as an apartment-building suburb, with large numbers of ground-plus-two-story structures coming up in this period. The first part of this chapter considers the reasons for this turnaround in the building trade and explains why the resulting buildings took the form of apartment buildings and not tenements. It identifies three reasons for the building boom that resulted in the apartment-building suburb: the revolution in building occasioned by RCC technology; the emergence of the first generation of Indian architects ready to build flats suited to Indian tastes; and finally, the regulatory activities of the Trust, which strangled the tenement and supported the apartment building in Dadar–Matunga.

The physical cityscape of apartment buildings was, however, only one part of the process that resulted in the Bombay apartment building. The middle-class residents of Dadar–Matunga embraced apartment living, but in doing so they also transformed the meaning of the spaces of the apartment building. The second part of this chapter moves to considering the ways in which the Bombay flat was property assimilated into the lower-middle-class upper-caste framework through a range of practices.

BUILDING MATUNGA

Reinforced Cement Concrete

A major technological transformation underpinned the feasibility of mass-built apartment buildings at low prices: the increasingly widespread availability of ever-cheaper cement and reinforced cement concrete. The growing availability of RCC meant that by the late 1920s, it was becoming possible in cities like Bombay to construct solidly built apartment buildings that married the fixity and permanence of the bungalow with the greater affordability of the multistory dwelling. It is not possible here to provide a comprehensive history of the introduction of concrete and the resulting transformation of the built environment in Indian cities, but a preliminary investigation suggests clearly that RCC was construed as the harbinger of a new urban environment. A few schematic observations suggest the increasingly prominent role that RCC and cement manufacturers came to play in the building industry in Bombay: by the late 1920s, there was an efflorescence of enterprises in Bombay supplying RCC. Due to an overcapacity in the market during the Depression years, the companies consolidated in 1936 to form a behemoth known as the Associated Cement Companies (ACC). Through a judicious adjustment of the supply of cement and concrete, ACC was able to establish a dominant position in the booming construction industry in 1930s Bombay.[1]

In many ways, the BDD housing project discussed in the previous chapter signaled the arrival of RCC construction in the city. Although RCC had been used previously, there had been some skepticism about its ability to withstand the corrosive effects of Bombay's monsoons and sea air, especially since a few RCC buildings had collapsed in the 1910s. Hence, before deciding to adopt RCC construction for their housing projects, the Bombay government had appointed a committee to study existing RCC buildings in the city; the study concluded that the buildings had collapsed because of defects in the application of RCC technology, not in the technology itself. The innovative use of RCC by the BDD's engineers, as Lawless Hepper elaborated, could revolutionize housing construction. Whereas previously concrete had to be poured or cast in situ, necessitating the use of costly shuttering (that is, wooden forms),

> the design evolved by Mr. Harvey . . . provides for a skeleton framework consisting of the columns, beams, floors and roof, which alone are poured in situ. The inner partitions and outer walls are formed of suitable concrete slabs made at a central factory, whilst all other details are similarly manufactured in standard sizes and brought, ready made, to the site of the work. As a result the skeleton framework, once completed, can be rapidly clothed to form the finished building.[2]

The method of construction outlined here was truly revolutionary. The building had now been disaggregated into discrete components—beams, columns, floors, walls—each of which could be separately manufactured according to standard specifications at a central factory and simply assembled according to particular configurations at a building site. The exterior and interior walls, formerly bulky, load-bearing components intrinsic to the structural integrity of the building, were now simply "clothing." The BDD chawls, especially in their distinctive use of RCC technology, thus initiated new modular building tech-

↝ FIGURE 4.1. *BDD's DeLisle Road* (A) *and Naigaum* (B) *chawls under construction. Note the scale of construction as well as the modular type of building referred to by Hepper in his inaugural speech. Courtesy of Gammon India.*

niques that would become crucial to the construction of apartment buildings within a decade.

By 1923 the PCACHS was already reporting that the increasing availability, at decreasing costs, of materials like iron and cement meant that the PCACHS was "introducing iron and cement, in place of timber, in [its] subsequent building works wherever practicable."[3] By 1936, construction costs had dropped almost to half their 1920 prices; structures that had cost fifty thousand rupees in 1922 could now be put up for twenty thousand to twenty-five thousand rupees, principally owing to the introduction of new building materials such as RCC.[4] Of course, such a dramatic reduction in building costs had unintended consequences for entities such as the PCACHS: the later buildings were built more cheaply and hence necessitated a lower economic rent, which in turn meant that the demand for older, more expensively built buildings was very low.[5]

Media representations of cement clearly associated it with the emerging built environment I have been trying to describe. Two representations from the 1930s suggest some links between RCC and the kind of urban modernism that Matunga embodied. Consider an advertisement for Katni Cement that appeared in the *Bombay Chronicle* (Figure 4.2). The advertisement links cement and modernization in the most direct and literal way and, while obviously proclaiming the alleged superiority of Katni Cement, makes a further and more general claim: the superiority of cement over other kinds of building materials.

Often the representations were a little more subtle. Consider an extraordinary image of the street that appeared in the *Indian Concrete Journal* (Figure 4.3). The illustration depicts a drawing of a street leading off into the distance. This street is an idealized representation of the planner's dream of functional separation of spaces: the center lanes of the street are labeled as being reserved for "fast moving traffic," here represented by drawings of automobiles. The outer lanes, closer to the pavements, are labeled as being reserved for "slow moving traffic," represented by bullock carts. The outermost strip of the road is reserved for parking. Outside this lane, separating the road from the sidewalk proper, is a lane reserved for cyclists, while pedestrians are to enjoy the right of way on the sidewalk. The caption reads, in bold art deco lettering, "NOT TODAY! NOT TOMORROW! BUT SOMEDAY!"

For promoters of cement and concrete, such as the publishers of the *Indian Concrete Journal,* the advantages of such paved and "concretized" streets were obvious. Yet here, the publication advertises its claim to the new and the modern by connecting the use of concrete with a new kind of use of space: it was no longer permissible to have functionally confused streets of the sort that actually characterized Indian cities. Instead, the street needed to be carefully demarcated into specific zones designed for specific purposes, here represented by traffic either stationary or moving at different speeds. While the caption acknowledges that such

FIGURE 4.2. *Advertisement for Katni Cement, marker of modernity.* Bombay Chronicle, December 23, 1929.

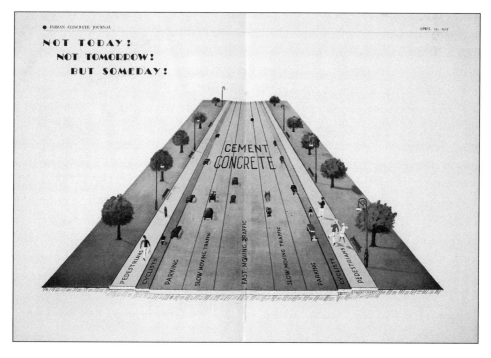

4.3. *Street fantasy in* Indian Concrete Journal *9, no. 4 (April 15, 1935).*

a functional disaggregation of space was as yet only an aspiration, in fact it was already in the process of being realized in the new suburbs of Dadar and Matunga. Space there was already demarcated as "residential," and the streets were designed with regard to the function they played in the ecology of the neighborhood.

At the All India Khadi and Swadeshi Exhibition, which the Tamil Nadu Congress Committee hosted in Madras in December 1939–January 1940, Indian concrete had its own impromptu coming-out party. Essentially, concrete received unexpected prominence at this exhibition because a devastating fire broke out, leading to the widespread destruction of less durable Swadeshi products and structures. A note appearing in the *Indian Concrete Journal* could barely cloak its glee under a layer of solemnity befitting the destruction that had been caused: it sought to provide a "description of the fire, the damage done, the structures which withstood its ravaging effects, and the fire-resistant qualities of cement and concrete products."[6] The fire started in one shed and then, owing to the "extremely imprudent use of coconut matting" to construct the roofs and the partitions between sheds, spread very quickly to envelop the entire exhibition ground. Even the Congress House was gutted. As the account in the *Indian Concrete Journal* went on to point out, all the major newspapers covering the event noted that the only structures to have survived the fire were the ACC shed with its bold sign ("curiously enough the letters ACC were more prominent after the fire than before") and the All-India Radio shed, which, although built of bricks and masonry, was coated with a layer of RCC.[7]

Yet such publicity in fact merely underscored the great revolution that had been playing out over the previous decade of the 1930s. Increasingly, even lower-middle-class and working-class structures were being constructed out of cement and concrete. Indeed, as the account of the BDD chawls earlier in the chapter indicated, RCC construction's revolutionary potential was initially deployed in a mass scale in the construction of working-class chawls. The apartment buildings built for the second Saraswat Cooperative Housing Society complex in Tardeo used a lot more RCC than had the first buildings, built in Gamdevi in 1916. Such buildings, designed for the cultural needs of specific communities, sometimes posed specific challenges. The Saraswats, for instance, wanted a residential building that also contained, on the ground floor, a meeting hall that extended the entire width and depth of the building.[8] The meeting hall also had to have a balcony running all along it at the first floor level. The second, third, and fourth floors were to be reserved for residential apartments, which were to be one- or two-bedroom units with interior bathrooms and kitchens. The challenge was that all the load of the three residential floors had to be born on the beams that spanned the meeting hall. This was further complicated by the fact that the rooms on the residential floor were obviously of much smaller size than the large meeting hall. This posed

~ FIGURE 4.4. *Gammon's Appabaug Building, circa 1926. The use of RCC columns, slabs, and beams made possible large rooms with relatively few supports. Courtesy of Gammon India.*

problems in the alignment of the columns on the ground floor. S. K. Nadkarni, a structural engineer who had designed the building, took great pride in revealing his solution to these engineering problems: the key element of his solution was the use of an RCC slab above the meeting hall, which helped sustain the weight of the three residential floors above. In such ways, specific cultural practices, such as the Saraswats' need for a community hall in their residential structure, were accommodated in the modern RCC apartment building.

It should be emphasized that the process by which RCC was incorporated into building practices was also a gradual one. Although, as the *Indian Concrete Journal* liked to proclaim, RCC was being used widely by the 1930s, and although, as we have seen, the BDD chawls were an early experiment with RCC-based modular construction in the early 1920s, many structures in Dadar–Matunga were actually hybrid structures, with only partial use of RCC elements. The firm of Marathe and Kulkarni, whose buildings were often featured in the *Indian Concrete Journal* and in the *Journal of the Indian Institute of Architects,* initially only used RCC slabs for floors and ceilings. RCC beams and columns were viewed with suspicion, and the walls in the firm's early buildings were traditional load-bearing walls made of brick masonry and lime mortar.[9] Indeed, in response to public pressure, the BMC decided to include, in its 1939 revision of the municipal bylaws, a provision whereby RCC specialists would have to undergo a certification process and get licenses.[10]

Even then the suspicion of RCC did not cease: on June 28, 1942, to the chagrin of RCC boosters everywhere, a large five-story RCC structure collapsed in the Churchgate Reclamation while still under construction, claiming several lives and provoking yet another inquiry into RCC technology.[11] While the prime focus of the investigation was the specific causes of the collapse, the city infrastructure's (in)ability to deal with emergencies of such a scale was another important concern. N. V. Modak, the BMC's chief engineer, who worked through the night after the crash trying to rescue trapped victims, reported on the scene in vivid terms to the Government of Bombay's committee of inquiry into the event: "[I have] seen many house collapses in the city before, but they were of the old buildings; but the building which collapsed was a new one built of steel and cement concrete and still it collapsed like a house of cards."[12] Thus, part of the issue was that RCC technology permitted structures of an unprecedented size and scale and hence posed potential risks. Should such structures collapse, then unparalleled damages would result, so new measures were necessary to prevent future collapses. Partly as a result of the inquiry into the Churchgate Reclamation House collapse, new measures were taken to regulate RCC construction, and gradually the building trade generally embraced the new technology.

Architects and the Profession

The new RCC technology was put to use in Dadar–Matunga by the first generation of Indian architects. Trained at the Sir J. J. School of Architecture in Bombay,
the first Indian institution associated with the Royal Institute of British Architects, a whole generation of architects appeared on the Bombay building scene by
the early 1930s, prepared to build and, if necessary, modify the form of the flat for
Indian tastes.

The role of architects in the building of residential buildings had not been significant. Even though the Trust had mandated that all structures built on lands
leased by the Trust be designed by an architect to ensure adherence to good design
principles, the actual role of architects had been minimal. A perspective on this
is offered by the Trust's decision to hire an official architect to design subsequent
projects.[13] The debate was sparked by an article in the *Times of India* urging the
Trust to hire an official architect who would supervise the overall aesthetic vision
of the Trust's projects. The article alluded to the success of the Hampstead Garden
City in Britain, which had recently been concluded, where the developing company had hired an architect to supervise and approve each design for each house to
ensure that it fit into an overall vision.[14]

In his note responding to the article, the Trust's former engineer, H. Kemball,
indicated the role that architects actually played in the design process. He noted
that average civil engineers were "quite incompetent" and that for all substantial
public buildings, the designs were referred to the government's consulting architect, George Wittet.[15] While it would be useful for the Trust to hire an architect to
provide free consulting services to all prospective builders seeking to erect buildings on Trust lands, it would be foolhardy to have the degree of supervision that
the Hampstead Garden City had imposed and that the *Times of India* article recommended. In Bombay, wrote Kemball, "conditions are absolutely different, the
same class of lessees and contractors being absent."[16] The practice of offering free
architectural consultation for the Trust's estates, however, would be good: even
though the Trust required that all builders get their plans approved by an architect, the architect's role was usually quite superficial at the time:

> Now the average Lessee of the Trust has very great confidence in his own ability in
> house planning and very little confidence in Architects good or bad. He only employs
> them because he must and when possible he confines them to drawing up plans under
> his direction and obtaining sanction for them from the Municipality and the Improve-
> ment Trust. As regards the construction of the building he, if possible, has an arrange-
> ment with them by which they give advice when asked and pose as his Architects when
> trouble arises owing to bad work. He pays them as little as he can and is quite ready to
> employ an incompetent architect if he thinks him capable to getting the plans passed,

and consequently capable Architects have to cut their fees in order to make a living and reduce their supervision.[17]

Kemball's note provides an insight into the superficial role of architects in building projects in the older parts of the city. Despite the fact that the Trust sought to make the use of an architect mandatory, developers had found ways to circumvent this attempt to regulate the design of residential structures. The architects only had real influence in the design of large public buildings. By the 1930s, however, things had changed, and architects began to play a more substantial role in the design of residential structures, not least because the Trust's practice of requiring architect-certified drawings for buildings was embraced by the BMC for its own lands as well.

A fascinating, ambivalent awareness of this transition among Indian architects is suggested in Janardan Shastri's remarkable essay "Traditional Domestic Architecture of Bombay," which appeared in 1939. With the development of the city and the rapid increase in population, he noted, it was necessary to disrupt the fabric of the old city and build new structures that could better accommodate the growing population, with its different needs. The resulting building could either be "airy and attractive flats," or else testimonies to the "absurdities of modern phantasy."[18] An architect trained in the Western tradition, Shastri felt compelled to make the obligatory genuflection to the dominant deco moderne building motifs of the 1930s, using the classic adjectives "airy" and "attractive" to describe the happier outcomes of this style of building. Yet Shastri also appeared to sense that something harmonious was being irrevocably destroyed by planned, regulated building of the sort undertaken by certified professional architects. The changes to the city's buildings "may be logical and for the better, yet it certainly closes the pages of Bombay's history that were formerly open and accessible to every way-farer."[19]

Shastri's essay began by breezily surveying the history of Bombay from ancient times to the present day, moving on to a general account of the people of Bombay and their relation to their dwellings, before settling upon detailed descriptions of certain houses. The descriptions came complete with line drawings, floor plans including elevations, and occasional drawings of detail elements. He selected houses he considered "typical" of some of the older neighborhoods of the city, such as the Fort, Kalbadevi, Girgaum, Parel, and Mahim.

The mediating link between the people and their dwellings was, for Shastri, religion or dharma. Hindu life was so saturated with the notion of dharma, a concept that cannot be abstracted into a category like "religion," that it also suffused the Hindu dwelling. Thus in traditional dwellings of the Hindus, the dictates of the dharma and the examples of their ancestors were faithfully reproduced in the design of the house. This was why, according to Shastri, the fundamental design of a Hindu house would not vary that much, whether it was in Ahmedabad, in

Nasik, or in Bombay. Only small changes, a function of local weather and space factors, could be detected.[20] Even though older towns and neighborhoods were also dirty and overcrowded, just as in modern cities, yet there was something in those older precincts such that "a high degree of beauty almost always marked the effect produced."[21] Shastri reflected on the effect of suddenly, while walking through a modern city, stumbling upon an older street or part of a street. He asks the reader to remember the pleasing effect such an experience produced. This effect was not necessarily due to the extraordinary design or exceptional execution of the buildings; rather, it existed because "there seems to have been in all a pervading instinct, or tradition, guiding the builders in past times, so that most of what they did contained elements of beauty and produced picturesque streets."[22]

With the coming of the Portuguese and then the British things changed, according to Shastri. The city eventually began to industrialize, necessitating the changes that prompted Shastri to compile this memorial to the city's traditional architecture. The full extent of Shastri's feelings regarding these developments is revealed in the following sentences:

> All the honor of Bombay's present glories goes to her English Masters and Portuguese Preceptors. Bombay, it seems, has been inclined to Occidental education from the very beginning. She did not go to seek it. It came floating on the waters of the Indian Ocean and she had to welcome it. It was God's wish to see a harmonious creation out of the combination between a Sea Prince and a Land Maiden. Yet, it was not to be. The maiden of the Land, as is the case with all Indian Maidens, forgot her own entity and identified with her Lord's. She bore Occidental children but they were neither Oriental nor Universal.[23]

Shastri's vertiginous use of metaphor appears here to teeter on the brink of incoherence. Yet it is clear that while he was nostalgic for a past when the buildings were authentically Indian, and while there was unmistakable resentment at colonization of India by the British, he was unable to easily characterize Bombay's contemporary architecture. The bastard child, if left in the hands of the untrained engineer, will bear neither the authenticity of the indigenous tradition nor the universalism of architectural modernism. But God's "harmonious creation" might still result, if only the architect could take the matter into his own hands.

Having described the old houses of Bombay, Shastri concludes with an attack on those unplanned suburbs appearing, like parasites, on the edges of Indian cities: instead of the old harmonies, we find

> a singular absence of planning, or conscious design in the laying out and an almost equal freedom to the individual builder to do as he likes is granted; but with what a different result? There is little thought bestowed on the individual buildings or on its adaptation to the site and surroundings, no imaginative fitting of it into a picture. . . . The one point apparently of import is whether the building can be done so cheaply as to yield a good

return on the outlay. Naturally therefore our towns and suburbs express by their ugliness the passion for individual gain which so largely dominates their creation.[24]

Here the villain was the profit-seeking builder/contractor/developer. In the absence of an overarching Hindu cosmology, redemption from the godless, profit-seeking purgatory that is the modern city is only offered in the synthetic vision of the architect.

The particular way in which the architecture in Bombay widened its ambit can be illustrated by considering a peculiar archival artifact: a series of unattributed occasional pieces in the *Journal of the Indian Institute of Architects* titled the Lesser Architecture of Bombay. Each feature consisted of a page or two on a particular building, with photographs, giving floor plans, the name of the client, costs and materials involved, and the names of the architects. Most of the buildings featured in these pages were modern residential apartment buildings built in the new middle-class precincts of Dadar–Matunga and Shivaji Park. They were built almost exclusively by Indian firms such as Patki, Jadhav, and Dadarkar; Master, Sathe, and Bhuta; Poonegar and Mhatre; and Marathe and Kulkarni.

THE LESSER ARCHITECTURE OF BOMBAY.

The building illustrated above has been erected for Mr. M. S. Balaram on Plot No. 579, Dadar-Matunga Estate, Bombay.

It consists of two room blocks, two on each floor, and built at a cost of Rs. 20,000 approximately.

This also a R. C. C. semi-frame type and with a pleasing outer effect.

The building was designed and supervised by Messrs. Marathe & Co., Architects & Civil Engineers, Bombay.

Owner.—M. S. Balaram, Esqr.
Architects.—Marathe & Co.
Plot No.—579, Dadar-Matunga Estate.
Cost.—Rs. 20,000 app. each Building.
2 room Blocks two on each floor.

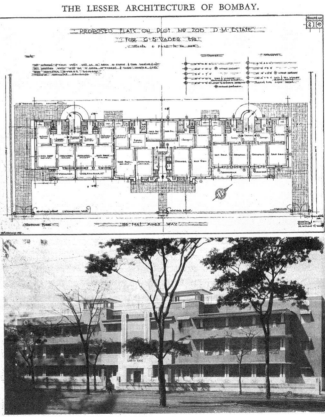

THE LESSER ARCHITECTURE OF BOMBAY.

FIGURE 4.5. *The Lesser Architecture of Bombay. Note the ground-plus-two-story construction of these buildings in Dadar–Matunga and the prominent compound walls. All three buildings were designed by Marathe and Company, which became Marathe and Kulkarni after Marathe was joined by the father of Ashok Kulkarni in 1939.* Journal of the Indian Institute of Architects, *April 1938, 367; April 1938, 366; January 1939, 73.*

This feature appears throughout the 1930s, but by the mid-1940s it peters out. I suggest that this is because the discipline of architecture has succeeded in consolidating itself by this point, to the extent that the pages of the journal are now filled with pieces on the "housing crisis," as though it were obvious that building new housing for the exploding population of Bombay in the postwar years would naturally be the provenance of architecture.

What is the significance of these curious pages? To the slight extent that they have been noticed before, they have generally been dismissed as evidence of the predominantly Anglo architectural establishment's reluctance to acknowledge the modernist endeavors of Indian architects.[25] Yet when we consider the hitherto limited role the architectural discipline had played in the building scene, such a dismissal misreads the significance of these pages. They represented an acknowledgment of the widening understanding of what constituted architecture in the Indian context. They also constituted a recognition, albeit reluctant and condescending, of the role played by Indian architects in the new field.

Further, the Lesser Architecture series points toward another feature of the buildings in these neighborhoods. The fact that most of the owners appear to have been Indian and the buildings' relatively low cost (usually between twelve thousand and twenty thousand rupees) suggest that the buildings provided a valuable instrument of investment in this period. Indeed, the availability of land leased out from the BIT on relatively less opaque terms ("transparent" would be too strong a word), constitutes an epochal moment in the history of the real estate market in Bombay.

Most importantly, this series adumbrates a compromise between "traditional" and "modern" dwellings. The buildings were apartment buildings, laid out in a suburban setting. In this they were very different from the house forms and layout of the village, but also from the chawl and *wadi* structure of the older parts of the city. But because this moment in the 1930s happened to be a time when the first generation of Indian architects was out and about looking for work, and because Dadar–Matunga offered a greenfields site (that is, with no prior development) for them to practice their craft, the layout of the flats differed in many small ways from the traditional European flat. Such changes in layout of the flat facilitated the move of Dadar–Matunga's lower-middle-class residents into the new dwellings.[26]

The lowering of building costs that RCC made possible meant, as discussed above, that by the mid-1930s apartment buildings could be constructed for as little as twenty thousand rupees. The Lesser Architecture of Bombay series indicates that most of the buildings in Dadar–Matunga were built for between fifteen thousand and twenty-five thousand rupees—less than half what such a building would have cost a decade earlier. In his 1939 *Modern Ideal Homes for India*, R. S. Deshpande noted that flats were becoming increasingly common in Bombay, especially among the middle classes. Deshpande explicitly links the rising popularity of flats with the lowered building costs, arguing that investing in such buildings now became an attractive option for middle- and upper-middle-class residents of older parts of the city such as Girgaum and Kalbadevi. By investing in such a building, and thus becoming landlords themselves, not only could they "be independent of the unreasonable demands of [other] landlords," but they could also be guaranteed a steady income:

> Many of the people who laid by some spare money, in service or in business, found a very safe and convenient investment in a building, part of which they could themselves occupy, and rent out the rest to people of their own status and thus, while living happily, could also earn rents, which in the boom period after the first Great War were high.[27]

Deshpande's observations explain the pattern of financing of the Dadar–Matunga building landscape. The vast majority of such builders were middle- and upper-middle-class residents of older parts of the city, who would often themselves take a unit on the top floor—or indeed, even the whole top floor—while renting out the other units to "people of their own status."[28] The buildings were often named after the investors' mothers or wives (thus the phenomenon of buildings changing names when changing owners). The primary sites where the building boom could take place were, of course, greenfields sites. These included the reclamations in south Bombay: Marine Drive and Colaba, where buildings for the upper classes were coming up by the late 1930s. As the cover of the March 15, 1939, issue of the *Indian Concrete Journal* announced, in screaming bold type, "Hundreds of modern buildings are under construction in Bombay." The photograph accompanying the caption depicts one of the new apartment buildings on Marine Drive, complete with art deco affectations. But the largest greenfields site, where construction along the new pattern began earliest, was the newly available land at Dadar–Matunga.

My account so far has sought to explain the particularities of the land market in the early 1920s that drove building upward in Dadar–Matunga, while also showing the emergent lower middle class's need for multiroom dwellings. Meanwhile, a series of developments over the course of the 1920s meant that, by the early 1930s, the toilet had moved inside the dwelling, firmly establishing what came to be called the Bombay flat. Over the course of the 1930s, lowered building costs and the emergence of Indian architects willing to design to Indian specifications meant that the building slump of the late 1920s was reversed into a building boom in the 1930s, sending up buildings all over newly available lands in the city, especially Dadar–Matunga. Initially, these buildings were tenement buildings, but soon the apartment building came to dominate the Dadar–Matunga landscape and, indeed, eventually became the middle-class residence of choice in Bombay. The next sec-

FIGURE 4.6. *A photograph of Deepak Mahal appeared on the cover of* Indian Concrete Journal *13, no. 3 (March 15, 1939). The caption for the photograph on the cover indicated that the building boom was under way.*

tion turns to considering a final aspect of the building trade: explaining how the regulatory actions of the Trust restricted the building of tenements and allowed the apartment building to emerge triumphant in Dadar–Matunga.

Regulations

The generalized use of cement and concrete created the conditions of possibility for vertical (and hence more affordable) building, but there were also other developments that shaped the form of the new structures to yield the Bombay apartment building. I turn now to consider the regulatory process through which tenement construction was banned. Chapter 1 has already argued the importance of Bombay's early history in subsequent attempts to control lands and building: the fact that, until 1865, the city was more interested in attracting residents than in controlling building activity. It sought to attract people by offering lands on extremely favorable terms, without specifying the conditions under which the state might resume the lands and without imposing any restrictions whatsoever on the building process. Indeed, until 1865, when the first protomunicipal legislation was enacted, enforcing some rudimentary building regulations, property holders could more or less do as they pleased. This had not posed serious problems of overcrowding previously since, as discussed above, the difficulty until the 1860s had always been to attract migrants to Bombay. Still, because of this earlier leniency, which came to be regarded as "custom," it subsequently became very difficult to regulate building practices.

The first major step in regulating development was the promulgation of the Bombay City Municipal Act of 1888, which permitted the enforcement of certain basic rules governing buildings. Most importantly, it sought to regulate the height and ventilation of rooms, tried to ensure that public streets were of a certain width, and enabled, in principle, the laying of setback lines.[29] On the strength of 1888 legislation, the first municipal bylaws were enacted in 1892. These sought to restrict the height of new buildings to 1.5 times the width of the street on which the building stood. The width of the street thus became an index and a regulator of the population density of the block. Crucially, however, there was no provision within these 1892 bylaws to regulate the height of *older* buildings. The landlord lobby had been able to limit the scope of the municipal regulation, and owners were free to keep making additions to their older structures.

The new urban spaces of Dadar–Matunga–Sion constituted a large expanse of open and "new" lands where landlords did not already have a stranglehold on the municipal regulatory process. Here the Trust's long-drawn-out and expensive strategy of physically acquiring the lands (discussed in chapter 1) began to yield some benefits in that the Trust was able to strictly regulate the height of buildings to three floors (ground plus two). Such regulation of the height, while conveying the aesthetic benefit of a uniform streetscape, also played the crucial role of controlling the density of population in a particular unit area. The perception that the older parts of the city were overcrowded, leading to disease, was after all what had gotten the whole enterprise of suburban development going in the first place.

It is possible to trace the actual process of the development of regulation and building in Dadar–Matunga thanks to a rare perspective offered by one of the key Improvement Trust officers involved with the regulatory process. H. B. Shivdasani had been the chief officer of the Improvement Trust during the 1920s and, following the incorporation of the Trust into the Municipal Corporation in 1933, he became the deputy commissioner of improvements of the Bombay Municipal Corporation.[30] When Shivdasani joined the Trust as chief officer, only one of the four large buildings ringing Khodadad Circle, in the southern part of the Dadar–Matunga Estate, had been built. This circle, along with King's Circle (referred to in chapter 1), was one of the key focal points of the entire development. Shivdasani's description of it marries the poetic and the technical—Khodadad Circle, he argued, "is perhaps the finest circle in Bombay with four large buildings of the same elevation on its four quadrants."[31] Shivdasani and his colleagues were able to impose a condition that the elevation of the remaining three buildings had to be exactly the same as that of the first building. King's Circle, which was developed a little after Khodadad Circle, had a condition written into its lease: all buildings around this circle would have to have their elevation and design approved by the chief engineer.[32]

Similarly, the Trust's officers and engineers were able to introduce clauses in the leases to these plots of land that controlled the elevation, setback, and, ultimately, even the kind of building that emerged. Shivdasani makes an especially revealing plea to the architects who constituted his audience. He noted that "owing to keen competition," some of the architects were undertaking any projects that came their way. Many speculators who had earlier leased plots along the important streets of Dadar–Matunga wanted to build tenement houses there, since previous experience in the old city had demonstrated that this building form was a surefire, low-maintenance (literally) investment. Even the most important boulevards—such as the Kingsway, over which the Trust's earlier stalwarts, including J. P. Orr, had fought fierce battles to ensure it was constructed as a grand boulevard—were to be marred by the construction of one-room tenement buildings.

Shivdasani noted that previously, leases had not contained any specifications as to the type of dwelling (flat or tenement) that would be constructed. This made it difficult to control the type of building that would arise on the plots of the new suburb. But clearly, according to Shivdasani, the tenement buildings that were sprouting up would have utterly compromised the whole enterprise of turning

Dadar–Matunga into a middle-class suburb; it would merely have been a distant extension of the slums of Pydhonie and Nagpada, packed with teeming tenement houses. Shivdasani and his colleagues were, however, able to exercise control over this process: following the erection of a couple of such tenement buildings, "it was therefore found necessary when leasing other plots, to impose a condition that one-room tenements will not be allowed, unless the City Engineer considers it desirable to permit them."[33] Shivdasani also urged his audience of architects to cooperate with the Trust's officers in enforcing this vision. He asked them not to simply accept any commission that came their way, especially if it involved compromising the overall vision.

The Trust was able to impose conditions on what kind of buildings could be built because it owned the lands in Dadar–Matunga and was only leasing them out to investors, even if the leases were for 999 years and hence, for all practical purposes, indefinite. One way the Trust did this was by only actually issuing leases after the potential lessees had built their buildings. In this way, the Trust was able to ensure two things: first, that buildings actually got built, and second, that lessees were not going to engage in "land hoarding" with a view to holding on to the land and selling as prices rose. This widespread practice subverted the Trust's mandate of providing housing for the middle classes in the new suburbs of Dadar–Matunga and thus relieving pressure on the housing stock in the south of the island. To deter such land hoarding, the Trust had a condition whereby potential lessees had to initially put down a security deposit of two years' ground rent as expression of interest in securing a lease. They then had to erect structures within eighteen to twenty-four months from the expression of interest. Only once they had erected structures, and after the Trust had ascertained that the buildings conformed to the Trust's regulations, did they actually receive the lease. In this way the Trust was able to achieve a second objective of regulating what kinds of structures got built and enforce a ban on single-room tenements.[34]

Shivdasani's account of the gradual development of the regulation of buildings in Dadar–Matunga is exceptionally revealing. It suggests the process through which apartment buildings came to dominate the landscape in Matunga, while also enabling us to understand why there are a few tenement buildings (such as the Paanch Buildings) in the apartment building–dominated environment. The Trust, as has been discussed, envisioned bungalows and villas as the primary residential unit, vaguely drawing upon British and German notions of garden cities. For various reasons, Bombay's middle classes did not wish to populate such bungalow-garden suburbs. Instead, as Shivdasani observed, real estate speculators were beginning to buy up plots and were beginning to construct tenement buildings. So when the Trust stepped in to regulate the construction of tenements in the late 1920s, the apartment building emerged as a compromise between the original vision of bungalows and the unfolding reality of tenement structures (and as a result of the economics of the housing market: there was no great demand for bungalows, but apartment buildings did well). By the mid-1950s, when the sociologist K. L. Mythili conducted an ethnography of the South Indian community in Matunga, 84 percent of her sample of three hundred families lived in flats, while only 16 percent lived in tenements.[35] Mythili's fieldwork among the South Indian community in Matunga, conducted in the mid-1950s, now constitutes an important archive of mid-twentieth-century life in the new suburbs and their apartment buildings.

The appearance and proliferation of the physical cityscape of apartment buildings was only one part of the process through which the Bombay flat became indigenized. Just as the physical spread of the Bombay apartment was shaped by the political economy of lands and buildings, so too were the ways of living in apartments conditioned by the cultural preoccupations of Dadar–Matunga's upper-caste residents. I turn now to consider some practices through which suburban residents appropriated and transformed the physical spaces of the apartment building.

APARTMENT LIVING

As has been described previously in this chapter, the buildings in the Dadar–Matunga area were generally three-story buildings consisting of two blocks. Each floor of each block had two flats.[36] Hence a typical building might consist of twelve flats, with each flat consisting of one or two "bedrooms," a "living room," a kitchen, a toilet, a bathroom, and, adjacent to the latter, a *nahani,* which was used for washing clothes and dishes.

During the 1930s, there were great efforts to promote apartment living. Perhaps the best known and most extensive effort was the festival known as the Ideal Home Exhibition, held in Bombay at the Town Hall, from November 3 to November 15, 1937. According to reports in the *Journal of the Indian Institute of Architects,* it attracted one hundred thousand visitors during this period.[37] The exhibition was organized by the Indian Institute of Architects with the support of a wide range of manufacturers, whose wares adorned the exhibits and who presumably hoped to encourage further consumption by impressed visitors.

In his speech at the opening of the exhibition, the director of the IIA, P. P. Kapadia, noted the strong connections between the growth of the building industry and the growth of the country's economy as a whole. In asking the first prime minister of Bombay Presidency to declare the exhibition open, the director firmly linked the impending development of the nation, represented by the newly established Home Ministry, to the proper development of the bourgeois household: "This Exhibition, like this Ministry, is a very great asset for nation building. You, Sir, and your Ministers will perhaps be responsible for giving us the ideal Home Government of the future. Let us, therefore, start building up side by side the ideal home of the future."[38]

Even if many of the visitors to the exhibition could not, at present, afford to make such "reforms" in their homes, Kapadia hoped that the exhibition would prove of "educational value." Indeed, the contradiction between the lushly appointed exhibit rooms, filled with Bauhaus-design furniture and modern appliances such as radios and typewriters, and the housing conditions of the majority of the city's residents was seized upon by the prime minister of Bombay, B. G. Kher. In his speech opening the exhibition, Kher spent much of his time detailing the alleged squalor of Bombay's slums and tenements. He urged the architects, manufacturers, and visitors to the exhibition to assist the municipality and the government in solving the problem of housing the poor. "While thinking of im-

FIGURE 4.7. *Matunga Building. Note the comfortable verandahs and art deco styling. Author's photograph.*

proving the home inhabited by the well-to-do people," he argued, "we [must] not lose sight of the very urgent problem of improving the homes of the working class people, who form the large majority of city's [sic] inhabitants."[39]

Perhaps anticipating such concerns over the disjuncture between the exhibition and Bombay's housing conditions, the director of the IIA had a ready response for Kher. In his closing remarks, Kapadia acknowledged that the finer details of room design might seem grotesque to "those far less fortunate . . . who live in squalor and dirt, not to say filth." Yet such experiments as the exhibition were necessary, he argued. Through their "carefully worked-out rooms," they allowed visitors to know "what to look for and what to demand when the subject of a *home* is in question." [40] The planners of the exhibition thus sought, through a staging of ideal domesticity, to actually work out the parameters of the home for all Bombay's citizens, not just for those few who could afford bath fittings by Garlick and Company or steel furniture by Allwyn and Company or Godrej Boyce and Company.[41]

The Ideal Home Exhibition represented a rare articulation in the Indian context of a certain kind of bourgeois fantasy: the disaggregation of private life into different functions, each represented by distinct private spaces. It argued for discrete spaces for sleeping, dining, relaxing, and cooking, instead of the multifunctional spaces of the traditional house. If, as Richard Sennett has eloquently put it, "the *ancien regime* house was like a covered street,"[42] then such modern apartments as those featured in the exhibition sought to subdue the unruliness of the street by judicious allocation and segregation of domestic space on the basis of function. The proliferation of suburban living meant that many Bombay residents were beginning to view the city as a set of functionally discrete spaces, which made communication between spaces *the* major problem for those concerned about the city. The Ideal Home Exhibition represents the extension of this logic of functional disaggregation into the private spaces of the home.

By the 1930s, hence, the state and Bombay's elite classes had arrived at a certain vision for Bombay, one in which a stable bourgeois order could be asserted through a regulation of public and private spaces. Of course, like other places where such order was sought, the regulation was invariably of an incomplete and distorted sort.

Apartment Living in Matunga

Even in "modern" spaces like Matunga, however, the pattern of living diverged dramatically from the vision sketched out by the planners of the Ideal Home Exhibition. The experience of K. P. Chari illustrates a reasonably typical trajectory of migration and settling in. Chari, an Iyengar from the area around Tiruchirapalli who was ninety-two in 2002, came to Bombay in 1927 as a young man of sixteen.

His older brother was already there, and Chari lived with him in a chawl in the industrial area of Naigaum. When I asked if this was difficult after the relative homogeneity of the *agraharam* (the traditionally Brahmin section of villages and small towns) from which he had come, he replied that it would have been a lot worse had it not been for the fact that all the families living on that floor of that chawl were also South Indian Brahmins. After seven years in this chawl, Chari moved to an apartment building in Dadar Hindu Colony, at the southwestern edge of the Dadar–Matunga Estate. In 1937 he moved into the adjacent building and has lived there ever since.[43] According to him:

> In those days there was no such thing as "living room," "bedroom." Anywhere where there was space, people would be sleeping at night. Only place that was special was kitchen, because here food was prepared and so was kept special. At night the mattresses would come out and people would sleep in the hall, the passages, the bedroom. Mornings the mattresses would be kept away, out of sight, up over the cupboards, because they are impure after we have bathed.

Chari lived in a "1 BHK" place—one bedroom, hall, kitchen—with his wife and two children, his brother and his brother's wife and three children, an unmarried nephew, and various itinerant visitors and guests over the years. As might be expected, such densities shattered any fantasies the Trust's planners might have had of middle-class nuclear families living in apartments with discrete separations between sleeping, living, and cooking areas.

The interiors of apartments were fluid and multifunctional. Echoing Chari's remarks, Mythili noted that "the functional separation of rooms is hardly ever maintained because of the size of the family. . . . The living room serves also as the bedroom in the nights when the furniture is pushed to the wall to make room for the beds to be spread."[44] Invariably, Mythili observed, however small the living space, at least one corner would be devoted to statues and portraits of gods, usually in the kitchen. This corner was where prayers would be performed. One element from the Ideal Home Exhibition had been firmly incorporated into even the lower-middle-class household: every apartment and tenement Mythili visited invariably had a stainless steel Godrej wardrobe.

Chari repeatedly emphasized how important ideas of purity were, especially for that early generation that had just come from the village. Yet his stories also underscored the ways in which such ideas of purity did not go unchanged but, rather, adapted themselves to the new kinds of living spaces that the apartment dwellers of Matunga found themselves in. I would initially pose questions of adjustment expecting a narrative of crisis and severe compromise as the Brahmin was forced to incorporate the impure into his world. Yet, more than anything else, I was struck rather by the relatively fluid mechanisms by which Brahmin families were able to adapt once they moved into these new apartment dwellings. Consider, for instance, one aspect of what it would have been like for a man to live with his family in one of the smaller apartments, of one bedroom or even just one room plus bathroom, and perform a daily practice such as shaving. In such a setting, certain extraordinary adjustments would have been necessary for caste-conscious Hindus. They would have already dealt with the fact that the toilet was within the dwelling. As Mythili notes, in the smallest apartments, the windowsill would serve as dressing table; a mirror hung on a nail in the wall, and a man would shave in the very room where food was prepared. In a village or small-town setting, where many early migrants would have come from, shaving would probably have been performed by a member of a specific caste and almost certainly would have been performed outside the living/cooking/eating space—either in the courtyard if the person lived in a large enough house, or out on the street if the person lived in a more modest dwelling. "In a Brahmin household, after a shave or haircut one never touches anything, much less enter[s] the kitchen, until he has a bath. But families here have to reorient their customs and traditions."[45]

Chari, for instance, was full of praise for the design aspect that located the *nahani* or dish- and clothes-cleaning area outside the kitchen. "Once we touch food, it is impure and it is not right to keep it in the kitchen." This was because the kitchen was invariably also the prayer room and hence was the most sanctified part of the home. Food and the containers in which it is held become impure once they have been touched, hence the imperative to remove the used dishes from the kitchen after eating. The disaggregated bathroom, with separate bathing area, sink/*nahani*, and toilet, meant that dishes could be removed immediately and placed in the sink or *nahani*.

The disaggregated bathroom provided certain advantages, and residents also appreciated the particular design feature that provided separate access to these areas. As noted in chapter 3, M. A. Rajagopalan, a longtime resident of Matunga, remarked upon the fact that many flats had two entrances, one that led into the main living room and another that opened into a passage going to the bathroom/*nahani*/toilet area. This meant that sweepers and cleaners could enter the dwelling and proceed directly to clean the *nahani* or toilet without entering the living area or bedroom. As also noted in chapter 3, architects and designers of the 1920s and 1930s deemed this design element to be very significant, with the author of several books on house construction, R. S. Deshpande, characterizing one design that had only one door leading into the living room as flawed.[46] Furthermore, as Ashok Kulkarni noted, this particular usage of the entry passage/lobby as a channel to funnel cleaning staff to the toilet/*nahani* area differed from the purpose of such spaces in English flats, where they served as insulating layers between the cold outdoors and the heated indoors.[47]

The door leading from the landing into the lobby—which played an important role both in facilitating the flexibility of use of the various rooms and in regulating the use of domestic space by permitting domestics and servants to proceed to the cleaning areas without needing to traverse the principal living areas—was not entirely an innovation of the Bombay flat builders of the 1930s. What Kulkarni suggests here is that a design element that had served a different function in European flat designs—minimizing the loss of heat once the front door was opened—was assimilated and redeployed to different effect in the Bombay context.

For M. A. Rajagopalan, as discussed above, the fact that the toilet, sink, and bathroom were separate, and were not part of an "attached bathroom," was crucial. It meant that these spaces were used with maximal efficiency. The "disaggregated bathroom" praised by Rajagopalan was the outcome of conscious design decisions by Bombay architects in the wake of the toilet's migration to the interior, described in chapter 3. Simply permitting the toilet entry into the dwelling was a revolutionary step. The advent of flushing technology and the campaigns of advertisers to promote their improved sanitary conveniences might have persuaded Indian middle-class city dwellers to consider inviting the toilet into the dwelling, but how could one have bathing (a ritually purifying practice) and toilet functions (ritually defiling) within the very same space? In addition, having all these functions within the same space meant that if one person used any of these appliances—the sink, bath, or toilet—then the other two items could not be used by any other person. Hence the integrated Shanks bathroom of the sort pictured in Figure 3.4 was disaggregated in the middle-class flats of Dadar–Matunga. The sink, bathroom, and toilet were discrete elements within the flat; they were located next to another, and each could be used independently of the others. As Deshpande put it, "It is a mistake to locate the w.c. inside a bathroom. It should always be in a separate closet or compartment with an access independent of the bathroom."[48] All designs for flats in the 1930s and 1940s in middle-class areas like Dadar–Matunga featured disaggregated bathing, washing, and toilet facilities, with certain specific features. Marathe and Kulkarni designs for the bathroom, for instance, would invariably contain features emphasized by Deshpande, such as a shelf to store coconut oil or soap, say, or a towel rod.[49] And these facilities were usually separated from the other rooms of the house by a small lobby, which acquired certain functions of its own. Ashok Kulkarni told me that a special feature of Marathe and Kulkarni designs in their early Dadar–Matunga flats—once again seemingly following Deshpande's principles of flat design—was the provision of batons on the walls of such lobbies, to which in turn hooks were attached to enable the clotheslines to be strung across the lobby. On these clotheslines were hung clothes that would have been washed either in the adjacent sink or in the bathroom. Drying clothes, which would once have taken place on the roof or in the courtyard of a house, could now take place within the apartment. Thus the designs disaggregating bathroom functions in Marathe and Kulkarni's flats married ritual considerations with efficiency of use for large families sharing a single set of facilities.

Another design aspect facilitated a more communal style of living, even within the modern apartment building. The passage or lobby into which the flat opened from the floor landing outside would often have another door that connected to the lobby of the neighboring flat. If relations between the two families were suitable, this connecting door would often remain open all day. Kamu Iyer told me that in the flat in which his family lived from 1931 to 1941, there was a very communal feel: "In the neighboring flat there was an Iyengar family. As soon as the men left for work in the morning, the door would be opened and people would treat the two flats as one unit. The connecting door would only be closed at night."[50] Kamu Iyer's account suggests the ways in which sociality in apartment buildings was gendered. As discussed in chapter 1, the suburban nature of Dadar–Matunga meant that men of working age would leave in the mornings for their offices in south Bombay, and "between 10 am and 4 pm is [women's] rajya [reign]," as one of Mythili's respondents joked.[51] During this diurnal women's *rajya,* there was an extensive flow of women and young children between the apartments. Men, on the other hand, claimed not to have too much interest in socializing; they might exchange some words across balconies but would not necessarily visit one another's flats.[52]

One especially revealing practice had to do with the informal—but strictly observed—regulations regarding the pounding and grinding of spices and flour. Mythili notes that for reasons of economy and caste orthodoxy, families would buy whole spices and whole grains and the women would then pound and grind these on stone slabs into powdered spices and flour. Since the pounding, especially, was a loud and intrusive activity, there was an agreement that it would take place only at certain times of day and always in one of the ground-floor apartments.[53] Such an arrangement, occasioned by the one-on-top-of-the-other nature of apartment living, ensured a certain gendered sociality. It is also illustrative of the conjuncture between the imperatives imposed by the built form, by caste considerations, and by the need for economies in household expenses. The purchasing of whole grains and whole spices illustrates the union of considerations of caste orthodoxy with a thrifty lower-middle-class sensibility; the pounding could only take place at a certain time of day, when the men were at work and thus away from their suburban homes; and it could only take place on the ground floor of the apartment buildings, since pounding on the upper floors would be noisy and might affect the structural integrity of the building.

If the distinctions within and between flats could be fluid in the ways described above, then the other spaces in the apartment building might also not conform to any ideal or typical model of cellular living that the apartment-building typology seemed to represent.[54] The inhabitants of apartment buildings in Matunga did perceive a sharp difference between apartment living and chawl living: one of Mythili's respondents proclaimed, "Neighbourly feelings you find more in chawls. In water tight flats, closed all the time against neighbours, there is no sharing of anything."[55] Servants, cooks, and their families, especially, inhabited the spaces "in-between" the interior of the dwelling and the exterior on the street, spaces such as landings and the areas underneath staircases. Mythili provides a vivid description of this practice:

> One never knows when one would put his foot on a servant who often makes the foot of the stairs or the landing his place of sleep. We have seen whole groups of Ramas [servants] keeping their belongings and cooking their food in the place under the staircase. They sleep in the passage even in the afternoon, during the short period of mid day rest they might get from their work. Where the passages are very narrow there is hardly any place to walk to reach the staircase.... *We were even informed that the Ramas pay some nominal rent for their dwelling namely the place below the staircase!*[56]

Not only did servants dwell in the intermediate spaces of the building, but such spaces also got commoditized, and occupants started to establish a legal right to live under the staircase, for example. Such rights even became transferable from one generation to the next. Such practices complicated the notion that the apartment buildings constituted a new kind of space distinct from the more fluid life of the chawl: in chawls, the "outside" space of the verandah was as important a living space for the residents as the "inside" space of the tenement itself. The ubiquitous presence of servants in the passages and stairwells complicated the fantasy that the move from the chawl to the apartment was some sort of necessary retreat into private domesticity, resulting in the realization of a proper middle-class bourgeoisie.[57] Swati Chattopadhyay has shown that one of the ancient truisms of colonial urbanism—that colonial cities like Calcutta and Bombay were separated into rigidly distinct "Black Towns" and "White Towns"—is in fact simply not true: the ubiquitous presence and residence of servants in the interstitial spaces of the "White Town" meant that they had more than a touch of "Black" in them. In analogous fashion, the seeming retreat of the middle classes into flats did not neatly result in a separation between private domestic space and public space; rather, the fluid relationship between inside and outside endured but was now strongly inflected by class. The lower-middle-class tenants of the apartment buildings did indeed live more "inside" in their flats than they would have in chawls, where a part of their lives would have been transacted on the verandahs, but the spaces outside the flats but within the building—landings, stairwells, and so on—were used by servants and domestics for living as well.

The relationship between the inside space of apartment buildings and the outside space of the street was further complicated by the compound, a distinctive feature of the Bombay apartment building. The apartment buildings of Dadar–Matunga were not quite the same as the residential precincts appearing in Europe at roughly the same time. In the classic European residential bourgeois street, the buildings presented a uniform facade to the street.[58] In suburbs like Dadar–Matunga–Sion (and indeed, in all subsequent developments all over Bombay), the facade presented to the street was not uniform and unbroken. Rather, each building stood within a plot, whose footprint was larger than the footprint of the building itself. The space between the edge of the building and the edge of the plot (at the sidewalk) was known as "the compound" and constituted an intermediary zone between the building interior and the street exterior.

The origins of this distinctive feature of the Bombay apartment building lay in the battles fought by the Improvement Trust against overcrowding. In particular, no one was more energetically engaged in combating overcrowding than the indefatigable J. P. Orr, chairman of the Trust in the 1910s. In his battles against overcrowding and resulting disease, Orr's chief argument was that because of the

FIGURE 4.8. *Typical Matunga streetscape with buildings and compounds. Note the residential quality of the street and the space of the compound. Author's photograph.*

proximity of buildings in the crowded areas of Bombay, tenements did not receive light and air, critical elements in the fight against disease.[59] Orr described extensively the process he called "the sweating of building sites"—the progressive growth of a house on a particular site into a tenement building. As the demand for housing rose, the owner of a house might decide that he could realize some additional revenues by building an additional wing or adding an additional floor and renting out these new rooms. In this way, what was originally a house surrounded by open space in a plot grew into a large building that occupied the entire plot and abutted the neighboring buildings with only very narrow passageways between. This, in turn, meant that only the rooms fronting the street would get any measure of light and air. Since the blocks were quite large, there would be structures between the buildings that fronted the street—in other words, structures that did not front on a street at all. This, of course, is the familiar pattern of the *wadi*: one enters the *wadi* from the street and then accesses dwellings in the interior through various passageways that wend through the *wadi*.

To attack this pattern of "sweating of building sites," Orr became a vigorous proponent of what he called the "63½° rule." Simply put, this was a rule that was guaranteed to control the density of buildings by indexing the height of the building to the size of the plot. What it meant was that for any given room in any floor of any building, the angle of incidence (the angle made with respect to the floor of the room) of light had to be at least 63½ degrees. This would guarantee that the size of a building would only be a fraction of the size of the plot, permitting light even into the rooms on the bottom floor. This rule had originated in urban-planning discourse in Britain and had already been adopted, in somewhat less restrictive form, in the city of Calcutta.[60]

Orr had succeeded in incorporating this rule into the Improvement Trust's estates. (It was a condition of leasing land owned by the Trust that developers abide by the Trust's building regulations, as opposed to the much laxer regulations of the Municipal Corporation. Here again the significance of the Trust's long battles to physically acquire lands becomes significant.) This meant that, effectively, only one-third of each plot in the Trust's new developments was built on. In 1919, Orr's efforts bore fruit in that the 63½ degree rule was incorporated into Bombay Municipal Corporation building regulations as Bye-Law 41(a).[61] Although the new municipal bylaw did not extend to the older parts of the city, which were still governed by the older regulations, the incorporation of the new bylaw did mean that all subsequent construction in the city, even buildings not on Trust lands, would now have to employ the familiar structure of a building emplotted within a compound.

The compound, the spatial outcome of the 63½ degree rule, played and continues to play an important role in mediating between the inside space of the building and the outside space of the street. Children, for instance, were permitted to play in the compound but were not permitted onto the street until they were older. Mythili identified the space around the buildings—that is, the compound—as the principal space where children played.[62] Women might come down into the compound to purchase vegetables from itinerant vendors wearing the long caftan-like dress called the "maxi" favored by housewives. They would not venture out into the street in such dress.

The compound also became the space where the corporate identity of the building was shaped. For instance, children would normally play cricket in the evenings or on weekends in the compound, but on particular match days, such as Sundays, a team from one building might play a match against a team from another building on the street or in a nearby field. K. V. L. Narayan, who lived in the BIT tenements in Matunga from the time he was a young boy in 1932, told me that in those days, when many of the plots were still not built upon, Sunday matches were a regular feature and the "BIT boys" would take on the boys from one of the buildings along, say, Bhandarkar Road, which was another stretch of the Dadar–Matunga Estate that featured early building.[63] There was no need to go to a field since so many plots were vacant in those days that they could play close to home.

Not only was the compound significant in these activities, but the compound wall itself played an important role. The nature of the wall was highly regulated by the BIT, which issued specific guidelines for the different walls that encircled the plot. According to BIT building regulations, which needed to be signed after each plot was leased:

> Each Plot shall be enclosed by a brick wall not exceeding five feet in height extending along the back and by a dwarf wall and railing extending along the two sides and the front, the height and design in all cases to be approved by the Engineer.[64]

The BIT clearly sought to sharply delineate the edges of the plot with the wall. It is noteworthy that while the rear of the building was to be enclosed by a solid brick wall "not exceeding five feet in height," the front and sides of the plot were to be bordered by a lower "dwarf wall and railing." This ensured that the wall was prominent enough to distinguish the interior of the plot from the street but not high enough to entirely shield the interior from the gaze of a passerby on the street. The BIT appears to have imposed these specific regulations to try to fashion the compound as an intermediate kind of space between the interiority of the interior and the exteriority of the street, in much the way the verandah was used in the colonial bungalow.

Residents of Dadar–Matunga used the compound wall in different ways, however. The relatively low height of the "dwarf wall" meant that housewives could transact with street cart vegetable vendors across it. The wall might serve as spectator "stands" during games within the compound, where children could sit and watch games of cricket or football. The wall might serve as an edge, and hitting the ball over the low compound wall might count as an "out." As a result, according to K. V. L. Narayan, players often developed stunted batting games, with either a strong legside offense or a strong offside offense, depending on the orientation of the pitch within the compound and on whether the wall lay to the offside or to the legside. In general, the organization of apartment buildings meant that the compound wall and the compound, rather than assisting in the fashioning of bourgeois individuality, actually served to consolidate the corporate identity of the building.

If the compound was a space where the "inside" space of the apartments penetrated and intersected with the "outside" space of the street, then the converse was also true. The activities of the street sometimes penetrated the "inside" space of the compound. Consider, for instance, the case of Tukaram Sawant, a sugarcane-juice vendor in Dadar–Matunga, which underscores the distinctive relationship between insides, outsides, and regulated spaces in Dadar–Matunga.[65] In 1956, one Kashibai Gandhi, the landlord of a building called Gandhi Bhuvan on Plot 321-A, had granted Tukaram Sawant permission to move his sugarcane-juice crusher from just *outside* the building compound to just *inside* it, near the entrance to the compound. From Sawant's point of view, this move was necessary since he was being harassed by the police for plying his trade on the sidewalk outside Gandhi Bhuvan. As a residential area in the regulated precincts of Dadar–Matunga, the street was theoretically to be kept free of commercial activity. Such an arrangement, while protecting Sawant from the police's enforcement of BIT street regulations, was of course still in violation of the BIT's regulation of compound spaces. The customary phrasing in BIT leases regarding compounds in Dadar–Matunga required the lessee

> not to use or permit to be used such portion of the land hereby demised as shall for the time being be unbuilt upon for any purpose whatsoever other than as a garden or open space without the previous consent in writing of the Board and not to place or store or permit to be placed or stored upon the land for the time being unbuilt upon or any part thereof any article or thing whatsoever which may interfere with the use of such land as a garden or open space.[66]

From Kashibai Gandhi's point of view, the unofficial license to Sawant earned her an extra fifteen rupees a month, the rent Sawant agreed to pay.[67] This arrangement continued for almost seventeen years, despite being in violation of the BIT's strict prohibition, with the rent paid by Sawant to Gandhi also increasing, to seventy rupees.

In 1973, the Gandhi family sold the building and the plot to the Shah family, which changed the name of the building to Shobha Sadan and proceeded to try to evict Sawant and his sugarcane-juice vending operation. Once the proceedings began, Sawant became concerned for the appearance and fixity of his juice business. He erected a tin roof over the juice crusher. Soon he felt that the tin roof was unattractive, and he covered the roof in cloth. Finding even this arrangement unsatisfactory, he added asbestos cement walls, followed shortly by signs in Marathi and Gujarati advertising himself and his business, as well as benches and chairs for his customers.[68]

Sawant's strategy was, of course, to make his juice operation appear permanent and fixed. His principal defense against the Shah family's efforts to evict him was that he was not a "licensee" but, rather, a "lessee" and was thus protected by the provisions of the Rent Control Act of 1948. The details of the arguments deployed by the parties to this case need not concern us here. The High Court ultimately ruled in favor of the Shah family and confirmed the eviction order that had been issued on Sawant, maintaining that the ultimate determining principle in the case should be the fact that commercial structures such as Sawant's were in violation of the BIT restrictions on how compound space might be used. What is interesting, however, is the fact that Sawant had first conducted his operation for seventeen years, from 1956 to 1973, with the blessing of the Gandhis and had then succeeded in continuing for another fifteen years until the High Court decision of 1988, presumably in the face of opposition from the Shah family. This suggests that while the BIT sought to use the compound to clearly delineate the interior space of the building from the exterior space of the street, landlords such as Kashibai Gandhi were able to bend regulations to permit a commercial activity such as sugarcane-juice vending within the compound. Further, Sawant himself appears to have resisted the Shahs' efforts to evict him for fifteen years. Undoubtedly he would have had support—perhaps through the Municipal Corporation itself—in this heroic resistance to the property owner. This suggests that the regulation of space through rules such as the BIT's building rules were significant, but were always liable to be subverted through the tactical use of political power.

From the point of view of the Trust's regulations, the main problem with Sawant's juice business was that it violated the residential character of the neighborhood while also misusing the space of the compound. The residential character of the buildings was specified in great detail in the BIT's leases, especially in Covenant 11, which stipulated that residents must

> use the buildings for the time being on the demised land for residential purposes only and not use the said premises or any part thereof or permit the same to be used for any business trade occupation or purpose whatsoever other than as aforesaid without the previous consent in writing of the Board and not at any time to permit stables factories

workshops or works-spaces on the demised land and in particular not to use the demised premises or any part thereof as a refreshment-room booth or shop.[69]

Sawant and the Gandhi family managed to subvert the Trust's zoning through their private arrangement. Alternatively, sometimes it was possible for residents of the suburbs to gain official permission to modify the residential character of the apartment buildings. Consider the case of the efforts by the South Indian Concerns to secure a plot in Matunga to carry out its business as a cooperative provisions society (see chapter 2; I discuss this again in chapter 5). The plot in question, Plot 401, was first leased from the Trust by B. V. S. Iyengar of Iyengar and Menzies, a firm of architects that had done extensive work in collaboration with the Trust and with the BMC. Indeed, this was a typical pattern, in which persons with inside knowledge of the Trust's operations would secure plots from the Trust at excellent rates, often at closed auctions.[70] Once he had secured the leasehold to this plot, Iyengar, who also held the leasehold to several other plots on the same street, sought to transfer the lease to the South Indian Concerns. He had already transferred leases to several other plots on this street, which became Telang Road, one of the principal streets in the South Indian part of Matunga. One of the leases was transferred by him to the South Indian Consumer Cooperative Society, another provisions cooperative just across the road from the proposed site for South Indian Concerns. Another became a residential building with principally South Indian tenants.

With the precedent of the Consumer Cooperative Society in mind, the chairman of the South Indian Concerns wrote to the Estates Department of the BMC asking for permission to change the name of the "user" of the plot from Iyengar to the South Indian Concerns.[71] The members of South Indian Concerns were chagrined, however, when the Estates Department turned down the request, citing the regulation that the building was zoned for residential purposes only and noting that the presence of a provisions store would entail commercial traffic, especially with the passage of shoppers through the compound on their way to and from the store.[72] The South Indian Concerns members wrote back emphasizing that it was not a commercial operation as such. Rather, they emphasized its community-oriented nature:

> Ours is more a public utility service run on mutual benefit basis, and is not at all intended for private profit. Our organization is conceived on the basis of the Trade Union. ... The shareholders in our Concern are the middle class office going public, who have found it necessary to organize this as an absolute social necessity.[73]

The South Indian Concerns members were thus making a subtle argument. While there would undoubtedly be persons who did not live in the building using the provisions store, they would not necessarily be "outsiders" as such. They were part of the community that the South Indian Concerns claimed to represent: a middle-class community of office-goers, who also happened to be South Indians. Thus, also included with this letter to the Estates Department was a copy of the "Articles of Association" of the South Indian Concerns coop society, underscoring that this was a community organization, that the officeholders received no payment, and that profits were returned to the members. Implicit in this letter, thus, was the argument that the people using the compound and the building where the store would be located were not going to be from outside as such, but were from within. They were drawing upon a slightly different understanding of what constituted the inside and the outside from the way of thinking that sought to draw a stricter line between the private spaces of individual families within the building and the public space of the street outside.

In addition, the South Indian Concerns assured the BMC that there would be no shop frontage, that the building and compound would conform to the residential regulations, and, of course, that "there would also be the compound wall." The arguments proposed were successful, and in his response sanctioning the change of user for Plot 401 from Iyengar to the South Indian Concerns, the secretary of the estates wrote that "since this business is to be carried out for the benefit of the members of the Society and not for profit, and since the building will be constructed like other buildings with a compound wall etc., there is no objection to the change of user."[74]

The spaces of the suburban apartment building were thus used in different ways by the lower-middle-class, upper-caste Indians who began moving there from the 1920s onward. The last example, of the South Indian Concerns, is especially interesting. In addition to illustrating how understandings of social space different from the conventional public/private distinction were deployed by the members of the society to gain permission from the BMC, the case also casts into relief the proliferation in the suburbs of new kinds of community. Who were the South Indians? Why did they organize themselves into cooperative societies? While chapter 2 has already discussed the migration and settlement of Matunga by South Indians, the discussion so far has not interrogated very closely the meaning of this category. Chapter 5 turns to an understanding of the meaning of "South Indian" in the context of Bombay in the period under discussion.

5 From Southern Indians to "South Indians"

WHEN I STARTED TO TALK TO LONGTIME RESIDENTS OF Matunga, people told me that I should meet K. V. L. Narayan as soon as possible. Narayan, it seems, moved into the neighborhood in 1932 and has lived continuously in the same tenement building ever since. His experience, I was told, was "typical" of the experience of the South Indians who moved into this neighborhood from the 1920s onward. Narayan was also one of the very few who had put any of his experiences in writing. In a letter to his grandchildren, in which he describes his childhood years in Bombay and which I quote here at length, Narayan writes:

> I was unhappy to leave my dearest ones in Singanallur. [But] Bombay was a beautiful and better place with a total population of only seven lakhs [700,000] of people. Roads used to be washed and cleaned on two days in a week. This was in the year 1932. My uncle CHUPPANA and KICHANNA were living in the same building. I was still sporting long flowing hair. Chupanna was very youthful and was nicknamed EROL FLYN [sic] because of his neatly cut moustache. He took me under his wing and decided to show me Bombay. I was thrilled to travel in train, bus, and trams which were cheap and not crowded. He showed me all important places and in the evening he took me to CAPITOL cinema and showed me the great movie *Rasputin and the Empress*. He entertained me at a restaurant with Falooda etc. Just before entraining at VT we visited a place in Capitol which was decorated with mirrors on all sides. I was made to sit on a chair. When my mind was engaged in looking round, the beautician took hold of my entire tuft [of hair] and cut it short. Down fell tresses of my long hair. Hell was let loose. I cried and cried that my BRAHMINHOOD has been destroyed as it was the first time I had a hair cut. I made my uncle miserable, crying without a break till we reached home. On reaching home I insisted to my mother that she return me to Singanallur.[1]

Narayan did not, however, leave Bombay; he moved into the same tenement apartment that he continues to live in. These sentences by Narayan capture many of the paradigmatic experiences of migrating to a city like Bombay: the sadness of leaving the native place, the cohabitation in the same building with other members of one's family and community; the excitement of taking modern transportation around the city and seeing the sights, especially the movies; the present-day nostalgia for an older, purer, Bombay; and finally, the moment of trauma when the conditions of the big city violate Brahminical notions of purity and pollution.

For Narayan, many of the difficulties of adjustment were ameliorated by the fact that he lived in Matunga, which he described to me as a "fully Southie area in those days."[2] It was the South Indian character of Matunga that created for Narayan (and others like him) a buffer zone between the home—where caste considerations could be controlled, as discussed in chapters 3 and 4—and the terrifying heterogeneity of the city. Yet this account appears to set up a tension between the relatively specific caste identity Narayan ascribed to himself (his "Brahminhood") and the seemingly general character of the Matunga community (its "Southie" or South Indian nature). "South Indian" could obviously mean a wide variety of things, ranging from fairly specific caste identities in some contexts to broader regional and linguistic associations in other contexts.

Previous chapters have discussed the ways in which, in Bombay by the 1920s, South Indians were discernible as a community that was employed in the white-collar sector and that made Matunga their neighborhood.[3] This chapter further interrogates the formation of this highly fluid and flexible category. In particular, I argue that the consolidation of South Indian identity entailed two parallel processes: on the one hand, a process of synthesis, through which earlier divisions based on highly specific caste and linguistic differences were transcended to generate the metacategory South Indian; on the other hand, a process of fragmentation as differences asserted themselves in different contexts and fractured the unity of the category South Indian. Urban ethnic identity as it constituted itself in the suburbs was thus not the result of an erosion of difference and the creation of the "urbanite" in some simplistic sense; nor was it the case that differences remain unaffected, that in this sense Indian cities were "urban villages." Rather, specific economic and political imperatives provided the context for the emergence of larger categories such as South Indian. Meanwhile, caste differences were displaced and restricted to specific domains of social life, such as marriage and dining.

The study of transformations in the idea of caste and community has an immaculate pedigree in South Asia scholarship. The pioneering work of Bernard Cohn argued that caste is not something that exists from time immemorial outside the sphere of politics, as scholars since G. W. F. Hegel have argued; rather, caste as we understand it today is very much an outcome of colonial politics.[4] As noted in the introduction, Arjun Appadurai developed some of the implications of Cohn's insights into the connection between knowledge-producing apparatuses such as the census and Indian understandings of community. Specifically, Appadurai made a far-reaching argument about the abstractive consequence of the colonial obsession with numbers: the ways in which notions of caste and community were disarticulated from specific spatial contexts. In a work primarily directed at rethinking nationalism, Manu Goswami made an important argument about the ways in which the logics of colonial practice and capital combine to produce a reinvestment of spaces with forms of identity.[5] The most recent scholarship of urban community identities all seek to identify the condition of displacement and ensuing mobility as the central factor in generating broad understandings of identity that are operationalized in the urban context.[6]

Such scholarship provides us with a broad account of the abstraction from space of community identities under colonialism, capitalism, nationalism, and now globalization. Yet while we have excellent accounts of the relationship between urban identity and the conditions of displacement and mobility, the subsequent connections between community identity, urban spaces, and institutions such as the cooperative housing society remain unelaborated. The apartment building suburbs of Dadar–Matunga constituted one new urban built environment in which community identity reconstituted itself. In this novel setting, the interwar years constituted a crucial period during which ideas of community were transformed in the context of the expanding city of Bombay. The cooperative society was a key institution in this reconfiguration of community, especially in the ways in which narrower caste distinctions were transcended to create metacaste identities such as the South Indian. Further, the history of communally organized cooperative housing societies provided the template for the subsequent expansion of the city of Bombay into Salsette Island following Independence, and hence also the pattern for the communalization of space.

The cooperative society formed a locus around which metacaste identities such as South Indian consolidated themselves; the diasporic condition of migrants in Bombay, and their physical location in the suburb of Matunga, also provided novel contexts within which they began to understand one another as members of a community. The spatial juxtaposition of Matunga with its neighbor Dharavi, also populated by low-caste Tamil speakers, provided an important context for the South Indians of Matunga to understand themselves as upper-caste and lower-middle-class South Indians as opposed to the lower-caste and laboring classes of Dharavi. Institutions such as temples and schools within Matunga, meanwhile, served as settings where new kinds of difference asserted themselves as Iyers from Palakkad confronted Iyers from Thanjavur and Tirunelveli.

This chapter proceeds by interrogating the category South Indian. The history of the cooperative movement in Bombay suggests ways in which the cooperative housing societies were institutional foci, so to speak, around which urban community identities such as the South Indian were constituted. I consider next the ways in which other institutional contexts in suburban neighborhoods like Matunga were the setting for assertions of difference and fragmentation within the category South Indian.

⁊ SYNTHESIS

How does a community constitute itself in Bombay? Some of the earliest references to the category South Indian occur in the context of the growth of cooperative societies in the first three decades of the twentieth century. Here is the registrar of cooperative societies, one V. S. Bhide, from a report of a tour he made in 1930:

> The South Indians seem to possess a special gift for successfully running a Consumer's cooperative society and during the year I was extremely pleased to pay a visit to see the progress of the South Indian Cooperative Consumer's society in Matunga. . . . The members are loyal to the institution and also very fortunate in securing the services of selfless and competent honorary workers for the Managing Committee.[7]

Who are the South Indians alluded to here? Clearly they have some quality that they share, which allows Bhide to represent them as a community predisposed to the institution of the cooperative society. I turn now to interrogate the category South Indian as it is used in the context of Matunga.

To get a sense of the world from which these people were coming to the city, consider Dr. K. Shankar's description of his boyhood years in the village of Kallarukocchhi, a small village in the Tirunelveli district in what was then Madras Presidency.[8] Dr. Shankar, who was born in Kallarukocchhi in 1921 and moved as a young boy to Bombay in the 1920s, is the son of Dr. S. S. Krishnan, described to me as a "pillar of Matunga." He told me at great length about the world of the Brahmin *agraharam* in which he was born, its rows of Brahmin houses, the canal at the edge of the village where he used to bathe. He remembered:

> There was a community there called the Pallans. They used to be untouchables. But it didn't cause any problems really, even when they had to go through the *agraharam* to the canal. If there were some religious person, they would say, as the untouchables went by, "*Theendadai, theendadai*" [Don't touch, don't touch].

From this world of the village, with its caste-saturated spaces, Dr. Shankar moved with his parents to Bombay in the 1920s. They first lived in a chawl in the working-class district of Parel, and in 1931 they moved into the South Indian Cooperative Housing Society in Matunga, blocks of apartment buildings where Dr. Shankar still lives. (Indeed, Dr. Shankar's father had been one of the original members of the society.) Such a move, from village to tenement in a working-class district to apartment building, would have been a fairly typical trajectory for migrants at that time. Once you moved to the city, according to Dr. Shankar, "you have to forget all these ideas about caste, not touching other people. My father and I had patients from all communities: Kutchis, Gujaratis, Parsis. They would invite us to their functions and everything. It was no problem." But when I asked him if non-Brahmins would come and eat in their house, Dr. Shankar paused and replied, "See, we hardly knew any non-Brahmins. They were all on the other side of the tracks, in Dharavi." (He refers here to the large slum of Dharavi, literally across the Central Railway tracks from Matunga, where many of the residents are migrants from southern India—low-caste Hindus, Christians, and Muslims.)

The contradiction in Dr. Shankar's account—between his earlier claim that in Bombay one had to forget about caste and that his family knew and socialized with all sorts of communities, and his later statement that actually they hardly knew any non-Brahmins—was a contradiction I encountered repeatedly in my attempts to understand the role of caste in the formation of modern ethnic categories such as South Indian. This contradiction expresses a fundamental process of urbanization in Bombay. Migrants like Dr. S. S. Krishnan were seeking to become residents of Bombay, a modern city. Engaged as they were in various white-collar occupations, they were forced to encounter and deal with the bewildering heterogeneity of castes, languages, and religions of the growing city of the 1920s and 1930s. At the same time, at least some of them were also engaged with the ideas of nationalist leaders such as Gandhi, who preached against casteist exclusion. They needed to compromise and modify their ideas of purity and pollution to deal with the circumstances of urban living.

The category South Indian emerged and developed in this period as a strategy for managing difference. When I began research on this project, I took the category South Indian entirely for granted and focused more on the spatiality of Matunga. But as I continued investigating, I noticed that while most accounts of this neighborhood would refer to it as "South Indian," the referent for this category varied wildly. A recent article on South Indians in Bombay by a Bombay historian in a local history pamphlet, for instance, takes it to mean anyone from any of the four states lying to the south of the Vindhya mountains: Karnataka, Tamil Nadu, Kerala, and Andhra Pradesh.[9] At the other extreme from this literalist reading is a 1959 Sociology Department Ph.D. dissertation on South Indians in Matunga. It does not articulate, explicitly, the question of caste, but buried in the text are allusions such as "an overwhelming majority of our migrants are Brahmins."[10]

A sense of the range of meanings this category might include is conveyed in the following confusing conversation I had with S. Ramachandran.[11] He was born in Matunga in 1938, in a nursing home two buildings away from where he now lives and where he has always lived. He used to be a municipal councilor representing F Ward, in which Matunga is located. He had been introduced to me as someone who, through this experience, had a good perspective on Matunga and the South Indian community. I asked him what kind of neighborhood Matunga was. "To understand Matunga," he said, "the chief thing to remember is the difference between coconuts and *puli* [tamarind]." Noting my blank look in response to this enigmatic answer, he went on to explain that the majority of migrants to Matunga in the 1930s were Tamil-speaking Iyer Brahmins from the Palakkad district in what is now the southwestern state of Kerala. Next came other Iyers from the Thanjavur district in the present-day southeastern state of Tamil Nadu. Since the Palakkad Iyers came from a more coastal region, they used more coconut in their food, whereas the "Chennai-side" Iyers used more tamarind. Ramachandran here maps an originary caste landscape onto the context of the city.

I asked him then if South Indians only included Palakkad Iyers and Thanjavur Iyers. He said not at all, there are also Iyengars, Namboodiris, Madhavas. These are other sorts of Brahmins, speaking, respectively, Tamil, Malayalam, and Kannada, from places in present-day Tamil Nadu, Kerala, and Karnataka. I asked him if Matunga is a Brahmin neighborhood. "What are you talking about?" he snapped irritably. "The oldest residents here are Kutchis and Gujaratis and there are also people from Andhra who are not Brahmin." Now thoroughly confused, I asked him to define South Indian. "These South Indians, they are basically middle-class people." When I suggested that this did not clarify matters for me, he said finally, "But South Indians are like that only."

The tautology of Ramachandran's retort was something I repeatedly encountered in various attempts to get people to define what "South Indian" meant. Invariably, people would begin with a very specific definition, usually Palakkad Iyers, but then slowly broaden their understanding, under duress, to include ideas of middle-classness, language, native place, and the kind of accommodations that people lived in. South Indian was clearly a category whose referent depended very much on the participants and the context of the discussion. At some kind of equilibrium state, "South Indian" generally referred to Brahmins, although also a couple of other high castes, who spoke Tamil, Kannada, and Malayalam, who came from Madras Presidency or Travancore or Mysore, who were employed in some sort of white-collar capacity, and who lived in one of the apartment buildings in Matunga. If the category South Indian appears unstable and blurred, the history of cooperative societies in Bombay suggests the imperatives demanding a fluid and flexible understanding of community.

✒ COOPERATIVE SOCIETIES

Cooperative societies were introduced in India in the early twentieth century following their success in England and the United States. Most of the early cooperatives were agricultural cooperatives, providing credit to poor farmers who had no access to regular lines of credit. In the 1910s, the colonial state attempted to promote cooperatives in growing cities such as Bombay, Madras, and Karachi. Such promotion took the form, for instance, of offering below-market-rate loans to building societies. In principle at least, these were part of the colonial state's attempt to develop an urban, white-collar middle class. The state did not actually extend very many such loans. It did so for a brief period during and after World War I, when the Bombay economy grew rapidly, but stopped following the retrenchment of 1922. Most building societies secured financing through loans from insurance companies (or loans from cooperative banks from the same community or from wealthy members of the community). However, the state's nominal support for cooperative societies should be understood in conjunction with its attempts to plan neighborhoods such as Matunga along the lines of garden suburbs. Marketed as a middle way between the two extremes of market society and socialism, cooperative societies were considered ideal institutions to allow new migrants to adjust to the conditions of urban living.[12]

The general workings of a cooperative society are familiar: members joined by purchasing shares, and this capital served as security against which the society could borrow money to buy land and erect buildings if it was a building society, or to purchase consumer goods for resale if it was a consumer society, or to give loans if it was a credit society. In India, however, these societies took a direction quite different from the original principles as elaborated in England, according to which membership in any co-op should be open to all. In India, through a provision in the Indian Cooperative Credit Societies Act of 1904, the colonial state allowed cooperative societies to organize themselves on the basis of community.[13] This has to do, of course, with the colonial state's understanding of caste and social difference as the central organizing principle in Indian society.

Indians seized upon this provision to allow them to define the borders of their community through cooperatives. At the second meeting of the Bombay Provincial Cooperative Conference in 1917, Vishwanath Narayan Jog, a stalwart of the cooperative movement, argued:

> It is said that mixed societies, wherever tried, have not been a success. . . . In other countries urban life usually involves a lack of cohesion and a want of fraternal feeling even among neighbours. In India there is the fellowship of caste and the discipline and a common interest of a caste. In India we find that in many instances occupations represent the castes. Ask an ordinary man what is his caste. The ready answer is I am a Teli, a Shimpi, a Kumbhar. Substitute a single caste for a single village, make caste as it were the urban unit and weld the units thus formed within one town into the powerful credit weapon which cooperative union is.[14]

Jog's social theory here seeks to deploy the progressive tool of the cooperative movement to reinforce a deeply conservative view of a caste-based society. Many of the early cooperative societies in Bombay rigorously applied this principle in restricting their membership.

The cooperative housing society allowed one to become urban without diluting one's caste identity, but in addition it was also seen as the best way to stabilize rents in the boom years after World War I, when most of Bombay's first wave of cooperative societies were started. Cooperative housing societies received concessions from the state in the period immediately following World War I. For one thing, they were permitted to lease the lands on favorable terms at less than market price on the condition that they limit their rents to within 6 percent of their total construction costs.[15] Such a well-meaning decision to peg rents to constructions costs could be a double-edged sword, especially if the construction took place during a building boom when all costs—land and building materials—were at record highs. When the boom subsided, and rents went down elsewhere, these societies ran into problems since they were unable to lower their own rents, which were pegged to high building costs.

Another way in which the state supported cooperative housing societies during the boom years was by extending loans on favorable terms. Normally, the members of a society could only put up about 15–25 percent of the costs of land and buildings, thus requiring loans of 75–85 percent of the costs. In 1919, the Bombay government agreed to extend loans of up to five lakhs of rupees (five hundred thousand rupees) to societies, and although the normal rate of interest would have been 6 percent, if "Government are satisfied that there are strong grounds for making a concession in this respect a lower rate of interest will be charged."[16] This practice continued for a few years but was suspended once the market subsided after 1922. Yet these practices—of extending loans and leasing out land on concessionary terms to cooperative housing societies—set an important precedent. When the real estate market crested the next time around, following Partition in 1947, it was through these very measures that the government sought to address the housing crisis.

In Bombay, if not in all of India, the Saraswat Brahmins were a pioneering community in terms of using cooperative societies to adjust to urban living. Starting with the Shamrao Vithal Cooperative Credit Society, registered in 1906, the Saraswat community set up a range of cooperative societies in Bombay and other places in the Bombay Presidency. They founded the Saraswat Cooperative Housing Society in 1915, the first cooperative housing society in Asia, restricted to members of the Saraswat Brahmin community.[17] Financing was secured through a loan from Sir Prabhashankar Pattani and a further loan from the Shamrao Vithal Cooperative Credit Society, which established the typical pattern wherein a community's cooperative credit society would finance the construction activities of its own cooperative housing society.

Attempts to restrict the various communities were also practiced by large agencies seeking to accommodate their staff. The Great Indian Peninsular Railway was one such organization. In 1918 the GIP approached the Trust with a proposal to lease lands in Dadar–Matunga for housing for its officers. It sought nothing less than to create a small colony for its staff and requested that no other lessee be permitted within the land leased to the GIP so that a railway colony could be formed, which could "make use of the central garden space and form athletic and social clubs, if desired, without having to give outsiders any rights of membership."[18] The GIP also proposed to build three types of buildings, at differing costs and thus differing rents, for its European, Hindu, and Parsi officers. The letter from the GIP also urged the Trust not to modify the submitted designs in any way because it was "very important that the scheme be carried out as designed to avoid an undesirable mixing of the classes."[19]

The restrictions imposed by such cooperatives had become an issue by the 1930s. Vaikunth L. Mehta, a stalwart of the cooperative movement and managing director of the Bombay Provincial Cooperative Bank, voiced his criticism of the communal basis of organization of the Saraswat cooperatives at a ceremony to unveil a portrait of Rao Bahadur S. S. Talmaki, the preeminent Saraswat cooperative activist. "In our country," said Mehta, "where there are ever so many divisions, cooperation should not be used to strengthen the diverting interests."[20] G. P. Murdeshwar, chairman of the Saraswat Cooperative Housing Society in 1940, also noted the critiques that had been made by "nationalists and social reformers" of the communal basis of the Saraswat societies. Yet he pointed to the failure of other cooperative housing societies that had attempted a wider definition of community. In particular, he pointed to the Hindu Cooperative Housing Society, which had taken extensive Improvement Trust lands in Matunga with an ambitious scheme but which had foundered, and he used the Hindu society's failure to support the Saraswat policy of restriction.[21] In fact the Bombay Hindu Cooperative Housing Society had been floated by S. S. Talmaki himself, the same person who had been the driving force in the Saraswat society. Talmaki had sought to broaden the definition of community and had applied to the Improvement Trust for several plots of land in Dadar–Matunga, probably hoping to attract a wider audience.[22]

Yet even if the early cooperative societies of the Saraswats were able to retain their restrictive membership policies, it must also be noted that the definition of community contained in the category Saraswat did not remain unchanged. Frank Conlon has noted that the Shamrao Vithal Cooperative Credit Society restricted participation not strictly to Saraswats but, rather, to a group defined as "members of the community of Shamrao Vithal." By defining the community thus, instead of using a strict *jati* (subcaste) definition, the society was able to avoid the critical issue of whether or not a particular section of excommunicant *Bhanaps* (a certain subset of Saraswat Brahmins) were properly part of the Saraswat *jati* and thus to widen the constituency of the credit society.[23] This represented an adjustment in strict *jati* definitions in order to secure a wider constituency within the urban context. Thus, a category as broad as "Hindu Cooperative Housing Society" was too broad to succeed, but a strict definition of "Saraswat" might be too restrictive and needed to be adjusted in order to recruit an adequate number of members.[24]

Such adjustments in the definition of community for the purposes of constituting sustainable cooperative societies were not uncommon; indeed, they became the norm. Another excellent instance of such an adjustment took place in the Parsi community, also very active in the settlement of Dadar–Matunga. The Parsi community was far more homogeneous and cohesive as a community than the South Indian. Tanya Luhrmann has shown, however, that even within the small and cohesive Parsi community differences arose over interpretations of doctrine, questions of assimilation, and so on.[25] For Luhrmann, such differences are functions of mobility and of the diasporic condition, where a community such as the Parsis, despite the fact that they have been settled in the Indian subcontinent for over a thousand years, still consider themselves "outsiders in an adopted land."[26]

Yet mobility yielded not just repeated assertions of difference but also moments when differences were submerged in order to adjust to circumstances that mobility had brought with it. Consider the case of the unwieldily named Parsi Central Association Cooperative Housing Society, one of the principal cooperative societies providing housing for Parsis in the Parsi Colony sector of Dadar–Matunga.[27] Founded during the years of the boom in land prices, the PCACHS struggled to attract membership in the years following the collapse of the boom. In 1925, in advance of the annual general meeting of the society, a critical item was introduced into the meeting's agenda: It was proposed to modify the bylaws of the society in the following way: "In bye-law 7 (i) (a) the words 'or Iranian' be inserted between 'Parsi' and 'community' and 'is a Zorastrian by faith' be added at the end."[28] This seemingly minor modification in an important bylaw that defined the community of persons who could belong to the cooperative society actually reflected a significant compromise. For a long time, the Parsi community had distinguished itself from the Irani community. The former were the descendents of the original migrants from Persia, who arrived in western India over a thousand years ago and prospered under British rule. The Iranis, on the other hand, were much more recent migrants from Persia, arriving in the nineteenth century, also Zorastrian by faith. For much of the nineteenth century and into the twentieth century, the Parsis had considered themselves "true" Zorastrians and deemed the Iranis' faith questionable. The proposed modification in the bylaws thus was extremely significant. Although the Iranis were not quite included into the category "Parsi," they were now acknowledged as "Zorastrian[s] by faith." The exigencies of cooperative living thus created a larger identity that straddled the Parsi–Irani distinction.

A similar pattern was discernible among the city's various Catholic communities. They were, along with the Saraswats and the Parsis, pioneering cooperators. During the boom period in cooperative housing, which coincided with the boom period in post–World War I Bombay, the city's various Catholic communities had attempted to form cooperative societies. The city's three main Catholic communities were the East Indians, the Goans, and the Mangaloreans. The East Indians were original inhabitants of the Bombay region converted by the Portuguese, while the Goan and Mangalorean Catholics, also converted by the Portuguese, came from Goa and Mangalore. Early attempts were thus organized on the basis of specific native place connections, which still seemed to be the dominant identities under which the city's Catholics understood themselves: the Mangalorean Christian Cooperative Housing Society, the Goan Colony, and so on. These attempts had foundered by the late 1910s, mostly because of difficulties in recruiting enough members. The different communities really came together in a self-conscious fashion under the "Catholic" banner when they formed the Bombay Catholic Cooperative Housing Society in Santa Cruz, a suburb in Salsette, in 1916.[29] This effort was followed shortly by the Salsette Catholic Cooperative Housing Society and the Saint Sebastian Homes Cooperative Society.[30] The significance of these institutions lay not just in the fact that they were early successful instances of cooperative housing societies but also in the fact that by naming themselves "Catholic" societies, they represented a significant shift in the self-understanding of the members of these societies. In response to the exigencies of urban living and specifically of founding a sustainable housing society, the members now saw themselves as Catholic in a broader sense, and not just as East Indians or Goans or Mangaloreans who also happened to be Catholic. Catholicism, thus, became a metacategory that now signified their presence in Bombay, and it was as members of the Catholic community that these people negotiated the other communities of Bombay.

South Indian had become such a metacategory by the late 1920s, even more encompassing in its sweep. The South Indians, as discussed earlier, started coming to the city later than the communities discussed so far: Saraswats, Parsis, and Catholic. Some of the Catholics were indigenous to the Bombay region while the Parsis were among the earliest settlers in the late seventeenth and early eighteenth centuries. The Goans and Saraswats, meanwhile, had been coming to Bombay from the mid-nineteenth century onward.[31] In Matunga there were at first three important cooperative societies: the South Indian Cooperative Credit Society, the South Indian Cooperative Housing Society, and South Indian Consumer Cooperative Society. Each of these, in different ways, sought to accommodate the special needs of its clientele.

The South Indian Cooperative Credit Society is the oldest society in Matunga. It was founded in 1919 in south Bombay and moved into its premises in Matunga in 1932. Conversations with longtime members of the society suggest that the membership in the early decades of its existence was exclusively Brahmin, although it included Palakkad Iyers, Iyengars, Thanjavur and Tirunelveli Iyers, and Namboothiris. The society, whose recent brochure advertises "85 years of ethnic banking," started off by taking jewelry as security and then making small loans to its members. Initially, as mentioned in chapter 2, these loans were made so members could pay for their annual trips home without resorting to drastic measures. Subsequently, these moneys would be used for things like paying rental deposits, conducting *poojas* (prayers and offerings to a deity), making trips back to the south, or paying for weddings or *arangethrams* (a celebration on the occasion of a girl's first public dance performance). I asked Raghavan Sarathy, the chairman of the bank and a third-generation member, whether providing such community-specific services gave the bank its "ethnic identity."[32] He replied, "Yes, yes, that is all true. But we also *give* them identity. Identity begins first when you can open a bank account. Identity begins when you get a ration card." For Sarathy the "ethnicity" of his bank did not consist only in reinforcing something called "culture." By drawing people into the bureaucratic web of the modern city—getting them bank accounts and ration cards—the bank is integrating them into the apparatus of an urban middle class. This also is part of ethnic banking.

If integration into the urban middle class was a part of becoming South Indian, the process also entailed a redefinition of community. I had initially thought that all the members of the South Indian Cooperative Housing Society were Iyers, since all the names of the people I had met were Iyer names. When I asked Ramachandran about this, he told me that the people who founded the building were all Southies. I mentioned to him that I had thought that they were all Iyers. He replied, "No, no, they were speaking different languages and all. There were two or three Kannadigas and all. That's where the adjustment takes place." I asked him what he meant by "adjustment," and he replied, "These fellows couldn't fully stick with the old ways. They had to adjust. Tamil or Kannada doesn't matter in the cooperative society. Important thing is that they feel they are from the same community. Most important for that is that non-veg food should not be taken."[33]

Ramachandran suggests that in the city, the old rigorous caste purity could not be maintained: sufficient members needed to be found who could afford to pay for their shares in the society, and if this meant that there had to be some Kannadigas involved, then it had to be so. A new baseline for caste purity needed to be established, and in the context of apartment buildings, with their greater densities, the decisive variable became food preparation. The odors of nonvegetarian food wafting through the corridors of the building became the line that could not be crossed. And so Saraswat Brahmins, who are Brahmins from the southern part of India, are often not included within the category South Indian because they are one of the three kinds of Brahmins, along with Kashmiri and Bengali, who are allowed to eat fish. (Incidentally, the original lease of the society indicates that of the thirteen charter members, four were non-Tamil Brahmins.)

The costs associated with cooperative societies would often necessitate a widening of the understanding of community. During the 1930s, for example, trouble beset the South Indian Consumer Cooperative Society. The annual reports of the Registrar of Cooperative Societies indicate a chronic difficulty, throughout the Depression-era 1930s, in securing funds and recruiting members. When I asked my three oldest informants—all of whom moved to Matunga as young men in the late 1920s or early 1930s—they said that it was difficult for them in those days to afford to purchase supplies from the store. Rajagopalan is the oldest person I spoke to; he moved to Bombay in 1928 as a young man of twenty. He described to me how much of a relief it was for him to move from his chawl (tenement) dwelling in Dadar to his flat in Matunga. For him the middle classes should not be living in chawls; they should be living in flats. (Paradoxically, he probably had less room in the flat than he had had in the tenement, since he moved into a one-bedroom apartment with his wife and two children and his brother's family of five. In the tenement he had shared the two rooms with five other single men.)[34]

But when I asked him whether he had been active in the South Indian Consumer Cooperative Society, he scoffed at the idea. "These people want you to pay up front. Where could we afford that. We were buying provisions from the *bania* [subcaste of money lenders] and paying on arrearage." As a result of considerations such as these, the Matunga cooperatives began to widen their membership base. They began to recognize the category of Brahmin from southern India as being more salient than Palakkad Iyer or Iyengar from Mysore.

While it made economic sense to widen the definition of the category South Indian, it also made good political sense. Such consolidation of identity could prove useful in the metropolis: at times conditions could lead a community to seek to define itself in much broader terms. Mention has already been made in chapter 2 of the nascent feeling of resentment among the Marathi-speaking middle class—as early as the middle 1930s—over the fact that the educated Brahmins from southern India were establishing a stranglehold on the clerical jobs in the city. As already noted in chapter 2, Bhonsle ascribed this dominance to the South Indians' seeming willingness to work for wages very close to those of the industrial working class and to their superior skills; his thoughts and language would be echoed thirty years later by Bal Thackeray when he launched the Shiv Sena in Shivaji Park, across the train tracks from Matunga.

A similar sentiment can be found in the following extract from a letter written by a native-born Bombay resident to the *Bombay Chronicle* newspaper. The letter was titled "Long Suffering Middle Classes of Bombay," and its writer, one S. Rajadhyax, argued:

In Bombay the number of educated unemployed is daily increasing. . . . Cruel poverty and privation are the lots of the educated Bombayites, who claim every right of citizenship as they were born and brought up in this Presidency. This is the state of affairs due to the negligence on the part of the Government and the leaders. They seem to have been above having a little bit of local pride.[35]

Rajadhyax wanted the government to restrict eligibility for jobs on the basis of region of origin—jobs in the Bombay Presidency should be kept for those "born and brought up" in the presidency. "Local pride" is a euphemism for nativism. He too was implicitly pointing to the overwhelming presence of people from southern India in those jobs that were most suitable for the educated—jobs as clerks, cashiers, accountants, and so forth.

In the face of such sentiment, by 1944, leaders of the South Indian community were already calling for solidarity among the South Indians in Bombay. At the South Indian Association's ball badminton tournament's prize-giving function, held in conjunction with the association's open carom tournament, the journalist and community leader V. K. Menon issued a "plea for unity among South Indians."[36] After praising the virtues of carom as offering leisure and relaxation to South Indian families in the big city, "where life was so crowded and the period of leisure and relaxation was so small," he moved smoothly to exhorting the unity of South Indians:

South Indians in Bombay constitute a considerable community. They live in all parts of the city and its near suburbs. Their conditions too vary according to the circumstances of their life and work. But removed as we all are from our homes—and in whatever conditions we may be placed—there runs within us all a chord of fundamental unity and comradeship. There are different associations in different parts of the city and suburbs which in one way or another contribute to our organization. Is it not possible for us to mould out of these various associations a unity of interest? As a first step, I would suggest efforts should be made to have a conference of all South Indians in this city and there develop a central body which can be made the basis of common activities of common interest and thus develop in the direction of all out unity. Such unity and the united endeavor that emerges out of it can alone serve as a sheet anchor for us in the difficult times through which we are passing, as also in the more difficult times that are ahead of us.[37]

This remarkable passage actually seeks to establish what it claims already existed. Consider how the passage begins: "South Indians in Bombay constitute a considerable community." Yet what was the nature of the community? As yet, it consisted of people who came from the southern parts of India. These people were divided by language, caste, and religion. Indeed, the speaker in this instance, a Malayalam-speaking Menon from Kerala, would have had caste, dietary, and linguistic differences from the Tamil-speaking Iyers who were the hegemonic component of the South Indian community, in addition to the class differences that would have differentiated persons of different means, and which Menon notes. Yet, despite all these caste, linguistic, and class differences, there still "runs within us all a chord of fundamental unity and comradeship." What would this consist of? The fact of being originally from a (very large) geographic region (southern India) and being in a condition "removed . . . from our homes" (that is, of having migrated to Bombay) are what Menon suggests are the bonds that South Indians share. The caste and linguistic differences would have been negotiated to some extent by the cooperative societies, as described earlier in the chapter. Yet what would truly constitute the "chord of fundamental unity and comradeship" among these highly disparate people thrown together in Bombay? What are the "difficult times" through which the South Indian community was passing, and what are the "more difficult times" that lie ahead?

An answer is provided in the remarks made by Pothan Joseph, an extremely well-known South Indian journalist in Bombay and editor of the *Dawn* newspaper. At a speech Joseph made in the Keraleeya Samaj, just about three weeks after these remarks by V. K. Menon, Joseph sought to trace the "story of immigration of South Indians" to Bombay.[38] The very fact that, by 1944, it was considered necessary to trace the history of South Indian migration to the city suggests that the community was already well consolidated. Joseph began by identifying some of the early pioneers of the community in Bombay, including some Keralite names—Joseph Mathai, Dr. Nair—as well as some Tamil Iyer names, such as K. S. Ramachandra Iyer (a well-known figure in the insurance business) and K. Natarajan (the founder of the *Indian Social Reformer* and a longtime social activist in Bombay). He identified the real beginning of mass South Indian immigration as the post–World War I period. Most telling in this speech was his attempt to address the criticisms, which clearly had been building up, that "people from the south" were undercutting wages in Bombay (as pointed out by Bhonsle) and taking away all the clerical/white-collar jobs. Joseph pointed to himself as evidence that South Indians were able to maintain a decent standard of living (and thus that they were not undercutting wages by living in sub-middle-class conditions, which presumably was what critics such as Bhonsle and Rajadhyax had been alleging). "We have been here and we have to remain here for a pretty long time because we cannot be bottled up in the south," he argued. He concluded by praising the work ethic of the "people from Malabar" and by urging them to keep up with their diligence and proficiency in the English language, the two factors that he identified as lying at the heart of their success in Bombay.

Joseph's account of South Indians is in some ways even more extraordinary than Menon's because, as his name indicates, Joseph was a Christian. He was thus even further removed from the Palakkad Iyers that considered themselves the core of the South Indian community. Yet what binds Joseph and all "people from Malabar" to the Palakkad Iyers is the fact that, as both Menon and Joseph indicate, they are perceived as a threat by "sons of the Presidency" such as Bhonsle and Rajadhyax. They were bound together in Bombay by the fact that despite the great disparities among them, they all happened to be well educated in English and had been able to take control of the white-collar sector in Bombay. This led them to be perceived as a threat by the educated Marathi- and English-speaking groups in the city. At the most general level, it was ultimately a shared white-collar lower-middle-class identity that bound the disparate groups of migrants from southern India together in the Bombay context. The most general definition of South Indian in Bombay—of a generally upper-caste, educated middle class—was thus generated in the context of the hostility faced by people from southern India on account of their rapid ascent in the new white-collar professions. The apprehensions expressed by Menon and Joseph here were borne out twenty years later when the Shiv Sena Party mounted its first campaigns on the basis of an anti–South Indian platform.

✒ FRAGMENTATION

Indeed, it is noteworthy that when the Shiv Sena did propel itself into the spotlight on an anti–South Indian springboard, using the term "South Indian" to designate the offending group, not all people from southern India were necessarily contained within this category.[39] Thus when Bal Thackeray ranted against the South Indians in the 1960s, he meant the upper-caste middle and lower middle classes of Matunga, who by virtue of their education had allegedly monopolized the white-collar jobs that Thackeray wanted to claim for the "sons of the soil." Such a definition of "South Indian" did not usually include the large non-Brahmin Tamilian population of Dharavi, across the train tracks to the west from Matunga.[40] Such a specific referent of the signifier "South Indian"—upper-caste middle class, living in flats in Matunga as opposed to huts in Dharavi or chawls in other parts of the city—was the outcome of a self-fashioning process that had been under way since the formation of the first South Indian cooperative societies in the 1920s and that continued in the discussions over the need to maintain South Indian unity in the face of local resentment. Such a self-fashioned South Indian identity was, crucially, upper-caste (mostly Brahmin) and middle-class. Hence, excluding lower castes and the working classes was part of the work of self-fashioning.

Excluding the lower castes and the working class was significant because Matunga was bounded to the south by the working-class areas of Parel and Lalbaug, with their streetscapes of mills and chawls, and to the west by the growing informal settlement of Dharavi. (Wadala to the east of Matunga and Sion to the north were not yet developed in the period under discussion.) Dharavi, to the west, especially, had a peculiar relationship to Matunga. A very large number of the residents of Dharavi were from the Tirunelveli district in Madras Presidency and were Tamil speakers.[41] But they did not fit into the hegemonic understanding of South Indian that was gaining circulation by the 1930s and that was deployed by South Indians themselves as well as by those who sought to demonize them, such as the Shiv Sena. Indeed, as will be argued below, the upper-caste lower-middle-class identity of South Indian Matunga was fashioned in opposition to the lower-caste laboring presence of Dharavi across the train tracks. The spatial location of Matunga in the north of the island city thus played a role in the constitution of South Indian identity.

The Tamils of Dharavi were either low-caste Hindu or Muslim or Christian. The Hindu Tamils were either Adi Dravidas, a scheduled caste; or Nadars, a toddy-tapper caste; or Thevars, an OBC (Other Backward Class) caste. Some of these Tamils came to Bombay as early as the late nineteenth century, but at least some of them were among the migrants who came to Bombay following a devastating famine outbreak in the Deccan in 1920.[42] When city officialdom pondered the problem of what to do with them, the possibility of their employment in the Trust's projects was brought up. The officers of the Trust appreciated such a ready-to-hand supply of labor, and soon at least 4,500 of these refugees were put to work in the arduous task of draining and clearing the lands of Dadar–Matunga for settlement.[43] These workers were housed in 1,200 "semi-permanent" rooms in Matunga from 1921 onward.[44] After a decade, however, as Matunga began to develop into a middle-class suburb, the huts of the laborers who laid the foundations of Matunga were perceived as an obstruction. They were moved literally across the tracks into a new labor camp in Dharavi. As Jamnadas Mehta, mayor of Bombay, recalled in an address he gave at the inauguration of the new labor camp in Dharavi in 1937:

> Recently, however, it was felt that the sheds [housing the laborers in Matunga] had run out of their life and it was no longer possible to keep them in good repair at reasonable cost. Further, in view of the development of the surrounding locality, a demand for the land on which these sheds stood was likely to arise in near future. The municipality, however, were reluctant to dishouse the people in occupation. It was, therefore, decided to provide suitable accommodation for them in the neighbourhood.[45]

The new labor camp, even though it was located in Dharavi, came to be called Matunga Labour Camp, presumably in view of its original location and also in view of the critical role that its inhabitants had played in the construction of Matunga.

A classic pattern was established: the labor force that was responsible for developing an area was initially housed there to minimize transportation costs and time. After years of being there, however, the workers' settlement was perceived as a blight on the middle-class landscape of the emerging neighborhood and needed to be relocated. Jamnadas Mehta sought to cast the relocation in a positive light by claiming that alternative accommodation was being provided for them "in the neighbourhood." Yet while Dharavi was and is physically proximate to Matunga, it would be very difficult to see these two places as "in the neighbourhood" of one another.

Where exactly in Dharavi were the laborers relocated from Matunga? It turned out that there had originally been a scheme to redevelop Dharavi along suburban lines just as there had been schemes for Dadar, Matunga, and Sion. But, as Jamnadas Mehta pointed out in his speech, since "the Dharavi scheme of the Trust had been abandoned . . . [this land] was considered suitable" for the purpose of rehousing the Matunga laborers.[46] The more elaborate Dharavi scheme had never taken off; it was replaced by Scheme 56, the Labour Camp, in the 1930s. In a certain sense, the original Dharavi scheme was sacrificed so that the Dadar–Matunga–Sion schemes could go on. At a critical juncture, when equipment for the ongoing projects in Dadar–Matunga was in short supply, certain key inputs were diverted from the Dharavi scheme to the Matunga scheme. Specifically, locomotives and rolling stock for work in Matunga "were obtained by transferring a portion of the plant brought out from England for the Dharavi scheme."[47] The Trust announced, opaquely, that "for motives of policy and finance it was decided to proceed slowly" with the Dharavi scheme.[48] It turned out that the Trust was actually moving slowly in Dharavi because it was already settled by tannery workers, who were putting up some resistance to being relocated.[49] This illustrates yet again two patterns in the Trust's operations: first, its ongoing difficulties in conducting operations in settled parts of the city (as argued in chapter 1, this was why the Trust had turned from redeveloping the inner city to developing the suburbs to begin with), and second, its favoring of the suburban schemes of Dadar–Matunga over schemes in poorer parts of the city, such as Dharavi.

The relocation of laborers from Matunga to Dharavi signified a process by which Dharavi and Matunga constituted one another (quite literally, in the sense of Dharavi's laborers laying the foundations of Matunga). If Matunga residents began to understand their neighborhood as middle-class and upper-caste people housed in apartment buildings, they did so in opposition to Dharavi, which consisted of laboring classes who were, importantly, of low caste, living in "semi-permanent" huts in areas that would soon be termed slums. I have been arguing that the suburbs were constitutive of the city. But there is a way in which the slum is prior even to this process, a way in which the whole idea of the city is constituted by its negation, the slum. For Matunga, this opposition was especially salient since the South Indian upper-caste middle classes of Matunga shared not only the Tamil language with some residents of Dharavi, but also origins in southern India.

A rare documented moment of interaction between the South Indians of Matunga and the Tamils of Dharavi took place in 1935, when the journalist and Congress Socialist leader C. K. Narayanswami was invited to open a Tamil reading room for tannery workers in Dharavi.[50] Narayanswami was a Tamil Brahmin from Matunga and was active in Gandhian political activities, especially the promotion of Khadi and of working toward "Harijan uplift."[51] Narayanswami's speech, as well as the speech of Purshottamdas Tricumdas, secretary of the Congress Socialists, were both filled with tirades against the "vested interests" in the Municipal Corporation who were responsible for the "scandalous housing conditions" and the "insanitary surroundings" in Dharavi. Narayanswami's address was especially significant. He began by saying how good it was to be back with the tannery workers, whom he had worked with five years earlier protesting wage cuts in Dharavi's leather factories. He recalled that "that agitation had a glorious end" in the formation of a union and the calling of a strike, which, in turn, had not only averted the wage cuts but secured wage increases. Following this success, however, due to their "ignorance and fear of losing their jobs," the class consciousness the tannery workers had displayed in forming the union had crumbled, and now they were once again exploited. "From the reading room to the study circle is only one step," noted Naryanswami, and he urged his audience to use the reading room to "create a new consciousness," which in turn would "give them the strength which was inherent in them."

Narayanswami was a remarkable man. Unlike many of his middle-class peers in Matunga, he threw himself into the anticolonial movement and was a committed Gandhian socialist.[52] (At times he appeared more socialist than Gandhian.) Although he was a prominent invitee and participant in functions of the South Indian community in Matunga, he seems to have maintained an oblique position with respect to the community. When he was invited to speak at the farewell ceremony for Krishna Iyer, another prominent member of the community who had been one of the forces driving the South Indian Cooperative Housing Society, Narayanswami took the opportunity to criticize the passive political stance of his fellow South Indians.[53] He was especially committed to fighting discrimination against untouchables. In recounting his involvement with the Provincial Conference in Kerala in 1923, following the Moplah Rebellion, Narayanswami recounted that he had participated in interdining with untouchables at the conference.[54] As a result, when he returned to his village in another part of Kerala, presumably the Palakkad district, he was "excommunicated and . . . asked to do certain propitiations and other ceremonies in order to purify [himself] from the pollution of having participated in the inter-dining."[55] (He refused.)

For all these reasons, it is all the more remarkable that in his speech at the opening of the Tamil reading room, he made no mention of the fact that the reading room was a *Tamil* reading room, that Tamil was his own language, and that thus, in principle, there could have been some connection between the tannery workers and himself. Indeed, it is not even clear that he addressed the tannery workers in Tamil. The article in the *Bombay Chronicle* reproduced the speeches of both Narayanswami and Tricumdas; Tricumdas would certainly not have been speaking Tamil, and the article made no mention of the speeches being in different languages.[56] For Narayanswami, the tannery workers, because of "ignorance and fear of losing their jobs," were obstructing the "mighty world force, the force of the organized workers of the world fighting for Socialism."[57] Narayanswami's view of the tanners exclusively as workers arose partly from his socialist leanings but also, I argue, from the way South Indian identity was constructed in Bombay. For upper-caste middle-class South Indians such as Narayanswami, their South-Indianness was firmly anchored in their caste and class backgrounds, as well as their residence in Matunga. Thus the Tamil language that he shared with the tannery workers, normally a powerful forger of bonds even among people separated by class position, was not adequate to make Narayanswami recognize the tannery workers as belonging to his own community. His perception of them as workers and only workers, not fellow Tamil speakers, was made possible by a specific understanding of his community as the South Indian community, which by definition could not have included low-caste laborers within it.

Caste difference as a critical factor marking the limits of inclusiveness of the category South Indian might seem obvious, but even within the group of people who considered themselves South Indians, fissures appeared and were emphasized over the years of living in Bombay. Cooperative societies were not the only kinds of institutions established by the South Indians in Matunga. A look at another category of institutions suggests that while there was a widening of community definitions through the cooperative institutions, there was also the establishment of difference within the community. Some of the well-known South Indian institutions in Matunga include temples such as Asthika Samaj and the Bhajana Samaj, cultural institutions such as the Shanmukhananda Sangeetha and Fine Arts Sabha, and educational institutions such as the South Indian Education Society. These institutions played important roles in the South Indian life of Matunga, but they tended to legitimate their presence in different ways. Some reify the presence, in Matunga, of people from southern India. A historical account of the Asthika Samaj, one of the most important and popular temples in the neighborhood, argues:

The historical importance of the place can be traced from the fact that the place now known as Matunga was previously the abode of Mathangarishi who after performing the Mahayagnas on the banks of the Pumpa acquired the coveted status of Maharishi. As a vestige of the ancient past, the Banyan tree exists even to this date fulfilling the desires of thousands of devotees.[58]

By locating the "historical importance of the place" securely in the cosmology of the current constituency of the temple before moving on to talk about the samaj's founding in 1932, the Asthika Samaj's self-understanding moves fluently from mythic time into historical time. In this understanding, the space of Matunga has always been of significance for the Brahmins of southern India, and it was only historical accident that delayed the founding of the building until the 1930s.

Another trend is the way the membership of some of these institutions, while using the "South Indian" label, actually tended to be dominated by members of certain subgroups, such as Palakkad or Tirunelveli Iyers. Indeed, there is a clear breakdown in the Matunga institutions: the Asthika Samaj, the South Indian Welfare Society, and the Model Cooperative Society tended to be dominated by Palakkad Iyers, whereas the Bhajana Samaj, the South Indian Education Society, and the South Indian Concerns tended to be dominated by Tirunelveli and Thanjavur Iyers.

The history of the Palakkad Iyers has not yet been written, but they are the dominant group in the larger community in Matunga that describes itself as "South Indian." Palakkad Iyers were the only community whose members asserted that they were the founding community in Matunga. Palakkad Iyers were themselves a subset of a larger community that described itself as "Kerala Iyers." These were Iyers from what is now Tamil Nadu (and what was then the Tamil-speaking parts of Madras Presidency) who migrated to the Malayalam-speaking areas around Cochin and Travancore, probably in the seventeenth and eighteenth centuries. They were drawn by attractive offers from the maharajas of these states, who, perhaps, were engaged in disputes with indigenous Brahmin castes such as the Namboodiris. Alternatively, they might have fled, one step ahead of the conquering Maratha armies. Indeed, this earlier history of migration was often adduced to explain the flexibility and adaptability displayed by the Palakkad Iyers in their migration to Bombay. As S. Ramachandran put it to me:

The Kerala Brahmin was the greatest immigrant, having migrated to Kerala from Thanjavur or Trichi. About three hundred years ago, when Shivaji Maharaj conquered that whole area. *Yenga appa sollava: Nanga Thanjavur lendu odi ponnom* [Our father used to say: we went running from Thanjavur].[59]

Ramachandran here represents a version of the often-repeated thesis regarding the Tamil Brahmin's distinctive attribute of mobility and adaptability. He also emphasizes the extra special qualifications of the Kerala Brahmins, who had already made the disruptive move to another linguistic world (to a Malayalam-speaking world) in the seventeenth century.

It was the architect Kamu Iyer who first argued to me that the Brahmin was always given to migrating, citing the examples of his great-grandfather, grandfather, and father, all of whom had taken jobs in various parts of Madras Presidency. They initially worked in the employ of various local rulers, and finally his father took up a job in an office in Bombay and settled down in Matunga. Indeed, Kamu Iyer's family's story shows how difficult it can be to identify the origins of some of these Brahmin families. Kamu Iyer's great-grandfather was originally "from" a place called Ramanathapuram near Madurai, where he was a poet and Sanskrit scholar enjoying the patronage of the local ruler. As was common practice, he had received a grant of some land in a place called Vettalaikondu, at the base of the Kodaikanal range, where Kamu Iyer's grandfather was born. Kamu Iyer's grandfather was schooled in Vettalaikondu but then made his way to Madras and managed to graduate from college, even though his own father had forbidden him to learn English (possibly an unusual case for Brahmins in Madras Presidency). He then joined the colonial Indian Educational Service, probably around 1895, and made a stop first in Pudukkottai and then in Tiruvayur, near Thanjavur, the birthplace of Sri Thyagaraja, which is where Kamu Iyer's father was born. The family then moved to Trichinopoly, where Kamu Iyer's father graduated from St. Xavier's College before coming to Bombay in 1921. In Bombay, he first lived in the Improvement Trust tenements in Matunga—the so-called BIT blocks. He then moved to Bandra, where he lived for a few years before returning in 1932 to live in an apartment building in Dadar Hindu Colony, on the very edge of Matunga. In 1941 he moved to the Gold Finch Building, which is across the Ambedkar Road from Matunga proper, to the apartment where Kamu Iyer still lives today. Kamu Iyer's maternal grandfather retired in 1935 as a deputy accountant general in the colonial service, a very high post for an Indian. As a result of his employment, he had moved around a great deal, to various postings including Delhi and Nagpur, and Kamu Iyer's mother had been born in Rangoon.

The degree of mobility displayed here might be partly attributed to the fact that Kamu Iyer's ancestors were highly educated and accomplished and availed themselves of opportunities all around the presidency. Yet it is reasonable to assume that a certain degree of mobility among such Brahmins would have been typical, rather than exceptional. "The Brahmin was not wedded to his land the way in which other castes were," Kamu Iyer asserted.[60] Indeed, many of my informants, when asked which temple in Matunga they visited regularly, would respond that in fact they never needed to visit temples since they carried their gods with them at home. Then they would point to the many portraits of the gods lining the walls of their homes.[61]

Two primary strands of Brahmins seem to have migrated to Kerala. The first are referred to as "TTKs"—Iyers from Trichy, Thanjavur, and Kumbakonam, the more northern parts of Tamil country, who migrated via Coimbatore and the Walayar Hills into the Palakkad district in present-day Kerala. Another group of Iyers from the southern parts of Tamil country—"TMs," or the Tirunelveli and Madurai group—migrated via Shenkottai Pass to the southern parts of Kerala, especially Cochin and Trivandrum. In Palakkad, the Iyers initially occupied a few villages, which soon multiplied to as many as ninety-six villages. Here they developed a syncretic culture, fusing the traditions of Smartha-Iyer Brahminism with the linguistic and cultural practices of the place they found themselves in.[62] The Malayalam language became an essential part of their world: in public life they would use Malayalam, whereas at home they spoke a kind of Tamil that incorporated significant elements from Malayalam. Most importantly, they wrote Tamil using the Malayalam script. Eventually this community would also spill over into the Trichur district, also in north-central Kerala.

When the Palakkad Iyers came to Bombay from the 1920s onward, they maintained their syncretic tradition. S. Ramachandran, who attended the South Indian Education Society's school all through his education, was in primary school in the middle of the 1940s. There were four Malayalam-language sections and two Tamil-language sections through fourth grade, after which the medium of education switched to English. The emphasis on Malayalam was primarily because of the heavy presence of the Palakkad Iyers in Matunga. Yet though the Iyers of Palakkad were stamped with a Malayali linguistic culture, the non-Iyer Keralites were also influenced by Tamil culture. S. Ramachandran told me of Narayana Menon, a past president of the Keraleeya Samaj.[63] Menon was not an Iyer and was a native Malayalam speaker, but whenever he ran into Ramachandran on the road, he would yell out in perfectly modulated Brahmin-dialect Tamil slang, "Yendaa Ramu, yenna pannindirkai?" (What's up Ramu? What are you doing with yourself these days?)

Ultimately, differences came to a head between the various groups in the SIES school. Just as there had been a break between the South Indian Consumer Cooperative Society (dominated by Palakkad Iyers) and the South Indian Concerns (dominated by the Tamil Iyers), similarly a civil war broke out among the trustees of the SIES. A walkout was staged, lead by Dr. S. R. Ramachandran, a sometime-textile commissioner and a leading light at the Victoria Jubilee Technical Institute and the University Department of Chemical Technology (and no relation to my present-day informant S. Ramachandran). The breakaway faction then formed the South Indian Welfare Society, which became a rival educational establishment to the SIES school.[64]

A similar divide developed between the Tamil Iyers and the Kerala Iyers over the issue of temples. As described in chapter 2, both the Asthika Samaj and the Bhajana Samaj were active by the mid-1930s. The Asthika Samaj, however, became associated more closely with the Kerala Iyers, whereas the Bhajana Samaj became more closely associated with the Tamil Iyers. The Asthika Samaj would have functions to celebrate Kerala festivals such as Onam and Vishu, on account of the syncretic culture of the Palakkad Iyers. The Bhajana Samaj, on the other hand, would not have marked the occasion of Onam in any special way; it would celebrate the traditional Tamil functions such as Pongal. In addition, the Asthika Samaj would invite Namboothiri Brahmins to conduct discourses on texts such as the Bhagavad Gita, as on the occasion in 1939 when the Asthika Samaj invited Brahmashree Vazhunnatha Vasudevan Namboodiri of Guruvayoor to conduct daily discourses on the Bhagavad Gita for an entire month.[65] Indeed, the Asthika Samaj and its patrons had always had a much stronger tradition of worship of Gurvayoorappan, the incarnation of Lord Krishna housed in the Guruvayoor Temple in the Thrissur district of Kerala (which was another stronghold of the Kerala Iyers). The Bhajana Samaj, on the other hand, was more oriented to Tamil Nadu–based deities.

All these differences notwithstanding, the context in which the category of South Indian was most thoroughly deconstructed was marriage. This was the domain of urban life where the most particularistic forms of identity would be asserted, with peculiar twists that could only occur in the context of a metropolis like Bombay. Usually, marriages were contracted through the offices of local astrologers. Parents might approach the astrologer with their offspring's horoscope. Upon looking at it, the astrologer would be able to draw upon a large selection of compatible horoscopes and offer them to the parents, who would work through them and possibly identify someone whose coordinates of subcaste, occupation and income, housing situation, and skin color were all suitable. The astrologer was thus different from a marriage broker. He established a basic harmony at the level of caste and so on, but considerable agency remained at the level of the parents. Further, the astrologer was never actually paid for his services; he would usually receive a gift of some sort. Indeed, usually the astrologers were retired men who had had successful careers in white-collar professions and then settled into astrology and matchmaking. S. Ramachandran, for instance, had had his match arranged by a local Matunga astrologer by the name of Pudukottai Joshiar. (The name is not very revealing: all it indicates is the name of the place where the person came from and his occupation. *Joshiar* is the Tamil word for "astrologer.") Another prominent astrologer was a man described to me as *Vakola mama* (literally, "Vakola Uncle"; Vakola is a suburb outside the island city, near Santa Cruz). One of my own informants, P. Chari, in his midnineties when I interviewed him, was very active as a *joshiar*.[66]

These marriages followed endogamy within the subcaste, but rigorous exogamy among *gotrams,* or clans. Consider, for instance, the following advertisement, which was placed in the Classified section of the *Bombay Chronicle* in 1938:

> Wanted: A bachelor of not over thirty years of age, in earning capacity, belonging to South Indian Brahmin community, Vadamma, other than Koundinya gotram, to marry a very fair accomplished and educated daughter of an officer in Bombay.[67]

In itself, the use of a classified advertisement was an anomaly; the usual course was to approach a local astrologer. The advertisement is revealing: it begins with a requirement that the prospective groom belong to the South Indian Brahmin community. Note that "South Indian Brahmin" is the way the community is defined: it is assumed that the three terms go together. It does not ask for a Brahmin from the South Indian community, for instance, which would allow for the possibility that there were non-Brahmins in the community of South Indians. But the specification does not end there; the next step is to specify the Vadamma subgroup, which is a subcategory of Iyers, itself a subcategory of Brahmins. And finally, the advertisement specifies that the prospective groom be from outside the Koundinya *gotram,* according to standard exogamy practice.[68]

Yet even this highly specialized degree of differentiation was not the end of it. In Matunga, a further division was opened up between the Palakkad Iyers and the Tamil Iyers. S. Ramachandran, for instance, told me that the main reason for the differences was because of the very different kinds of food: "the Palakkad Brahmin was gregarious, garrulous, hard working, and a great eater. 100 percent there is a difference in the cuisine of Palakkad and Chennai. *Ange puli thaan. Ingay irikarai vegetables* . . . any number of vegetables." (There [among the Tamil Iyers] the food is all about tamarind. Here the variety of vegetables . . .). This difference in the food was, according to Ramachandran, a crucial factor in determining marriage alliances:

> The Kerala Brahmin would not give his daughter to a Chennai Brahmin. *Patni podavaalaam.* They will be starved. *Avarrodu vitulai Pappadam podavalaam. Rasatha vepaalaam. Pulivalatha vapalaam Vadaam podavaal.* Vegetable *onnum kadaikyadu.* [They will starve. In their houses, (the Chennai Brahmin) will serve pappadams, rasam, all things with tamarind, vadaams. [You] won't get any vegetables.][69]

Although Ramachandran's emphasis on food here might be overstated, it clearly indicates that food represented a distillation of the differences between the Palakkad Iyers and the Tamil Iyers. And food also distinguished the Iyers from Iyengars. In her ethnographic study of Matunga in the 1950s, K. L. Mythili noted, "The Iyengars start with rice and then serve other dishes—this is an idea of eternal ridicule for the Iyers who serve rice last."[70] Such differences were transcended to solve large urban problems such as housing (cooperative societies), but in the domain of marriage, they asserted themselves in the most acute and specific ways—ways that may not even have been relevant in the context of Madras Presidency itself, where interaction between Tamil Iyers and Palakkad Iyers would not necessarily have been as dense as they were in Matunga.

Indeed, though the Palakkad Iyers held the cuisine of the Tamil Iyers in low esteem, the Tamil Iyers also could be picky. Consider the following advertisement seeking a match, which appeared in 1947:

> Wanted, a South Indian Tamilian Vadama sect healthy Brahmin bachelor or an issueless widower under 30 years of age, of non-Sreevathsa gothram and non-Malabaree, well settled in life to marry an orthodox South Indian Tamil Brahmin bride aged 18. She is a matriculate of the 11th class of Bombay University and well versed in all north Indian languages. No dowry.[71]

This advertisement takes trouble to emphasize the Tamil-ness of the prospective bride and the sought-after groom. It is not adequate that the latter be a Vadama Iyer of "non-Sreevathsa gothram" (which was the degree of specificity desired in the previous classified advertisement discussed); the prospective groom must also be a "non-Malabaree." In other words, he should not be a Kerala Iyer.

CONCLUSION

I have tried to suggest that the 1930s witnessed the emergence of a new kind of urban community. This community, rather than being determined exclusively by caste and subcaste, drew upon notions of caste, class, native place, and neighborhood in order to understand itself. I have also suggested that the institution of the cooperative society was an important institutional kernel around which these various concerns articulated themselves. Such a synthetic drive, leading to the creation of the South Indian identity, was propelled by both economic and political concerns. Pressed by the need to secure credit, housing, and consumer goods, migrants from southern India to Bombay set up these societies. Once the societies were set up, however, they became the site upon which the borders of community were redefined. In part the redrawing resulted from the simple need to broaden the understanding of community and hence to secure enough members. But the redrawing also resulted from the recognition of some kind of connection between Iyers from Palakkad and Iyers from Thanjavur or Iyengars from Mysore. Similarly, in the face of growing recognition (and resentment) of their dominant position in the white-collar sector, South Indians also perceived the need to consolidate and present themselves as a unified front.

Yet such processes of consolidation did not mean that differences were erased. As I have sought to demonstrate, new kinds of differences based on native place, language, and food asserted themselves in the urban context. Such difference was, however, articulated in more restricted domains—marriage was probably the aspect of social life where the most specialized forms of identity confronted each other.

In constituting themselves as a South Indian community, migrants to Matunga embraced institutions such as the cooperative society and the modern apartment building, bulwarks of the colonial state's project of creating an urban white-collar middle class. Yet they also set some of their own terms, widening their understanding of community in response to a series of local constraints. They participated in a project of late-colonial modernity, which, in its seeming turn away from the determinism of caste, was also a project of nationalism and the postcolonial state. Yet the nature of their participation was only partial and enabled them to recalibrate their ordering of difference in response to the conditions of urban life.

Following World War II and Independence/Partition in 1947, large new waves of migrants from Punjab, Sindh, and the northern state of Uttar Pradesh flooded into Bombay. The further expansion of Bombay into Salsette to accommodate these migrants followed the pattern initiated in Matunga: colonies of apartment buildings run by cooperative societies organized along the lines pioneered in Matunga. Metacaste forms of identity that incorporated ideas of caste, class, native place, language, and dwelling in their self-understanding flourished in neighborhoods like Khar, Santa Cruz, and Andheri in Salsette. Indeed, Punjabi, Sindhi, and even North Indian are categories that today have wide currency and that share similar shifting edges, depending on context, as the category South Indian. I turn now to consider the expansion and suburbanization of Salsette.

6 *Toward Greater Mumbai*

ON FEBRUARY 1, 1957, AN UNUSUAL CEREMONY TOOK PLACE AT a high school hall in Malad, a suburb of Bombay in Salsette. Until that day, Malad had been an autonomous municipal entity. In the second of two expansions that took place between 1950 and 1957, Bombay's municipal limits were widened to incorporate the surrounding areas, and Malad, along with other local bodies in the island of Salsette, was amalgamated into Greater Bombay. At the high school hall in Malad, a small group of municipal councilors and executive officers were gathered together in the presence of journalists.[1] Kunverbhai Patel, president of the soon-to-be-defunct Malad Municipality, using "rustic, picturesque language," compared the event to the *varat* ceremony, an important (and sad) final moment in the traditional wedding where the bride departs with the groom for his family's home and, in effect, leaves her own family. Patel himself played the father of the bride within the terms of his own metaphor, handing over Malad to Bombay and asking the latter to treat the former well.

"Our *Kanya* is not sophisticated. She is not much good in the finer points of law, but she is sincere at heart and brings you a lot of dowry," averred Patel, alluding to the fact that Malad, the *kanya,* or bride, was an important producer of bricks, mortar, stone, and sand, all of which would be of great use to the rapidly expanding Bombay of the 1950s.[2] In return, Patel requested the bridegroom, the city of Bombay within the metaphor, to "treat her well. Don't let her feel she is at her '*sasara*' [in-laws' place]."[3] What would it take to make Malad feel at home, and not bossed around by her mother-in-law? Water, it turns out, was the most pressing need of Malad and other suburbs like it. It was the promise of a water supply scheme, to be implemented by the Greater Bombay Municipal Corporation, that finally persuaded Malad and other suburban entities to cede their sovereignty and come under the jurisdiction of Greater Bombay. The idea of an entity called Greater Bombay, containing the original island city of Bombay as well as large parts of adjacent Salsette and floated in various forms since the early 1910s, thus was finally realized in 1957.

The formation of Greater Bombay in the 1950s was a seminal event in the history of the city, one that has received little attention and is little understood. As a result of the division of academic labor in writing about Bombay discussed in the introduction, there is a great difference between the "Greater Mumbai" studied by scholars of the contemporary city and the "colonial Bombay" of urban historians. When historians of the city speak of colonial Bombay, they refer to an island of roughly 22 square miles of which only about two-thirds had been developed until 1918. When anthropologists, sociologists, and geographers speak of present-day Greater Mumbai, they refer to a metropolitan area of almost 186 square miles, which includes the suburbs of Dadar–Matunga and Mahim, on Bombay Island, and most of Salsette Island and Trombay. The (sub)urbanization and eventual incorporation of the island of Salsette into Bombay is the subject of this chapter.

Previous chapters have considered different aspects of the formation of suburbs in the island city of Bombay. Chapter 1 began with the critical problem faced by the Improvement Trust of acquiring and converting land to urban use. Subsequent chapters investigated the migration of a new kind of upper-caste white-collar grouping, predominantly South Indians, who were drawn to the suburban landscapes of Matunga. The book then moved to considering the formation of a distinctive dwelling typology of the suburbs—the apartment building—before turning to examining more closely the constitution of new kinds of community identity in the suburbs of Dadar–Matunga.

The book so far has focused on suburbanization in the island city of Bombay. By historical accident, when the Portuguese made over Bombay to the British in the seventeenth century, the territorial extent of the city was much greater than the tiny portion that was actually settled. As the city grew and expanded over the course of the eighteenth and nineteenth centuries, new space for the city was created through filling in and reclaiming the swampy marshy lands between the original seven islands and thus creating the island city of Bombay. When the Bombay Municipal Corporation was formed in the second half of the nineteenth century, its jurisdiction was the town and island of Bombay, an area that was much larger than the portion that was actually settled. Hence, as the city expanded over the course of the second half of the nineteenth century, the challenge was one of rendering lands in the island city suitable for habitation, not necessarily one of annexing new lands to the city.

As the city continued to expand over the early years of the twentieth century, and as the Dadar–Matunga–Sion schemes of the BIT for the suburbanization of the northern part of Bombay Island gradually got underway, the issue of whether the existing lands within Bombay's city limits could contain the growing population began to receive the attention of the provincial government as well as of Indians in the BMC. Meanwhile, one of the outcomes of the plague epidemic of 1896–1900 had been the flight of many of the city's residents out of the island city of Bombay into the neighboring big island of Salsette, where they settled into chawls and cottages in the areas around the railway stations of the BBCI line. Ef-

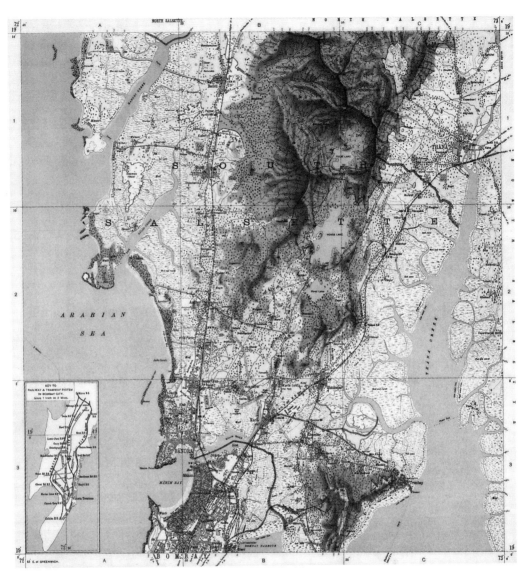

~✒ FIGURE 6.1. *Salsette in 1930. Note the size of Salsette in comparison to Bombay Island, the top third of which is visible here, showing development in Dadar–Matunga. Courtesy of Regenstein Library, University of Chicago.*

fectively an extension of the city's working populations into Salsette, such settlements, by virtue of their allegedly insanitary nature, precipitated the issue of state control over these areas. It was thus in the context of mechanisms through which the colonial government could extend control of building in what was clearly, by the early 1900s, the urbanizing island of Salsette that one of the critical aspects of suburbanization—the extension of the city's municipal limits—was first posed.

As Salsette began to urbanize in the first two decades of the twentieth century, the existing revenue administration—consisting of the familiar mechanism of the district collector with attendant powers and responsibilities—gradually began to be supplemented with or replaced by varieties of municipal government with a different mandate. The land price boom of 1916–1922, which had impressive effects in shaping the nature of building in Dadar–Matunga, also drove up land prices in Salsette, as speculators bet that the "land famine" in the island city would inevitably drive urban expansion northward into Salsette.

The discussion of the "suburbanization" of Salsette in this chapter thus addresses a crucial aspect of the suburbanization process not encountered so far in the book: the question of municipalization and extension of municipal limits. As will be demonstrated, suburbanization in Salsette presented itself in three aspects. First, over the course of the first half of the twentieth century, the revenue administration of Salsette was slowly supplemented with varying levels of municipal government, raising varying concerns among different constituencies. Second, from at least as early as 1907, the question of annexing parts of Salsette to the city of Bombay had been posed and underwent various modifications, before finally being implemented in two stages, in 1950 and 1957. Finally, the question of the physical transformation of Salsette into suburbs was attempted through a different mechanism than had been used in the island city of Bombay. Whereas the BIT had relied on the Land Acquisition Act to physically acquire and transform lands in Dadar–Matunga, the colonial state relied upon town planning to effect the physical transformation of Salsette. That the physical transformation of Salsette depended upon town planning rather than compulsory acquisition of lands was a function of the increasing municipalization of urban politics and of the greater participation of Bombay's residents in matters concerning local self-government. This chapter argues that the physical transformation of Salsette, which entailed converting vast swathes of agrarian and quasi-agrarian land to urban building sites, cannot be understood outside of the political and administrative transformation entailed by municipalization. The first part of this chapter thus reviews the changing administrative logic of urban governance. The second part of the chapter moves to examine the process by which agrarian lands were converted to urban use through town planning. The final part examines the changing housing scenario in the aftermath of Partition and increased migration into the city and suggests ways in which the patterns of suburbanization examined so far endured into the 1950s and 1960s.

A SHORT HISTORY OF GREATER BOMBAY

In January 1957, Padmakar Balkrishna Samant, a resident of Goregaon, filed an unusual petition against the state of Bombay. Samant's object was to challenge a law that was about to come into effect that would have extended the city of Bombay's municipal limits to encompass Goregaon, resulting in the dissolution of the Goregaon village panchayat (a local self-government body).[4] Under the aegis of the unwieldily named Bombay Municipal [Further Extension of Limits and Schedule BBA (Amendment)] Act, 58 of 1956, the state of Bombay sought to bring eighty-two square miles and thirty-three villages of Salsette Island, previously in the Thana Collectorate just north of Bombay, into the welcoming embrace of the city of Greater Bombay. Such an expansion of city limits came on the heels of the 1950 expansion of city limits under the Bombay Municipal (Extension of Limits) Act of 1950, through which sixty-eight square miles of Salsette and fifty-three villages were annexed to Bombay to form Greater Bombay. Within a few short years between 1950 and 1957, thus, Bombay, both city and island, initially consisting of a mere 25 square miles, grew first to 93 square miles to form Greater Bombay, and at the time of Samant's petition on the eve of the second annexure, it was about to expand into a behemoth of 175 square miles.

Samant's reason for challenging the annexure was fairly common among some of the residents of the areas about to become part of Greater Bombay. Although his petition evoked the integrity and progressive nature of the Goregaon village panchayat and bemoaned its impending dissolution, he was ultimately concerned about taxation without adequate representation in the Greater Bombay Municipal Corporation. He claimed that each resident would have to bear an additional annual municipal tax burden of twenty rupees while the entire eighty-two-square-mile region annexed to Greater Bombay would only receive six seats' worth of representation on the Municipal Corporation.[5] In his petition, Samant requested a writ or directive from the Bombay High Court restraining the state of Bombay from enforcing the provisions of the act, an injunction restraining the Municipal Corporation from acting under these legislations, and a declaration of the continued validity of the Goregaon village panchayat.[6]

More interesting than Samant's reason for challenging the state of Bombay was the legal argument deployed by his lawyers, R. A. Jahagirdar and M. V. Paranjpe. Although Samant's petition was swiftly dismissed within a day by Justices Shah and Gokhale, it raised the important issue of competing sovereignties within the framework of urban expansion, which will frame the discussion in this chapter. Their petition, thus, did not target the municipal legislation directly. Rather, evoking the Constitution of India, they challenged the composition of the Bombay provincial legislature constituted through the States Reorganization Act 137 of 1956, recently passed by the Parliament of India. Their petition sought to contest the manner in which the Bombay state legislature was constituted, and thus the latter's competence to pass any sort of legislation whatsoever.[7]

Samant's legal team seized upon a highly specific moment where certain provisions of the States Reorganization Act intersected with the passage of acts by the Bombay provincial government. As part of the reorganization of states, certain members elected in Kutch were transferred to the Bombay State Legislative Assembly. But Article 170 of the Constitution of India, the petitioners argued, mandated that members must be directly elected to the legislative assemblies. Hence, the transfer of members from Kutch into the Bombay assembly was unconstitutional. Further, the petitioners contended that as a result of the transfer of members from Kutch, there were 456 members in the Bombay State Legislative Assembly in 1956 instead of the 396 mandated by the States Reorganization Act. Hence, even by the standards established in that act, the Bombay legislature was incorrectly constituted in 1956, when the Municipal Corporation Amendment Act was passed.[8]

Justices Shah and Gokhale swiftly dismissed Samant's petition on the grounds that in their interpretation of the States Reorganization Act, the members transferred from Kutch to Bombay were to be deemed "elected in Bombay." Further, since Parliament had formulated the States Reorganization Act, and since Parliament had broad powers to interpret the Constitution in doing so, there was nothing irregular about the constitution of the Bombay legislature.

Samant's petition is of great interest, however, because it draws upon several levels of governance and sovereignty in framing its ultimately unsuccessful argument. Seeking to protect the integrity of the Goregaon village panchayat against the encroaching Greater Bombay Municipal Corporation, the petition challenged the composition of the Bombay state legislature on the basis of both the Constitution of India and a law drafted by the Parliament of India. Virtually every level of governance, from the village to the nation, was thus brought into the argument. Samant's petition underscores the shifting terrains of governance in the 1950s. While great attention has been given—with justification—to the transition from colonial state to independent nation in 1947, much less is known of the other reorganizations in governance that were also taking place at the municipal and regional levels. Samant's petition brings into focus two such reorganizations: the reorganization of the states in 1956, and the emergence and subsequent expansion of Greater Bombay in 1950 and 1957.

This chapter is concerned with the emergence of Greater Bombay. Samant's evocation of the integrity of the Goregaon village panchayat in his petition underscores a fundamental administrative transformation accompanying urbanization in South Asia. As an area urbanized, an agrarian administrative logic driven principally by land revenue concerns was gradually replaced by a municipal administrative logic driven by the concerns of managing the infrastructure of the urbanizing area. A classification of space based on the district, *taluka,* and village was replaced by one in which the municipality and the ward were the principal organizing factors. In Salsette, this happened within the span of about fifty years. Such a relatively rapid superimposition of a municipal administrative structure over the older revenue structure has imparted a peculiar "two-faced" character to the present-day city and, especially, to Salsette. Partly because of its history of expansion through annexure alluded to above, Greater Mumbai exists as two distinct legal entities, one municipal and the other revenue. From a municipal point of view, the city is a unitary entity: Greater Mumbai, comprising in territorial terms the old island city and the annexed portions of Salsette Island, falls under the jurisdiction of the Municipal Corporation of Greater Mumbai (MCGM). The MCGM deals with several critical aspects of urban life: water supply, sanitation, property taxes, building regulation, public health, roads and streets, and education are all within its ambit. Day-to-day operations are executed through the Administrative Wing under the command of an Indian Administrative Services (IAS) officer appointed by the government of Maharashtra State, but the overall authority rests with the Deliberative Wing under the control of 227 locally elected and 5 nominated councilors or corporators.

From a revenue point of view, however, the picture looks different. From this perspective, Mumbai exists as two distinct entities. Mumbai City, consisting of the old island city of Bombay, is under the jurisdiction of the Mumbai City Collectorate in south Mumbai; the Mumbai Suburban District is under the jurisdiction of Mumbai Suburban District Collectorate located in Bandra East. Both collectorates are run by district collectors, who are IAS officers, and their staffs. Purely executive officers not accountable to local electorates; they are representatives of the government of Maharashtra and thus represent a regional scale of governance. The collectorates are responsible for overseeing an arcane grab bag of legislations, including laws dealing with the taxation of marriage, explosives, betting, entertainment, and advertising. The collectorates also act as representatives of the central and state governments in overseeing elections to the Lok Sabha (the lower house of the Parliament of India) and to the Maharashtra Legislative Assembly and in issuing various identity cards and caste certificates (including, for qualified applicants, a "Non-Creamy Layer Certificate"). For many residents of the city, the collectorate looms large as the keeper of land records. It is the Collector's

Office that is responsible for determining the integrity of titles to land and for recording property transfers. Some important aspects of urban life, not necessarily the responsibility of the collectorate, are nonetheless organized on the basis of the revenue perspective on the city. Power for the island city, thus, is supplied by the municipalized Brihanmumbai Electric Supply and Transport Company (BEST), while the Mumbai Suburban District used to get its power from the nonmunicipal Bombay Suburban Electric Supply, which has now been bought by Reliance Infrastructure.[9]

Such a doubled legal existence of the city—as municipal and as revenue entities, often not in communication with one another—leads to perplexing situations. For instance, the fact that water bills—which can help establish title to land—are collected by the Municipal Corporation while property records are maintained by the Collector's Office can mean problems for city residents seeking the cooperation of both faces of the city in order to establish title to land. Studying the relatively rapid municipalization of Salsette over the first half of the twentieth century permits us to disaggregate these different modes of urban and suburban governance and underscores the significance of Salsette in the suburbanization of Bombay.

The rest of this section elaborates the two faces of the administrative transformation of Salsette. On the one hand, the various townships in Salsette began to form local bodies with increasing powers and responsibilities. On the other hand, Salsette's suburban character and its dependence upon Bombay increased over the early decades of the twentieth century to the point where the administrative annexure of Salsette to Bombay was proposed. All along, taxation, urban crime, and public services came to play increasingly significant roles in the debates over the municipalization of Salsette. An important aspect of these discussions was that, beginning in the early 1920s, the middle classes were starting to perceive municipal governance as "their" sphere, a domain in which they could assert their local interests against more distant regional authorities.

A rural area such as Salsette was under the jurisdiction of Thana District until the early twentieth century, and the Thana collector oversaw large tracts of lands with interspersed villages, which had panchayats to handle local affairs. As the city approached, areas that were perceived as likely to urbanize were "notified," and "notified area committees" were nominated by provincial governments to tackle increasingly complex administrative matters. In 1920, the 140 villages of Salsette were divided into South and North Salsette, with 54 and 86 villages respectively. North Salsette *taluka* remained part of Thana District, but South Salsette was reconstituted into the Bombay Suburban District (BSD) in anticipation of the continued expansion of the city of Bombay. South Salsette was broken into two *talukas,* and BSD now consisted of Borivli and Andheri *talukas,* with 33 and 53 villages respectively.[10]

At roughly the same time, in recognition of the increasingly urban character of Salsette, the provincial government created a new category of urban self-government through the Bombay Municipal Boroughs legislation of 1925. Former district municipalities that were growing, such as Bandra, Andheri, and Kurla, were now promoted to the status of borough municipalities. Borough municipalities had greater powers than district municipalities, which were governed by the 1901 Bombay District Municipal Act and which included Ghatkopar and Juhu. Borough municipalities were operated by a standing committee instead of a managing committee and had wider powers, including the right to levy certain special taxes over and above those levied by the district municipalities, such as a drainage tax and an education tax. By the mid-1920s, thus, a bewildering variety of local self-governmental bodies dotted Salsette Island: borough municipalities, district municipalities, notified area committees, and sanitary beach committees were responsible for "urban" areas, and district local boards and village panchayats were responsible for "rural" areas. (Both "urban" and "rural" areas were, of course, all part of the BSD.)[11]

A telling example of the suburban public's growing awareness of these varying levels of government and of impending changes in urban governance was provided in a letter written to the editor of the *Bombay Chronicle* in 1923.[12] The letter writer, who called himself "Muddy Pedestrian," made a common and unexceptional complaint: the road leading from the southern end of the Santa Cruz railway station to join the north–south Ghodbundar Road was in atrocious condition. "To count the holes and the pits full of muddy water on this small road," wrote Muddy Pedestrian, no doubt hyperbolically, "would be as impossible as to count the stars in the sky and to speak of the slush and dirt on it would hardly be possible in decent language." The source of the problem, according to Muddy Pedestrian, lay in the fact that the authority responsible for the road was the Thana District Local Board, an authority located twenty-five miles away on the GIP line. For Muddy Pedestrian, no doubt daily doused with mud and slush on his way home from the suburban Santa Cruz railway station, it was useless to ponder "the mysterious considerations of State policy that perhaps necessitated this ridiculous arrangement" whereby what was so clearly an urbanizing area like Santa Cruz should be under a distant authority such as the Thana District Local Board. But he noted that while a sum of 1.3 million rupees had been "squandered" on improving the Ghodbundar Road linking Bandra to Andheri, authorities couldn't find the thousand rupees that would have been needed for the station road. Attributing such disproportionate expenditure to the fact that "rich citizens who own motor cars" used the Ghodbundar Road and could influence the priorities of distant local board authorities, Muddy Pedestrian concluded his impassioned letter with a plea for the Santa Cruz Notified Area Committee to receive its own municipality, so that the residents "could look after their own interests and affairs." A municipality was a body with far greater powers than a notified area committee and could theoretically allow local residents to act in their own interests.

In 1935 the provincial Government of Bombay attempted to address the problem of varied forms of local self-government by attempting a consolidation of some of the different administrative units in the BSD. (Muddy Pedestrian would have been deeply unhappy with their plan.) Such a consolidation was deemed necessary as early as in 1925, shortly after Muddy Pedestrian's letter, when a committee reported on the reorganization of local self-government in Salsette. A "concerted action" was needed to combat the challenges posed by sanitation, water supply, roads, and drainage.[13] Concerted action meant addressing the highly complex and variegated pattern of municipalization in Salsette, with its gram panchayats (village panchayats), notified area committees, district municipalities, and borough municipalities, each with different kinds of jurisdictions and different levels of power. The committee initially proposed a scheme—similar to the London County Council—in which the local bodies would have continued to exist but certain crucial infrastructural matters would have fallen under the jurisdiction of a newly constituted Central Board.

The local authorities of Salsette had fought the recommendation of the 1925 committee, however, and nothing had happened at that time. This led the provincial government in 1935 to forcibly attempt a consolidation of the local bodies. Specifically, the limits of the Bandra Municipal Borough were expanded to include the Santa Cruz area, and Santa Cruz's status as a notified area was dissolved. Similarly, the Vile Parle Notified Area was merged into the Andheri Municipal Borough.[14] The proposed consolidation generated much resentment, principally revolving around the issues of giving up sovereignty in self-government and of paying higher taxes. J. K. Mehta, a resident of Santa Cruz, was outraged at the planned amalgamation.[15] Declaring the amalgamation to be a "gross abuse of the rights of self-government," he challenged the logic of the amalgamation. Santa Cruz was a solvent entity about to embark on a critical drainage scheme, he maintained. If it were to be merged into the financially less-sound Bandra Municipality, then not only would the drainage scheme be indefinitely postponed, but Santa Cruz residents would have to subsidize, through their taxes, the profligacy of the Bandra Municipality. A. X. Moraes, president of the Santa Cruz Notified Area Committee and an engineer in the Public Works Department, claimed that the voice of Santa Cruz would be "practically drowned by an overwhelming majority on the other side." The drainage scheme for Santa Cruz, which he had personally worked on for three years, now "seem[ed] a hopeless affair."[16]

Residents of the Vile Parle Notified Area Committee, which was to be merged into the Andheri Borough Municipality, raised a different kind of objection. The residents of Andheri, claimed S. N. Kalbag, president of the Vile Parle Notified Area Committee, consisted of capitalists and speculators, while Vile Parle was essentially a middle-class community. Vile Parle had been developed according to town planning principles, whereas Andheri was an old village that had grown in haphazard fashion. What would happen to Vile Parle and its middle-class residents when the township came within the jurisdiction of the larger Andheri Municipality, controlled by Andheri's speculators?[17]

Chunilal Barfivala of Andheri, the president of the District Local Board of the BSD, took a measured position on this consolidation. Sensitive to the concerns of residents of the notified area committees that were about to be dissolved, such as Mehta, Moraes, and Kalbag, he nonetheless asserted that something needed to be done to address the proliferation of local self-government bodies in Salsette, whose very multiplicity was hindering coordinated development.[18] Two solutions were possible, he argued: either the various local bodies could retain their autonomy and a central board could be set up for Salsette-wide concerns, on the model of the London County Council, or further amalgamation of local bodies would have to take place on the lines proposed by provincial government. For Barfivala, the former idea, of a loose federation of local bodies, was fundamentally flawed; he saw further consolidation of the various local bodies as the only way forward.

Whereas concerns over autonomy and taxation were arguments against further consolidation, middle-class concern over crime in the suburbs became an argument for greater consolidation. By the 1920s residents of Salsette were complaining vigorously about what they called "Pathan terrorism" in the suburbs and searching for ways to check the "Pathan menace."[19] One solution that gradually began to gain currency was the notion of extending the jurisdiction of the Bombay City Police and the Bombay High Court to the BSD. This was the first concrete step taken in the extension of the city of Bombay's jurisdiction into Salsette.

The notion of expanding the understanding of Bombay city to create a larger municipal entity dates at least as far back as 1907, when the provincial Government of Bombay solicited the views of various Bombay constituencies on a variety of matters having to do with the infrastructural needs of the city, including the possible development of adjacent Trombay Island into a suburb for the wealthy classes.[20] This proposal did not go anywhere, but the idea of expanding the municipal definition of the city to include the larger Salsette Island to the north was subsequently considered in greater detail by the Bombay Development Committee, appointed by the Government of Bombay in 1913.[21]

In 1918 C. H. Cowan, the Salsette development officer, recommended the inclusion of Kurla within Bombay's municipal limits because of the alleged mismanagement of sanitary affairs by that local body, which could have affected the public health of Bombay itself.[22] Nothing was made of this recommendation, and indeed, even though various proposals to expand city limits were made in 1925, 1933, 1936, and 1938, nothing was realized from these various ideas. It was not until 1945 that, under pressure to crack down upon the criminal element in the BSD, ambitious legislation was passed expanding the jurisdiction of the Bombay City Police and the Bombay High Court to a portion of the BSD: the Greater Bombay Law and the Bombay High Court (Declaration of Limits) Law, 1945. But only the Andheri *taluka* of the BSD—north up to Jogeshwari on the western side and Ghatkopar on the eastern side—was to fall within what basically amounted to the first juridical expression of Greater Bombay.

Residents of Borivli *taluka*—that is, those residents of the BSD excluded from the Bombay Police and High Court jurisdiction—were not pleased with this exclusion. They wanted to be included in this first expression of Greater Bombay because they feared that criminal elements would now make their municipalities—within easy physical reach of Greater Bombay but just out of legal reach—the base for criminal gangs. Such, at least, were the opinions of Jeshtaram Kapadia, chairman of the Borivli Notified Area Committee, and S. V. Iyer, member of the Malad Notified Area Committee:[23]

> The area excluded from Greater Bombay is an integral part of the City of Bombay, with which it is united economically, socially, industrially, commercially, educationally, and otherwise. This excluded area has nothing in common with Thana District to which it is now arbitrarily annexed against the wishes and in spite of the protests of the people of the Bombay Suburban District.[24]

This was quite an extraordinary statement to have made in 1945, considering that it had only been in 1920 that the Borivili and Andheri *talukas* had been separated from Thana District to form the Bombay Suburban District. Yet it indicated how even distant areas like Borivli and Malad had become strongly identified as suburbs of Bombay. Beneath these middle-class concerns over law and order lay a broader fear of the administrative implications of transferring, for the purpose of land revenue, all these villages in the Bombay Suburban District to Thana District. The Bombay Suburban District Local Board, responsible for the administration of the various villages in the BSD, would now have to be dissolved and those regions would now fall under the authority of the Thana District Collectorate. A process of municipalization that had begun with the establishment of the district local boards would now be reversed. In those areas of the BSD that were to revert to Thana District after 1945, the regional revenue administration was going to reclaim jurisdiction from the local municipal administration.

By 1945, thus, the expanded jurisdiction of the Bombay High Court and the Bombay City Police provided the blueprint for the first expansion of municipal limits in 1950 to yield Greater Bombay. The postwar committee appointed to look into the development of suburbs indicated that it would be necessary to take over vast swathes of land to accommodate the future needs of the city: not just the Bombay Suburban District, but a much larger region that included portions of Thana District and Thana Municipal City Limits should be encompassed. For the reason of feasibility, though, the committee proposed that initially—over the course of five years—only the area under the jurisdiction of the Bombay High Court and police be included within city limits.[25]

Some of the proposals of the postwar committee came under ferocious attack from the residents of Salsette, most vividly by Chunilal Barfivala, who had been a member of the committee.[26] Barfivala, echoing the interests of his middle-class and landowning constituencies, felt that the proposed extension of city limits went both too far and not far enough. On the one hand, the outright annexation of the various local bodies of Salsette he termed a "ruthless sacrifice of the corporate life of the annexed communities."[27] Barfivala saw a two-tiered federation on the model of the London County Council as the only solution to the problem of urban expansion.[28] (Note that this was basically an about-turn from his position in 1935, discussed above, when he had rejected the two-tiered model in favor of suburban amalgamation. No doubt this had to do with the fact that in 1935, it was another local body—Vile Parle—that was being amalgamated into his own municipality of Andheri. In 1945, on the other hand, it was being proposed that Andheri, along with other local bodies in the Andheri *taluka,* be merged into Greater Bombay.) Further, Barfivala argued that it would be absurd to expect the whole of the Bombay Suburban District—with its vastly varied levels of development—to pay the same taxes as the island city. It would be a long time before the infrastructure in the suburbs approached the levels of the city. On the other hand, Barfivala felt that the piecemeal approach recommended in the committee's report was ill conceived. The only way to go about the program of expansion was to do so in one swift stroke. The city's needs for space were such that it would very quickly overflow the proposed initial added area.

Barfivala seems to have won some of his battles. The tax structure for the annexed portions, for instance, was graded in a highly specific way, and residents of villages paid the least, while residents of areas like the Bandra Municipality, which along with Ghatkopar was the only area in Salsette that had a sewerage system in 1950, paid the same as the island city. But the two-tiered model was rejected in favor of outright annexure. And even though the initial expansion of 1950 was followed in 1957 by a further expansion of the Borivli *taluka,* the proposed annexure of Thana Municipal Corporation and areas north of Bassein did not take place.

The actual process of expansion was delayed by Partition in 1947, which resulted in waves of refugees flooding the city. Both the BMC and the provincial government were engaged with managing the ensuing housing crisis, and it was not until 1950 that the first extension of municipal limits was actually achieved. On the morning of April 15, 1950, the governor of Bombay, Raja Maharaj Singh, in the company of Local Self-Government Minister G. D. Vartak and Mayor S. K. Patil, formally crossed the line separating Bombay from Greater Bombay at Mahim Causeway.[29] In Mayor Patil's speech on the occasion, he claimed that "the citizens of both parts of Greater Bombay were equally ready to welcome one another as brothers and sisters of one greater city."[30]

The municipalization of Salsette as discussed above needs to be understood in the context of the changing meaning of municipal governance between the 1910s and 1950s. Until the end of the 1910s, the municipal franchise was restricted to rate-payers, or property owners. Following the Montague–Chelmsford reforms, which made local self-government a "transferred" subject, the franchise was extended to rentpayers as well, provided that rent was greater than ten rupees per month. In 1935, following the Government of India Act, the franchise qualification was further lowered and persons paying five rupees or more per month in rent could vote. It was at around this time that the Congress Party first began to contest municipal elections in Bombay: in a tentative fashion in 1934–1935 and then in a full-fledged way in 1939.[31] Full franchise was extended at the municipal level in 1942. Oddly, though, despite this transformation of rural administrative units into urban units, Salsette retains another classification system than that of wards. For instance, from the revenue point of view in the Mumbai Suburban District Collectorate, it is still perceived as consisting of three *talukas*: Andheri, Borivili, and Kurla.

URBAN EXPANSION AND TOWN PLANNING

As chapter 1 has elaborated, suburbanization emerged in the early twentieth century as an "indirect attack" on the problem of overcrowding in the older parts of the city. One distinctive feature of the Trust's intervention strategy—in the old city as well as in the suburbs—was its preference for physically acquiring all the required land and then laying out an orderly street pattern, with each plot subject to strict building regulations, designated open spaces, and reserved spaces for schools and public institutions. In order to acquire lands for such projects, the Trust used the Imperial Land Acquisition Act of 1894, which authorized the state to acquire lands for public purposes.

Beginning in the 1910s, however, in the face of increasing calls for self-determination from Bombay's residents, renewed resistance from landowning elites, and weakening political resolve of the colonial state in matters of urban intervention, urban authorities embraced town planning as a new legislative framework within which to effect (sub)urban growth. Town planning distinguished itself from previous urban interventions (such as those attempted by the Bombay Improvement Trust) in that it was, in principle, a collaborative venture. Town planning did not entail wholesale land acquisition by the state or planning authority through the Land Acquisition Act. Confronted by urbanization, the owners of agrarian lands at the urban edge, in conjunction with local authorities and regional planning authorities, could decide to undertake a so-called town planning scheme, through which an urban streetscape and building plots were imposed on the agrarian landscape. Crucially, suburbanization within a town planning framework meant that landholders retained ownership of their lands and also had a say in determining whether the development scheme went ahead to begin with.

Following the plague epidemic in Bombay at the end of the nineteenth century, waves of the city's residents fled to Salsette. Speculators began buying up agricultural land in the vicinity of railway stations on the BBCI line and began to apply to the Thana District collector for permission to convert those plots of land into residential building sites. Among the earliest such speculators was J. N. Tata, who in 1899 bought up large pieces of land in Bandra and applied for permission to reclaim portions of the foreshore and build dwelling houses.[32] It was during this correspondence that the collector of Thana, J. P. Orr, realized that the provincial government did not have an effective mechanism to convert land from agricultural to urban/residential use.[33]

Shortly thereafter, several other speculators began buying up plots of agricultural land and applying for permission to convert these lands into building sites. Since the lands were agricultural plots, they were highly irregular in shape and were not served by roads. Orr identified these features, especially the absence of street frontage, as the principal obstacle to granting permission to convert these sites into residential dwellings and sought to impose punitive building fines on landowners who had gone ahead with residential construction anyway. Irregular plot shapes meant that owners were less likely to provide adequate open space around the buildings, which would lead to an undesirably dense building pattern. Irregularity in plot size also meant that plots were more difficult to service with streets.[34] Lack of street frontage posed problems. In addition to the self-evident fact that it meant access was restricted, lack of street frontage was critical since streets were emerging as critical indices through which the heights of buildings and the amounts of open space around them were being regulated (this observation is developed in chapters 1 and 3). Thus, from the point of view of colonial public health officials, allowing buildings to go up without street frontage was tantamount to licensing indiscriminate building.

As early as in 1900, just two years after the founding of the Bombay Improvement Trust, the colonial officer W. C. Hughes (the first chairman of the Improvement Trust) conducted a detailed study of city improvement schemes in Britain while on home leave.[35] Hughes, trained as an engineer at King's College in London, noted that most "street schemes" of the sort he studied in Britain were street-widening schemes, designed to accommodate new infrastructure such as tramways. At this early and optimistic moment, the Bombay Improvement Trust believed that it could execute similar street schemes in Bombay, though less with the intention of adding infrastructure and more with the goal of "ventilat[ing] congested areas in the Native Town."[36] However, Hughes also studied comprehensive city extension schemes of the sort attempted by the BIT in Schemes 4, 5, and 6, notably the Blackley scheme in Manchester, England. Planning authorities in British cities expressed admiration for the comprehensiveness of the Bombay schemes and regretted that sufficient schemes of this sort were not being planned for British cities.[37] Hughes noted one crucial feature of the British schemes: the absolute secrecy that was maintained regarding the specific details of each scheme. Secrecy was important because advance knowledge of a scheme, especially details regarding the valuations of lands to be acquired for its implementation, could result in speculative acquisition of lands by residents in the area and thus could drive up the costs of executing any scheme to prohibitive levels. Hughes emphasized the need to maintain secrecy in Bombay, noting that already the Trust's activities were being slowed down owing to lengthy acquisition processes resulting from speculation in advance of the scheme.[38]

Hughes's warning, it turned out, proved prophetic. As the BIT continued with its activities over the first decade of the twentieth century, it proved incapable of maintaining secrecy, and speculation in advance of the Trust's schemes, along with the growing assertiveness of Bombay's increasingly empowered landowners, meant that land acquisition proved to be a cripplingly arduous process. The English town planning bill was proposed and subsequently passed as an act in 1909; a draft town planning bill was drawn up for Bombay in that same year.[39] When this draft bill came up for discussion by the trustees of the BIT, Orr, formerly collector of Thana and appointed chairman of the Improvement Trust in 1908, assumed an unmistakably weary tone in comparing town planning with the existing mode of urban intervention through the Improvement Trust legislation:

> The acquisition of property under the City of Bombay Improvement Act [which derived its powers of acquisition from the Land Acquisition Act] involves a long and expensive inquiry into title, much friction between the Trust and the land-owners on account of dispossession and disputes as to the adequacy of compensation, the expenditure of capital sums, and . . . great risk by reason of the land being left undisposed of on the Trust's hands long after it is acquired.[40]

While earlier suburban schemes had pitted the colonial state seeking new lands on its own terms against owners of agrarian lands at the edge of the city, town planning featured a collaborative model of urban expansion in which agrarian landowners at the city's edge themselves sought to convert their lands to (sub) urban use. Indigenous capital was thus mobilized for the project of urban expansion. As Orr put it:

> The main difference in practical policy between the City of Bombay Improvement Act and the Town Planning Act is that, whereas under the former the Trust have to buy up land and lay it out, under the latter all land except what is acquired for roads and open spaces is left in possession of its owners.[41]

Town planning, as a mode of land use conversion, thus offered advantages over the Improvement Trust Act as well as over the Bombay Municipal Corporation Act, which were the two existing legislations that contained the provisions for imposing street grids and building plots on formerly agrarian lands. Orr compared the relative ease of execution of town planning schemes, where the problem of land acquisition did not have to be confronted, with the Trust's own ruinously expensive suburban schemes in the island city of Bombay.

The growing numbers of applications to convert agricultural plots into building sites in Salsette—and the imperative of administrators to control the pattern of building—led the provincial government in 1908 to appoint an ICS officer by the name of P. J. Mead to conduct an extensive survey of Salsette's potential for suburban development.[42] The problem in Salsette was that there existed only a very weak piece of legislation to handle the impending urbanization of the large island. This was the 1901 District Municipalities Act, promulgated to allow for the creation of municipal bodies to regulate growth in newly urbanizing areas.[43] Most importantly, this legislation contained no effective provision to regulate building on private lands. While bylaws could be framed, the penalty for infringing them was so low as to be irrelevant.

Mead's ambitious and wide-ranging study of Salsette provides an extraordinary portrait of Salsette in its early stages of urbanization, with descriptions of the various villages and townships scattered across the island, now recognizable as large urban neighborhoods. Beginning with an account of the topographical features of Salsette, Mead's detailed assessment of the various infrastructural assets and liabilities in the development of Salsette emphasized the problem of water supply and the malaria-prone lands on the eastern parts of the island.[44] However, the principle obstacles to the orderly development of Salsette were similar to the issues raised by Orr. First, the lack of developed street patterns meant that little back land had been developed, while congested ribbon development took place along the existing street frontages. Second, the absence of any suitable mechanism to pool lands—especially small or irregularly shaped plots—served as a severe disincentive to permitting lands to come to market in an orderly fashion.[45]

Mead's influential report recommended the formulation of town planning legislation on the lines of the English town planning legislation then under discussion before Parliament, but with some key differences. Mead recommended two important German laws, the Fluchtliniengesetz of 1875 and the Lex Adickes of 1902, arguing that the provisions of these laws were especially important given the landholding patterns in Salsette. Mead's recommendations were taken seriously by the Bombay provincial government, which sent another Bombay ICS officer, B. W. Kissan, on a study tour of German cities. Kissan conducted an extensive study lasting three months, resulting in the publication of his *Report on Town Planning Enactments in Germany,* in which he echoed Mead's recommendations.[46]

Dinshaw Vacha, the Municipal Corporation's representative on the board of the Improvement Trust, argued that the draft town planning bill was "confiscatory in its character and calculated to destroy all just and fair rights and interests in private property."[47] Since the franchise at this time was restricted to ratepayers and since the Bombay Municipal Corporation consisted of the Indian representatives of the franchise-bearing ratepayers, it is reasonable to assume that the landowners had a dominant interest in the BMC. Wacha was unsuccessful in his attempt to sink the town planning bill altogether, but landowners were successful in restricting the scope and ambition of town planning in the Bombay context. For one thing, Wacha argued that town planning "shall in no way apply to the City of Bombay"; rather, it would only apply to entirely undeveloped portions of the city and to areas on the urban edge outside city limits.[48] Town planning could only be applied to any areas within the island city upon the express request of the BMC itself. In winning this last exclusive right to determine the applicability of town planning within the island city, Wacha won a battle against Orr and other British trustees of the BIT, who sought joint authority with the BMC in determining the applicability of town planning to the island city.[49] Wacha and other landowners thus asserted the status of the BMC as the sole local authority in any application of town planning within the municipal limits of Bombay. Finally, after six years of deliberations in the Bombay Presidency legislature and elsewhere, where landowning interests contested the provisions, the Bombay Town Planning Act was finally passed in 1915. It was the first town planning act in India and was followed by the Madras Town Planning Act in 1919. Other presidencies subsequently passed their own versions. From 1915 until 1964, town planning remained the principal mechanism through which agrarian lands at the city's edge were converted to urban use in Bombay.

After the passage of the Bombay Town Planning Act in 1915, A. E. Mirams, a surveyor active in city expansion schemes in Bombay, gave a lecture in 1919 to the Town Planning Institute in London on town planning in Bombay.[50] Mirams had served as arbitrator in all of the first ten town planning schemes notified in

Salsette, so he had a good perspective on the issues. Mirams adopted a somewhat servile tone and begged the indulgence of the "august assembly of expert professional Town Planners" before him. He assured them that despite the fact that his town planning experience was in "the lands of jungles and tigers," there "were still advantages which would accrue as the result of copying the Town Planning methods of the East." According to Mirams, the Bombay Town Planning Act was superior in some respects to the English Town Planning Act.

When Mirams addressed the British Town Planning Institute in 1919, he emphasized the fact that although Salsette landowners initially expressed great hostility toward town planning, their attitudes changed "from open hostility to undisguised gratitude for the benefits conferred" by the new legislation.[51] What he did not mention in his lecture was the fact that the market for urban lands had changed dramatically between the early 1910s, when the town planning bill was being debated (and opposed), and the period from 1916 onward, when new circumstances served to give a major boost to town planning's principal agenda of converting agrarian lands into urban use.

The economic boom of 1916–1922—especially the speculation in land—meant there was keen interest in bringing new lands in Salsette to market. The specific nature of town planning in Bombay, with its emphasis on the powers of local authorities, also dovetailed with the increasing sovereignty of Indians in the sphere of local self-government. For four years after the passage of the Town Planning Act in 1915, the Revenue Department of the provincial Government of Bombay served as the central authority overseeing town planning schemes, while the various notified area committees, district municipalities, and borough municipalities of Salsette served as local authorities. In 1919 at the height of the boom in the Bombay economy at large and in the land and housing markets in particular, the Government of Bombay created the Bombay Development Department, an executive department of regional government, to oversee the orderly development of the city in a time of overall growth. As mentioned in chapter 3, in addition to the projects of reclamation of foreshore lands and construction of industrial housing, the BDD was also entrusted with the work of suburban development.

Although the first two projects of the BDD have received some attention, little is known about the BDD's work on the suburbanization of Bombay.[52] The BDD had an ambitious two-pronged suburbanization strategy.[53] Most of the development along the west of Salsette, around the areas that already had some settlement in the vicinity of railway stations, was to be carried out by town planning schemes, initiated by and largely executed by local authorities, with the BDD playing the role of approving the schemes and providing the arbitrator. On the eastern side of the island, on the other hand, where there was much less development to begin with and where the lands were principally agricultural, the government proposed to proceed through what it called suburban schemes. Here, the method to be followed was different from town planning. More reminiscent of the BIT's operations in the island city, the Development Department proposed to acquire large tracts of land through the Land Acquisition Act and then to construct garden suburbs. This strategy was driven by the landholding pattern in Salsette, which consisted of numerous small farms. In such a setting, it was unlikely that a single large builder or corporation could acquire one large plot of land and construct a suburban estate, as had been the practice in England. The BDD's attempts to acquire large plots of land and construct suburban estates was thus a distorted attempt to replicate the "municipal socialism" of German cities, whereby German local authorities, to overcome the challenge of small farms, would regularly acquire plots of land and encourage orderly development on liberal terms. This practice of local authorities purchasing large lands had been approvingly noted by both Mead and Kissan.[54] The BDD's attempt at municipal socialism was severely distorted, however, because the BDD was an executive organ of provincial government and thus part of the revenue city. It was not answerable to local authorities or subject to the mandate of local populations; it was not municipal at all.

The fact that the BDD was an executive organ of regional government and not subject to local mandate did not escape the notice of the residents of Salsette. Criticism of the suburban schemes centered on the BDD's use of the Land Acquisition Act, which was perceived to be a high-handed and arbitrary instrument of state power. Consider, for instance, the lengthy diatribe in a letter to the editor of the *Bombay Chronicle* by a resident of Salsette who called himself "Kalina."[55] In appealing to the government to restrict the acquisitions of the BDD, Kalina made special note of the fact that several of the landholders whose lands had been appropriated were the holders of *Khoti Inams,* which were older tenures granted by the East India Company in the early nineteenth century and which were not subject to resumption by the state. Kalina was essentially challenging the legality of eminent domain–like legislation such as the Land Acquisition Act and its right to supersede older forms of tenure. Meanwhile, another critic, who called himself "Pro Bono Publico," wrote a scathing letter about the planned garden city in Trombay, an island lying just east of Salsette.[56] Pro Bono Publico's critique of the BDD was premised on the fact that development of Trombay and eastern Salsette went against the advice of experts such as Mead, who had warned of the malarial conditions of eastern Salsette and had noted the presence in this area of noxious trades such as tanneries and slaughterhouses. The improbable fantasy of constructing a garden city in such a setting would only have the effect of dispossessing the poor agriculturalists of Trombay, without any meaningful suburban development. This critique was echoed by G. B. Trivedi, a Salsette resident and member of the provincial legislative council. Trivedi, in a letter to the editor of the *Bombay Chronicle,* provided a rare view of the BDD's efforts to sell plots and houses in the garden suburb in Trombay:

> Middle class people go there every Saturday morning in the hope of finding a solution of their housing problem. I met a group which returned last Saturday from inspection of model Bungalows and they all expressed their disappointment. They thought they could own a bungalow for Rs. 5000 to be paid in easy monthly instalments but they now find that they have to pay the price of the land at Rs. 3/8 per sq yard. The bungalow too is disappointing: the plinth is low, bricks are sundried and mud is used in place of *chunam* [a kind of mortar].[57]

Trivedi ended his letter with an appeal to the provincial government to cease the suburban schemes, which relied upon compulsory acquisition through the Land Acquisition Act, and instead proceed through the mechanism of town planning, which gave greater discretion to local authorities.

The weight of public opinion against the suburban schemes, combined with the larger problems of the BDD as it got embroiled in scandal and failure with the better-known reclamation and industrial housing schemes, meant that the BDD's suburban schemes faded away after 1925, when the BDD itself lost its energy; it was folded into the Revenue Department of provincial government by the end of the decade. Only two of the suburban schemes seem to have been carried out: the Khar Model Suburb, in Khar in western Salsette, and the garden city in Trombay, which is now in Chembur.

More successful than the suburban schemes were the town planning schemes, many of which were proposed and framed in the boom years between 1916 and 1922, predominantly on the western side of Salsette. If an area were deemed ready for urbanization, then the relevant local body would, in conjunction with landholders, notify regional government of its intention to frame a town planning scheme. If regional government approved such intention, then the local authority would frame a draft town planning scheme. If government approved the draft scheme, then it appointed an arbitrator to verify landowners' titles, to assess the lands, and to oversee the process of converting the draft scheme into a final scheme. A board of appeal was appointed where the arbitrator's award could be challenged. There were thus numerous exchanges between the local authority and the regional authority in the framing of a scheme. The landowners concerned surrendered their original plots and were awarded equivalent plots after the scheme was completed. The local authority would assume some of the lands in the scheme for the construction of a street pattern and also for public spaces such as gardens, schools, and clinics. This was all part of the distinctive redistribution system permitted within the Bombay Town Planning Act. Thus, the final plots awarded to landowners would be smaller than the original plots and might even be located elsewhere within the scheme, but they were presumably of much greater value because of the urban infrastructure now in place. A portion of the enhanced value of the final plots was taken by the local authorities in the form of betterment charges to pay for the costs of laying down streets and other infrastructure. In essence, a town planning scheme had little to do with any overall aesthetic vision for the city, as noted above. It was essentially about changing the way land was perceived and treated. Whereas previously a logic of soil fertility and irrigation had determined the value of land, town planning imposed a new set of rules whereby value was determined by street frontage.

In a general sense, different observers pointed out that town planning entailed changes in the perception of the land and property. At the talk given by Mirams at the British Town Planning Institute in London, discussed above, one of the members of the audience had been H. V. Lanchester, an English architect and town planning pioneer who had spent time in India and who had given lectures on town planning in Madras.[58] Lanchester noted that whereas in Britain it was common to associate a single plot of land with a single owner or controlling interest, in India the situation was different, with families and clans having joint ownership of land.[59] In such a case, where some members of the family with an interest in the land might be physically quite distant, pooling and redistributing lands would raise specific challenges. Specifically, how might family members residing somewhere else, who might have an interest in a particular plot of land, react to the redistribution and reparceling of land under a town planning scheme? Essentially, the problem raised by Lanchester was that in India, models of property were to be encountered that were different from the liberal idea of ownership that had developed in Europe, where a single person was considered to be the owner of a piece of property. In the case of improvement schemes, such as had been operated by the BIT and the Madras Improvement Trust (with whom Lanchester had worked), the problem did not arise since land was forcibly acquired through the Land Acquisition Act. But since town planning entailed, in principle, the consensus of the landowners, then the redistribution effected by town planning raised the problem of securing consent from a wide and amorphous group of family or clan members who may have an interest in a piece of land that was about to become part of a town planning scheme.

A different kind of change in the perception of land arose from the fact that within a town planning scheme, the value of the land was to be determined by street frontage. As has been described above, this was a function of the fact that planned suburbanization entailed the penetration of the street networks into agrarian lands. Streets served not only in their more obvious capacity as channels of communication, but also as the bearers of urban infrastructure such as gas and electricity lines. Crucially, streets also served to regulate the height and shape

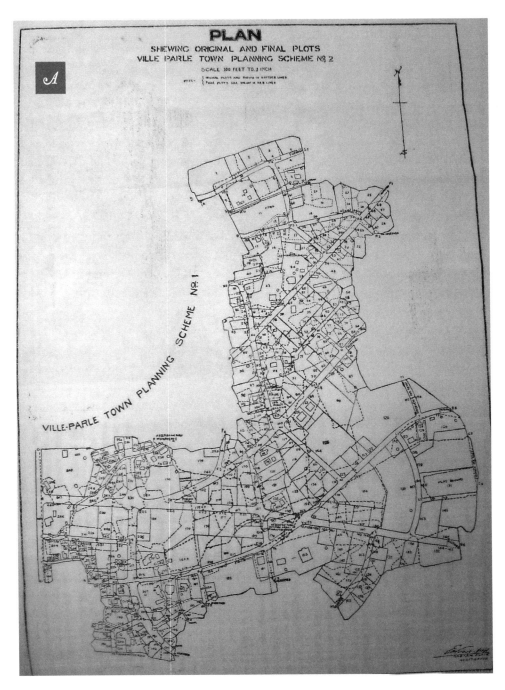

PLAN
SHEWING ORIGINAL AND FINAL PLOTS
VILLE PARLE TOWN PLANNING SCHEME № 2

SCALE 100 FEET TO 1 INCH

VILLE-PARLE TOWN PLANNING SCHEME № 1

𝒜 FIGURE 6.2. *A Vile Parle town planning scheme* (A) *and a Mahim town planning scheme*
(B). *These images show how town planning imposed a new street grid on a preexisting
fabric. In Vile Parle, irregular agrarian plots are reshaped into regular building plots, and
a street pattern is superimposed. In Mahim, an older street and building pattern is replaced
by a new, more regular pattern. Vile Parle scheme from* Local Self-Government Gazette,
*May 1923, between pages 242 and 243; Mahim scheme from Government of Bombay, Local
Self-Government Department,* Bombay City No. II (Mahim Area) (Final).

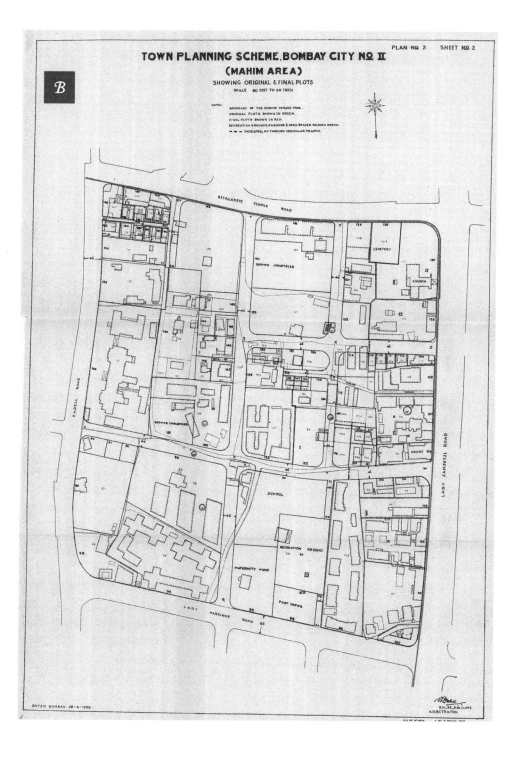

TOWN PLANNING SCHEME, BOMBAY CITY Nº II
(MAHIM AREA)
SHOWING ORIGINAL & FINAL PLOTS

SCALE   80 FEET TO AN INCH

NOTE:-
BOUNDARY OF THE SCHEME VERGED PINK.
ORIGINAL PLOTS SHOWN IN GREEN.
FINAL PLOTS SHOWN IN RED.
RECREATION GROUNDS, GARDENS & OPEN SPACES WASHED GREEN.
INDICATES, NO THROUGH VEHICULAR TRAFFIC.

DATED BOMBAY 28-4-1955.

B.Sc., B.E., B.Sc. (LON.)
ARBITRATOR

of buildings—and thus the physical shape of the suburb—because height and set-backs were indexed to the width of the street.

From British planners' point of view, increased street frontage meant increased value for a plot of land. This was why betterment charges taken from owners of plots within a town planning scheme were a function of the street frontage that was provided to their plots within the scheme: the more street frontage a plot received, the greater was the betterment charge. From the planners' point of view, this method of valuing land was so self-evident as to need no further elaboration. Yet there is reason to think that Indian landholders did not necessarily perceive land in this way. Rather, at least in some situations, Indian landholders seem to have believed that *less* street frontage was preferable to more. One way this alternative perception of the value of land manifested itself was in the idea of so-called *Vaagmukhi* land. *Vaagmukhi* land, as explained to me by various builders and architects, was land shaped like the head of a tiger with gaping jaws in profile. (*Vaag* is the word for "tiger" in Hindi, Marathi, and several other Indian languages, while *Mukh* is the word for "face.") In terms of street frontage, this was a piece of land that had a lot of street frontage (the space between the gaping jaws) in relation to a narrower rear portion (the rear of the tiger's head). *Vaagmukhi* land was always contrasted to *Gaimukhi* land, or land shaped like the head of a cow (*Gai*) with its jaws shut. In terms of the street, this was a plot of land that had less of the land in the front portion along the street (the clamped jaws of the cow) and a greater portion in the rear of the plot (the bulk of the head of the cow).

References to *Vaagmukhi* land are fragmentary but consistent in their suggestion that such land was undesirable, despite possessing excellent street frontage. In the hearings of the board of appeal for one of the Bandra town planning schemes, for instance, Leo Rodrigues, a major landowner in the area, mentioned the undesirability of *Vaagmukhi* land. Arguing against the betterment charges levied on the owner of the plot (Final Plot 22) by the arbitrator of the town planning scheme, Rodrigues claimed that the plot in question was a "*Waghmukhi,* and nobody is willing to purchase the same."[60] As can be seen on the top-right portion of the map of Bandra Town Planning Scheme 4 (Figure 6.3), on Plot 22, the side fronting the street is slightly wider than the side away from the street. Rodrigues was questioning the high final value (and thus high betterment charges) assigned to the plot under the scheme and was arguing that since the plot was *Vaagmukhi*, it would not be attractive despite having street frontage. It is difficult to understand exactly why *Vaagmukhi* land was undesirable. Most builders and architects seem to think that it had to do with superstition and the imprecise notion that the cow was associated with good fortune whereas the tiger was associated with ill luck. This appears to be borne out in the following allusion to *Vaagmukhi* by Soli Sorabjee, an eminent jurist and columnist for the *Indian Express* newspaper. Writ-

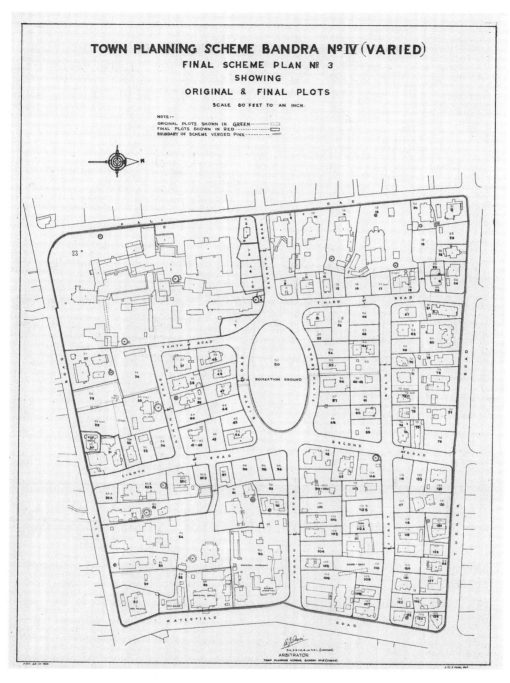

FIGURE 6.3. *Bandra Town Planning Scheme 4, Plan 3. Government of Bombay, Local Self-Government Department,* Bandra Town Planning Scheme, No. IV (Varied) (Final).

ing about the abuse of superstitions in the real estate business, Sorabjee wrote, "If the shape of the land projects *Waghmukhi* (tiger's face), it forebodes ill-luck and would be disastrous to purchase."[61] That *Vaagmukhi* was more than idle superstition was borne out by the fact that people were willing to back out of real estate transactions and undergo court proceedings if a property was so described. This was the case of one Ratanchand Hirachand, who in 1946 entered into a legal agreement to purchase a piece of land with a house upon it in the Walkeshwar area of Bombay. After having entered into a binding agreement, however, Hirachand was "unwilling to complete the transaction" because the property was known to be *Vaagmukhi,* and it "was a common superstition that a *vagmukhi* house brings ill-luck to the owner."[62]

Regardless of the exact etiology of the negative associations of *Vaagmukhi* land, the discussion above illustrates how local ways of perceiving land value did not always converge with town planners' assumptions, which equated enhanced street frontage with enhanced land value. However, this did not mean that Bandra landowners entirely rejected the logic of street frontage, either. Indeed, almost immediately after Rodrigues had contested one plot valuation on the basis of its *Vaagmukhi* character, he challenged another plot valuation on the basis that this plot—Plot 91, observable in the bottom-left portion of the map—"was an interior plot having no real road frontage."[63]

While landowners might have occasionally rejected the practice of valuing land on the basis of street frontage, mostly they were concerned with bringing their lands to market at the optimal moment. Thus, while the land price boom of 1916–1922 witnessed a whole slew of schemes being proposed and sanctioned for various parts of Salsette—almost exclusively along the stations of the railway line running along the western side of the island—the collapse in land prices after 1922 meant that landowners sought to stall and derail town planning schemes that had been proposed but had not yet been brought into effect. The rapid municipalization of Salsette meant that increasingly enfranchised landowners were able to stall town planning schemes until the land market turned more favorable in the 1940s. It is to this shift in the land and housing markets that I now turn.

THE 1940S AND ONWARD

From the 1940s onward, a variety of factors combined to transform the nature of the demand for land and housing in the suburbs of Bombay. As late as the mid-1940s, the supply of housing in the suburbs appears to have outstripped the demand. Informants regularly reported that the Apartment to Let signs were ubiquitous in Dadar–Matunga in this period, at least until the end of World War II.

Such stories were recounted to me by informants with a keen appreciation for the difference between that time and the present day, when housing is shockingly scarce and expensive and rental housing is almost nonexistent. Specifically, four features served to transform the nature of the housing market and set the stage for the rapid development of Salsette from the late 1940s onward, leading to its annexure to Bombay, as described above, but also to the proliferation of town planning schemes.[64]

The famous Rent Control Act of 1947 is usually adduced to explain the tightening of the rental housing market. Yet while there had actually been some sort of rent control in Bombay more or less since 1918, except for an interlude between 1928 and 1939, we only see a crunch in the supply of middle-class housing from the late 1940s onward. Besides, opinions differed in the 1950s upon the precise implications of the Rent Act for housing construction. Tenants' associations insisted that it was the high cost of building materials and land that had created housing shortages, whereas, unsurprisingly, landlords maintained that it was the Rent Act that was the principle damper on building activity.[65] The 1947 Rent Act is, therefore, a necessary but not a sufficient factor in explaining the shortage of housing.

A second important factor was the government's control of building materials. As argued in chapter 3, Bombay's growth upward was made possible by the increasingly widespread availability of RCC from the late 1920s onward. It is well known that with the launching of the First Plan in 1951, the state commandeered essential materials such as cement and steel for the purpose of constructing the large hydroelectric power projects so well loved by Jawaharlal Nehru. What is less well known is that such state control of building materials fit in seamlessly with what had been official practice for the previous decade: in 1941, the wartime colonial government passed the Defence of India Act, which, among other things, reserved the majority of cement and steel for the war effort and strictly controlled the supply of cement and steel to the building industry. From this time onward, anyone seeking to purchase cement—even for some minor repair in his or her own house—needed to apply to municipal authorities for a "certificate" before becoming eligible to purchase. Such controls put a damper on the building industry. Even the Bombay Municipal Corporation, seeking to celebrate its assimilation of a large area to the north of the city limits and its subsequent transformation into the Municipal Corporation of Greater Bombay in 1956 by adding a new Victorian Gothic wing, was forced to slow down the plan due to the shortage of cement.[66] Such shortages arising from the central government's planning priorities were compounded by its decision in 1957 to cease the import of cement.[67] Famously, shortages led to the notorious black market in cement that culminated in the downfall of the government of Maharashtra's chief minister, Abdul Rehman Antulay, in 1981–1982.

A third important factor specifically affecting building in the 1940s and 1950s was the imposition by the provincial Bombay government of the Urban Immoveable Property Tax in 1939, in effect until the mid-1950s, which placed a further damper on the market by temporarily disincentivizing house building as a form of investment. Much of the growth of Bombay's housing stock in the 1930s had been driven by the emergent practice among the middle class of putting their savings into an apartment building, an argument I elaborated in chapter 4. They would usually occupy one unit while renting out the others and thus assure themselves a steady if not spectacular income. The imposition of the Urban Immoveable Property Tax put a damper on this practice, prompting Claude Batley, mandarin of the Bombay housing scene for forty years, to remark that the tax had "proved a very severe set back in the provision of housing throughout Bombay, except for a few luxury flats and private residences."[68] The imposition of the tax was deemed a serious enough threat to housing that, as a preemptive move, the Bombay provincial government imposed the Bombay Rent Restriction Act of 1939 to prevent landlords from passing on the burden of the property tax to their tenants.[69]

The preceding factors adversely affected the supply of housing stock to the market. Meanwhile, Bombay witnessed a spectacular growth in population—with a resultant increase in the demand for housing—in the two decades between 1941 and 1961. The population went from about 1.8 million in 1941 to almost 3 million in 1951 and to almost 5 million in 1961. In these two decades the annual growth rate of the population was 5.1 percent and 3.3 percent, respectively, two of the three highest annual growth rates posted over the entire century. Partition in 1947, followed by an influx of refugees from Sindh and Punjab, constituted the immediate shock; but a more broad-based diversification of the industrial and commercial base of the city's economy beginning during World War II—with significant growth especially in petrochemicals and electricals—meant that increasing numbers of migrants were attracted to the city looking for work.

The extraordinary growth spurt between 1941 and 1961 is partially to be explained by the two annexures of

YEAR	Population of Bombay (in thousands)	Annual rate of growth over decade
1901	928	——
1911	1149	2.1
1921	1380	1.8
1931	1398	0.1
1941	1801	2.5
1951	2994	5.1
1961	4994	3.3
1971	5971	3.6
1981	8243	3.2
1991	9926	1.9

FIGURE 6.4. *Population of Bombay. From* Census of India: Primary Census Abstracts for Greater Bombay, 1901–1991; *reproduced in S. Deshpande, "Evidence of Under-enumeration in 1991 Census," 1539–1541.*

Salsette in 1950 and 1957 to create Greater Bombay, a larger census entity than existed previously. But another important reason for the increase in population was the migration into the city of large numbers of refugees from Sindh and Punjab. These factors combined to result in a situation in the 1950s in which a dramatically increased number of migrants sought housing in a market where supply of the predominant form of housing—rentals—was curtailed.

Such a changed housing market spurred the demand for housing in the suburbs of Bombay. In addition to continued southern Indian migration to Sion and Matunga, large colonies of Sindhis and Punjabis arose in Sion and Wadala. A part of the old Koli fishing village in Sion, for instance, was taken by the BMC to put up camps for two groups of Sindhi and Punjabi refugees.[70] Town planning schemes in Salsette, stalled since the 1920s, were reactivated, and new schemes were proposed. The combined logic of community considerations and economy that had driven building upward rather than outward in Dadar–Matunga, as elaborated in chapter 3, was also reproduced in the town planning schemes of Salsette. Much like Dadar–Matunga in the original colonial vision of the 1910s, Salsette as developed through town planning was envisioned as a suburb of bungalows and villas. All town planning schemes had strict bylaws that restricted construction to only one-quarter of the area of the plot, which meant that only ground-plus-one structures were possible. Indeed, one of the factors that tilted planning officials in favor of town planning was the fact that town planning schemes could be used to enforce new and more rigorous bylaws.

However, as in Dadar–Matunga, pressure from landowners forced alteration of building regulations, resulting in multistory housing. In Dadar–Matunga, as demonstrated in chapter 3, the Trust's original plan to restrict building to ground-plus-one structures was modified under pressure from landowners in the late 1910s to permit ground-plus-two buildings, an early precondition for the rise of the self-contained flat. In response to further pressure from landowners and the perception of a heightened housing shortage in the late 1940s, in 1949 the Bombay Municipal Corporation once again changed the terms of its leases in Dadar–Matunga and Shivaji Park to permit construction of another floor upon payment of increased ground rent.[71] The multistory building with ground plus three floors became still more common, and the suburban cottage receded still further into the realm of colonial planners' fantasy. From 1949 onward, owners of buildings in Dadar–Matunga and other suburbs increasingly added an extra floor to their ground-plus-two structures to yield incrementally taller buildings.

Municipal authorities permitted the construction of taller buildings on plots in the suburbs in the hope that this would add to the supply of low-income housing to accommodate the rapidly expanding population of the city, many of whom were either working-class migrants or impoverished refugees from Sindh and

FIGURE 6.5. *Matunga buildings with added floors. Author's photographs.*

Punjab. Such a contribution by the private sector was supposed to complement the government of India's own planned housing schemes for low-income residents of the city. However, the self-contained flat had already become hegemonic, and the result was to tilt new housing construction toward what were called self-contained blocks of flats of the sort described in chapter 3. Despite the concessions in increased building heights made to landowners, the municipal commissioner complained in 1953 that

> there was no improvement in the acute shortage of housing accommodation as there was no response from private enterprise for the construction of one or two room tenements which are required for low income group families. The tendency of the house owners is towards the construction of blocks which are beyond the reach of low income group.[72]

The problem was that as a result of the changes in the housing market discussed above, landowners were increasingly motivated to add capacity in the middle- and higher-income brackets rather than in the low-income bracket. Blocks of self-contained flats, rather than one- or two-room tenements, were the most common new additions to the housing stock.

The case of a town planning scheme in Bandra illustrates how the pattern toward middle- and upper-income apartment housing in Dadar–Matunga was reproduced in the town planning schemes of Salsette. This scheme had been sanctioned in 1937, but in the wake of changed housing conditions in the 1940s, landowners succeeded in pressing local authorities to "vary" the scheme in 1948 and change some of the regulations contained in it.[73] At the heart of the varied scheme was landowners' desire to change the original regulations, which only permitted one-quarter of the plot to be built upon, and only with ground-plus-one structures. Such regulations would have permitted only small cottages even within a fairly large plot. Landowners sought, successfully, to vary the scheme to permit construction on one-third of the area of the plot and to permit ground-plus-two buildings, to bring the regulations more in line with the prevailing regulations in other suburbs of Bombay, such as Dadar–Matunga and also the lands in Salsette owned by the collector. (These would have been the suburban schemes in Khar and Chembur discussed above.) Increasing the footprints and the heights of the buildings, as these varied regulations did, meant that apartments were now more likely to be built than cottages or bungalows. An important secondary purpose of varying the scheme was to lay in sewerage lines and also to pave the roads and construct storm drains. While landowners were successful in increasing the permissible built-up area to facilitate the construction of multistory buildings, the *kind* of multistory buildings that were imagined by landowners is also interesting. One landowner, the same Leo Rodrigues who appeared in an earlier discussion of this scheme, repeatedly challenged the incremental value assigned by the arbitrator on the grounds that to fully take advantage of the regulations in the scheme and the provision of sewerage, landowners would have to make substantial investments in transforming their dwellings. Most importantly, they would have to invest in changing the existing outhouses based on either the basket privy or a septic tank into internal toilets on the flushing system.[74] In other words, landowners such as Rodrigues imagined that the new structures they would erect on the town planning scheme would be apartment buildings of self-contained flats rather than tenements.

The middle- and upper-middle-class suburbs developing along the western edge of Salsette thus gradually began to physically resemble the suburbs in Dadar–Matunga as multistory apartment buildings with self-contained flats became more common than bungalows and villas. Independence and Partition in 1947 were significant in that they prompted a gigantic spurt of migration by Sindhis and Punjabis into the city, but the patterns of urban growth did not change significantly. Town planning continued as the principal mechanism through which the city expanded physically until 1964, when a far-reaching new development plan for Greater Bombay was promulgated, seeking to bring the entire city and region within its planning ambit. Meanwhile, state support for middle-class housing used the measures taken by the colonial state during the previous housing crunch of 1916–1922: support for cooperative housing societies through a combination of help with land acquisition and cheap loans. As a result of state support for cooperative housing societies by the independent government of India in the 1950s, the cooperative movement received a major boost, and increasingly migrants from Sindh and Punjab organized themselves into cooperative housing societies of the sort pioneered in the suburbs of Bombay.[75]

There is reason to believe that migrants from Sindh and Punjab living in cooperative housing societies in suburban Bombay began to see themselves as "Sindhis" and "Punjabis" in this very particular context. Thus, large metacaste forms of identity such as the South Indian, incorporating regional, linguistic, caste, and class aspects, became increasingly significant in the cosmopolitan ethos of Bombay in the 1950s. While notions such as "Sindhiyat" and "Punjabiyat" undoubtedly had to do with these communities' diasporic and refugee predicament, equally significant in shaping these identities were the material and cultural environments of Bombay.[76]

While the imperatives of living in cooperative housing societies might have resulted in the creation of larger regional identities such as Sindhi, it was also the case that the waves of migration after Partition, especially by Sindhis, resulted in changes to the nature of the cooperative housing societies. As discussed above, support for cooperative housing societies was the mechanism through which the postcolonial Government of Bombay sought to deal with the problems of middle-class housing, especially the housing of refugees. Migrants from Sindh seized upon governmental incentives such as low-interest loans and help in land acquisition and quickly began to establish cooperative housing societies. In the climate of acute housing scarcity of the late 1940s and the early 1950s, where rent control and other factors disincentivized new rental construction, the cooperative housing society quickly became the principal form of new housing construction.

Sindhi entrepreneurs transformed the nature of the cooperative housing society by putting it on a fully commercial basis. As has been described in chapter 5, the cooperative society was a peculiar institution expressly designed to permit migrants to meet urban imperatives such as housing and banking while maintaining their community identity. In the original model pioneered by the Saraswats, the Parsis, and the South Indians in the 1910s and 1920s, an already-constituted community formed a cooperative society and then approached a builder or architect to construct an apartment building. This model was followed in the early Sindhi cooperative housing societies such as Shyam Niwas and Nanik Niwas on Warden Road. By the 1950s, however, Sindhi entrepreneurs started offering flats in apartment buildings to anyone who was seeking housing and could afford it.

The commercialization of cooperative housing societies meant that societies had less control over who lived in their buildings, as the logic of purchasing power gradually supplemented communal affinity in organizing the composition of buildings. This trend was further exacerbated by the new legislation passed by the government of Maharashtra in 1961, legislation that, in keeping with the secular agenda of Nehruvian India, sought to disallow discrimination on the basis of community in the membership of cooperative societies. While earlier cooperative housing societies such as the Saraswats, Parsis, Catholics, and South Indians had been able to explicitly restrict admission on the basis of community, the commercialization of cooperative housing in the 1950s, combined with the state's efforts to disallow such discrimination, meant that the new housing societies could not serve as effectively in physically policing the boundaries of community.

Perhaps for this reason, specific communities among migrants from Sindh established formal caste institutions to preserve their distinctive identities. One such association was the Khudabadi Amil Panchayat, formed among the Amils of Bombay in 1952. The Amils are one of the two principal Sindhi Hindu communities, and they formed a large portion of the migrants to Bombay after Partition. Interestingly, Amils as a community appear to have originated not as one of the traditional subcastes of the subcontinent but, rather, out of the various Hindu communities that migrated to Sindh during Mughal rule and succeeded in educating themselves and entering government service.[77]

According to the reminiscences of a senior member of the community and one of the original members of the Khudabadi Amil Panchayat, in cities such as Hyderabad, where Amils used to be concentrated, the members of the community lived in close proximity to one another:

> In Hyderabad all lanes named after our ancestors like Advani, Kripalani, Mansukhani, etc., were interconnected with each other as neighbourhood. . . . The result and advantage of being [physically] well knit was that on occasions such as deaths, marriages, childbirths etc. all Amils could attend together as a community, finding of grooms within the community and finalizing of marriage was convenient.[78]

In Punwaney's account, the sheer physical proximity of Amils in towns such as Hyderabad and Karachi was an effective means of maintaining the integrity of the community. In large heterogeneous cities like Bombay, however, the physical dispersion of people across the space of the city made it impossible to have proximity determine the boundaries of community:

> In course of time Amils along with other displaced persons went on settling down wherever they were able to get accommodation all over Bombay. Bombay is a vast city of distances. Getting accommodation in locations of one's choice with a view to be

near friends, relatives or even where other Amils are settled has always been a difficult proposition. Even chance meeting on the roads or in buses or trains between friends, relatives were a rarity.[79]

In Punwaney's account, the physical sprawl of the city meant that even a community that prided itself on its education and progressive nature was forced to embrace a seemingly traditional institution such as the caste panchayat. (A greater irony may lie in the fact that, by Punwaney's own account, the Amils may not even have been a "caste" at all.)

The Khudabadi Amil Panchayat sought to reinforce the "joy and sense and feeling of belonging to the known community"[80] by organizing meetings and conferences to address challenges facing the Amils in Bombay. The meetings were meant to reinforce feelings of community, to resolve disputes among families within the community, and, finally, to meet the great challenge of organizing matrimonial alliances within the community. Such meetings were held in those areas where significant numbers of Amils lived, such as Bandra, Sion, Warden Road, and Churchgate. Thus, even though the Amils did not live in areas that were large enough to be distinctly identifiable as "Sindhi neighborhoods" (although there were certainly "Sindhi buildings" and even "Sindhi lanes" in neighborhoods), through such meetings dispersed across the space of the city, they were nonetheless able to establish the physicality of their presence in the city.

Even while working to establish the integrity of the Amil community, though, the Amils acknowledged the imperative of synthetic identity described previously in the formation of "South Indian" identity. Thus, while membership in the Khudabadi Amil Panchayat was restricted to Khudabadi Amils, the constitution of the panchayat retained the right to admit any Sindhi Hindu provided he or she "has relationship or affinity with any family or brotherhood recognized by the Khudabadi Amil Panchayat of Hyderabad Sind or Karachi."[81] In this way, the Amils acknowledged a larger Sindhi identity in the Bombay context while asserting the particularity of Amil identity.

In the years after Independence, the patterns of suburbanization in Bombay and Salsette at the level of lands, dwellings, and communities elaborated and modified patterns that had been pioneered in the suburbs of Dadar–Matunga. Town planning emerged as an alternative mode of land use conversion to the more authoritarian land acquisitions of the Bombay Improvement Trust. While cooperative housing societies in multistory apartment buildings overwhelmingly became the norm in the new suburbs, the very nature of the cooperative housing society changed and became more commercially oriented. In defining communities of "Sindhis" and "Punjabis," new migrants to the city residing in these apartment buildings exhibited some of the same forms of fragmentation and synthesis exhibited by South Indians in Matunga. Yet changes in the nature of the cooperative society in cosmopolitan Nehruvian Bombay meant that some of the mechanisms used by South Indians were not available to Sindhis and Punjabis, necessitating the formation of formal caste associations such as the Khudabadi Amil Panchayat of Bombay. Here too, though, oscillating between highly specific understandings of the community as Khudabadi Amils in some contexts and a broader understanding of the community as Sindhi in other contexts remained an enduring pattern of urban identity in postcolonial Bombay.

Conclusion

OVER THE PAST TWENTY YEARS, FAR-REACHING CHANGES HAVE transformed the economic, material, and sociocultural environments of Mumbai. Deregulation of the Indian economy and of the built environment in the city has meant that the city's physical and demographic face is changing at an astounding rate. Indeed, the very idea of "suburb," while still in use, means something entirely different than it did in the early and mid-twentieth century. As the city has expanded relentlessly northward into Salsette and further north and east into Thane District on the mainland, the original suburbs of Dadar–Matunga are now part of south-central Mumbai. The "suburban" character of many of the suburbs has also changed. While Dadar–Matunga remains resolutely residential, parts of many of the suburbs to the north have, over the last decade, been transformed into white-collar office parks. Many of the suburbs to the northeast, developed as industrial suburbs in the 1950s and 1960s, have struggled to cope with the deindustrialization that has been the pattern since at least the 1980s.

The areas to the north of Dadar–Matunga have changed dramatically, and the same can certainly be said for those to the south. Formerly the industrial working-class areas of Parel, Lalbaug, Chinchpokli, and Byculla, these places have witnessed a staggering transformation in just the last ten years. Factories have come down to be replaced by office and residential towers. Alternatively, factories have been repurposed as fashionable nightclubs or galleries. Entire districts such as Lower Parel have been rebranded by real estate agents as Upper Worli in order to disassociate the space from the working-class connotations of the place-name Parel and instead associate it with the fashionable address of Worli, where the Improvement Trust planned an exclusive upper-class residential enclave in the 1920s.

There has been an inexorable drift of the center of gravity of the city northward, from the "city" to the "suburbs," to the point where the latter actually constitutes the former. With the establishment of gigantic new commercial districts in Bandra, Andheri, and New Bombay, once-distant suburbs in Salsette and Thane are now where many people go to work. A long-standing visual signifier of the city's working life—the sight of overcrowded suburban trains bearing workers south in the mornings and north and northeast to the suburbs at the end of the day—is no longer as predictable as it once was. The suburbs are now the center of the city.

Dadar–Matunga and its apartment buildings have also changed. From an out-lying suburb that had trouble attracting residents in the 1930s because of its distance from the city to the south, Dadar–Matunga has now become extremely desirable precisely because its location means that it is equally well-connected both to the older parts of the city to the south and to the sprawling suburbs to the north and east. The very desirability of Dadar–Matunga has increased the pressure on the suburban character of the neighborhood, resulting in changes in the regulations governing building height that had been zealously protected for so long. The ground-plus-three apartment buildings that had been a constant of the neighborhood are increasingly being replaced by much taller structures, some as many as fourteen stories high. Figure C.1, a photograph, taken in 2005, of a new building under construction adjacent to an older building on Bhau Daji Road in the heart of Matunga, tells the story of the changing patterns of middle-class housing since the end of the period covered by this book.

The older building to the right of the image shows a classic older ground-plus-two building with its compound. A third floor has been added to it, probably at

✒ FIGURE C.1. *New building on Bhau Daji Road next to older building. Author's photograph, circa 2005.*

some point in the 1950s or early 1960s, to take advantage of an increase in the permissible building height. The newer top floor remains unpainted, probably because of a dispute between the tenants and the owner of the building. Since the tenants pay very low rents as a result of rent control, owners have no incentive to maintain buildings. Hence, many older buildings are in highly dilapidated and precarious condition, which has prompted the state to extend substantial incentives to builders to redevelop such older buildings. Incentives are usually extended in the form of permission to build much higher and more densely than the regulations permit, which is why the newer buildings, such as the one on the left side of this image, are so much taller and broader than older buildings. However, developers themselves often run out of money while executing such projects, resulting in stalled or frozen structures, such as the one we see here: only very desultory activity was taking place when I walked by almost daily for a period of several weeks in 2005. Once the market picked up, however, the developer quickly pushed the project through, and the building seen under construction here has long been occupied, as are several new similar structures that have come up in the vicinity since this photograph was taken.

The buildings have changed, and the demographic character of the neighborhood is also in transition. Consider the sign shown in Figure C.2, found prominently displayed at the entrance to a Punjabi restaurant not far from the buildings pictured in Figure C.1. This sign was no doubt put up by the annoyed owner of the restaurant, fed up with being asked, repeatedly, whether *idlis* and *dosas* (popular South Indian dishes) were served there. Yet the persistent demands for *idlis* and *dosas* did not mark the enduring presence of South Indians in Matunga (who would have been less likely to eat such food at restaurants); rather, they pointed to the significant Gujarati population that has moved into the neighborhood and embraced the attractions of Matunga, especially the many establishments serving vegetarian South Indian snacks. South Indians, meanwhile, had begun moving northeast, to suburbs in Chembur, Mulund, Vashi, and Dombivili. While many middle-class South Indians still live there, Matunga itself now has a definitely moneyed feel to it.

Such changes notwithstanding, the suburbs of Dadar–Matunga represented a pioneering transformation in middle-class ways of inhabiting the city. From the 1920s, when the first migrants moved in, until the 1960s, when the first significant wave of retirees used their public provident fund payouts to move from the rental housing of Matunga into ownership flats in the northeast suburbs, Matunga evolved into a prototype of middle-class urban living in Bombay. Apartment buildings consisting of ethnically organized cooperative housing societies in residential neighborhoods became the template for future middle-class expansion. The growth and proliferation of informal settlements was one dominant narra-

⌐🙰 FIGURE C.2. *Sign outside a Punjabi restaurant. Author's photograph.*

tive of urban growth in the postcolonial city, but the ethnically marked apartment building suburb was another, less noticed, pattern.

House, but No Garden has sought to demonstrate the significance of suburban apartment living. In doing so, it visually and analytically links the colonial city with the postcolonial city. In elaborating the significance of apartment building suburbs, it analyzes one of the two most significant changes in the built environment in Bombay from the 1920s onward. (The other is the proliferation of informal settlements.)

House, but No Garden has argued that understanding this form of middle-class living offers insight into three significant shifts in urban life: at the levels of land, dwellings, and communities. At the level of land, the challenge of converting lands at the urban edge from agrarian to urban use resulted in new constellations of relations among the state, landholders, and other residents of the city. In acquiring lands for the suburbs of Dadar, Matunga, and Sion, the Bombay Improvement Trust, founded in 1898, also became one of the first entities in colonial India to deploy the powerful new imperial Land Acquisition Act of 1894. In determining the conditions under which lands could be resumed from landholders by the state in the public interest, the eminent domain–type acquisitions of the Improvement Trust also had the paradoxical effect of clarifying the meaning of urban "property" in land, of facilitating the commodification of land. After 1915, however, partly in response to the withdrawal of the colonial state from urban intervention, suburban lands in Salsette were created through the mechanism of town planning, a more collaborative system of land-use conversion where landholders retained ownership of their lands. Both forms of land-use conversion resulted in new ways of perceiving land. These two phases of suburban expansion—through land acquisition by the Improvement Trust in Dadar–Matunga and through town planning in Salsette—thus represented two distinct modes of state intervention in urban lands. One mode did not replace the other in any consistent fashion; rather, the state's role in urban intervention over the course of the twentieth century oscillated between these two modes of land-use conversion. This book suggests that thinking through when and in what way the state acquires land offers a new way of thinking about the state's role in urban intervention.

At the level of dwellings, apartment living in self-contained flats represented a departure from living in houses and tenements, where toilets were external to the dwelling. A novel form that made its first sustained appearance in the suburbs of Dadar–Matunga in the 1920s, the apartment or flat became the hegemonic mode of dwelling, moving from the suburbs back into the city. But the Bombay flat was not simply available as a form of dwelling and as a practice of urban living that had already been developed in Europe. Rather, the Bombay flat and apartment living assumed shape as a category and set of practices in the suburbs of Dadar–Matunga through the conjuncture of the political economy of land and housing, on the one hand, and the caste and class considerations of the suburbs' lower-middle-class, upper-caste residents, on the other. Specifically, the movement of buildings "upward" and the movement of the toilet "inward" into the dwelling distinguished the apartment from the house and the tenement. Representing not only a culmination of technological and infrastructural developments over the 1920s, the toilet-in-the-dwelling was also a significant conceptual shift for upper-caste suburban residents. The positive aspects of control over sanitation offered by the internal toilet were juxtaposed with the negativity associated with the polluting nature of bodily functions, making the toilet an uneasy but defining presence in the middle-class household. Understanding how modern built forms such as the apartment building are assimilated into the South Asian urban setting offers a critical perspective on the idea of a universal urban modernity.

The embrace of a public health view of bodily functions, and apartment living more generally, was part of a broader transformation in ideas of community that began in Dadar–Matunga. Many of the early residents of the new suburbs in the 1920s were upper-caste (principally Brahmin) migrants from Madras Presidency, Cochin, and Travancore in southern India. Under the often-conflicting imperatives of seeking to maintain the exclusivity typical of caste and subcaste, while also needing to form large enough collectives to be viable in the urban setting, these migrants combined caste with class, type of work, and residence to forge new metacaste forms of community identity. Migrants from southern India became "South Indians," a fluid and flexible category that served to redraw the boundaries of inclusion within and exclusion from the community. Critical to the refashioning of identity was the novel suburban environment of apartment buildings, where residence was distinct from work. In contrast to older parts of the city, where work was visible and the community identity of a neighborhood could be read from visible markers of the dominant caste or subcaste group residing and working there, the residential character of Dadar–Matunga made possible an abstraction from the specificity of caste and occupation. Such metacaste forms of identity became the norm as subsequent waves of migrants flooded the expanding city after decolonization. The book has thus suggested that examining the ways in which ideas of caste and community are transformed in the context of the spaces of the modern city is an important way to think about modern urban identity in South Asia.

Acknowledgments

🙦 ᷐᷐ᷤ᷑ᷤ᷑ MY INTEREST IN HOUSING AND SUBURBAN GROWTH IN BOMBAY
developed while I was writing my dissertation in the Department of History at
the University of Chicago. Dipesh Chakrabarty, Ron Inden, and Moishe Post-
one, the members of my committee, were patient and indulgent advisers. Dipesh
encouraged me to think critically about the seeming universality of apartment
living as a form of urban dwelling; his insistent questioning of the apparent lacuna in the urban historiography of the period after 1918 pushed me to make this
critical period the heart of the book. Ron inspired me to approach problems in
unconventional ways. Moishe urged me to think about political economy and to
consider Bombay in the context of other cities. Ralph Austen and Prasenjit Duara
provided advice and support. Survival in graduate school was possible thanks to
my friends and fellow travelers in the Chicago South Asia scene of those years,
including Spencer Leonard, Rochona Majumdar, Prithvidatta Chandrashobhi,
Riaz Khan, Whitney Cox, Suzanne Morrison Cox, Amanda Hamilton, Daisy
Rockwell, Aaron York, David Clingingsmith, Simon Mkrtschjan, Bali Sahota,
Manan Ahmed, Rajeev Kinra, and Blake Wentworth. Research in India for my
dissertation was supported by an American Institute of Indian Studies junior research fellowship as well as by grants from the University of Chicago's Committee on Southern Asian Studies.

Arjun Appadurai and the late Carol Breckenridge guided me in my developing
interest in the city they knew so well. Carol played a key role: in helping me see the
physical distinctiveness of Dadar–Matunga and in noting the novel form of community that emerged there, she was crucial in helping me conceptualize this book.
Sadly, she will not be able to see my attempt to follow through on her insights.

Frank Magilligan, Mona Domosh, and the Department of Geography at Dartmouth College, where I taught as an adjunct instructor while writing my dissertation and where I spent a portion of my leave year writing this book, offered me an
excellent alternative institutional home. Manuel Rota and Nora Stoppino played
important roles as interlocutors and hosts at a critical stage of the project. Adrian
Randolph, then director of the Leslie Center for the Humanities, and Isabel Weat-
herdon, the center's administrator, made the center's resources available to me
during my leave year in 2009–2010. The librarians at Dartmouth were extraordinarily helpful in procuring materials. I'm especially grateful to Hazen Allen for

his heroic efforts in this regard and to Miguel Valladares. I'm also grateful to the librarians at the University of Chicago's Regenstein Library, especially James Nye, Chris Winters, and the staff at the Map Collection, and to the staff at Special Collections, as well as to the staff at the Center for Research Libraries in Chicago.

Douglas E. Haynes played a crucial role in the emergence of this book. He read the entire manuscript and offered support in innumerable ways, from encouragement and steady assurance to sharp-eyed and thoughtful critique.

Wellesley College has been an extraordinary institutional home. Support from Wellesley made possible several research trips to Mumbai. My colleagues in the Department of History have been gracious and supportive during the challenging process of writing a book. Lidwien Kapteijns and Alejandra Osorio, especially, offered not just support but important observations and helped me think about Mumbai from a comparative perspective.

Eric Beverley and Shekhar Krishnan have been invaluable friends and fellow South Asian urbanists. Shekhar Krishnan established the Urban South Asia workshop at MIT. Most of my dissertation was subjected to close reading by members of this workshop. Michael M. J. Fischer of MIT attended most of these sessions and encouraged me to take ethnography and oral history as seriously as historians' more conventional sources. Eric Beverley and Erik Ghenoiu helped me see Bombay in the context of other cities in South Asia and elsewhere.

This book could not have been written without the help and support of Shekhar Krishnan. Interested in similar aspects of the city, Shekhar helped me in almost every possible way: from discussing ideas and broad themes, to suggesting sources, to helping me meet people in Matunga, to reading and commenting on portions of my manuscript. I'm fortunate to have known someone as obsessively preoccupied with Bombay in general and Dadar–Matunga in particular as I was.

My parents, extended family, and friends greatly facilitated my research and stays in Mumbai. I thank my uncle Raju Bharatan, whose encyclopedic knowledge included an invaluable appreciation of the city in the 1950s. I also acknowledge my aunts Girija Rajendran and Kavita Bharatan, who each expressed interest in the book and cooked for me countless times, but who sadly are not here today. My cousin Raju Srinivasan, who also is no more, and his wife Padma helped me by introducing me to people in Matunga, where they lived for many years.

Too many people in Matunga helped me and obliged me with their time for me to acknowledge them individually. I would like to make special note of Kamu Iyer and S. Ramachandran. Kamu Iyer met with me dozens of times and offered me the invaluable perspective of a lifelong South Indian resident of Dadar–Matunga who is a highly regarded and experienced architect. He introduced me to many people who in turn helped me further. S. Ramachandran, a former municipal corporator and a lifelong resident of Matunga, helped me think about the locality in the broader context of the city. Other people in Matunga I acknowledge are Dr. K. Shankar; V. Shankar, secretary of the South Indian Education Society in 2000; M. A. Rajagopalan; K. P. Chari; I. G. Gopalakrishnan; and Zarine Engineer.

The staff at the Maharashtra State Archives, especially Shri Ashok Kharade, who supervised the reading room during my time there, was extraordinarily helpful. I thank the staffs at the Asiatic Society Library and the library of the Indian Institute of Architects. I'm grateful to S. A. Reddi of Gammon India for talking to me about the illustrious history of this firm in the Bombay construction industry, and to Abhijit Rajan, chairman and managing director of Gammon India, for granting me permission to reproduce images from Gammon's remarkable collection of photographs of buildings under construction.

Other people in Mumbai who helped me include the late V. Subramaniam, former secretary, Housing Department of the Government of Maharashtra; N. V. Iyer; Shri Vasant P. Prabhu, deputy municipal commissioner, MCGM; Anirudh Paul, director of the Kamala Raheja Vidyanidhi Institute of Architecture; and Prasad Shetty of the Kamla Raheja Vidyanidhi Institute for Architecture and Environmental Studies (KRVIA) Design Cell. I am especially grateful to Ashok Kulkarni of the pioneering architectural firm Marathe and Kulkarni, who spent many hours talking to me about his father's and his own experiences and showed me his collection of architectural drawings. Other friends in Mumbai who helped me in ways direct and indirect include Vaishnavi Chandrashekhar, Namita Devidayal, Naresh Fernandes, Jeannie and Mark Koops-Elson, Rina Agarwala, Carsten Stendevad, Rohan Sippy, Rajeev Samant, and Pratish Motwane.

This book has relied heavily on the writings and ideas of scholars of Bombay and other cities. I would like to thank Frank Conlon, Gyan Prakash, the late Rajnarayan Chandavarkar, Mariam Dossal, and William Glover; each took time to talk to me about the city and my book, and some read parts of the book manuscript. I especially thank Sharon Marcus; not only was her pioneering book *Apartment Stories* an inspiring study of apartment living, but she thoughtfully engaged with me in my attempts to distinguish the South Asian apartment experience from the European one. I'm grateful to the editors and members of the H-Urban and H-Asia communities, who offered valuable advice in response to my queries.

Pieter Martin at the University of Minnesota Press has been a wonderful editor. Kristian Tvedten helped me prepare the manuscript for publication, and Kathy Delfosse did an extraordinarily thorough job copyediting it. I'm grateful to everyone at the Press for their patience, responsiveness, and help throughout this process.

This book is dedicated to my parents Kamala and Raghunatha Rao. Patient, loving, and supportive, they reserved judgment as I veered off the engineering track and wandered onto a path then very unfamiliar to them. They have always been steady and unflinching in their support, and I hope that this book in some small measure acknowledges my immense and unrepayable debt to them.

Veronika Fuechtner has been a rock for me over the years. She listened patiently, cooked for me, and did innumerable other things to help during critical periods of the writing of this book. She read countless drafts, chapters, and passages, in varying degrees of unfinishedness, and offered thoughtful and measured advice. Unfamiliar with India before she met me, she took the plunge into the subcontinent and immersed herself in the life of Mumbai. I could not have done it without her.

Notes

INTRODUCTION

1. The first suburbs of Dadar–Matunga were within municipal limits. As the suburbanization of Salsette Island to the north of Bombay city progressed, discussions over the possible amalgamation of Salsette with the city ensued, culminating in the annexure of large parts of Salsette in 1950 and 1957 to create Greater Bombay.

2. Some European cities experienced suburbanization in the form of multistory dwellings, especially workers' housing estates. For such instances in Germany and Austria, see von Saldern, "The Workers' Movement and Cultural Patterns," and Blau, *The Architecture of Red Vienna.*

3. As a result of historical accident, the physical entity of Bombay Island, and later the municipal entity of Bombay, greatly exceeded in size the developed city of Bombay. Suburban development in the north of the island filled out the city to encompass the island.

4. This point is made by Brian Ladd with reference to the growth of German cities. Ladd, *Urban Planning and Civic Order in Germany,* 78.

5. Chandavarkar, *The Origins of Industrial Capitalism in India.*

6. The only exceptions were small private professional practices: a medical clinic, say, or an accountancy practice was permissible on the ground floor as long as it was a private practice.

7. *Wadis* and *mohullas* are neighborhood units in older parts of the city. They tend to have dense building patterns organized around a lane or group of lanes and are usually mixed use, combining work and residence. They are often associated with a particular caste or community.

8. William Glover's essay "Construing Urban Space as 'Public' in Colonial India" shows how modern ideas of the municipal public negotiated older, indigenous ideas of the collectivity in Punjabi towns between the 1870s and the 1920s.

9. Glover, *Making Lahore Modern*; Chattopadhyay, *Representing Calcutta*; and Chopra, *A Joint Enterprise.*

10. There were, of course, limitations to these measures of sovereignty, since the supply of funds to undertake public works and so on were still controlled almost entirely by the British.

11. The works of Clive Dewey provide a good general background for this important shift in British policy and the resultant wartime and postwar boom. Dewey, "The Government of India's 'New Industrial Policy'" and "The End of the Imperialism of Free Trade." For an account that elaborates the diversification and expansion of the Bombay economy, especially the emergence of the white-collar sector, see Gordon, *Businessmen and Politics.*

12. Two recent works address this lacuna in South Asian urban historiography. Gyan Prakash's *Mumbai Fables,* esp. chaps. 3 and 7, considers links between the city's politics and land-use decisions. Mariam Dossal's *Theatre of Conflict, City of Hope* emphasizes the changing status of land as Bombay Is-

land urbanized and the city expanded over a 350-year period.

13. Appadurai, "Number in the Colonial Imagination," 329.

14. Warner, *Streetcar Suburbs*, vii.

15. So, for instance, an excellent new survey of industrialization and urbanization in Europe has chapters examining various aspects of urbanization in European cities and then one final chapter on "imperial and colonial cities." The authors' aim, of course, is to show how the colonial experience decisively shaped both metropolitan and peripheral cities. Yet one unintended effect of such a treatment is to suggest that all colonial cities share the same single problem—that of being colonial—and do not need the kinds of variegated analysis that other cities merit. Lees and Lees, *Cities and the Making of Modern Europe*.

16. This literature is immense. Some works include Sam Bass Warner, *Streetcar Suburbs*; Fishman, *Bourgeois Utopias*; Jackson, *Crabgrass Frontier*; Kruse and Sugrue, *The New Suburban History*; and Archer, *Architecture and Suburbia*.

17. This has also recently been pointed out by Richard Harris. See his "Meaningful Types in a World of Suburbs."

18. Jackson, *Crabgrass Frontier*, 8–9.

19. For two recent accounts, see Davis, *Planet of Slums*, and Neuwirth, *Shadow Cities*. It is noteworthy that most such studies focus on present-day squatter settlements. We have very little historical understanding of how such settlements are constituted. It is obviously very difficult to write histories of squatter settlements since such settlements are, by definition, irregular, and thus historical source materials can be difficult to find.

20. Chandavarkar, "Bombay's Perennial Modernities," in his *Culture, History, and the Indian City*; and Prakash, *Mumbai Fables*.

21. This was the framing problematic of a special issue of the journal *Seminar*: "The Problem: A Short Statement on the Issues Involved," in "City of Dreams: A Symposium on the Many Facets of Bombay," special issue, *Seminar* 528 (August 2003). For studies that elaborate and complicate this problematic, see Hansen, *Wages of Violence*, and Appadurai, "Spectral Housing and Urban Cleansing."

22. Hansen, *Wages of Violence*. The Shiv Sena is a regionalist political party that emerged in the late 1960s on the platform of targeting migrants from other regions of India.

23. Joshi, *The Middle Class in Colonial India*.

24. In addition to some of the essays in Joshi's edited volume, Anne Hardgrove's study of the Marwari community is an excellent example of the ways in which certain communities combine caste and occupation in large heterogeneous urban settings to forge metaforms of identities. Hardgrove, *Community and Public Culture*.

25. Kidambi, "Consumption, Domestic Economy, and the Idea of the 'Middle Class.'" This essay first appeared in Haynes et al., *Towards a History of Consumption in South Asia*.

26. Chatterjee, "Are Indian Cities Becoming Bourgeois at Last?" and Kaviraj, "Filth and the Public Sphere." Chakrabarty's "Of Garbage, Modernity, and the Citizen's Gaze," in his *Habitations of Modernity*, is another fine study of this problem. Here I focus on Chatterjee and Kaviraj since they discuss the *changing* ways in which social spaces are perceived and used in postcolonial India.

27. This distinction is elaborated in

Chatterjee, "On Civil and Political Society in Postcolonial Democracies."

28. Kaviraj, "Filth and the Public Sphere," 108.

29. The Marathi *Manoos* is, of course, the allegedly downtrodden Marathi-speaking everyman in whose name the Shiv Sena has constructed its nativist platform, beginning in the 1960s by targeting South Indians, then Muslims, and now, most recently, North Indians. The category of the Marathi *Manoos,* seemingly an ethnic category, cannot be understood without considering not only struggles over language and culture but also, equally, struggles over housing and employment.

30. It is thus no coincidence that when the municipal franchise was widened in 1922, the basis of the franchise shifted from ratepayers to rentpayers: housing, rather than property, now became the defining feature of the citizenry.

✣ 1. AN INDIAN SUBURB

1. Bombay Improvement Trust, *Annual Administration Report* (henceforth BIT, *Annual Administration Report*), for the year 1920–1921, 1.

2. The Trust's Dadar–Matunga suburbs were not by any means the first instance of city extension undertaken by the colonial state. Especially when it came to the attempted transformation of older cities such as Lahore, Delhi, or Hyderabad, what William Glover has called a "colonial spatial imagination" came into play. Such an epistemology rendered the native city opaque and unknowable, thus prompting British authorities to turn their attention to the edges of existing cities, building cantonments and civil lines for themselves

in these peripheries, while also seeking to transform the more comprehensible villages to be found in this region. See Glover, *Making Lahore Modern,* chap. 2. What distinguished Dadar–Matunga was, first, that it was undertaken with full consciousness—among both British and Indians—that mass suburbanization was an accepted response to the problems of industrialization, and second, more importantly, that these suburbs were intended entirely for Indians.

3. The mere fact that no one has undertaken to investigate the Trust's project of suburbanization in any detail indicates the disconnect between the Trust and the suburbs of Bombay.

4. Hazareesingh, "The Quest for Urban Citizenship."

5. Ibid., 812.

6. There is now an excellent body of work on Bombay in the late nineteenth and early twentieth centuries. For accounts of the Trust, see Kidambi, *The Making of an Indian Metropolis,* esp. chap. 2; and Hazareesingh, *The Colonial City and the Challenge of Modernity,* esp. chap. 2. Chopra's *A Joint Enterprise,* Prakash's *Mumbai Fables,* and Dossal's *Theatre of Conflict, City of Hope* all have good accounts of aspects of the Trust's activities.

7. From the promulgation of the Bombay Act I of 1888, considered the most significant piece of legislation underpinning the Bombay Municipal Corporation, until the enactment of Act 6 in 1922, there was no widening of the municipal franchise in the city of Bombay. Only property owners—those who paid "rates" (that is, municipal property taxes) on their properties—were permitted to vote. Only from 1922 onward was the franchise extended, significantly, to include "rentpayers"—those who paid

a monthly rent of ten rupees or more. See Rahimtoola, "The Corporation." Sandip Hazareesingh has shown that the franchise from 1888 to 1922—consisting of the ratepayers—was a meager 1 percent or so of the total population. Even after the extension of the franchise in 1922, it still consisted of little more than 7 percent of the population. See Hazareesingh, "Colonial Modernism and the Flawed Paradigms of Urban Renewal." See also Gordon, *Businessmen and Politics*, esp. 117–122, for a good account of the landlord–industrialist–merchant control of the Municipal Corporation.

8. The composition of the board was as follows: There were fourteen trustees in total, comprising three ex officio trustees (the commanding military officer of Bombay District, the collector of Bombay, and the municipal commissioner); seven elected trustees, of whom four were to be elected by the Municipal Corporation, one by the Bombay Chamber of Commerce, one by the Port Trust of Bombay, and one by the Bombay Millowners Association; and three trustees and a chairman nominated by the Government of Bombay. See *Report of the Select Committee Appointed to Consider Bill No. I of 1898*, Legislative Department, Government of Bombay, Maharashtra State Archives (henceforth MSA)/ General Department (henceforth GD)/ Vol. 27/1898.

9. *Mumbai Vaibhav*, in *Report of the Native Newspapers*, February 5, 1898, 22.

10. There is a peculiar way in which the miasma theory of the proliferation of disease thrived in Bombay long after the germ theory of disease had become generally accepted. For an analysis of the disjuncture between theories of disease and the Trust's practices, see Kidambi, "'An Infection of Locality.'" There is a large literature on

the Bombay plague. See Arnold, "Plague: Assault on the Body," in his *Colonizing the Body*, 200–239; Chandavarkar, "Plague Panic and Epidemic Politics in India, 1896–1914," in his *Imperial Power and Popular Politics*, 234–265; Klein, "Urban Development and Death"; and Catanach, "'Who Are Your Leaders?'"

11. The Bombay City Improvement Trust awaits a comprehensive history. Meanwhile, see the works of Hazareesingh and Kidambi cited above, as well as Kidambi, "Housing the Poor in a Colonial City."

12. The most explicit elaboration of this strategic shift is in Orr, "Social Reform and Slum Reform," a lecture delivered to the Social Service League in Bombay, September 3, 1917.

13. BIT, *Annual Administration Report, 1917–1918*, 114. The summary of the board's proceedings on this page contains excellent back-and-forth on this issue between the colonial board members such as Orr and Hepper, on the one hand, and the Indian landowners such as Rahimtulla, Vacha, and Cowasji Jehangir, on the other. The list of slum areas in the city is on pages 108–113.

14. Glover, *Making Lahore Modern*, chap. 2.

15. *Bombay Chronicle*, January 4, 1938, 2.

16. From the late nineteenth century onward, the Collector's Office identified certain tenures where it would have had little or no chance of resuming the land and proceeded to "redeem" the lands. This meant that the property holder could convert the basis of the tenure into something resembling freehold if he or she paid up a capitalized sum equal to a certain number of years' worth of rent, depending on the nature of the tenure.

17. Interpretation and understanding of

the various classificatory systems was only possible through conversations with various persons. In particular, I am grateful to the people working in the so-called Strong Room of the Mumbai Collector's Office, where old survey charts are kept, who explained the meaning of the various survey numbers.

18. For the early history of Bombay, see da Cunha, *The Origin of Bombay*; Edwardes, *The Rise of Bombay*; and Tindall, *City of Gold*.

19. The history of the land tenures of the city of Bombay is staggeringly complex and, astoundingly, has been only sparsely treated by modern scholarship. One account, which leaves much unexplained, is Edwardes's version in volume 3 of *The Gazetteer of Bombay City and Island*. Perhaps the best account, however, is D. R. Vaidya's 1914 preface to *The Bombay City Land Revenue Act No. II of 1876. As amended by Acts III of 1900, I of 1910, IV of 1915, II of 1919, 49 of 1947, and 9 of 1949, 1–147*. Vaidya writes in his preface, "I have endeavoured to write the 'Introduction' at some length, and I shall feel that my labours are sufficiently compensated if the respective rights of the Government and the holders of land in Bombay are removed from the domain of uncertainty and surmise." Mariam Dossal's recent *Theatre of Conflict, City of Hope* is the best scholarly treatment of the problem of land tenures in Bombay.

20. The standard sources are Baden Powell, *The Land Systems of British India*; Guha, *A Rule of Property for Bengal*; and Stein, *Thomas Munro,* on the *ryotwari* system. Significantly, none of these volumes treats the specific cases of the cities in Bombay, Bengal, and Madras Presidencies that were ceded to the British prior to the Company's establishing control over the

subcontinent: the cities of Bombay, Calcutta, and Madras still await their respective revenue histories.

21. Thus Alexander Rogers's massive *The Land Revenue of Bombay* does not address Bombay Island at all, although it provides an exhaustive *taluka*-by-*taluka* breakdown of the revenue structure of the rest of the presidency. (A *taluka* is a land revenue administration unit below the district.) There was initially an attempt to include the city of Bombay in the Bombay [Presidency] Revenue Officers' and Land Revenue Code Bill, but "as the land revenue administration of the Presidency Town differed widely from that of the Mofussil it was afterward thought more satisfactory to embody the necessary provisions for the former in a separate Bill." *The Bombay City Land Revenue Act No. II,* 148.

22. Between the seventeenth century—when Bombay consisted of seven islands—and the mid-nineteenth century, the marshes, swamps, and waters separating the islands were slowly filled in and reclaimed to create the "island of Bombay."

23. MSA/Revenue Department (henceforth RD)/Vol. 77/1843, 1.

24. Letter of Grant to Reid, April 29, 1843, MSA/RD/Vol. 77/1843, 7.

25. Edwardes distinguishes between *fazindari,* pension and tax; *foras,* quit and ground rent; *inami*; *sanadi*; and "Salt Batty," or *toka*.

26. For accounts of Bombay's growth and expansion from the 1840s onward, see Dossal, *Imperial Designs and Indian Realities,* and Chopra, "The City and Its Fragments." Dwivedi and Mehrotra's *Bombay* remains a good account of the changing physical form of the city.

27. "Report upon the Completion of the Survey of the Town and Island of Bom-

bay," Colonel G. A. Laughton to Colonel J. T. Francis, November 23, 1872, MSA/RD/Vol. 50/1873, Comp. 1025, 259.

28. The discussion of the Trust's method of land valuation and the opposition it faced is drawn from a letter from Orr, chairman of the BIT, as well as from several other disputes that appear in the General and Revenue Department files in the Maharashtra State Archives. Orr to Secretary, General Department, Government of Bombay, MSA/GD/Vol. 31/1909, Comp. 411, 21–27.

29. Ibid., 21.

30. Ibid., 22. Orr's claim that the plots were often fully developed for the neighborhood's needs raises an interesting paradox: why, if the gross demand was being met, was there a need for more housing? Of course, the Trust proposed to build cleaner and more healthful stock, but it also sought to justify itself on the grounds that there was a dire need for more housing stock.

31. "Vacant" and "empty" and "waste" were words used to describe lands that did not, in fact, appear to have been either vacant or empty. These lands in the north of the island appear to have been occupied—albeit quite sparsely—by a variety of small rice cultivators, fishing villages, Bhandari toddy-tappers, and so on. The deploying of words like "empty" and "vacant" to describe land that was populated by peoples who did not fit into the Trust's idea of the modern city constituted a discursive erasure, which in turn served as a preamble for literal evictions.

32. Memo of Robertson, MSA/GD/Vol. 31/1909, Comp. 411, 54–55.

33. W. C. Hughes, *Notes on City Improvement Schemes in England,* February 12, 1901, MSA/GD/Vol. 40/1901.

34. As recorded in the report of Tate and Dickinson: "Report on the Completion of Survey of Bombay Island," MSA/RD/Vol. 12/1828.

35. The preceding account of the history of the *toka* tenure is from Vaidya's introduction to *The Bombay City Land Revenue Act No. II,* 106–109. A *moora* is a measure of crop equivalent to about one hundred bushels.

36. Letter of F. F. Arbuthnot to E. W. Ravenscroft, MSA/RD/Vol. 99/1877, 313–329.

37. Letter of M. S. Bharucha, Land Manager, to Chairman, January 28, 1908, MSA/GD/Vol. 48/1912, 197.

38. Ibid., 199.

39. Details of the case are taken from the letter of G. W. Hatch, collector of Bombay, No. L. R. 1584, February 29, 1908, MSA/RD/Vol. 219/1908, 37.

40. The following documents make it possible to piece together this history: Report of the Land Acquisition Committee, No. 10, August 2, 1911, declaring the Improvement Trust's decision not to acquire Cases 1-B and 1-C, which, as Sanghani's subsequent petition indicates, were the cases pertaining to his land. MSA/GD/Vol. 48/1912, 391. This note is accompanied by a plan showing the affected properties, which it is possible to correlate with later maps as the areas not included in the schemes. Petition of Keshavlal Sanghani to Governor of Bombay, January 18, 1912, MSA/GD/Vol. 48/1912, 423–437.

41. "Proposed Development for Scheme VI," MSA/GD/Vol. 48/1912, 341–347.

42. In his two petitions, Sanghani documents the series of purchases in this vicinity made by himself and his partners. He appears to be have been well-known to government and Trust employees: a scribbled note in the margin by a government official notes that Sanghani "is in the habit

of petitioning Govt. and the India Office on various subjects." MSA/GD/Vol. 48/1912, 463.

43. The details are provided in Sanghani's lengthy second petition to the government. Petition of Keshavlal Sanghani to Governor of Bombay, November 15, 1912, MSA/GD/Vol. 48/1912, 443–457.

44. As outlined in his second petition.

45. Bombay Improvement Trust, *Minutes of Proceedings,* report of conference between Bombay Improvement Trust trustees and the government (henceforth BIT *Minutes*), January 31, 1913, MSA/GD/Vol. 34/1913, 20.

46. Land manager's letter to trustees, reporting details of the Matunga Residents' Association's letter, in BIT *Minutes*, April 1, 1913, MSA/GD/Vol. 34/1913, 63.

47. Deputy land manager's letter, in BIT *Minutes*, April 22, 1913, MSA/GD/Vol. 34/1913, 93.

48. Ibid.

49. All details from the case, including direct quotations, taken from BIT, *Annual Administration Report*, 1917–1918, 90–91.

50. Government of Bombay, Legislative Department, *Report of the Select Committee Appointed to Consider Bill No. I of 1898,* MSA/GD/Vol. 27/1898, 14.

51. Petition of the landowners of the village of Sion, January 17, 1906, MSA/GD/Vol. 48/1912, 87.

52. Ibid.

53. Letter of G. O. W. Dunn to Secretary, General Department, No. 1522, March 5, 1906, MSA/GD/Vol. 48/1912, 125–131; quotation on page 127.

54. No. 1967, March 31, 1906, MSA/GD/Vol. 48/1912, 169.

55. The various petitions of the ratepayers are contained in MSA/GD/Vol. 29/1908.

56. BIT *Minutes,* August 18, 1903, MSA/GD/Vol. 29/1908, 193.

57. Unsigned marginal note, MSA/GD/Vol. 29/1908, 94.

58. The details of Tata's petition and the Trust's response are summarized in an excerpt from the Proceedings of BIT, February 16, 1900, MSA/GD/Vol. 29/1908, 111.

59. Ibid.

60. BIT, *Annual Administration Report,* 1921, 55.

61. Ibid., 8.

62. BIT *Minutes,* January 11, 1910, MSA/GD/Vol. 47/1910, 16–18, 20–22. This particular schedule included Catholic names such as Bastian Martin Borges; various Maharashtrian caste names such as Vaidyas and Mogres and Teles; and Gujarati and Kutchi Bhatia caste names, both Muslim and Hindu, such as Essaji Moosaji and Dharamsey Meghji.

63. The discussion of the construction of Eastern Avenue is contained in BIT *Minutes,* December 6, 1910, 294–298, MSA/GD/Vol. 47/1910; and in MSA/GD/Comp. 217 Pt. I/1916.

64. BIT *Minutes,* December 6, 1910, MSA/GD/Vol. 47/1910, 295. The road already existed in a rudimentary form, and figures like Orr wanted to turn it into a grand boulevard suitable for automobiles. By the 1930s it was called, variously, Mohammed Ali Road (the section at the beginning, wending through the Muslim areas of Pydhonie, Dongri, and Bhendi Bazaar), Eastern Avenue, Parel Road (these names were used for stretches that went through the industrial districts of Parel and Lalbaug), Vincent Road, and Kingsway (in Matunga and Sion; see especially Chandavarkar, "Police and Public Order in Bombay, 1880–1947," in Chandavarkar, *Imperial Power and Popular Politics,* 180–233). The

plan was to construct a 150-foot-wide road from Sion down through Matunga and Dadar to the Elphinstone Road; from there, entering the industrial districts, which were more congested, the road would be a little narrower, at 120 feet; from Byculla onward, when the road would encounter the most crowded and congested parts of the city, all the way to Crawford Market, the road might have to be restricted to 100 feet in width.

65. "Excerpts from Mr. Kemball's Note," MSA/GD/Comp. 217 Pt. I/1916, 146–151.

66. Ibid., 146.

67. Ibid., 150.

68. BIT *Minutes,* December 6, 1910, MSA/GD/Vol. 47/1910, 295.

69. Ibid., 295–296

70. BIT, *Annual Administration Report,* 1920–1921.

71. Ibid., 295.

72. Minute of R. J. Kent, in ibid., 296.

73. The plan is in BIT, *Annual Administration Report,* 1915–1916.

74. Ibid., 297.

75. Ibid.

76. "Bombay Corporation: Parel Street Scheme," clippings from the *Times of India* (n.d., circa June 4, 1915), MSA/GD/Comp. 217 Pt. I/1916.

77. This was the substance of Orr's argument in an extremely lengthy (one and a half hours long) speech he gave on the floor of the Corporation. "Parel Road Scheme: Hon. Mr. Orr's Views," clippings from the *Times of India,* July 20, 1915, MSA/GD/Comp. 217 Pt. I/1916, 99–105.

78. Ibid., 105.

79. Gordon, *Businessmen and Politics.*

80. Such "sweating of building sites" and the challenges it posed to property prices, not to mention public health, was one of Orr's favorite topics. For one especially vivid statement of his argument, see Orr, "The Need for Co-operation between Neighbours in the Development of Building Estates."

81. "Proposed Development for Scheme VI," MSA/GD/Vol. 48/1912, between 341 and 347. Unfortunately, it was not possible to satisfactorily reproduce this plan owing to its extremely fragile condition. According to a note accompanying the plan, this was the vision of Scheme 6 as of March 1911. See the letter from Secretary, City of Bombay Improvement Trust, No. 1992, March 31, 1911, MSA/GD/Vol. 48/1912, 347.

82. See BIT, *Annual Administration Report,* 1916.

83. Some of the people I spoke to resided in these tenements, which date from about 1922 or 1923.

84. Citizen, letter to the editor, *Bombay Chronicle,* December 6, 1934, 8. The occasion for this letter was a lecture given at the Nagpada Neighbourhood House by H. B. Shivdasani, a former chief officer of the Trust, on the workings of the Trust.

2. PEOPLING THE SUBURBS

1. The voluminous correspondence (six hundred plus pages) surrounding this survey is collected in MSA/GD/Vol. 28/1909/Comp. 218 Pts. I and II.

2. These unsolicited letters are included in the archival compilation cited in note 1, but, interestingly, they were omitted in the printed version that came out a few years later as *Report of the Bombay Development Committee,* which nevertheless contains hundreds of pages of written and oral testimony on Bombay's infrastructure.

3. General Department Press Note No.

3022, June 14, 1909, MSA/GD/Vol. 28/1909, 613. This note is a summary of the hundreds of pages of correspondence received in response to the questionnaire.

4. Written Statement of R. J. Kent, November 16, 1913. *Report of the Bombay Development Committee,* 138.

5. Ibid.

6. Letter of V. P. Vaidya to R. E. Enthoven, April 29, 1908, MSA/GD/Vol. 28/1909, 331–340.

7. Letter of R. E. Enthoven, Secretary, General Department, No. 7382, December 9, 1907, MSA/GD/Vol. 28/1909, 30.

8. Letter of V. P. Vaidya to R. E. Enthoven, April 29, 1908, MSA/GD/Vol. 28/1909, 333.

9. Ibid.

10. Ibid., 335.

11. Kaji, "Housing Conditions among the Lower Middle Class in Bombay (South)."

12. Ibid., 106.

13. Ibid., 108.

14. This observation was related to me by numerous informants. Consider also Frank Conlon's study, in *A Caste in a Changing World,* of Saraswat Brahmins, who would have started coming to Bombay about fifty years before the South Indians and who also seem to have followed a similar pattern, only becoming involved in the cooperative movement (and hence more permanent settlement in the city) from the 1910s onward.

15. *Jam-e-Jamshed,* October 17, 1912, in *Report of the Native Newspapers,* week ending October 19, 1912.

16. Ibid. Here the critics of suburbanization were contradicting themselves shamelessly—on the one hand, they criticized the Trust for building roads and other infrastructure leading to the suburbs; on the other, they criticized the suburbs as

unsuitable because they lacked infrastructure. It is true that the main mode of accessing the northern suburbs was Eastern Avenue, discussed earlier, which was designed for use by automobiles. But it was also intended to have a tramway, which would have rendered the suburbs a little more democratically accessible. The suburbs were designed to be mixed-income neighborhoods. But many of the critics of suburbanization were from the old city's landlord class, whose properties stood to lose value with the addition of housing stock to the city.

17. *Parsi,* October 14, 1912, in *Report of the Native Newspapers,* week ending October 19, 1912.

18. The most complete study of the morphology of the Indian middle class in the nineteenth century remains Misra's *The Indian Middle Classes.*

19. *Report on an Enquiry into Middle Class Family Budgets in Bombay City* (henceforth *Enquiry into Middle Class Family Budgets*) and *Report on an Enquiry into Middle Class Unemployment in the Bombay Presidency* (henceforth *Enquiry into Middle Class Unemployment*).

20. Bhonsle, "Clerks in the City of Bombay."

21. The educated unemployed were perceived as the primary instigators of anticolonial agitations at least as far back as the Swadeshi movement of the early twentieth century. See Sarkar, *The Swadeshi Movement in Bengal.*

22. *Enquiry into Middle Class Unemployment,* 2.

23. Ibid.

24. Ibid., 20, 21. Other occupations listed as "middle class" include storekeeper, manager, accountant, salesman, and draftsman.

25. *Census of India, 1931*, vol. 11, *Cities of the Bombay Presidency.*

26. Ibid., 51.

27. *Bombay Chronicle*, November 8, 1939.

28. The 1951 census tables appear to indicate the ballooning of the equivalent category—whose "source of livelihood" was "services and miscellaneous sources"—to a point of incoherence. Almost 75 percent of the enumerated population of the city of Bombay and Bombay Island of 1,480,883 seem to fall into this category. Still, at the very least we can take this to indicate a further dramatic expansion of the clerk/service population over the 1930s and 1940s. See *Census of India, 1951, Greater Bombay District Census Handbook*, 2: 154–161.

29. Bhonsle, "Clerks in the City of Bombay," 5.

30. Ibid., 2, 3.

31. Of the report's survey sample, 49.4 percent were Brahmin and some 70 percent consisted of upper and middle castes such as Marathas. Parsis were disproportionately high in representation at 9.4 percent, while Muslims were disproportionately low at 3 percent. *Enquiry into Middle Class Family Budgets*, 2.

32. Bhonsle, "Clerks in the City of Bombay," 60. It is noteworthy that at this point in the 1930s, Bhonsle uses "Madrasi" to designate those people who probably understood themselves as South Indians.

33. Ibid., 39. The relative paucity of South Indian clerks in his sample might have had to do with the fact that most of the clerks he surveyed lived in the older precincts of the city, in Wards B and C. Most of the relatively recent migrants from southern India lived in the northern wards, especially F Ward. The terms "Madrasi"—referring to someone from Madras Presidency in southern India—and "South

Indian" seem to have been used interchangeably at this point.

34. Ibid., 40

35. *Bombay Chronicle*, June 15, 1934.

36. *Bombay Chronicle*, June 26, 1935. This article describes the accomplishments of the South Indian Association as displayed in the latter's recently issued annual report, so we may assume that the resolution to the dispute was actually arrived at in 1934.

37. *Bombay Chronicle*, July 1, 1935, 1.

38. Bhonsle, "Clerks in the City of Bombay," 40 (emphasis added).

39. In any case, the 1931 census acknowledged itself to be guilty of underenumeration and underreporting on account of the extensive disturbances associated with the civil disobedience movement of that year.

40. *Census of India, 1931*, 16, 17. Incredibly, some 75.6 percent of those enumerated were born outside the city of Bombay in 1931.

41. Ibid., 38. Infuriatingly and inexplicably, this particular table does not include any data on native speakers of Tamil.

42. Ibid., 178. There were high numbers of people born in these regions of India residing in E and G Wards as well, but they were low-caste Telugu and Tamil speakers, respectively, and would not have fallen into the lower-middle-class stratum that so typified the South Indians of F Ward.

43. Due to World War II and anticolonial unrest, the 1941 census did not contain detailed statistics at the city level.

44. *Census of India, 1951*, 2.

45. Ibid., 103–107.

46. Ibid., 104–105. There were about 11,000 Sindhi speakers, 6,000 Punjabi speakers, and 5,500 Kutchi speakers.

47. Ibid., 160–161. The number of per-

sons reporting this occupation was 48,821, as against 80,530 persons for all other occupations combined. This particular table contains disaggregated Ward-level figures, which allowed me to calculate numbers just for Matunga and Sion tracts within F Ward and omit Lower Parel and Worli tracts.

48. Mahaluxmivala, *The History of the Bombay Electric Supply and Tramways Company*, 92.

49. Letter of the general manager of BEST, October 7, 1927, contained in ibid., 111–112.

50. Mahaluxmivala, *The History of the Bombay Electric Supply and Tramways Company*, 113.

51. *Bombay Chronicle*, September 12, 1933, 10.

52. *Bombay Chronicle*, July 4, 1934, 8.

53. These events are reported in a statement issued by the GIP in which the railway pleads with passengers to resort to accepted methods of presenting their grievances—in writing, through authorized representatives. *Bombay Chronicle*, January 6, 1939, 5.

54. This event merited the front-page lead headline: "Satyagraha Holds Up Suburban Trains." *Bombay Chronicle*, January 12, 1939, 1.

55. *Bombay Chronicle*, January 13, 1939, 12.

56. *Bombay Chronicle*, January 16, 1939, 7.

57. Ibid.

58. Ibid.

59. Ibid.

60. *Bombay Chronicle*, January 18, 1939, 4. The negotiations with the railways were conducted at a high level, with congressional supremos such as Home Minister K. M. Munshi and S. K. Patil, a member of the Legislative Assembly, also in attendance.

61. "Passengers' Satyagraha Succeeds!" *Bombay Chronicle*, January 20, 1939, 3.

62. Statement of Bhulabhai Desai, *Bombay Chronicle*, January 20, 1939, 5.

63. K. V. L. Narayan, interview with the author, September 14, 2003.

64. M. T. Rayan, interview with the author, October 31, 2001.

65. *Bombay Chronicle*, July 11, 1934, 8.

66. Ibid. Throughout the 1910s, 1920s, and 1930s, the Municipal Corporation was engaged in an attempt to shift cattle stables out of the city.

67. *Bombay Chronicle*, August 8, 1934, 3. *Mawali* is a common term used in Bombay for "ruffian" or "hooligan."

68. As reported in the *Bombay Chronicle*, January 14, 1939, 10.

69. It was to prevent people from resorting to such drastic means of securing funds for travel that the South Indian Cooperative Credit Society, which became the South Indian Cooperative Bank, was first set up: its earliest business was in advancing loans to finance people's trips back home.

70. *Bombay Chronicle*, January 14, 1939, 10 (emphasis added).

71. This account of Gopalakrishnan's experience of migration to Bombay is taken from my essay "Changing Cities, Aging Men."

72. *Bombay Chronicle*, May 27, 1939, 2.

73. The account of Viswanatha Iyer's lodging house is drawn from part 3 of Ramachandran, "Matunga Musings."

74. The account of the Trichur Mess and the meal and full tickets is taken from the memoir-history of the Matunga area by Vaidyanathan, "Wadala Whispers."

75. Rayan, interview with the author. Rayan was the younger brother of Salevateeshwaran, better known in Bombay simply as "Salivati." A "meal set," also known as a "rice plate," would consist of a serving

of rice, some lentils in the form of sambhar or rasam, one or two dry vegetable curries, and a papadam.

76. The significance of the cooperative societies is treated more fully in chapter 5.

77. S. Ramachandran, interview with the author, September 18, 2003. *Sapaddu* is a Tamil word for food. Ramachandran's father was one of the founders of this society, along with longtime Matunga political stalwart and subsequent mayor of Bombay, M. Madhavan Nair.

78. Advertisement for the South Indian Concerns, Ltd., *Mysore Association Silver Jubilee Annual Report,* 24.

79. Numerous accounts circulate of the acrimonious split between the Palakkad Iyers, on the one hand, and the Thanjavur and Tirunelveli Iyers, on the other. See, for instance, the memoir of P. P. Ramachandran, "Matunga Musings," part 3. I heard this version on many different occasions, and it was confirmed for me by K. V. Vaidyanathan (the author of another Matunga memoir, "Wadala Whispers") in an e-mail communication, July 15, 2006. See also the amusing memoir by V. Mahadevan, "Matunga—The Malgudi in Mumbai." He writes that "the Palghat [Palakkad] boys would not budge from [South Indian Consumer Cooperative] Society, tantalizing [South Indian] Concerns notwithstanding."

80. *Bombay Chronicle,* June 11, 1934, 2.

81. I have heard conflicting accounts of the medium of instruction at the SIES. It seems clear that within a few years the school had switched completely to instruction in English. In the early years, however, instruction at the junior levels appears to have taken place in Tamil, Kannada, and Malayalam, before moving to English by year six.

82. There were four Malayalam sections and two Tamil sections for each grade. Education continued in Malayalam and Tamil through fourth grade, after which it switched to English. Students began learning English as a second language even in the first four years when instruction was in Malayalam or Tamil.

83. *Bombay Chronicle,* December 10, 1929, 3.

84. *Bombay Chronicle,* June 13, 1934, 3.

85. Ramachandran, "Matunga Musings," part 3.

86. *Bombay Chronicle,* January 5, 1938, 3.

87. *Bombay Chronicle,* August 18, 1934, 8, 10.

88. K. S. Narahari's letter to the editor of the *Bombay Chronicle,* June 25, 1935, provides a brief and helpful history of the cultural offerings available to South Indians. He notes that until quite recently, the only cultural offerings for South Indians were restricted to musical performances organized by outfits such as the South Indian Sangeetha Sabha. Very recently, certain cinemas had also occasionally started screening Tamil-language talkies. He then gets to his point: the Surya cinema in Parel was to begin screening a Tamil talkie entitled *Valli's Wedding,* but the predatory proprietor of the cinema house, sensing the demand in the community, had raised the prices just for this particular film. Narahari maintained that this had "cast a gloom over the entire community" and pleaded with the proprietor not to charge extortionate rates, especially in light of the "trade depression and [resulting] unemployment" among the members of the community. *Bombay Chronicle,* June 25, 1935, 8.

89. *Bombay Chronicle,* April 18, 1942, 5.

90. Vaidyanathan, "Wadala Whispers," part 3.

91. Luminaries as varied as Duke Ellington with his Big Band and Zubin Mehta with the New York Philharmonic have performed there over the years.

92. *Bombay Chronicle*, June 10, 1934, 3.

93. *Bombay Chronicle*, June 17, 1934, 5.

94. *Journal of the Indian Institute of Architects* (henceforth *JIIA*) 1, no. 2 (July 1934): 68. The notice came under a special category of notices titled "The Lesser Architecture of Bombay," which I consider in further detail in chapter 4.

95. *Bombay Chronicle*, January 16, 1937, 3. The performance also featured Madura Krishnamaswamy on violin and Tanjore Krishnamurthy Rao on mridangam.

96. The *pandal* was the alternative to the Asthika Samaj, especially when the event was drawn out over several days and was projected to attract very large audiences.

97. *Bombay Chronicle*, January 14, 1939, 10. Sri Thyagaraja Swamy was a late-eighteenth-century composer, born in Tiruvayur near Thanjavur, and was one of the great trinity of composers of Carnatic music, along with Muthuswamy Dikshitar and Shyama Sastri.

98. *Bombay Chronicle*, March 20, 1939, 11. The performance also featured Krishnamswamy Iyengar on violin and Mani Iyer on mridangam.

99. *Bombay Chronicle*, April 22, 1944, 3. The concert was held at the Don Bosco School in Matunga, a Catholic school established by the Salesian Society. Tickets were available at the Café Madras and at the Madras Brahmins' Coffee Hotel, both in Matunga. Seats for men ranged in price from two to almost seven rupees, and for women from two to four rupees.

100. Vishwanath Menon, interview with the author, August 12, 2001. Menon was a longtime cook at the Indian Gymkhana. He claimed that sports, unlike food or religion or even education, was a universal pastime and hence should not be defined on the basis of community.

101. *Bombay Chronicle*, January 5, 1939, 5. The Indian Gymkhana team won the match handily.

102. *Bombay Chronicle*, January 10, 1939, 3. The tournament was called the Ramanujam Challenge Shield Ball Badminton Tournament. The eponymous T. V. Ramanujam, one of the legendary figures of Matunga, would later go on to endow a basketball tournament that came to be called the Ramu Memorial Cup. This became the most important basketball tournament in the city, and for several decades the cup was furiously contested and shared by teams from the Indian Gymkhana, on the one hand, and from the Nagpada Neighbourhood House and the Mastan YMCA in Nagpada, on the other. The competition between these teams was nothing less than a competition between dramatically different ideas of the city—the middle-class Hindu South Indians from the middle-class suburb of Matunga fought it out with Muslims from the inner-city neighborhood of Nagpada. Indeed, this was the opposition that the Improvement Trust sought to create: the suburbs of Dadar and Matunga were built as a countervision to the perceived aporias of Nagpada. My essay "Hoops, Hunger, and the City" explores this opposition further.

103. *Bombay Chronicle*, January 17, 1939, 5. The reporter writes, witheringly, "The play was very dull at the beginning and far below the standard expected of the champions. . . . The play as a whole was marred

by the hits to the boundaries and innumerable missings by both the players."

104. *Bombay Chronicle*, January 18, 1939, 4. Fifteen out of the eighteen competitors in men's singles had South Indian—predominantly Iyer—names. Two of the other three, curiously, bear the name Sanghani. It will be recalled that Keshavlal Sanghani was the name of the speculator discussed in chapter 1 who had acquired lands in Matunga in advance of the Trust's acquisition. Quite possibly the Sanghanis participating in this badminton tournament were relatives.

105. *Bombay Chronicle*, June 25, 1935, 8. The paper's account contains an overview of the annual report of the South Indian Association.

106. *Mysore Association Silver Jubilee Annual Report*, 18, 19.

107. *Keraleeya Samaj, Golden Jubilee Souvenir*, 4.

108. *Bombay Chronicle*, January 19, 1939, 2.

109. Two short general accounts of the dispute are available: N. Iyer's letter to the editor, *Bombay Chronicle*, July 11, 1934, 8; and the statement by K. F. Nariman, president of the BPCC, in which he summarizes the details of the dispute in seeking to come to a resolution, *Bombay Chronicle*, July 21, 1934, 5.

110. "Matunga Vyayam Shala" translates as "Matunga Exercise School." Many well-known Congress Party "activists" and "social workers" were involved in physical culture and could be counted upon to mobilize warm bodies when needed. Perhaps the most dramatic instance of this was the case of Keshav Dada Borkar, a well-known gangster of the industrial districts, who ran on the Congress ticket in the Mazagaon/Tadwadi Ward in the Municipal

Corporation elections of February 1939, the first time the Congress Party ran for a municipal-level office in Bombay. Borkar is described in the Congress Party publicity material as a "long time social worker." *Bombay Chronicle*, January 28, 1939. Raj Chandavarkar has given a detailed and nuanced portrait of this fascinating character and the various roles he played in the life of the industrial working-class districts. B. N. Maheshwari himself appears to have been a long-standing political activist. He was earlier active in the Mandvi Ward, in the southern parts of the city, under the mentorship of Vithalbhai Patel, Vallabhbhai Patel's brother. He moved to Matunga in the late 1920s and was very active there: the Congress Party describes him as a "veteran publicist and a fighter in the public life of Bombay." In 1939, he stood for election to the Municipal Corporation from Matunga and was elected. See the short profile of Maheshwhari in the *Bombay Chronicle*, January 27, 1939, 3. Today one of the nodal points of Matunga—the King's Circle—is renamed after him as Maheshwari Udyan (Maheshwari Gardens).

111. B. N. Mahes[h]wari, letter to the editor, *Bombay Chronicle*, July 4, 1934, 8.

112. K. Rajagopalan, letter to the editor, *Bombay Chronicle*, July 5, 1934, 8.

113. N. Iyer, letter to the editor, *Bombay Chronicle*, July 11, 1934, 8.

114. B. G. Horniman, quoted in "Thanksgiving at Matunga," *Bombay Chronicle*, July 16, 1934, 5.

115. Ibid.

116. The historical record is not clear as to why, exactly, the MTCC wanted to exercise its autonomy from the FDCC. A part of it no doubt had to do with the fact that Matunga was primarily a middle-class area, whereas, as indicated earlier, substantial

portions of F Ward were heavily working-class districts. Partly it might have been an issue of community, with the Tamil Brahmins, Parsis, and Marathi-speaking Brahmins of Matunga wanting to separate themselves from the lower-caste districts to the south.

117. Details of the deal are contained in Nariman's press statement, *Bombay Chronicle*, July 21, 1934, 5.

118. "'F' Ward Dispute Takes New Turn," *Bombay Chronicle*, July 21, 1934, 7. A letter to the editor from one N. Subramanian gleefully relishes the disorder in the FDCC: "It is rather a pity that . . . they cannot put their own house in order on a matter of a little deficit in an accommodative spirit." *Bombay Chronicle*, July 24, 1934, 8.

119. "Polling Booth for Matunga," *Bombay Chronicle*, August 4, 1934, 5. The letter was signed by K. Vithal Rao and sixty other Congress Party members "resident in Matunga." K. Vithal Rao was one of the founding members of the South Indian Cooperative Housing Society and an active political figure in ward and municipal politics. By the time of the municipal elections of 1939, he was the secretary of the Matunga–Sion Congress Municipal Election Committee. *Bombay Chronicle*, January 20, 1939, 11.

120. "'F' Ward Polling Station," *Bombay Chronicle*, August 5, 1934. Excerpts from both the letter of refusal by the FDCC and the rebuttal by the MTCC are contained within this report.

121. *Bombay Chronicle*, August 6, 1934, 5.

3. THE RISE OF THE BOMBAY FLAT

1. Manju Mehta, "Soon: A Hot Upscale Residency Called Dharavi," *Indian Express*, August 24, 2003.

2. Ibid.

3. Ibid.

4. Ibid.

5. Edwardes, *The Gazetteer of Bombay City and Island*, 1:199.

6. Ibid.

7. Mehta, "Domestic Architecture in India," 116–117. Also cited in Evenson, *The Indian Metropolis*, 119.

8. Mehta, "Domestic Architecture in India."

9. My sense is that buildings housing Hindu flats were not purpose-built but, rather, resulted from the addition of floors to single-family houses that became, as a result, multifamily, multistory dwellings.

10. There are no studies of the rise of apartment living (as opposed to tenement living) in South Asian cities. One important study of the rise of apartment living in New York, which elaborates the argument tracing the rise of apartment living to a compromise between space constraints and the middle class's search for privacy, is Elizabeth Collins Cromley's *Alone Together*. See also her articles "The Development of American Apartment-Houses from the Civil War to the Depression" and "New York, Paris, and the French Flat." Another interesting study of the origins of apartment living in U.S. cities—seeking to deploy ideas of transience and mobility to explain apartment living rather than the more commonly deployed framework of a quest for permanence and privacy—is Andrew Sandoval-Strausz's "Homes for a World of Strangers." For Toronto, see

Richard Dennis's "Interpreting the Apartment House," and for London see the same author's "'Babylonian Flats' in Victorian and Edwardian London."

11. A classic study in this vein, which also seeks to complicate the commonly assumed duality of public/private, is Sharon Marcus's extraordinary *Apartment Stories*. Another work exploring dwelling practices in a very different cultural setting and in a place whose cities are today closely associated with apartment living is Jordan Sand's *House and Home in Modern Japan*. Interestingly, in the period under consideration, when Bombay was witnessing the rise of the apartment building, Japanese cities featured the more commonly waged battle between the house or cottage and the tenement. The apartment was not as common, and Sand quotes the pubic housing historian Otsuki Toshio's claim that only twenty-four apartment houses were built in all of Japan between 1925 and the war. Sand, *House and Home in Modern Japan*, 197.

12. On toilets and indoor plumbing, see Ogle, *All the Modern Conveniences*. On toilet practices, see George, *The Big Necessity*.

13. Cromley, *Alone Together*, 95. She also writes of late-nineteenth-century New York: "It is hard to find consistent differences between tenement and French-flat entries in the docket books [she is speaking of the New Buildings Docket books maintained by the city's Buildings Department]. . . . Bathroom and toilet facilities may have been a deciding factor in making distinctions between them—privies in the rear yard or water closets in the common halls for tenements, and bathrooms within the unit for French flats—but this information is not recorded in the docket books." Cromley, *Alone Together*, 72.

14. Gyáni, *Parlor and Kitchen*, 125.

15. W. R. Davidge, "Re. Bombay Housing Schemes," MSA/[RD] Development Department (henceforth DD)/File 31/2/1924, 4.

16. Letter from E. M. Gilbert-Lodge, Land Manager, Development Department, to Deputy Director, Development Department, March 2, 1921, MSA/[RD] DD/File 125/1921, 1–3.

17. Such speculation in land in advance of proposed acquisition by the government was, of course, a long-standing practice, as discussed in chapter 1.

18. Letter from the E. M. Gilbert-Lodge, Land Manager, Development Department, to Deputy Director, Development Department, March 2, 1921, MSA/[RD] DD/File 125/1921, 2, 3.

19. Letter from A. G. Viegas to George Lloyd, governor of Bombay, November 3, 1919, MSA/[RD] DD/File 36/1919–1920, 9–10. Viegas's numbers amount to a sixteenfold increase in land prices in the span of a few months.

20. Bhuta, "Rise of Value of Land and Other Properties in Bombay in Recent Times," 797–805, esp. 802–803.

21. City of Bombay, *Municipal Retrenchment and Reform*, 1.

22. W. R. Davidge, "Re. Bombay Housing Schemes," MSA/[RD] DD/File 31/2/1924, 8.

23. Ibid., 7.

24. Letter of E. G. Turner to Deputy Director of Development, "Re. Proposal to Introduce a System of 'Zoning' for the Island of Bombay," MSA/[RD] DD/File 31/2/1924, 27.

25. Letter of J. W. Mackison, Special Engineer, Development Works, to Deputy Director, Development, "Re. Proposal to Introduce a System of 'Zoning' for the

Island of Bombay," MSA/[RD] DD/File 31/2/1924, 35 (emphasis added).

26. These investors sought to play it safe and initially tried to construct tenements on these lands, a safe and low-maintenance investment. Chapter 4 will consider how the Improvement Trust was able to enforce apartment buildings as a compromise, as it were, between the initially desired cottages and the "safe bet" tenements that investors sought to erect in recessionary times.

27. Letter of J. W. Mackison, Special Engineer, Development Works, to Deputy Director, Development, "Re. Proposal to Introduce a System of 'Zoning' for the Island of Bombay," MSA/[RD] DD/File 31/2/1924, 35.

28. BIT, *Annual Administration Report*, 1931, 2.

29. Parsi Central Association Cooperative Housing Society, *Annual Report* (henceforth PCACHS, *Annual Report*), for the year 1922–1923, 1.

30. Memorial of the Zorastrian Association to governor of Bombay, July 1, 1924, MSA/[RD] DD/File 19/2/1924, 68–69.

31. As described in PCACHS, *Annual Report*, 1922–1923, 2–3.

32. For other brief accounts, see Conlon, "Industrialization and the Housing Problem in Bombay," 164–165, and Hazareesingh, *The Colonial City and the Challenge of Modernity*, 48–50.

33. The suburban schemes of the BDD are treated in chapters 1 and 6.

34. One of the truly extraordinary innovations was in the industrialization of the housing-production process, which will be treated in greater detail in chapter 4.

35. These are the figures presented by T. A. J. Ayyar, manager of the Development Department chawls in the mid-1930s, in "Industrial Housing in Bombay," in Man-

shardt, *Some Social Services of the Government of Bombay*, 91–92.

36. Conlon, citing the BDD annual report of 1925, quotes a figure of 16,864 one-room tenements in 207 chawl buildings. Conlon, "Industrialization and the Housing Problem in Bombay," 165. Ayyar, on the other hand, gives a figure of 16,197 single-room tenements and 327 shops in 207 chawls in his 1937 piece. Ayyar, "Industrial Housing in Bombay," 92. Hazareesingh comes up with a figure of 16,544 one-room tenements in 207 buildings, citing Government of Bombay Proceedings from 1925. Hazareesingh, *The Colonial City and the Challenge of Modernity*, 49. The discrepancy in the number of single-room tenements, while the number of buildings remains consistent, may have had to do with the fact that several of the single-room tenements were converted to multiroom tenements after 1925, as will be discussed later in this section.

37. The most exhaustive critique of the BDD chawls is contained in Manu Subedar's "Dissenting Report" contained in the "Report of the Special Advisory Committee to the Industrial Housing Scheme," MSA/RD [DD]/File 141/1926–27, 17–84. His summary of the critique of the design of the chawls is on pages 28–37.

38. Speech of Sir Lawless Hepper at inauguration of Worli BDD chawls, November 22, 1922, MSA/[RD] DD/File 53/1/Pt. I/1922, 89.

39. Conlon, "Industrialization and the Housing Problem in Bombay," 164.

40. Letter to the editor, *Bombay Chronicle*, May 25, 1923, 9.

41. S. K. Bole, Dissenting Minute, "Report of the Special Advisory Committee to the Industrial Housing Scheme," MSA/RD [DD]/File 141/1926–27, 20–21.

42. Ibid.

43. I. Newton, C. Rebello, J. Moses, P. K. Pereira, N. Lopes, D. Fernandes, and J. Obedia, letter to the editor, *Bombay Chronicle,* April 30, 1924, 4.

44. Note of BDD land manager in response to letter to *Bombay Chronicle,* MSA/[RD] DD/File 53/Misc./1924, 101.

45. Letter of Dinshaw Burjorji, Junior Assistant Land Manager, to Land Manager, Development Department, MSA/[RD] DD/File 53/Misc./1924, 50.

46. The Advisory Committee to the Industrial Housing Scheme reported that by the mid-1920s most of the criticized designs discussed so far had been modified: *nahanis* had been added to all tenements, windows and shutters had replaced the concrete louvers, and so on. "Report of the Special Advisory Committee to the Industrial Housing Scheme," MSA/RD [DD]/File 141/1926–27, 109.

47. Kaji, "Housing Conditions among the Lower Middle Class in Bombay (South)," 106.

48. Details of this meeting are drawn from a letter written by a member of the delegation, E. Woodfall, to the editor of the *Bombay Chronicle,* April 22, 1925, reproduction in MSA/[RD] DD/File 53/30/Pt. I/1926, 82–83.

49. As reported in anonymous memo, MSA/[RD] DD/File 53/30/Pt. I/1926, 77. The presence in the BDD chawls of Rebello, Newton, and the other letter writers mentioned above, even though they did not belong to the working class, was thus explained by the BDD's practice of not enforcing the restriction to working classes.

50. Note of A. W. Mackie, Secretary to the Government, Development Department, September 10, 1926, MSA/[RD] DD/File 53/30/Pt. I/1926, 133.

51. Government of Bombay, Development Department, *Report on the Working of the Development Department for the Year Ending 31/3/1929,* 29.

52. Ayyar, "Industrial Housing in Bombay," 93. Ayyar, the manager of the BDD chawls at that time, wrote that these modifications were made "with a view towards meeting the needs of the better class of people in those localities."

53. Ibid., 95.

54. Deshpande, *Modern Ideal Homes for India,* 131.

55. Ibid.

56. Batley, *Bombay's Houses and Homes.* Interestingly, and tellingly, the Cement Marketing Company of India sponsored the publication of this book. It is important to note that Grant's Buildings were not purpose-built as apartment buildings. They appear to date from at least the late 1850s and are visible in photographs taken when the Fort walls were still up in the early 1860s. It is likely that Grant's Buildings housed shops and offices associated with the cotton green (a patch of "green" ground where bales of cotton were stacked prior to trading) that lay in this part of Colaba from the mid-nineteenth century until the early 1920s. After that point it is possible that some of the units had been converted into flats and also retrofitted with internal toilets.

57. *Bombay Chronicle,* February 5, 1916, 2. This is the earliest advertisement I have seen that explicitly promised the "latest sanitary arrangements."

58. *Bombay Chronicle,* January 13, 1916, 2.

59. Details of the Saraswat Cooperative Housing Society in Gamdevi are presented in "Cooperative House Building in Bombay," *Local Self-Government Gazette* 2, no. 4 (April 1916): 320–325.

60. *Bombay Chronicle,* November 8, 1920, 3.

61. Ibid.

62. Vijay Prashad gives a critique of such colonial policies, which he suggests offer technological fixes for social contradictions. See his "The Technology of Sanitation in Colonial Delhi."

63. See Klein, "Urban Development and Death." He writes that by the turn of the century, the older parts of the city to the south of Dadar–Matunga had a "growing sewer network" but that these were of limited utility owing to a "want of house connections." Klein, "Urban Development and Death," 743.

64. In 1920–1921, 309 such "sullage connections" were made serving 188 premises; in 1921–1922, 840 sullage connections were made serving 265 premises; in 1924–1925, 258 sullage connections were made serving 452 premises. Bombay Municipal Corporation, *Administration Report,* for the years 1920–1921, 1921–1922, and 1924–1925, pages 167, 156, and 190 respectively. Sullage refers to waste water distinct from actual sewerage—that is, waste water generated from sinks and taps, but not from sewage. Extending sullage connections into the house was the first step to extending actual sewerage connections.

65. Bombay Municipal Corporation, *Administration Report,* for the year 1921–1922, 156.

66. BIT, *Annual Administration Report,* 1916–1917, 8.

67. Bombay Municipal Corporation, *Administration Report,* 1919–1920, 14. The outfall was a pipe going out deep into the sea to deposit the city's waste water. The city already had one large pumping works and outfall in the Love Grove Station in central Bombay.

68. Ibid.

69. Bombay Municipal Corporation, *Administration Report,* 1934–1935, 200.

70. Bombay Municipal Corporation, *Administration Report,* 1921–1922, 156.

71. As reported in Bombay Municipal Corporation, *Administration Report,* 1940–1941, 192.

72. Bombay Municipal Corporation, *Administration Report,* 1938–1939, 192.

73. Ibid., 194.

74. Ibid., 235.

75. Glover, *Making Lahore Modern,* 113.

76. *Bombay Chronicle,* February 21, 1921.

77. Deshpande, *Residential Buildings Suited to India,* 235–254.

78. Ibid., 240, 241.

79. Ibid., 244.

80. Three of the eight flat floor plans in *Residential Buildings Suited to India* featured this flexible design. See pages 247–248, 250, and 253.

81. Deshpande, *Modern Ideal Homes for India,* v (emphasis added).

82. Ibid., 63.

83. Thus, Glover notes that in Lahori houses, where the latrines were usually on the terrace, the staircases were kept distinct from the interior of the house to permit sweepers to make their way up to the terrace to clean the latrines. Glover, *Making Lahore Modern,* 113.

84. For a savage attack on the failures of the Indian state and polity in addressing this issue, see Thekaekara, *Endless Filth.*

85. Deshpande, *Cheap and Healthy Homes for the Middle Classes of India,* 182.

86. Ibid.

87. Gandhi, *Autobiography,* 149–150. In all Gandhi's writings on latrines, there is a link between caste and bad toilet practices, which amount to bad sanitary practices.

88. Deshpande, *Cheap and Healthy Homes for the Middle Classes of India,* 183.

89. M. A. Rajagopalan, interview with the author, August 2, 2002. He was ninety-five when I conducted this interview.

90. Deshpande, *Residential Buildings Suited to India,* 240.

91. Ashok Kulkarni, interview with the author, August 10, 2007. Many of the flat designs presented by Deshpande in *Modern Ideal Homes for India* are Marathe and Kulkarni designs for their buildings in Bombay.

92. Ashok Kulkarni, interview with the author, August 10, 2007 (emphasis added).

93. Deshpande, *Modern Ideal Homes for India,* 138. In the early 1930s, when the attached toilet was still new, the injunction to isolate the toilet in one corner of the flat might have been rigidly adhered to; however, over the course of the decade things seem to have loosened up a bit, and there are Marathe and Kulkarni designs from the late 1930s that sometimes locate the toilet next to the kitchen.

94. Yorke and Gibberd, *The Modern Flat,* 36.

95. "Alleged Nuisance: Sequel to Increased Rents," *Bombay Chronicle,* May 18, 1918, 7.

96. Ibid.

97. "Harassing Tenants by Stopping Water Supply," *Bombay Chronicle,* June 18, 1918, 9.

98. "Landlord Fined Rs. 50: Parallel to Dr. Shroff's Case," *Bombay Chronicle,* June 27, 1918, 5.

99. N. R. Iyer, "Water Supply," letter to the editor, *Bombay Chronicle,* November 23, 1920, 5 (emphasis added).

100. "Cooperative Housing Scheme: Matunga South Indian's Move," *Bombay Chronicle,* December 10, 1929, 5. As chapter 5 demonstrates, the South Indians were actually predominantly Brahmins.

4. THE SPREAD OF APARTMENT LIVING

1. See the short account titled "The Cement Merger" by F. E. Dinshaw, who led the effort at consolidation but passed away shortly before the formal merger took place on August 1, 1936.

2. Speech of Sir Lawless Hepper at Inauguration of Worli BDD chawls, November 22, 1922, MSA/[RD] DD/File 53/1/Pt. I/1922, 90.

3. PCACHS, *Annual Report,* 1922–1923, 5.

4. Dwivedi and Mehrotra, *Bombay Deco,* 277.

5. PCACHS, *Annual Report,* 1927–1928, 2.

6. "The 7th All-India Khadi & Swadeshi Exhibition, Madras, 1939–1940," *Indian Concrete Journal* (henceforth *ICJ*), supplement to the May 15, 1940 issue: 1.

7. Ibid., 2.

8. This account is taken from the description by the structural engineer who designed the building: S. K. Nadkarni, "The Saraswat Cooperative Housing Buildings in Tardeo," 370–371.

9. Ashok Kulkarni, interview with the author, August 10, 2007.

10. Municipal Commissioner for the City of Bombay, *Administration Report,* 1938–1939, 189.

11. The crash and the subsequent inquiry were extensively covered in the *Bombay Chronicle.* The hearings in the investigation began in mid-July.

12. Testimony of N. V. Modak as reported in "Reclamation House Collapse Echo," *Bombay Chronicle,* July 28, 1942, 3.

13. As far as I have been able to deter-

mine, the Trust did not actually end up hiring an architect because it faced a storm of criticism from the Municipal Corporation over the expense.

14. "The Honour and Dignity of Bombay," cuttings from the *Times of India,* April 26, 1909, MSA/GD/Vol. 51/1910, Comp. 1026, 17–25.

15. Handwritten note of H. Kemball, April 6, 1909, MSA/GD/Vol. 51/1910, Comp. 1026, 41.

16. Ibid., 46.

17. Ibid., 42–43.

18. Shastri, "Traditional Domestic Architecture of Bombay," 94.

19. Ibid.

20. Ibid., 96.

21. Ibid., 136.

22. Ibid.

23. Ibid., 96.

24. Ibid., 140.

25. Dalvi, "'Domestic Deco' Architecture in Bombay," 14.

26. For an account of the activities of G. B. Mhatre, the best known of this first generation of Indian architects, see Kamu Iyer's "G. B. Mhatre."

27. Deshpande, *Modern Ideal Homes for India,* 131–132.

28. The overwhelming majority of buildings were built for rental purposes. Only a very, very small minority of buyers chose to actually purchase flats through cooperative housing societies. These were pioneers, nonetheless, and they set up the pattern that came to dominate post-Independence Bombay. Such cooperative housing societies are considered in chapters 5 and 6.

29. The evolution of Bombay's municipal bylaws remains a murky and inadequately explored subject. A short but good introduction is contained in the lec-

ture delivered before the Indian Institute of Architects by G. P. Dandekar, special officer of the Bombay Municipality, and unglamorously titled "Revision of Bombay Municipal Building Regulations and Bye Laws with a View to Bringing Them Up to Date." Dandekar was acutely aware of the problems posed to planners when their predecessors had followed lenient policies with building regulations. He urged his audience to "always bear in mind this difference between our city and newly laid out cities like Washington, Canberra, and New Delhi, where there was open undeveloped land like a blank sheet of paper and where you could plan your city first and then commence construction according to that plan." See also the overview by N. V. Modak, "Notes on 'Greater Bombay,'" in Bombay City and Suburbs Post-War Development Committee, *Preliminary Report of the Development of Suburbs and Planning Panel,* 117–281, especially 133–137.

30. Shivdasani, "'City Improvement,' a Paper Read before the Indian Institute of Architects on October 20, 1938," 84–87.

31. Ibid., 86.

32. Ibid.

33. Ibid.

34. The information on the BIT's leasing policies is taken from the account by the chairman, J. P. Orr, "The Dishousing and Rehousing of the Middle Class Slum Population," 215–222, especially 220.

35. Mythili, "A Socio-ecological Study of an Immigrant Community."

36. With the passage of the first development plan in 1964, new floor space index regulations were introduced to allow another floor. According to the latest modifications to the Development Control rules, promulgated in 2001, builders can now build up to seven, fourteen, or twenty

floors, depending upon the exact location and size of the plot. This means that a neighborhood specifically designed to support three-story buildings will now have to cope with structures that are much higher. But that is another story, so to speak.

37. *JIIA* 4, no. 3 (January 1938): 319.

38. Ibid., 320.

39. B. G. Kher's speech, as summarized and quoted in ibid., 321–323.

40. Ibid., 324 (emphasis in the original).

41. Ibid., 324–325.

42. Sennett, *The Conscience of the Eye*, 26–27.

43. K. P. Chari, interview with the author, July 8, 2002.

44. Mythili, "A Socio-ecological Study of an Immigrant Community," 206. As indicated earlier, Mythili's fieldwork in Matunga in the 1950s constitutes an important archive of dwelling practices among South Indians in this neighborhood. The built environment is not her principal concern, but I use her ethnography to develop an account of how people lived in apartment buildings.

45. Mythili, "A Socio-ecological Study of an Immigrant Community," 220.

46. Deshpande, *Residential Buildings Suited to India*, 240.

47. Ashok Kulkarni, interview, August 10, 2007.

48. Deshpande, *Modern Ideal Homes for India*, 57.

49. Ashok Kulkarni, interview with the author, August 10, 2007; Deshpande, *Modern Ideal Homes for India*, 56.

50. Kamu Iyer, interview with author, September 16, 2003.

51. Mythili, "A Socio-ecological Study of an Immigrant Community," 252.

52. Ibid., 253.

53. Ibid., 253.

54. Ibid., 187.

55. Ibid., 236.

56. Ibid., 205 (emphasis added).

57. As discussed earlier, this had been the position of observers of the housing scene in the 1920s urging for multiroom dwellings for the new lower middle class.

58. There was, of course, great variety possible in the "European bourgeois street." In Paris, as is well known, the streets were not entirely residential, with small shops and commercial establishments lining the ground level. In Berlin, on the other hand, bourgeois residential neighborhoods that developed in the late nineteenth and early twentieth centuries were predominantly "residential," with small shops and markets clustered in the vicinity of the local transport hubs such as tram and later train and bus stops. In both cities, an essential attribute of the street was the fact that the buildings presented a uniform facade. James Holston has linked such a facade—and the strict distinction it creates between the "inside" space of the apartment and the "outside" space of the street—with a certain kind of bourgeois subjectivity. In his book about the design of Brasilia he argues that the Le Corbusier–influenced architects Oscar Niemeyer and Lucio Costa sought to shatter precisely such notions of subjectivity through their high-rise buildings emplotted onto gigantic plazas. Holston, *The Modernist City*.

59. Orr was a prodigious public speaker who seemed to never tire of voicing his opinions in any forum that would have him. The best way to approach his ideas is through the four public lectures he gave over the course of the 1910s: *Light and Air in Dwellings in Bombay*, June 27, 1912; "How to Check the Growth of Insanitary Conditions in Bombay," January 1914; "Density

of Population in Bombay," September 1914; and "The Need of Co-operation between Neighbours in the Development of Building Estates," August 1914.

60. The correspondence between the Trust and the commissioner of the Calcutta Municipal Corporation is included in appendix B in Orr, *Light and Air in Dwelling in Bombay,* 27–31. Also included is an interesting comparison by R. J. Kent, the Trust's engineer, of the Calcutta municipal regulations, the Bombay municipal regulations, and the Improvement Trust's regulations on its own estates (33–38). Kent concludes that the Calcutta regulations, were they enforceable, would be the most stringent in this regard; but they were not actually enforced, whereas the Trust's regulations were enforceable because the Trust owned the lands on which its buildings stood.

61. Dandekar, "Revision of Bombay Municipal Building Regulations and Bye-Laws with a View to Bringing Them Up to Date," 118.

62. Mythili, "A Socio-ecological Study of an Immigrant Community," 225.

63. K. V. L. Narayan, interview with the author, September 14, 2003.

64. Bombay Improvement Trust, *Dadar–Matunga Estate: Building Rules,* 2.

65. Bombay High Court, *Tukaram Sawant vs. Mangalalaxmi Chinubhai Shah and Others on 14/12/1988,* 1989 (3) BomCR 313. All details of the case are taken from this judgment and cited by paragraph number.

66. *Deed of Indenture between Bombay Improvement Trust and South Indian Cooperative Housing Society, Limited,* December 20, 1933, Covenant 2; in the author's possession. This same passage is quoted in Bombay High Court, *Tukaram Sawant,* para. 11, indicating that these restrictions were generally applied to all buildings in Dadar–Matunga.

67. Bombay High Court, *Tukaram Sawant,* para. 10.

68. Ibid., para. 13.

69. *Deed of Indenture between Bombay Improvement Trust and South Indian Cooperative Housing Society, Limited,* December 20, 1933, Covenant 11.

70. The information and citations for this particular case are derived from the BIT plot file for Plot 401, Dadar–Matunga Estate.

71. Letter of chairman, South Indian Concerns, to secretary, Estates Department, June 2, 1936, Estates Department, BMC. BIT plot file for Plot 401.

72. Estates Department's objections as recapitulated in a second letter from chairman, South Indian Concerns, to secretary, Estates Department, December 26, 1936, BIT plot file for Plot 401.

73. Ibid.

74. Letter of municipal secretary, Estates Department, to chairman, South Indian Concerns, February 4, 1937.

5. FROM SOUTHERN INDIANS TO "SOUTH INDIANS"

1. K. V. L. Narayan, letter to grandchildren, May 1, 2003, 5 (all emphases in the original). Narayan is referring to the tuft of hair that Brahmin boys customarily wore.

2. K. V. L. Narayan, interview with the author, September 14, 2003. "Southie" is a Mumbai term for people from southern India and is always rendered in English.

3. "Matunga South Indians Make Their Move," *Bombay Chronicle,* December 10, 1929, 10.

4. Cohn, "The Census, Social Structure, and Objectification in South Asia," in

his *An Anthropologist among the Historians,* 224–254.

5. Goswami, *Producing India.* See especially chapter 3, "Mobile Incarceration: Travels in Colonial State Space," 103–131, where she demonstrates the ways in which recalibrated notions of caste, class, race, and gender are mapped onto railway spaces in the nineteenth century.

6. Tanya M. Luhrmann's scholarship on Parsis, for instance, emphasizes the diasporic condition of this community as constitutive of their self-understanding. Luhrmann, *The Good Parsi.* Anne Hardgrove's study of Marwaris in Calcutta also emphasizes their diasporic condition. Hardgrove, *Community and Public Culture.* Mark Anthony Falzon's study of Sindhis and Srijana Mitra Das's study of the representations of Punjabis in Bollywood films both emphasize the condition of exile and mobility as constitutive of, respectively, Sindhi and Punjabi identity. Falzon, "'Bombay, Our Cultural Heart'"; Das, "Partition and Punjabiyat in Bombay Cinema."

7. V. S. Bhide, Bombay Cooperative Societies, *Annual Report,* 1929–1930, 62.

8. Dr. K. Shankar, interview with the author, September 29, 2003.

9. Ramanna, "South Indian Settlers in Mumbai," 25.

10. Mythili, "Little Madras in Bombay City," 242. This piece is an extract from Mythili's Bombay University Ph.D. dissertation, "A Socio-ecological Study of an Immigrant Community." It turns out that 93.3 percent of her sample in the latter work was Brahmin. What is extraordinary is that she did not need to foreground this detail at the very beginning; see page 329. Other castes included in the sample were non-Brahmin but were more or less high castes: Nairs, Menons, Mudaliars, and Chettiars.

11. S. Ramachandran, interview with the author, September 16, 2003.

12. For a contemporary elaboration of how cooperative societies provided an ideal way for middle-class Indians to adjust to urban living, see the paper by R. C. Ewbank, registrar of cooperative societies in Bombay Presidency, titled "Cooperative Housing Societies." He writes, "It is of the first importance that the members of a society should be bound to each other by common interests and pursuits, and therefore they should, as a rule, belong to a single community, caste, class, or profession, and should be of about the same social standing" (800).

13. Such thinking is already adumbrated in the quotation from R. C. Ewbank in note 12. See also Conlon, *A Caste in a Changing World,* 185.

14. Bombay Provincial Cooperative Conference, *Proceedings of the Bombay Provincial Cooperative Conference Held in Poona, September 18th and 19th, 1917,* 13.

15. As indicated in BIT, *Annual Administration Report,* 1919–1920, 19–20. In that year, of 1,819 plots to be leased by the Trust, no fewer than 465 were "agreed to be leased" to copartnership housing societies. Of course, as the unwieldy phrasing "agreed to be leased" indicates, many, perhaps most, of these leases did not come to fruition, for many, perhaps most, of these cooperative societies were found to be unviable. Precise details of the concessions extended to the societies are contained in appendix O-2 of BIT, *Annual Administration Report,* 1920, 112.

16. Press note, Government of Bombay,

reproduced in *Bombay Chronicle*, February 13, 1919, 5.

17. Conlon, *A Caste in a Changing World*, 187–188.

18. Letter from agent, GIP, no. 361-C29, April 26, 1918, in BIT, *Annual Administration Report*, 1918–1919, 134.

19. Ibid.

20. "Speech of Vaikunth L. Mehta on 30 November 1940," in Saraswat Cooperative Housing Society, *Silver Jubilee Souvenir*, 35. Mehta goes on to say that he still believes that cooperative societies should not be organized on a communal basis, but in light of the tremendous success of the Saraswat societies, he conceded, "It is not impossible to serve wider interests while working on communal institutions."

21. "Speech of G. P. Murdeshwar on the Silver Jubilee of the Saraswat Cooperative Housing Society," April 20, 1940, as reported in Saraswat Cooperative Housing Society, *Silver Jubilee Souvenir*, 21–22.

22. Some details of Talmaki's proposal, on a considerably larger scale than the initial Saraswat projects in Gamdevi, are contained in BIT, *Annual Administration Report*, 1918–1919, 135–136.

23. Conlon, *A Caste in a Changing World*, 185.

24. In 1920 the following societies were given plots on the Improvement Trust's Dadar–Matunga estate: the Bombay Hindu Housing Association (the one that subsequently went defunct), the Zorastrian Society, the Hindu Association, the Chandraseniya Kayastha Prabhu Society, the Bombay Cooperative Housing Association, the Kutchi Visa Oswal Society, and the Telugu Building Society. BIT, *Annual Administration Report*, 1919–1920, 35.

25. Luhrmann, "Evil in the Sands of Time." See also her book-length study *The Good Parsi*.

26. Luhrmann, "Evil in the Sands of Time," 861.

27. The formation of the Parsi Colony in Dadar–Matunga and the role of the PCACHS is discussed in chapter 2.

28. PCACHS, *Annual Report*, 1923–1924, 1.

29. Teresa Albuquerque, in her wonderful account of the Bombay suburb of Santa Cruz, notes that a doctrinal compromise between the Bishopric of Goa and Daman, on the one hand, and representatives of the Holy See in Rome, on the other hand, was necessary before true cooperation among the various Catholic communities became possible. "Thus was ushered in an era of cooperative effort among the Catholics of Bombay," she writes, following the compromise. Albuquerque, *Santa Cruz That Was*, 19.

30. Albuquerque, *To Love Is to Serve*, 15.

31. Conlon, *A Caste in a Changing World*, 174–175.

32. Raghavan Sarathy, interview with the author, October 15, 2003.

33. S. Ramachandran, interview with the author, September 16, 2003.

34. The implications of such preferences are discussed in detail in chapter 3.

35. S. Rajadhyax, letter to the editor, *Bombay Chronicle*, June 13, 1934, 8.

36. "Plea for Unity among South Indians," *Bombay Chronicle*, March 13, 1944, 2.

37. This extract from V. K. Menon's speech is reproduced in ibid.

38. *Bombay Chronicle*, April 21, 1944, 33. The article is titled, tellingly, "Do Not Lose Grasp of Reality." Pothan Joseph's remarks are excerpted within the article.

39. For a discussion of the way the South

Indian or the Madrasi figured as the target of the Sena's ire in these years, see Hansen, *Wages of Violence*, 46–47.

40. Of course, this is not to suggest that Sena strongmen would not bash low-caste Tamilian tannery workers from Dharavi for being "South Indians" if they needed to.

41. Kalpana Sharma estimates that even today, after decades of post-Independence migration into Dharavi from northern India, perhaps one-third of Dharavi remains Tamil-speaking. In the 1930s and 1940s the proportion would have been greater. Sharma, *Rediscovering Dharavi*, 47.

42. The majority of these refugees were from the region of the Deccan around Ahmadnagar.

43. As reported in BIT, *Annual Administration Report*, 1921, 12.

44. Ibid., 13.

45. Speech of Jamnadas Mehta is reported in "7 Lakh Scheme to House City's Poor: Mayor Opens New Labour Colony," *Bombay Chronicle*, January 11, 1937, 8.

46. Ibid.

47. BIT, *Annual Administration Report*, 1921, 13.

48. Ibid.

49. "City Improvement Trust: Dharavi Street Scheme," *Bombay Chronicle*, May 6, 1923, 5. This article reported a familiar pattern: the owners of the tanneries demanded what were, in the Trust's view, highly inflated prices for their lands in Dharavi. The haggling over these lands appeared to have deflated the Trust's enthusiasm for the scheme, and in the recessionary years after 1922, the scheme fell by the wayside.

50. An account of this gathering, including summaries of the speeches delivered by Narayanswami and Purshottamdas Tricumdas, secretary of the Congress Socialists, is contained in "Tamil Reading Room for Tannery Workers," *Bombay Chronicle*, January 12, 1935, 5.

51. He also ran for political office from the F Ward, which included Matunga.

52. It has been possible to reconstruct Narayanswami's political activities through the transcripts of an oral history recorded and transcribed by Uma Shanker in 1969. Transcript of conversations between C. K. Narayanswami and Uma Shanker (henceforth Narayanswami Oral History), September 14, 1969, 1–31, University of Cambridge Centre of South Asian Studies, Oral History Archive.

53. "South Indians Bid Farewell to Mr. Krishna Iyer," *Bombay Chronicle*, July 11, 1934, 5.

54. Narayanswami Oral History, 4.

55. Ibid., 5.

56. Of course, Narayanswami, a journalist, might have written the article himself and supplied his own translation. But then it is even more noteworthy that he made no mention of the Tamil language.

57. Narayanswami Oral History, 5.

58. *Asthika Samaj Matunga Souvenir*, 4.

59. S. Ramachandran, interview with the author, September 23, 2003.

60. Kamu Iyer, interview with the author, September 16, 2003.

61. Both P. Chari and M. Rajagopalan, two of the oldest of my informants, and both of whom claimed to be deeply religious, made exactly this assertion, and Kamu Iyer also said as much in a different context.

62. S. R. Ramachandran illustrated this synthesis by referring to the statesman Sir C. P. Ramaswami Iyer, *dewan* (chief minister) of Travancore State from 1936 to 1946. Ramaswami Iyer was already a classic case of a Tamil Brahmin recruited as an admin-

istrator into the court of a Malayali ruler. Ramachandran described him to me, unself-consciously, as "Pakka Tamil, but pure Malayalam," and also as "highly modernistic, but terribly casteist also." S. Ramachandran, interview with the author, September 23, 2003.

63. The Keraleeya Samaj, also housed in Matunga, was an association of persons from what is now Kerala but what in the 1930s and 1940s would have consisted of the princely states of Cochin, Travancore, and the Malabar district of Madras Presidency. This association was primarily non-Iyer in composition and included Christians because of Kerala's distinctive history.

64. These details were told to me by S. Ramachandran (September 18, 2003), but I heard this story repeatedly. Invariably I was told that the South Indian Welfare Society school was more oriented to a Palakkad Iyer clientele.

65. *Bombay Chronicle*, January 19, 1939, 5. Namboodiri Brahmins are Malayalam-speaking Brahmins from Kerala. They are indigenous to Kerala and, unlike the Kerala Iyers, are not recent migrants. An admittedly unscientific survey of announcements in the *Bombay Chronicle* from the 1930s and 1940s suggests that the Asthika Samaj was much more likely to advertise events that bore a distinctive Kerala stamp, such as the discourse by the Namboodiri cited here or musical events featuring musicians from Kerala.

66. Indeed, my efforts to interview him were constantly interrupted by visitors anxiously bearing the horoscopes of their children for his examination. At one point he insisted on reading my horoscope.

67. *Bombay Chronicle*, June 3, 1938, 2.

68. The Iyers, like other Hindu castes, believe that they are descended from one of eighteen *gotrams*, which are named after eighteen sages who are supposed to have founded the clans. Hence it is necessary for members of a particular *gotram* to marry outside that *gotram* in order not to commit incest.

69. S. Ramachandran, interview with the author, September 23, 2003. Pappadams and vadaams are varieties of crisp, fried lentil batter.

70. Mythili, "A Socio-ecological Study of an Immigrant Community," 154.

71. *Bombay Chronicle*, October 17, 1947, 8.

6. TOWARD GREATER MUMBAI

1. As reported in "New Greater Bombay Inaugurated," *Bombay Chronicle*, February 2, 1957, 3.

2. Ibid.

3. Ibid.

4. Bombay High Court, *Padmakar Balkrishna Samant vs. State of Bombay and Ors on 31/1/1957*, (1957) 59 BOMLR 355. The petition was admitted to the Bombay High Court by Justices Shah and Gokhale. Further citations will be to paragraph numbers from the text of the judgment.

5. As reported in "Further Extension of City Limits Challenged," *Bombay Chronicle*, January 31, 1957, 3.

6. Bombay High Court, *Padmakar Balkrishna Samant*, para. 1.

7. Ibid., para. 2.

8. Ibid., paras. 4 and 5. A summary of the petitioners' arguments also appears in "Further Extension of City Limits Challenged."

9. Since 1926, though, BEST has sourced its power from Tata Electric Companies. Tata Power, one of the Tata Electric Com-

panies, also has an odd relationship with Reliance Infrastructure, its biggest rival: since Tata Power is a net generator of power and Reliance Infrastructure cannot meet its demand, the latter buys the former's surplus power at a regulated price (although, most recently, this arrangement is in jeopardy).

10. A short account of this consolidation can be found in "Local Self-Government," in Government of Maharashtra, *Maharashtra State Gazetteers: Greater Bombay District*.

11. Chunilal Barfivala, "Minute of Dissent," April 11, 1946, in Bombay City and Suburbs Post-War Development Committee, *Preliminary Report of the Development of Suburbs and Planning Panel*, 77.

12. Muddy Pedestrian, "A Santa Cruz Grievance," *Bombay Chronicle*, June 22, 1923, 2. All subsequent citations from the Muddy Pedestrian are from this article.

13. This was the observation of the Reorganization of Local Self-Government in Salsette Committee, also known as the Bell Committee, in 1925. As reported in *Bombay Chronicle*, August 11, 1925.

14. "New Scheme of Suburban Amalgamation," *Bombay Chronicle*, January 18, 1935, 5.

15. "'Gross Abuse of Rights of Self-Govt.' J. K. Mehta Denounces Suburban Municipal Amalgamation," *Bombay Chronicle*, January 17, 1935, 8.

16. Ibid.

17. S. N. Kalbag, as reported in ibid.

18. "Towards Greater Bombay: Barfivala on Suburban Municipal Unification," *Bombay Chronicle*, January 21, 1935, 13.

19. In the mid-1920s there were letters and articles in newspapers practically every week complaining about crime, allegedly perpetrated by Pathan frontiersmen, who evaded the jurisdiction of the Bombay City Police by making their base in the suburbs. See, for instance, "Pathan Terrorism in Malad," letter to the editor, *Bombay Chronicle*, March 20, 1923, 12; see also "Pathan Terrorism in Bombay: A Grave Scandal," *Bombay Chronicle*, May 3, 1924; and "Insecurity in Ghatkoper: People in Panic," *Bombay Chronicle*, June 4 1924, 5.

20. The original letter inviting opinions, dated December 9, 1907, and the voluminous subsequent correspondence is contained in MSA/GD/Vol. 218 Pt. I/1909.

21. The findings and recommendations of this committee are contained in the *Report of the Bombay Development Committee*.

22. A short overview—just a time line, really—of the various Greater Bombay schemes is contained in the introduction to the report of the Post-War Development Committee. Bombay City and Suburbs Post-War Development Committee, *Preliminary Report of the Development of Suburbs and Planning Panel*, 1–4.

23. "Resolutions Passed at the Conference of the Member of Bombay Suburban Local Bodies, December 1st, 1945." Appendix to Barfivala, "Minute of Dissent," 107–108.

24. Ibid., 107.

25. Bombay City and Suburbs Post-War Development Committee, *Preliminary Report of the Development of Suburbs and Planning Panel*, 56.

26. See Barfivala's incendiary "Minute of Dissent," 65–96.

27. Ibid., 66.

28. Ibid., 68.

29. "Greater Bombay Will Be Born Today," *Bombay Chronicle*, April 15, 1950, 2.

30. "Make Bombay the Pride of the East: Mayor's Call to Citizens," *Bombay Chronicle*, April 15, 1950, 2.

31. Chapter 2 deals with municipal elections in an early suburb within the island city.

32. The correspondence relating to this piece of speculation is contained in "Proposal of Mr. J. N. Tata to Reclaim Certain Un-assessed Un-occupied Lands in the North of the Island of Bombay," MSA/RD/Vol. 186/1905.

33. J. P. Orr was an Indian Civil Service officer who, after serving as collector of Thana, went on to serve in the city of Bombay and was the energetic chairman of the Bombay Improvement Trust in the 1910s.

34. These conclusions were worked out in an extensive correspondence among landowners, the Thana collector, and the Revenue Department of the provincial government, contained in "Assessment of Land Appropriated for Building Sites," MSA/GD/Vol. 55/1902.

35. His study was published as W. C. Hughes, *Notes on City Improvement Schemes in England,* in MSA/GD/Vol. 40/1901. Hughes was a long-serving engineer and bureaucrat in Bombay and served in important positions in the Public Works Department and the Improvement Trust and as chairman of the Port Trust.

36. Hughes, *Notes on City Improvement Schemes,* 2.

37. Ibid.

38. Ibid., 1.

39. The bill was discussed by the trustees of the BIT in March 1910: BIT, *Proceedings,* March 8, 1910, MSA/GD/Vol. 7/1910, 111. All subsequent references to these BIT *Proceedings,* unless otherwise noted, use the page numbers from this GD volume, where they are compiled.

40. BIT, *Proceedings,* March 8, 1910, 112.

41. Ibid. Note that although Orr refers to the "Town Planning Act," in fact the legislation remained a bill in Bombay until 1915, when it was finally passed in the legislature and became an act of government.

42. Mead, *Report on the Possibilities of Development of Salsette as a Residential Area* (a report for the Government of Bombay).

43. Ibid., 7.

44. Ibid., 1–5.

45. Ibid., 7.

46. Kissan, *Report on Town Planning Enactments in Germany* (a report for the Government of Bombay). For a fuller elaboration of the ways in which German urban thinking was incorporated into the Bombay Town Planning Act, see my article "Towards Greater Bombay."

47. BIT, *Proceedings,* March 15, 1910, 133.

48. In thus effectively restricting the meaning of Town Planning to city extension and suburbanization, rather than urban planning and redevelopment in built-up areas, Bombay's landowners appear to have done something similar to what British landowners did with the first English Town Planning Act of 1909, which effectively became a city-extension legislation. See S. Martin Gaskell, "'The Suburb Salubrious': Town Planning in Practice," in Sutcliffe, *British Town Planning,* 41.

49. BIT, *Proceedings,* March 15, 1910, 133.

50. Mirams, "Town Planning in Bombay under the Bombay Town Planning Act."

51. Ibid., 50.

52. The Industrial Housing Scheme is discussed in Conlon, "Industrialization and the Housing Problem in Bombay," and Hazareesingh, *The Colonial City and the Challenge of Modernity.* The scandal-ridden Backbay Reclamation Scheme is discussed in Prakash, *Mumbai Fables.*

53. "Suburban Development in Salsette and Bombay," draft annual report of De-

velopment Department for 1921–1922, Public Works Department (DD)/File 26/1922, 183.

54. Kissan, *Report on Town Planning Enactments in Germany,* 27. Kissan noted that in places where municipalities had been active in such purchasing of lands, there was less need for reparceling legislation such as the Lex Adickes.

55. Kalina, "Development in South Salsette: Abuse of Land Acquisition Act," letter to the editor, *Bombay Chronicle,* April 29, 1921, 5. Kalina was one of the villages in south Salsette that was affected by the land acquisitions.

56. Pro Bono Publico, "A Garden City in Salsette," *Bombay Chronicle,* May 8, 1924, 10.

57. G. B. Trivedi, "Suburban Development," *Bombay Chronicle,* May 26, 1924, 11.

58. Lanchester, *Town Planning in Madras.*

59. Mirams, "Town Planning in Bombay under the Bombay Town Planning Act," 59. The question-and-answer session following Mirams's lecture is reproduced in ibid., 57–63. Rachel Sturman has discussed some ways in which ideas of the family in nineteenth-century western India transform the meaning of the subject of property. See Sturman, "Property and Attachments."

60. Government of Bombay, Local Self-Government Department, "Board of Appeal Proceedings," in *Bandra Town Planning Scheme No. IV (Varied) (Final),* 24.

61. Soli Sorabjee, "Decriminalisation of Politics," *Indian Express,* September 12, 2004, http://www.indianexpress.com/oldStory/54934/ (accessed July 21, 2010).

62. Bombay High Court, *Ratanchand Hirachand vs. Commissioner of Income Tax and Others on June 30th, 1959,* (1960) 38 ITR 76 Bom, para. 1.

63. Government of Bombay, Local Self-Government Department, "Board of Appeal Proceedings," 25.

64. For an analysis of how changed housing conditions in the aftermath of World War II led to the rise of ownership-based housing, as opposed to rental housing, see my article "Uncertain Ground."

65. Government of Bombay, *Report of the Committee Appointed to Inquire into the Workings of the Bombay Rents, Hotel, and Lodging House Rates Control Act, 1947,* 9.

66. Bombay Municipal Corporation, *Annual Administration Report,* 1955–1956, vii.

67. "Cement Shortage May Increase," *Bombay Chronicle,* January 24, 1957, 7. According to this article, the demand for cement had gone up from 2.6 million tons in 1950–1951 to 6.5 million tons in 1955–1956. The cement shortfall for 1955–1956 was estimated at 1.5 million tons.

68. Batley, *Bombay's Houses and Homes,* 21.

69. Government of Bombay, *Report of the Committee Appointed to Inquire into the Workings of the Bombay Rents, Hotel, and Lodging House Rates Control Act,* 5.

70. Bombay Municipal Corporation, *Annual Administration Report,* 1948–1949, 18.

71. Bombay Municipal Corporation, *Annual Administration Report,* 1948–1949, vi.

72. Bombay Municipal Corporation, *Annual Administration Report,* 1952–1953, 182.

73. Government of Bombay, Local Self-Government Department, *Bandra Town Planning Scheme No. IV (Varied) (Final),* 1. "Varying" a scheme was the standard procedure for changing regulations within the scheme and entailed the same elaborate procedure as described above for framing a scheme. The "variation" resulted in a "varied" scheme.

74. This argument was made repeatedly

by Rodrigues and others. See, for example, Government of Bombay, Local Self-Government Department, "Board of Appeal Proceedings," 25.

75. For a more extensive exploration of the spread of cooperative housing societies in Bombay after 1947, see my article "Uncertain Ground."

76. On the place of Bombay in fashioning Sindhi self-understanding, see Falzon, "'Bombay, Our Cultural Heart.'" On "Punjabiyat" and its connection to the Bombay cinema, especially of the 1950s, see Das, "Partition and Punjabiyat in Bombay Cinema." One critical aspect of "Punjabiyat," argues Das, is the "construction of a curious Punjabi world almost exclusively occupied by Hindu Khatris" (453).

77. Punwaney, "The Origins of Amils."

78. Punwaney, "How Amils lived in Sind before Partition."

79. Punwaney, "Activities in Mumbai."

80. Ibid.

81. Khudabadi Amil Panchayat of Bombay, "Constitution and Rules."

Bibliography

⊱ ARCHIVES

Maharashtra State Archives, Mumbai
   Development Department
   General Department
   Revenue Department
University of Cambridge Centre of South
   Asian Studies, Oral History Archive

⊱ OFFICIAL GOVERNMENT PUBLICATIONS

Bombay, City of. *Municipal Retrenchment and Reform: Final Report of the Retrenchment Advisor.* Bombay: Indian Daily Mail Press, 1925.

Bombay City and Suburbs Post-War Development Committee. *Preliminary Report of the Development of Suburbs and Planning Panel.* Bombay: Government Central Press, 1948.

The Bombay City Land Revenue Act No. II of 1876. As amended by Acts III of 1900, I of 1910, IV of 1915, II of 1919, 49 of 1947, and 9 of 1949. Bombay: Government of Bombay, 1948.

Bombay Development Directorate. *Annual Administration Reports.*

Bombay, Government of. *Report of the Committee Appointed to Inquire into the Workings of the Bombay Rents, Hotel, and Lodging House Rates Control Act, 1947.* Bombay: Government Central Press, 1953.

Bombay, Government of, Development Department. *Report on the Working of the Development Department for the Year Ending 31/3/1929.* Bombay: Government Central Press, 1929.

Bombay, Government of, Local Self-Government Department. *Bandra Town Planning Scheme No. IV (Varied) (Final).* Bombay: Government Central Press, 1960.

———. *Bombay City No. II (Mahim Area) (Final).* Bombay: Government Central Press, 1962.

Bombay High Court. *Padmakar Balkrishna Samant vs. State of Bombay and Ors on 31/1/1957.* (1957) 59 BOMLR 355.

———. *Ratanchand Hirachand vs. Commissioner of Income Tax and Others on June 30th, 1959.* (1960) 38 ITR 76 Bom.

———. *Tukaram Sawant vs. Mangalalaxmi Chinubhai Shah and Others on 14/12/1988.* 1989 (3) BomCR 313.

Bombay Improvement Trust. *Annual Administration Reports.* Bombay: Government Printing Press, various years.

———. *Dadar–Matunga Estate: Building Rules.* Estates Department, MCGB, 1936.

Bombay Municipal Corporation. *Annual Administration Reports,* various years. Bombay: Times Press.

Bombay Provincial Cooperative Conference. *Proceedings of the Bombay Provincial Cooperative Conference Held in Poona, September 18th and 19th, 1917.* Poona: Government Central Press, 1918.

Census of India, 1931. Vol. 11, *Cities of the Bombay Presidency.* Bombay: Government Central Press, 1931.

Census of India, 1951. Greater Bombay District

Census Handbook. Bombay: Government of Bombay Printing, 1952.

Kissan, B. W. *Report on Town Planning Enactments in Germany.* Bombay: Government Central Press, 1913.

Maharashtra, Government of. *Maharashtra State Gazetteers: Greater Bombay District.* http://www.maharashtra.gov.in /english/gazetteer/greater_bombay /local.html. Accessed June 10, 2010.

Mead, P. J. *Report on the Possibilities of the Development of Salsette as a Residential Area.* Bombay: Government Central Press, 1909.

Report of the Bombay Development Committee. Bombay: Government Central Press, 1914.

Report on an Enquiry into Middle Class Family Budgets in Bombay City. Bombay: Government Central Press, Labour Office, 1928.

Report on an Enquiry into Middle Class Unemployment in the Bombay Presidency. Bombay: Government Central Press, Labour Office, 1927.

Report on Working Class Budgets in Bombay City. Bombay: Labour Office, 1924.

⊰ PERIODICALS AND PAMPHLETS

Asthika Samaj Matunga Souvenir. Bombay: 2003.

Bombay Chronicle.

Bombay Cooperative Societies, *Annual Report, 1929–1930.*

Bombay Explorer.

Indian Concrete Journal (ICJ). Mumbai: Associated Cement Companies (ACC).

Journal of the Indian Institute of Architects (JIIA). Bombay: Indian Institute of Architects.

Journal of the Royal Institute of British Architects. London: Royal Institute of British Architects.

Keraleeya Samaj, Golden Jubilee Souvenir. Bombay: 1977.

Laws of Incorporation of the South Indian Cooperative Housing Society. Bombay, n.d.

Local Self-Government Gazette. Bombay: All-India Institute of Local Self-Government.

Mysore Association Silver Jubilee Annual Report. Bombay: 1951.

Parsi Central Association Cooperative Housing Societies, *Annual Reports, 1921–1942.*

Saraswat Cooperative Housing Society, Ltd. *Silver Jubilee Souvenir.* December 15, 1940.

⊰ THESES, ARTICLES, AND BOOKS

Albuquerque, Teresa. *Santa Cruz That Was.* Bombay: Teresa Albuquerque, 1981.

———. *To Love Is to Serve: Catholics of Bombay.* Bombay: Heras Institute, 1986.

Appadurai, Arjun. "Number in the Colonial Imagination." In *Orientalism and the Postcolonial Predicament: Perspectives on South Asia,* edited by Carol Breckenridge and Peter van der Veer, 314–339. Philadelphia: University of Pennsylvania Press, 1993.

———. "Spectral Housing and Urban Cleansing: Notes on Millennial Mumbai." *Public Culture* 12, no. 3 (2000): 627–651.

Archer, John. *Architecture and Suburbia: From English Villa to American Dream House, 1690–2000.* Minneapolis: University of Minnesota Press, 2005.

———. "Colonial Suburbs in South Asia,

1700–1850, and the Spaces of Modernity." In *Visions of Suburbia*, edited by Roger Silverstone, 26–54. London: Routledge, 1997.

Arnold, David. *Colonizing the Body: State Medicine and Epidemic Disease in Nineteenth Century India*. Berkeley: University of California Press, 1993.

Baden Powell, B. H. *The Land Systems of British India*. Oxford: Clarendon Press, 1892.

Batley, Claude. *Bombay's Houses and Homes*. Bombay: National Information and Publications, 1949.

Bedarida, François, and Anthony Sutcliffe. "The Street in the Structure and Life of the City." *Journal of Urban History* 6, no. 4 (1980): 379–396.

Begg, John. "The Indian Master Builder." *Journal of Royal Institute of British Architects*, 3rd ser., 20 (November 23, 1912): 59.

Bhonsle, Ramkrishna Narayan. "Clerks in the City of Bombay." Master's thesis, Bombay University, 1938.

Bhuta, O. K. "Rise of Value of Land and Other Properties in Bombay in Recent Times." *Local Self-Government Gazette* 5, no. 11 (November 1919): 797–805.

Blake, Stephen. "Shahjahanabad: Cityscape of an Imperial Capital." In *Delhi through the Ages*, edited by Robert E. Frykenberg, 66–105. New Delhi: Oxford University Press, 1986.

Blau, Eve. *The Architecture of Red Vienna, 1919–1934*. Cambridge: MIT Press, 1999.

Burnett-Hurst, A. F. *Labour and Housing in Bombay: A Study of the Economic Conditions of the Wage Earning Classes of Bombay*. London: P. S. King, 1925.

Catanach, I. J. "'Who Are Your Leaders?' Plague, the Raj, and the 'Communities' in Bombay, 1896–1901." In *Society and Ideology: Essays in South Asian History Presented to K. A. Ballhatchet*, edited by Peter Robb, 196–221. New Delhi: Oxford University Press, 1993.

Chakrabarty, Dipesh. *Habitations of Modernity: Essays in the Wake of Subaltern Studies*. Chicago: University of Chicago Press, 2002.

Chandavarkar, Rajnarayan. *Culture, History, and the Indian City: Essays*. New York: Cambridge University Press, 2009.

——. *Imperial Power and Popular Politics*. Cambridge: Cambridge University Press, 1998.

——. *The Origins of Industrial Capitalism in India: Business Strategies and the Working Classes in Bombay, 1900–1940*. Cambridge: Cambridge University Press, 1994.

Chatterjee, Partha. "Are Indian Cities Becoming Bourgeois at Last? Or, If You Prefer, We Could Exclaim: Are Indian Cities Becoming Bourgeois, Alas?" In *Body.City: Siting Contemporary Culture in India*, edited by Indira Chandrasekhar and Peter C. Seel, 171–185. New Delhi: Haus der Kulturen der Welt/Tulika Books, 2003.

——. "On Civil and Political Society in Postcolonial Democracies." In *Civil Society: History and Possibilities*, edited by Sudipta Kaviraj and Sunil Khilnani, 165–178. Cambridge: Cambridge University Press, 2001.

Chattopadhyay, Swati. *Representing Calcutta: Modernity, Nationalism, and the Colonial Uncanny*. New York: Routledge, 2006.

Chopra, Preeti. "The City and Its Fragments: Colonial Bombay, 1854–1918." Ph.D. diss., University of California, Berkeley, 2003.

——. *A Joint Enterprise: Indian Elites and the*

Making of British Bombay. Minneapolis: University of Minnesota Press, 2011.

Cohn, Bernard. *An Anthropologist among the Historians, and Other Essays.* New Delhi: Oxford University Press India, 1990.

Conlon, Frank. *A Caste in a Changing World: The Chitrapur Saraswat Brahmans, 1700–1935.* Berkeley and Los Angeles: University of California Press, 1977.

———. "Industrialization and the Housing Problem in Bombay, 1850–1940." In *Changing South Asia,* edited by Kenneth Ballhatchet and David Taylor, 153–168. Hong Kong: Asian Research Service for SOAS, 1984.

Cromley, Elizabeth Collins. *Alone Together: A History of New York's Early Apartments.* Ithaca, N.Y., and London: Cornell University Press, 1990.

———. "The Development of American Apartment-Houses from the Civil War to the Depression." *Architectura* 21 (1991): 47–52.

———. "New York, Paris, and the French Flat." *Architectura* 21 (1991): 53–67.

da Cunha, J. Gerson. *The Origin of Bombay.* Reprint, Delhi: Asian Educational Services, 1992. First published 1900.

Dalvi, Mustansir. "'Domestic Deco' Architecture in Bombay: G. B.'s Milieu." In *Buildings That Shaped Bombay: Works of G. B. Mhatre,* edited by Kamu Iyer, 14–21. Mumbai: Kamala Raheja Vidyanidhi Institute of Architecture, 2000.

Dandekar, G. P. "Revision of Bombay Municipal Building Regulations and Bye Laws with a View to Bringing Them Up to Date." *Journal of the Indian Institute of Architects* 5, no. 4 (April 1939): 117–118.

Das, Srijana Mitra. "Partition and Punjabiyat in Bombay Cinema: The Cinematic Perspective of Yash Chopra and Others." *Contemporary South Asia* 15, no. 4 (December 2006): 453–471.

Davis, Mike. *Planet of Slums.* London: Verso, 2007.

Dennis, Richard. "'Babylonian Flats' in Victorian and Edwardian London." *London Journal* 33, no. 3 (November 2008): 233–247.

———. "Interpreting the Apartment House: Modernity and Metropolitanism in Toronto, 1900–1930." *Journal of Historical Geography* 20, no. 3 (1994): 305–322.

Deshpande, R. S. *Cheap and Healthy Homes for the Middle Classes of India.* Poona: Aryabhushan Press, 1935.

———. *Modern Ideal Homes for India.* Poona: United Book Corporation, 1939.

———. *Residential Buildings Suited to India.* Poona: United Book Corporation, 1931.

Deshpande, Sudha. "Evidence of Under-Enumeration in 1991 Census." *Economic and Political Weekly* 32, no. 36 (June 28, 1997): 1539–1541.

Design Cell, Kamla Raheja Vidyanidhi Institute for Architecture and Environmental Studies. "Documentation and Preparation of Heritage Conservation Guidelines for Dadar–Matunga Scheme V—Parsi Colony & Hindu Colony Precincts." Unpublished Report for Mumbai Metropolitan Region Heritage Conservation Society, Mumbai, 2000.

Dewey, Clive. "The End of the Imperialism of Free Trade: The Eclipse of the Lancashire Lobby and the Concession of Free Trade to India." In *The Imperial Impact: Studies in the Imperial History of Africa and India,* edited by C. J. Dewey and A. G. Hopkins, 35–67. London: Athlone Press for Institute of Commonwealth Studies, 1978.

———. "The Government of India's 'New Industrial Policy,' 1900–1925: Formation and Failure." In *Economy and Society: Studies in Indian Economic and Social History,* edited by K. N. Chaudhuri and C. J. Dewey, 215–257. New Delhi: Oxford University Press, 1978.

Dinshaw, F. E. "The Cement Merger." *Indian Concrete Journal,* March 15, 1936: nonpaginated insert.

Dossal, Mariam. *Imperial Designs and Indian Realities: The Planning of Bombay City, 1845–1875.* Bombay: Oxford University Press India, 1991.

———. *Theatre of Conflict, City of Hope: Bombay/Mumbai, 1660 to Present Times.* Bombay: Oxford University Press India, 2010.

Dwivedi, Sharada, and Rahul Mehrotra. *Bombay: The Cities Within.* Mumbai: India Book House, 1995.

———. *Bombay Deco.* Bombay: Eminence Designs, 2008.

Edwardes, S. M. *By-Ways of Bombay.* Bombay: D. B. Taraporewalla and Sons, 1912.

———. *The Gazetteer of Bombay City and Island.* Vols. 1–3. Reprint, Bombay: Cosmo Publications, 2001. First published Bombay: Times of India Press, 1909–1910. Page citations are to the reprint edition.

———. *The Rise of Bombay: A Retrospect.* Bombay: Times of India Press, 1902.

Evenson, Norma. *The Indian Metropolis: A View toward the West.* New Haven: Yale University Press, 1989.

Ewbank, R. C. "Cooperative Housing Societies." *Local Self-Government Gazette* 2, no. 10 (1916): 799–805.

Falzon, Mark Anthony. "'Bombay, Our Cultural Heart': Rethinking the Relation between Homeland and Diaspora." *Ethnic and Racial Studies* 26, no. 4 (July 2003): 662–683.

Fishman, Robert. *Bourgeois Utopias: The Rise and Fall of Suburbia.* New York: Basic Books, 1987.

Gandhi, Mohandas. *Autobiography: The Story of My Experiments with Truth.* London: Dover, 1983.

George, Rose. *The Big Necessity: The Unmentionable World of Human Waste and Why It Matters.* New York: Holt, 2009.

Glover, William J. "Construing Urban Space as 'Public' in Colonial India: Some Notes from the Punjab." *Journal of Punjab Studies* 15, no. 1 (Fall 2007): 1–14.

———. *Making Lahore Modern: Constructing and Imagining a Colonial City.* Minneapolis: University of Minnesota Press, 2007.

———. "Making Lahore Modern: Urban Form and Social Practice in Colonial Punjab, 1849–1920." Ph.D. diss., University of California, Berkeley, 1999.

Gordon, A. D. D. *Businessmen and Politics: Rising Nationalism and a Modernizing Economy in Bombay, 1918–1933.* New Delhi: Manohar, 1978.

Goswami, Manu. *Producing India: From Colonial Economy to National Space.* Chicago: University of Chicago Press, 2004.

Guha, Ranajit. *A Rule of Property for Bengal: An Essay on the Idea of Permanent Settlement.* Paris: Mouton, 1963.

Gupta, Narayani. "Military Security and Urban Development: A Case of Delhi, 1857–1912." *Modern Asian Studies* 5, no. 1 (1971): 61–77.

Gyáni, Gábor. *Parlor and Kitchen: Housing and Domestic Culture in Budapest, 1870–1940.* Translated from Hungarian by Miklos Bodoczky. Budapest: Central European University Press, 2002. First published in Hungarian in 1998.

Hansen, Thomas Blom. *Wages of Violence: Naming and Identity in Postcolonial*

Bombay. Princeton: Princeton University Press, 2001.

Hardgrove, Anne. *Community and Public Culture: The Marwaris in Calcutta, c. 1897–1997.* New York: Columbia University Press, 2004.

Harris, Richard. "Meaningful Types in a World of Suburbs." In "Suburbanization in a Global Society," edited by Mark Clapson and Ray Hutchinson, special issue *Research in Urban Sociology* 10 (2011): 15–47.

Haynes, Douglas E., Abigail McGowan, Tirthankar Roy, and Haruka Yanagisawa, eds. *Towards a History of Consumption in South Asia.* New Delhi: Oxford University Press, 2009.

Hazareesingh, Sandip. *The Colonial City and the Challenge of Modernity: Urban Hegemonies and Civic Contestations in Bombay, 1900–1925.* Delhi: Orient Longman, 2007.

———. "Colonial Modernism and the Flawed Paradigms of Urban Renewal: Uneven Development in Bombay, 1900–1925." *Urban History* 28, no. 2 (2001): 235–255.

———. "The Quest for Urban Citizenship: Civic Rights, Public Opinion, and Colonial Resistance in Early Twentieth-Century Bombay." *Modern Asian Studies* 34, no. 4 (2000): 797–829.

Heitzman, James. *Gifts of Power: Lordship in an Early Indian State.* New Delhi: Oxford University Press, 1997.

Holston, James. *The Modernist City: An Anthropological Critique of Brasilia.* Chicago: University of Chicago Press, 1989.

Howard, Ebenezer. *Garden Cities of Tomorrow.* Edited by F. J. Osborn. Reprint, Cambridge: MIT Press, 1965. First published 1898.

Irschick, Eugene. *Politics and Social Conflict in South India: The Non-Brahman Movement and Tamil Separatism, 1916–1929.* Berkeley and Los Angeles: University of California Press, 1969.

Iyer, Kamu. "G. B. Mhatre: The Man and His Work." In *Buildings That Shaped Bombay,* edited by Kamu Iyer, 22–29. Mumbai: Kamala Raheja Vidyanidhi Institute of Architecture, 2000.

Jackson, Kenneth. *Crabgrass Frontier: The Suburbanization of the United States.* New York: Oxford University Press, 1985.

Joshi, Sanjay, ed. *The Middle Class in Colonial India.* New Delhi: Oxford University Press, 2010.

Kaji, H. L. "Housing Conditions among the Lower Middle Class in Bombay (South)." *Local Self-Government Gazette* 11, no. 2 (1925): 105–110.

Kaviraj, Sudipta. "Filth and the Public Sphere: Concepts and Practices about Space in Calcutta." *Public Culture* 10, no. 1 (1997): 83–113.

Khudabadi Amil Panchayat of Bombay. "Constitution and Rules." http://www.amilsindhis.com/constitution.html. Accessed October 9, 2011.

Kidambi, Prashant. "Consumption, Domestic Economy, and the Idea of the 'Middle Class' in Late Colonial Bombay." In *The Middle Class in Colonial India,* edited by Sanjay Joshi, 132–156. New Delhi: Oxford University Press, 2010.

———. "Housing the Poor in a Colonial City: The Bombay Improvement Trust, 1898–1918." *Studies in History,* n.s., 17, no. 1 (2001): 57–79.

———. "'An Infection of Locality': Plague, Pythogenesis, and the Poor in Bombay, c. 1896–1905." *Urban History* 31, no. 2 (2004): 249–267.

———. *The Making of an Indian Metropolis:*

Colonial Governance and Public Culture in Bombay, 1890–1920. London: Ashgate, 2007.

King, Anthony D. *The Bungalow: The Production of a Global Culture.* New York: Oxford University Press, 1995.

——. *Colonial Urban Development: Culture, Social Power, and Environment.* Boston: Routledge and Paul, 1976.

——. "The Westernization of Domestic Architecture in India." *Art and Archaelogy Research Papers* 11 (1977): 32–41.

Klein, Ira. "Urban Development and Death: Bombay City, 1870–1914." *Modern Asian Studies* 20, no. 4 (1986): 725–754.

Kracauer, Siegfried. *The Salaried Masses: Duty and Distraction in Weimar Germany.* Translated by Quintin Hoare. First published in German in 1930. Reprint, London: Verso Books, 1998.

Kruse, Kevin, and Thomas Sugrue, eds. *The New Suburban History.* Chicago: University of Chicago Press, 2006.

Kumar, Nita. "Work and Leisure in the Formation of Identity: Muslim Weavers in a Hindu City." In *Culture and Power in Banaras,* edited by Sandria B. Freitag, 147–170. Berkeley: University of California Press, 1989.

Ladd, Brian. *Urban Planning and Civic Order in Germany, 1860–1914.* Cambridge, Mass.: Harvard University Press, 1990.

Lanchester, H. V. *Town Planning in Madras.* London: Constable, 1918.

Lees, Andrew, and Lynn Hollen Lees. *Cities and the Making of Modern Europe, 1750–1914.* New York: Cambridge University Press, 2007.

Lewandowski, Susan. "Changing Form and Function in the Ceremonial and the Colonial Port City in India." *Modern Asian Studies* 11, no. 2 (1977): 183–212.

Luhrmann, Tanya. "Evil in the Sands of Time: Theology and Identity Politics among the Zorastrian Parsis." *Journal of Asian Studies* 61, no. 3 (August 2002): 861–889.

——. *The Good Parsi: The Fate of a Colonial Elite in a Postcolonial Society.* Cambridge, Mass.: Harvard University Press, 1996.

Mahadevan, V. "Matunga—The Malgudi in Mumbai." *Mahadevan's Monologues* (blog), June 21, 2007. http://plmahadevan.blogspot.com/2007/06/matunga-malgudi-in-mumbai.html.

Mahaluxmivala, P. D. *The History of the Bombay Electric Supply and Tramways Company, Limited, 1905–1935.* Bombay, [probably 1936].

Manshardt, Clifford, ed. *The Bombay Municipality at Work: A Symposium.* Bombay: Nagpada Neighbourhood House, 1935.

——. *Pioneering on Social Frontiers in India.* Bombay: Lalvani, 1967.

——, ed. *Some Social Services of the Government of Bombay.* Bombay: Taraporevala and Sons, 1937.

Marcus, Sharon. *Apartment Stories: City and Home in 19th Century Paris and London.* Berkeley and Los Angeles: University of California Press, 1999.

Masselos, Jim. *The City in Action: Bombay Struggles for Power.* New Delhi: Oxford University Press, 2007.

——. "Power in the Bombay Mohulla, 1904–1915: An Initial Exploration into the World of the Indian Urban Muslim." *South Asia* 6 (1976): 75–95.

Mehta, Hansa. "Domestic Architecture in India." Paper read at the Indian Institute of Architects, February 19, 1936. In *Journal of the Indian Institute of Architects* 2, no. 4 (April 1936): 116–117.

Mirams, A. E. "Town Planning in Bombay under the Bombay Town Planning Act, 1915." *British Town Planning Institute,*

Papers and Discussions 6 (1919–1920): 43–63.

Misra, B. B. *The Indian Middle Classes: Their Growth in Modern Times*. London: Oxford University Press, 1961.

Mythili, K. L. "Little Madras in Bombay City." In *Urban Sociology in India: Reader and Sourcebook*, edited by M. S. A. Rao, 235–243. New Delhi: Orient Longman India, 1974.

——. "A Socio-ecological Study of an Immigrant Community." Ph.D. diss., University of Bombay, 1959.

Nadkarni, S. K. "The Saraswat Cooperative Housing Buildings in Tardeo." *Indian Concrete Journal*, October 15, 1940: 370–371.

Nair, Janaki. *The Promise of the Metropolis: Bangalore's Twentieth Century*. New Delhi: Oxford University Press, 2005.

Neuwirth, Robert. *Shadow Cities: A Billion Squatters, a New Urban World*. London: Verso, 2006.

Ogle, Maureen. *All the Modern Conveniences: American Household Plumbing, 1840–1890*. Baltimore: The Johns Hopkins University Press, 2000.

Oldenburg, Veena. *The Making of Colonial Lucknow, 1856–1877*. New York: Oxford University Press, 1990.

Orr, J. P. "Density of Population in Bombay." Lecture delivered before the Bombay Cooperative Housing Association, September 1914.

——. "The Dishousing and Rehousing of the Middle Class Slum Population," *Local Self-Government Gazette* 5, no. 4 (April 1919): 215–222.

——. "How to Check the Growth of Insanitary Conditions in Bombay." Lecture delivered before the All India Sanitary Conference in Lucknow, January 1914.

——. *Light and Air in Dwelling in Bombay*. Lecture delivered before the Bombay Sanitary Association. Bombay: Bombay Gazette Electric Printing Works, June 27, 1912.

——. "The Need for Co-operation between Neighbours in the Development of Building Estates." Lecture delivered before the Bombay Cooperative Housing Association, August 1914.

——. "Social Reform and Slum Reform." Lecture delivered before the Social Service League in Bombay, September 3, 1917. Pts. 1–4. *Local Self-Government Gazette* 3, no. 10 (October 1917): 740–750; 3, no. 11 (November 1917): 805–816; 4, no. 2 (February 1918); 77–88; 4, no. 3 (March 1918): 174–187.

Prakash, Gyan. *Mumbai Fables*. Princeton: Princeton University Press, 2010.

Prashad, Vijay. "The Technology of Sanitation in Colonial Delhi." *Modern Asian Studies* 35, no. 1 (February 2001): 113–155.

"The Problem: A Short Statement on the Issues Involved." In "City of Dreams: A Symposium on the Many Facets of Bombay." Special issue, *Seminar* 528 (August 2003).

Punwaney, Doulat. "Activities in Mumbai." Edited by Asha Idnani and Menka Shivdasani. http://www.amilsindhis.com/activities-in-mumbai.html. Accessed October 9, 2011.

——. "How Amils Lived in Sind before Partition." Edited by Asha Idnani and Menka Shivdasani. http://www.amilsindhis.com/how-amils-lived-in-sind-before-partition.html. Accessed October 9, 2011.

——. "The Origins of Amils." Edited by Asha Idnani and Menka Shivdasani. http://www.amilsindhis.com/origin-of-amils.html. Accessed October 9, 2011.

Rahimtoola, Hoosenally M. "The Corporation: What It Is, How It Works, and What It Does." In *The Bombay Municipality at Work: A Symposium,* edited by Clifford Manshardt, 1–13. Bombay: Nagpada Neighbourhood House, 1935.

Ramachandran, P. P. "Matunga Musings." http://www.keralaiyers.com/mm3 .html.

Ramanna, Mridula. "South Indian Settlers in Mumbai." *Bombay Explorer* 33 (December 2000): 24–30.

Rao, Nikhil. "Changing Cities, Aging Men." *Man's World* 1, no. 12 (February 2001): 88–93.

———. "Hoops, Hunger, and the City." In *Bombay Meri Jaan: Writings on Mumbai,* edited by Jerry Pinto and Naresh Fernandes, 101–111. New Delhi: Penguin Books, 2003.

———. "Towards Greater Bombay: Town Planning and the Politics of Urban Growth, 1915–1964." Unpublished paper.

———. "Uncertain Ground: The 'Ownership Flat' and Urban Property in 20th Century Bombay." *South Asian History and Culture* 3, no. 1 (Winter 2012): 1–25.

Rogers, Alexander. *The Land Revenue of Bombay: A History of Its Administration, Rise, and Progress.* London: W. H. Allen, 1892.

Sand, Jordan. *House and Home in Modern Japan: Architecture, Domestic Space, and Bourgeois Culture, 1880–1930.* Cambridge, Mass., and London: Harvard University Press, 2003.

Sandoval-Strausz, Andrew. "Homes for a World of Strangers: Hospitality and the Origins of Multiple Dwellings in Urban America." *Journal of Urban History* 33, no. 6 (September 2007): 933–964.

Sarkar, Sumit. *The Swadeshi Movement in Bengal, 1903–1908.* New Delhi: People's Publishing House, 1973.

Sennett, Richard. *The Conscience of the Eye.* New York: Knopf, 1990.

Shah, Mayank. "*Chawls*: Popular Dwellings in Bombay." Master's thesis, Massachusetts Institute of Technology, 1981.

Sharma, Kalpana. *Rediscovering Dharavi: Stories from Asia's Largest Slum.* New Delhi: Penguin Books, 2000.

Shastri, Janardan. "Traditional Domestic Architecture of Bombay." Parts 1 and 2. *Journal of the Indian Institute of Architects* 5, no. 3 (January 1939): 93–98; 5, no. 4 (April 1939): 136–141.

Shetty, Prasad, and Rupali Gupte. *Housing Typologies in Mumbai.* Mumbai: Collective Research Initiatives Trust, 2007.

Shivdasani, H. B. "'City Improvement,' a Paper Read before the Indian Institute of Architects on October 20, 1938." *Journal of the Indian Institute of Architects* 5, no. 3 (January 1939): 84–87.

———. "The Work of the Improvements Department." In *The Bombay Municipality at Work,* edited by Clifford Manshardt, 23–33. Bombay: D. B. Taraporevala and Sons, 1935.

Shoosmith, A. G. "Present Day Architecture in India." *Nineteenth Century and After* 123 (1938): 206–207.

Siddiqi, Asiya. "Ayesha's World: A Butcher's Family in Nineteenth-Century Bombay." *Comparative Studies in Society and History* 43, no. 1 (January 2001): 101–129.

———. "Ayesha's World: The Territory of a Family of Butchers in 19th Century Bombay." Paper presented at the seminar Religious Imagination and Practices in the City, Bangalore, December 18–19, 1995.

Stein, Burton. *Thomas Munro: The Origins of the Colonial State and His Vision of Empire.* Oxford: Oxford University Press, 1989.

Sturman, Rachel. "Property and Attachments: Defining Autonomy and the Claims of Family in Nineteenth Century Western India." *Comparative Studies in Society and History* 47, no. 3 (July 2005): 611–637.

Sutcliffe, Anthony, ed. *British Town Planning: The Formative Years.* New York: St. Martin's Press, 1981.

——, ed. *Multi-storey Living: The British Working-Class Experience.* New York: Barnes and Noble, 1974.

Thekaekara, Mari Marcel. *Endless Filth: The Saga of the Bhangis.* Bangalore: Books for Change, 1999.

Tindall, Gillian. *City of Gold: A Biography of Bombay.* London: Temple Smith, 1982.

Vaidyanathan, K. V. "Wadala Whispers." http://www.keralaiyers.com/kv_ww1.html.

Vidler, Anthony. "Scenes of the Street: Transformations in Ideal and Reality, 1750–1871." In *On Streets,* edited by Stanford Anderson, 29–111. Cambridge: MIT Press, 1986.

von Saldern, Adelheid. "The Workers' Movement and Cultural Patterns on Urban Housing Estates and in Rural Settlements in Germany and Austria during the 1920s." *Social History* 15, no. 4 (October 1990): 333–354.

Warner, Sam Bass. *Streetcar Suburbs: The Process of Growth in Boston (1870–1900).* Cambridge, Mass.: Harvard University Press, 1978. First published 1962.

Yorke, F. R. S., and Frederick Gibberd. *The Modern Flat.* London: Architectural Press, 1937.

Index

Nikhil Rao is associate professor
of history at Wellesley College.